D0929622

THE *FAST TIMES* OF
ALBERT CHAMPION

THE *FAST TIMES* OF
ALBERT CHAMPION

FROM RECORD-SETTING RACER TO DASHING TYCOON, AN UNTOLD STORY OF SPEED, SUCCESS, AND BETRAYAL

PETER JOFFRE NYE

Prometheus Books

59 John Glenn Drive
Amherst, New York 14228

Published 2014 by Prometheus Books

Cover design by Jacqueline Nasso Cooke
Cover photo courtesy of Kerry Champion Williams

Inquiries should be addressed to
Prometheus Books
59 John Glenn Drive
Amherst, New York 14228
VOICE: 716–691–0133
FAX: 716–691–0137
WWW.PROMETHEUSBOOKS.COM

18 17 16 15 14   5 4 3 2 1

Library of Congress Cataloging-in-Publication Data

Nye, Peter, 1947–
    The fast times of Albert Champion : from record-setting racer to dashing tycoon, an untold story of speed, success, and betrayal / by Peter Joffre Nye.
        pages cm
    Includes bibliographical references and index.
    ISBN 978-1-61614-964-2 (hardback)—ISBN 978-1-61614-965-9 (ebook)
    1. Champion, Albert, 1878–1927. 2. Champion Spark Plug (Company) 3. Automobile supplies industry—United States—History. 4. Racers (Persons)—France—Biography.
5. Businessmen—France—Biography. I. Title.

HD9710.3.U54C435 2014
338.7'629258—dc23
[B]
                                                                        2014023876

Printed in the United States of America

To Valerie

CONTENTS

PROLOGUE

No more colorful figure than Albert Champion ever has been developed in the automobile industry, which is saying plenty, for this business has produced many brass hats who started at the bottom of the ladder and climbed to the top.

—CHRIS SINSABAUGH,
Who, Me? Forty Years of Automobile History[1]

Never before had there been such a sight in America. Frenchman Albert Champion crouched like a jockey over his new motorcycle, his mop of blond hair windblown over goggles as he tore around the Empire City Race Track in Yonkers, New York, and threw up a tall dirt cloud. It was Memorial Day 1903.[2] Spectators in their Sunday finest filled the enormous steel grandstand hugging the home straight of the oval built for sulky racing. Champion circled a lap to build speed for a flying start. When he rocketed in front of the grandstand, his unmuffled engine popped loudly and perfectly. In his wake lingered the pungent odor of oil and gasoline. Thousands of heads turned in unison to watch him approach. The audience, sheltered under the slanting roof from the blazing afternoon sun, studied him in profile. Then he set off on his three laps for the mile. He leaned so precariously through flat turns on the 350-pound Gladiator that the *New York Sun* described his ride as "hair-raising."[3] He would either set a world record, or crash and die.

The Gladiator throbbed with three times the power of anything made on this side of the Atlantic.[4] Its mighty engine harnessed the muscles of a team of fourteen horses. Raucous New Yorkers applauded, cheered, and tooted horns until an official, crowned in a yellow boater, slashed the air over the start/finish line with a checkered flag. A hush fell.

Three dedicated timers holding stopwatches in their palms as if they possessed something magical conferred in the judges' stand on the infield with the announcer. The announcer picked up a megaphone so long he needed both hands and aimed it at the grandstand. He broke the silence by bellowing that Champion had set a new world record—1 minute 4 and 1/5 seconds, a breathtaking fifty-five miles per hour (55 mph).[5] The audience shouted approval. Champion waved back from his Gladiator and beamed his showman's smile.

In this era, if a city or town had a speed limit, it was 10 mph, as much in deference to the hegemony of the nation's eighteen million horses and mules as to the terrible state of roads.[6] The prospect of driving a machine a mile a minute embodied the holy grail of speed. Champion had been hired from his native Paris to race for a bicycle manufacturer in suburban Boston. He had competed on outdoor board-cycling tracks, called velodromes, on the Eastern Seaboard when cycling rivaled baseball as this country's most popular spectator sport. However, the cycling craze recently had sputtered out, and sales had plummeted. His employer planned to cease making bicycles and terminate his contract. Now Champion was desperate to break through the minute, a symbolic barrier.

Champion won the one-mile time trials open to gas-combustion, electric, and steam cars weighing less than a thousand pounds.[7] Victory stoked his ambition to reinvent himself as a racecar driver, but autos were far too expensive. He reckoned with unwavering confidence that he could pilot a Gladiator 60 mph around a velodrome. The resulting publicity for his daring and skill could impress an auto company that would hire him. It was a gamble, but it was his only option.

Later that Saturday afternoon, Champion watched the main event from the infield and gazed in awe upon an exceptionally loud vehicle that careened around turns, rear wheels sliding sideways some fifty feet, tires snarling in the dirt and throwing off tall rooster tails of sand and stones when the noisemaker wasn't caroming down the straights and raising dust clouds. He heard the car before he saw the driver, Barney Oldfield. Just when the air would clear, Oldfield would charge back around and set off fresh dirt plumes.

Through the dusty haze everyone saw the goggled driver perched on a bucket seat behind an exposed four-cylinder engine. Its gas tank, fuel lines, hoses connected to air-intake valves, and exhaust valves belching black smoke all hunkered down along a boxy wooden frame, ten feet long and painted bright red—a desperate cosmetic touch. The radiator, flat as a door, squatted between the front wheels like a shield. Oldfield hunched his shoulders. He steered a prototype called 999 after the celebrated steam locomotive, the Empire State Express No. 999, a buzzword for speed. The racecar's designer was an obscure Detroit mechanic named Henry Ford.[8]

Oldfield had a folksy manner, and his lopsided awe-shucks grin was part swagger and part pal. He liked to stick out his hand to greet strangers or wave to crowds, saying, "You know me! I'm Barney Oldfield!"

He and Champion had celebrated their twenty-fifth birthdays that spring, but their backgrounds could not have been more different. Champion grew up in the City of Light near the Arc de Triomphe; Oldfield came from a farm outside Toledo. The Frenchman stood to the American's nose and weighed at least sixty pounds less. Upon meeting at the Empire City Race Track, they recognized they were brothers in speed. Champion knew about the deadly price of speed. He had crashed in a race and caused two fatalities. Yet nothing deterred his passion for speed, the metaphor for his life and Oldfield's life. Driving to push the limits of man and machine, if they overshot a turn, they wanted to be remembered for going like hell when their chariots took them over the bank.

America's auto industry was so nominal that the 1900 US Census had lumped auto manufacturing in the category of "miscellaneous."[9] Oldfield used to pooh-pooh autos as a fad.[10] Such a sentiment was widespread. Autos were playthings of upper-class city people, notorious for breaking down, and cursed for spooking horses. However, Champion had immigrated for the 1900 season well aware of the growing popularity of motor vehicles on the continent. The United States lagged about a decade behind France, England, Germany,[11] and even little Belgium in production. The modern automobile had been introduced in Paris. For a decade, French engines had been mounted on the front for better balance to negotiate turns with a round steering wheel. Americans made horseless carriages; engines fastened under the high chassis, and the front wheels turned with a tiller that replaced the reins of a horse.

Oldfield, like Champion, had been a pro cyclist. He drove for the first time in an October 1902 auto meet on the Grosse Point horse track outside Detroit when he had filled in at the last minute for his buddy, who owned 999. On that chilly, overcast afternoon, Oldfield strong-armed 999 like a nightclub bouncer with a rowdy customer. He never let up on the gas in the contest against four rivals, and he vanquished them. He enjoyed a victory lap, then stopped at the end of the finishing straight before he shut off the engine.

Henry Ford had watched everything from the grandstand. He marched over and posed with Oldfield in his bucket seat for a photograph. Then Ford left to call on newspaper offices and claim credit as 999's designer. News coverage about the triumph of 999 over three other cars helped Ford secure financial backing to found the Ford Motor Company.

A cascade of newspaper coverage had changed Oldfield's attitude about autos. On Memorial Day 1903, at the Empire City Race Track, he was driving in the five-mile pursuit. He and his opponent had begun on opposite sides of the track to chase one another, ensuring that one of the thunderous contraptions flashed past the grandstand every twenty seconds. His adversary piloted a Peerless Greyhound, made in Cleveland and crafted with a hood over the engine and an upholstered leather seat wide enough for a passenger.

From the start, Oldfield had stomped on the gas pedal. Like a brawler throwing haymakers, he swung 999 wide before every turn then cut in again on the straights. All of his six-foot, 190 pounds of brute strength went into taming the 2,800-pound mechanical monster.[12] The back wheels slid and threw up a dirt storm that forced spectators standing behind the fence to flee.

His opponent steered the Greyhound through turns with finesse. But Oldfield won the first five-mile heat with an impressive average of 56 mph. In the next heat, both cars went even faster. The crowd went wild as Oldfield charged through the second mile in 1 minute 1-3/5 seconds, 59 mph.[13] The announcer barked through his megaphone that Oldfield had set a world one-mile record around an elliptical track.

Oldfield won the second five-miler for two straight victories, which gave him the match.

Of the forty or so drivers in five events in Yonkers, and other motor-mad enthusiasts in cities from coast to coast infected with mile-a-minute fever that summer, Champion and Oldfield led the chase. Neither suspected that driving 60 mph would soon become passé. Or that the friendship they had forged from that day would cause Champion to pay with his life.

1

BALANCING ON ONE WHEEL

*IN THE BUILDING OF THIS AUTOMOBILE INDUSTRY,
PERSONALITIES PLAYED A MAJOR PART. THERE WAS
THE IDEA OF A SELF-PROPELLED ROAD VEHICLE,
CRUDE AS IT IS GRANTED, BUT TO PICK UP THAT
IDEA AND CARRY ON TOOK MEN OF IMAGINATION,
MEN WITH THE COURAGE OF THEIR CONVICTIONS,
RESOURCEFUL, COLORFUL, AND LAST-DITCH
FIGHTERS.*

—CHRIS SINSABAUGH, *WHO ME? FORTY YEARS
OF AUTOMOBILE HISTORY*[1]

By the age of forty-nine, Albert Champion employed three thousand five hundred workers in his AC Spark Plug Company in Flint, Michigan, and they all passed every workday under his photo portrait, which hung in a large frame over the portal leading into the factory.[2] They called him The Chief.[3] He looked every inch the chief in his tailored dark suit—fashionable, trim with an air of Gaulic insouciance, stylish Arrow collar points, cuffs showing just so with links of gold, a diamond pin winking in his necktie, hands resting in the pockets of pleated trousers. His attire perpetuated his reputation as a lady's man. He was of medium height with a commanding presence, accustomed to being stared at by women for his distinguished appearance, enhanced by a fringe of gray hair hugging the sides of his head, and by men for his athletic bearing. This stolid corporate image failed to portray the fame and heroics of his youthful trans-Atlantic energy celebrating that trait so essential to Frenchmen of his generation, *la gloire*! The man with a predestined name was born in Paris, hard by the Arc de Triomphe, on April 5, 1878,[4] upon sawdust.

Paris had such high infant mortality that the law required parents to take newborns in person with two witnesses to city hall to register them. Champion's birth certificate, in flowing longhand penned with a quill nib, indicates that his parents, Alexandre Champion, a coachman, and Marie Blanche Carpentier Champion,[5] a washerwoman, waited two weeks to bundle him up before they left their home at 11 Avenue MacMahon for city hall in the Seventeenth Arrondissement, a neighborhood known as Batignolles. Witnesses Henri Genet, a metalworker, and Eugène Belly, a laborer, attended to verify the identity of the couple's legitimate son: Albert Joseph Champion.

This portrait of The Chief hung over the portal of his AC Spark Plug Company in Flint, where three thousand five hundred workers passed through to work in the factory. *Photo courtesy of Kerry Champion Williams.*

Albert, the couple's firstborn, could now be counted among the City of Light's two million residents.[6] Avenue MacMahon, a tribute to the former soldier-statesman and president of France, Patrice de MacMahon, stretches as one of a dozen streets laid out like spokes of a wheel radiating from Place de l'Étoile, the hub encircling the Arc de Triomphe. Emperor Napoléon had erected the monument in the early nineteenth century to glorify the armies of the empire and to mark the western entry into Paris.[7] Avenue MacMahon marked twelve o'clock on the circle, above Avenue des Champs-Élysées, perhaps the most famous boulevard in the world, which intersected at three o'clock. Other thoroughfares honored greats, such as Avenue Victor Hugo for France's grand man of letters. Champion may have been born to humble parents, but they put him in the center of la gloire!

In the spring of 1889, on his eleventh birthday,[8] Champion was strolling on a sunny afternoon at the end of the chic Avenue de la Grand Armée when he spotted a crowd watching a slim dark-haired young man riding a unicycle. The unique one-wheel contraption without anything whatsoever to steer was enough to make anyone stop whatever they were doing to look. It was the latest gadget, a simple piece of equipment, and the wheel held a neat standard-issue hard-rubber tire. The rider sat with his back in perfect posture, chin up, and appeared completely at ease, as though he were born on that wheel. Although the avenue was lined with tempting sidewalk cafés and boutiques offering fashionable clothes and jewelry, Champion could see that the cluster of elegantly dressed men and women had their eyes fixed on the acrobat. His legs rolled the machine's short crank arms forward a yard or two, then he abruptly pedaled backward exactly to where he had started—as though pulled by an invisible cord. The stunt incited applause and shouts of *bravo*! The unicyclist spun around like a coin on a tabletop. People gasped. Then with a slight forward dip of his torso, he zoomed ahead and made four sharp square turns that took him back to where he had started. His movements looked silky smooth and magical. Spectators clapped and cheered. They tossed franc coins into a cloth cap on the sidewalk, the coins so plentiful that each new deposit clinked.

Champion stuck around until the performer in due course popped off his unicycle and landed on his feet, one hand holding the device by its leather saddle. The acrobat graciously smiled and bowed his head, nodding and thanking everyone before he bent down to pick up the cap and tips. Champion enthusiastically introduced himself to Alexandre Tellier.[9]

Tellier looked at the eager youngster, curly blond hair parted down the middle of his head in the fashion of the day, gray eyes flashing with excitement, asking an outburst of questions.[10] Champion had a build that a journalist described as resembling the Greco-Roman statues bequeathed to posterity for admiration in museums.[11] Something about him impressed Tellier. He volunteered good-naturedly to mentor the lad. They were in the neighborhood of Porte Maillot, the entrance to the Bois de Boulogne, the magnificent park on Paris's west end. Tellier and Champion found a grassy section to get started.

There Tellier instructed his protégé on the proper basics of mounting the unicycle and riding—head held straight on the neck, backbone upright as though it were an extension of the seatpost holding the saddle, lean forward slightly, arms out for balance, and legs pedaling. The trick was to keep the wheel rolling and to point with your chin to where you want to go. You can set a wheel rolling and it will continue on its own until it slows down. Tellier had him practice on the grass. Most everyone can learn the basics of riding a regular bicycle in less than an hour, but a unicycle can require at good day or two of concentrated trial and error. It takes that long to sense that your center of balance lies just below your navel.

Fortune smiled upon young Champion. He caught the eye of Henri Gauliard,[12] a civil engineer in his late thirties with a bike shop in the eastern township of Noisy-le-Sec. Gauliard happened by chance to visit the Porte Maillot neighborhood on business.[13] He was struck by Champion's agility and vigor.[14] He offered the precocious youngster employment to perform acrobatics outside his bike shop in Noisy-le-Sec to lure in customers. Champion could not afford to buy a unicycle, but Gauliard, the father of two girls,[15] and sensing a business opportunity, offered to provide one. Champion quickly accepted. They shook hands.[16]

As promised, Gauliard built Champion a unicycle.[17] As the weather warmed, Champion practiced every day. He became adept performing on the sidewalk and the street in front of his boss's bike shop. He learned how to draw onlookers and hold their attention. They encouraged his flair for showmanship. He experimented and added more stunts to his repertoire. Removing a foot from the pedal to push the top of the tire to propel him was always a crowd pleaser. Each day, Gauliard paid him some francs. Gauliard started lending him out to other proprietors to do exhibitions for their businesses. That summer he became a second Tellier.

Champion's getting out and around brought him onto the Boulevard des Batignolles, a main thoroughfare extending east to Montmartre, the Eighteenth Arrondissement. He encountered a grocery store with a wine section run by a couple whose daughter Albert Champion would marry.

A reporter knew him around this time and said he kept his nose in the air like the Parisian he was. "This one-of-a-kind street urchin with a little face to go along with it, alert and lively as a monkey, seemed to have quicksilver coursing through his veins."[18]

Champion had discovered the value of self-improvement. He would apply that principle again and again.

His family was living on rue Debarcadere,[19] near the Avenue de la Grande Armée. The neighborhood of Batignolles is shaped like a croissant sitting on the Right Bank of the Seine, with a flank sprawled over the city's northwestern edge and one corner under the Arc de Triomphe. Batignolles had been annexed into Paris in 1860. Unlike central Paris, with its straight, broad avenues conducive to flowing traffic of horse-drawn carriages, Batignolles was filigreed with crooked, narrow brick and stone lanes. Small vineyards defied the city's expansion. Cheap rents and flower-bedecked picturesque houses with mansard roofs of slate contributed to a bohemian ambiance.

The locale was more than a coachman and washerwoman with Albert and three younger brothers could afford, but his parents worked in service for a family that provided lodging. No records remain about his parents' employer. Champion's nature was to plunge with formidable energy headlong into life and work, without pausing for introspection. Years later, as his business in the United States thrived and expanded to England and France, he reminisced with colleagues over dinners, wine and champagne, and cigars at trade shows, sales conferences, and in the Pullman restaurant cars of passenger trains swaying across the country. Yet he only provided topical sketches of his background. He was more intent on the future. *Automobile Topics Illustrated*, a New York–based trade publication, described him as "perpetually afire with new ideas and ever reaching for further achievements. If he was without patience, hot tempered, erratic at times, he was also versatile, amusing, brilliant, and delightfully companionable."[20]

During his childhood, his father rose six mornings a week to heave into the uniform and boots of his livery and tramp out the door so early that the gaslights still illuminated the streets. Alexandre trudged back late, redolent of leather and straw and manure. He was a working-class native of central Paris,[21] the First Arrondissement, the ancient Île de la Cité. Alexandre grew up in the squalid, congested area that Victor Hugo rendered in his novel *Les Misérables*.[22] Alexandre was forced out among twenty-five thousand inhabitants displaced by the radical demolitions by Baron Georges Eugène Haussmann to make way for the gracious public spaces and attractive metropolis we know today.[23]

Before the advent of electricity, washing clothes was outdoor labor as strenuous as tilling farm soil.[24] Marie Champion's morning began by pulling off the heavy wooden lid set at the end of the previous workday over the top of the well to keep out the rats. A wooden bucket holding three or four gallons attached to the end of a rope was dropped into the well, filled with water until it weighed twenty-five or thirty pounds, and hauled up, hand over hand, to the surface. Water buckets were lugged some fifty yards from the well to pour into a big vat suspended over a large roaring fire that heated the water to a boil. Before putting clothes and bedding into the vat, washerwomen bent over a washboard and scrubbed out dirt and stains, often grunting from the effort. The laundry tossed into the vat's soapy water was stirred around with wooden poles like broom handles. Sopping-wet fabric was heavy. Stirring the poles strained backs, shoulders, and arms. Next, laundry had to be lifted from the vat and held up for long minutes, with the pole leveraged against the side of the vat, for most of the dirty water to drip away before the load was dropped into the rinsing tub. Then every piece of laundry had to be wrung by hand to squeeze out excess water. Finally the laundry was hung to dry on rope lines, creating alleys in which Albert ran and played.

Alexandre Champion and Marie Blanche Carpentier had met in Batignolles, likely when they were living in service at 16 rue de Tillsit, an upscale address near the Arc de Triomphe. They published their wedding banns on October 18, 1873.[25] Alexandre and Blanche had some evenings and Sundays together. They explored local cafés and cabarets noisy with other *classes laborieuses*, poets, musicians, and artists drawn to districts where the rent was cheap. They married on January 17, 1874.[26]

In the year Albert learned to ride the unicycle, he was the big brother of Louis and Henri, named after French Kings, and Prosper, honoring Marie's father and paternal grandfather.[27] The family ate simple meals, mostly baked bread and herbs, supplemented with copious amounts of red onions, garlic, and sorrel. A seasonal dish included dandelion salad garnished with slices of hard-boiled egg. It was typical to finish with a piece of cheese. They also would have indulged in the fare of the Paris poor: horsemeat.

He grew up when neighbors still seethed about the shelling of Paris by Prussian artillery in 1871 during the Franco-Prussian War.[28] At gatherings around dining tables and in cafés and cabarets people spewed passionate recollections about citizens who had grabbed picks and shovels and rushed to protect the Arc de Triomphe.[29] Residents of Batignolles had filled tons of sandbags and stacked them up the monument's height of 164 feet and breadth of 148 feet. The Arc de Triomphe escaped harm. However, the Prussian artillery siege cut off the supply of food for three months. Starving citizens resorted to eating all of the animals in the zoo, then dogs, cats, and crows, every horse, and—after consuming all options—people resorted to eating rats.[30] France capitulated to Prussia and was forced to pay ruinous compensation, which set off a wave of business failures. Revolutionaries in the leftist Commune of Paris had set up a provisional government and fought a civil war on the streets. Sections of the city went up in flames. In May 1871, some twenty thousand citizens were massacred or court-martialed and summarily shot.[31]

When Champion came to possess a unicycle, Paris was hosting a world's fair—the *Exposition Universelle* of 1889. Government officials and business leaders organized it to rejoice over the city's recovery from the Franco-Prussian War, remember the centenary of the 1789 storming of the Bastille, and display France's culture with the new painting movement called Impressionism.

The exposition's symbol was bridge builder Gustave Eiffel's tapering steel tower, soaring up 984 feet,[32] an audacious icon. During two years of construction, his spectacle of 7,000 tons, held together with 2.5 million rivets, rose rudely above Paris's ocean of slate roofs. Intellectuals expressed outrage. They gathered in the streets and grumbled that Eiffel's structure violated the city profile; many circulated petitions and wrote letters of protest to newspapers. Yet supporters rallied in greater numbers, expressing pride that Paris now possessed the tallest building in the world, surpassing America's Washington Monument, a marble obelisk 555 feet tall in Washington, DC.[33] Adoring advocates boasted that the Eiffel Tower represented modern France. Champion, looking south from Batignolles across the city, could see the Eiffel Tower going up, higher and higher. This was among his cherished memories from childhood.

His father lived to see the Eiffel Tower completed, but he died of pneumonia at home three days after Christmas—December 28, 1889.[34] He was forty-seven, about the average life expectancy for his generation. Aside from his wedding banns and marriage, he left behind no records of paying taxes, voting, or serving in the military.[35] (France had a compulsory two-year military conscription. If he had served, which is likely, he would have been a lowly enlisted man, a *poilu*, among the faceless undocumented.)

On top of Albert's mother taking over all the family responsibilities, she likely realized she had scant chance of ever remarrying. Her sons became the center of her life.

The father Albert had was no longer going to offer guidance. He struggled with the gloom of *le réveil mortel*, the uncompromising reality of death, unaware he had lost his childhood innocence. Aunts and uncles and cousins on the Champion and Carpentier sides of his extended family provided whatever emotional support they could, but they were hard pressed to do much for Alexandre's widow and sons. The experience formed Albert's character. For the rest of his life, he threw himself into work, forever escaping into the task at hand, keeping busy, always planning new projects, in time building up a business with factories in three countries and offices of his own.

What little is known of Champion's childhood can be gleaned from a lifetime of journal articles and an outpouring of hundreds of French and English obituaries with recollections from friends, fellow athletes, and auto executives on both sides of the Atlantic. He grew up in public as a celebrity, like today's young rock stars. An itinerant bicycle racer competing on the pro circuit's banked cycling tracks, called vélodromes, he enjoyed immense popularity and money by the fistful. The press corps flocked around him, keen to capture quotes or describe his actions. Before he immigrated to America, he already had been closely tracked in a steady cascade of articles. He was cited in books published in Paris. He kept a scrapbook of his racing career.

In the spring of 1890, Champion was working as a unicycle acrobat for Henri Gauliard. Champion commuted to work and back home, some six miles each way, on his unicycle. The ride would have been rough from the hard-rubber tire on his wheel. "I was earning my own living and part of my mother's and brothers' when I was twelve years old,"[36] he later told the *Detroit News*. It may have been the only time he ever mentioned his siblings, although without naming Henri, Louis, or Prosper.

He was twelve when he ended formal schooling, common among kids from impoverished families. City boys flocked to factories, rural youths toiled on farms or in mines; girls and some boys found household domestic service, wearing servant uniforms. Their milieu required always acknowledging their place below the upper ranks of the social order. They lived under the protocol of being seen but not heard from unless spoken to directly by someone of higher authority. Any speaking out of turn or misbehaving put them at risk of getting a sharp slap on the ear or sacked outright.

Proud, Champion had no interest in service employment. Yet he lacked family or social connections that would allow him to enter a trade, like baking or printing. No opportunities beckoned where he could expect to support himself and improve conditions for his mother and brothers. His mother's diligence and the sacrifices she made on behalf of him and his brothers weighed on him. His brothers looked up to him.

Self-reliant and a natural showman, he created an ambitious publicity stunt. Gauliard publicized the event and charged admission. On a Saturday in May, Champion would pedal his unicycle for ten hours around a high-school cinder running track and cover one hundred miles—the distance equivalent to what a carriage drawn by four horses would cover in two days. The audacity of the self-propelled, one-wheel venture filled the stands. He pedaled round and round the track from seven o'clock in the morning to 5 o'clock in the evening, crank arms spinning, hands waving to the crowd. Champion went 101 miles (162 kilometers),[37] averaging a brisk 10 mph.

He earned more than five hundred francs—about as much as a school teacher was paid in three months—and burnished his local fame. Yet the future of unicycle riding was uncertain. Sooner or later the novelty would wear off and he would have to make a career choice—either move up as an acrobat performing in a circus act or try something else. He faced his predicament during the *Belle Époque* following the end of the Franco-Prussian War. Peacetime nurtured advances in technology, the arts, and literature. Mechanical innovations were raising the quality of daily life for many while creating new employment possibilities and greater productivity. Steam engines operated looms, threshing machines, power tools, and locomotives pulling passenger trains. Wind-powered, ocean-going ships were overtaken by faster, more reliable steamships. Thanks to Thomas Edison, light bulbs were replacing malodorous coal-oil lamps. After the introduction of electric elevators, hotel customers no longer had to climb flights of stairs. Technical advances bolstered international commerce. They generated additional revenue in national economies, broadened meritocracy, thawed class mobility, and prepared society for the coming of motorcars and airplanes.

Yet Champion lived outside of all this progress. He had no means to enter. It took a locksmith to let him in.

2

THE FEARLESS KNIGHT

MONSIEUR CLÉMENT ALWAYS HAD THE WELL-
BEING OF HIS WORKERS IN MIND. THE FACTORY
WAS SPACIOUS, WELL LIT, AND HEATED IN THE
WINTER.

—CITATION FOR CHEVALIER
DE LA LÉGION D'HONNEUR, APRIL 2, 1894[1]

Adolphe Clément left his village in northern France at sixteen, right after the Franco-Prussian War, with 30 francs in his pocket and his possessions in a canvas backpack.[2] He became a manufacturer in Paris, a man at the heart of the genius of the nation's sweeping changes in transportation—pneumatic tires, bicycles, motorcycles, automobiles, and airplanes. From the introduction of each revolutionary advancement, Clément took an aggressive approach to funding its development and seeking creative new ways to promote advancement. Always restless, he hustled from one board of directors meeting to another, offering advice to a broadening circle of associates, sharing experiences, mentoring the next generation. He was known as a father to his workers when that trait was rare and respected.[3] He created such prosperity in French industry that he was awarded the highest civilian honors, la Légion d'Honneur, by three presidents.[4]

One day in November 1890, before anyone beyond Paris ever heard of him, Clément was in north London's Camden Town, attending the annual Stanley Show of Cycles in the spacious Royal Agricultural Hall.[5] He ambled over the stone floor, which amplified the din of hundreds of people gathered under the high ceiling at the trade show. The convivial Frenchman renewed acquaintances, met new friends, and checked out exhibits of gleaming bicycles mounted on stands among the aisles and steel wheels, leather saddles, wool apparel, and additional merchandise heaped on tables. He stood a little over five feet in height. In his thirty-three years he had experience making and repairing locks, shoeing horses, fixing broken watches, operating every piece of machinery in his factory, driving a bargain for shipments at a specific delivery date, closing a contract for a new supplier, and passing judgment on a question of manufacturing or sales policy of his Clément Cycles Company. Within a decade his business grew to one hundred fifty workers.[6] Photos captured a gleam in his eyes, as though excited about a new discovery, like the one he made at the Stanley Show.

Among the merchandise exhibits was the Dunlop Pneumatic Tyre Company, Ltd., a start-up from Dublin, Ireland. William Harvey du Cros Sr., an accountant who served as president, and his adult son, Arthur, displayed Dunlop pneumatic tires on their table. Most in the crowd swarmed past them without casting a glance. A few paused long enough to take a cursory look at the Indian-rubber tread or to talk briefly with the elder du Cros about his product. But they soon snorted or guffawed and abruptly bolted away.[7] "Actually, they made fun of us," Arthur du Cros later reminded journalists.[8]

It was not that the Irishmen's brogue or their manner had put anyone off. Harvey du Cros, as the senior du Cros was known, wore a bespoke suit and a fresh, crisp, white collar over his cravat. His nearly tamed mustache adorned a clean face under a high forehead. The faint lines on his dignified visage testified to a career of working indoors. Now in his fifties, he could still slip into the trunks he used to wear as Ireland's lightweight boxing champion, and he retained the physical grace of a tournament fencer. Arthur looked like a twenty-something version of his father, with the exception of a broader mustache, its ends waxed into submission.

The skepticism came from hearing the tires were filled with air. They were inflated by a soccer-ball pump. The younger du Cros could pump quick strokes of air into the tube, making the tire swell (resembling contemporary mountain bike tires). However, anybody seeing his demonstration scoffed that the tire looked like a sausage and turned away before either du Cros could explain that pneumatic tires offered a smooth ride over rough roads. English businessmen from cycling manufacturing centers in Coventry, Birmingham, and Nottingham felt free to point a finger at the Dunlops and laugh out loud, mocking them, as if to call attention to a prank or a scam.

"The public in Ireland and the cycle trade in England were unbelievers,"

Arthur du Cros wrote in his 1938 memoir *Wheels of Fortune*. "The ridicule and derision with which the tyre had been received was almost unanimous."[9]

Existing tires on bicycles, wagon wheels, and everything else that rolled used a neat strip of solid rubber, about an inch wide and deep, glued to steel rims—still common on grocery carts and farm tractors. Cyclists bounced over urban streets of cobblestones, crisscrossed with train rails, or had their hands jerked from handlebars shaken by rutted rural dirt roads, but without giving any thought to discomfort. A London cycling magazine took a snarky view of Dunlop pneumatics and sniped that they "should last at least a season."[10]

Clément took a longer perspective. He had traveled to the Stanley Show for a preview of innovations that had thrust England to the forefront of the flourishing bicycle industry. English engineers had improved steel—lighter, stronger, and more abundant than ever. New miracle steel enabled Eiffel to build his tower. Artisans in Coventry took advantage of recent steel to introduce early bicycles and unicycles, followed by tricycles with rack-and-pinion steering along with a novel gearing differential, which allowed wheels on the same axle to turn at different speeds around corners—technical breakthroughs that before long would prove indispensable for automobiles.

Clément sized up that the Dunlop pneumatic tires were dismissed by traditionalists content with solid rubber. The man had a habit of rebelling against traditions. Christened Gustave-Adolphe Clément in the village of Pierrefonds, he had dropped use of Gustave at a young age,[11] rejecting it due to its frequent designation among paternal ancestors and his disdain for the extravagant French penchant for compound first names, like his father's name, Léopold-Adolphe. At a time when the overwhelming majority of men wore a beard, Clément, completely at ease with hand tools, shaved daily with a straight razor, taking care to maintain a neat mustache. After the arrival of the safety razor at the turn of the century, beards became passé, but then he stopped shaving and let his beard grow full and bushy for the rest of his life.

Some of Clément's defiant leanings developed while growing up in Pierrefonds, home to a fifteenth-century castle; the castle's walls and corner towers had languished in ruins until his childhood, when an aristocrat restored it to resemble a palace with rounded turrets fit for a fairy tale.[12] Clément and his older brother had apprenticed to their father, who eked out a living as the village locksmith and blacksmith. Adolphe Clément was seven when his mother, Julie Alexandrina Roussette Clément, died.[13] Two years later, his father remarried and added to his trade a grocery shop that sold seasonal novelties.[14] The youth yearned to leave the complacent petit bourgeois provincial life for opportunities in Paris, a universe unto itself—the national capital, center of France's arts and letters, source of international fashion and cuisine, and the absolute essence of style.

His generation grew up learning about France's legendary Pierre Bayard, renowned in folklore as *le chevalier sans peur et sans reproche*, the knight without fear and without reproach.[15] Bayard was also remembered as generous and kindly. In one famous account, Bayard was a lieutenant general under King Francis I in 1521 and commanded a thousand soldiers in the ancient town of Mézièrs against German King Charles V's invading army of thirty-five thousand troops.[16] Mézièrs, a farming community on the Meuse River, where it meanders alongside the Belgian border, served as a critical defense between Germany and Paris. Bayard's men withstood heavy cannon fire in a six-week siege, giving King Francis enough time to collect an army that drove out the Germans. Such gallantry aroused Clément's imagination.

One frigid winter morning in early 1872, sixteen-year-old Clément had pulled on his backpack and walked away from his home on rue du Bourg to embark on the traditional *compagnon du tour de France*, a journeymanship to become a master locksmith.[17] The francs in his pocket were sufficient to buy bread and essentials for no longer than a couple weeks. He trekked clockwise around the country in the custom of *compagnons*—among them tinsmiths, cabinetmakers, stonemasons, and plumbers. They stayed in hostels or residences of "mothers" doing their part in a guild network by arranging accommodations and local work stints.[18] Compagnons put in long hours for low pay as they acquired regional techniques and used area materials over stretches of weeks or months. Clément studied under several masters. Now and then when it was time to leave for his next destination, a rowdy procession of drummers and fiddlers accompanied him out of town—an informal graduation rite.[19] Provincials like him thought nothing about walking fifty miles in a day.[20] He concluded his *tour de France* with a year in the Loire Valley region, south of Paris, among its fertile vineyards and a thousand old chateaux, enough to keep a battalion of locksmiths busy.[21]

He had Sundays to make daytrips to Paris by train. Paris had recovered from the Franco-Prussian War and had resumed its usual bustle. Clément found monuments galore, trendy boutiques with ingénues waiting on customers, and cafés that served lattés and cappuccinos sipped by men and women alike, all of them dressed to the nines.[22] At sunset, an army of lamplighters spread out to the city's almost one thousand streets.[23] Glowing whale-oil street lamps distinguished Paris as *La Ville Lumière*, the City Of Light.[24] Streetlights created a robust nightlife, which Parisians exploited by going about their lives after the sun went down—visiting friends and relatives, attending theaters, shopping, and exploring restaurants.

Compagnons, as a rule, went back home when they finished their tour, but Clément, a rebel to his core, chose to stay in Paris. He put down roots in Montmartre,[25] charmed by its vista over the city, low rents, and the chance to catch glimpses of artists coming and going, like Henri Toulouse-Lautrec, Marius Utrillo, Utrillo's mother Suzanne Valadon, and Raoul Dufy. Pierre-August Renoir painted *The Garden of the Rue Cortot in Montmartre*. Erik Satie played his soft piano compositions at Montmartre's hip cabaret Le Chat Noir. By 1878, Clément had secured a shop at 20 rue Brunel, in the tall, imposing Saint Ferdinand Building.[26] His choice was strategic. As a tradesman, he could starve without attracting enough customers. Instead, he gained some notice by moving next door to the atelier and print shop of acclaimed poster artist Jules Chéret, at 18 rue Brunel, commanding the Saint Ferdinand Building's other half.[27] Clément required a shop sign to hang over his front door to inform even illiterates of his locksmith services, but he could not afford the artist's rates. He befriended one of Chéret's understudies to paint a sign depicting an open padlock.

Around the time Clément settled in, he noticed upper-class sportsmen perched on high-wheeled bicycles cruising Paris's boulevards. The machines were imported from Coventry, England. Their oversized front wheel and rear wheel like a dinner plate led to the English nickname Penny-Farthings, after the big penny and the smaller, less valuable farthing. The sight of the English two-wheelers had a profound effect on the master locksmith of twenty-three. They had swept into Paris one spring like schoolchildren running to the playground.

He learned that front-wheel sizes depended on the owner's leg inseam. Most front wheels and their long, spidery steel spokes had a diameter of about fifty inches, which fit the average man, about five feet seven. It was fashionable for cyclists to pose standing next to their machine for photos, the top of the big wheel even with the owner's shoulder.

The steel frame curved up over the front wheel and accommodated the handlebars and leather saddle. The high center of gravity made the front wheels susceptible to snagging on ruts, sticks, and stones. They became notorious for pitching riders headfirst over the handlebars. Nevertheless, these newfangled machines caused people seeing them rolling along the street to watch and point.

Small wonder. Unlike horses, these novel contraptions did not deposit tons of manure every day on Paris thoroughfares. Clément later told associates that he was awestruck at how even a portly cyclist could overtake a fast runner in one hundred meters and catch almost anyone on a horse in two kilometers.[28] That meant something special to Clément. He was aware that for generations dreamers and tinkerers had fashioned various hobbyhorses with wheels, but they had been crude. Until now. Clément recognized that the high-wheelers whipping around Paris boulevards were what the dreamers had in mind for a self-propelled way to get around.

Clément had learned a lot about metals and had paid attention to advances in steel from Sheffield, England. He studied the high-wheelers that droves of young men were pedaling in the Bois de Boulogne, the park spread out in western Paris with paths, avenues, and waterfalls. He bought some of the new lighter, hollow English steel tubing and built his own two-wheeler, which the French called *un grand-bi*.[29] He took it out for a spin in the Bois de Boulogne. With the wind rushing across his face and the sense of balance and fluid movement, he felt exhilarated. Always a businessman, he sold his machine to buy parts to make two more.[30] He bought a drill press, a lathe, and tools for gas welding to braze tubes together. He sold the next two he made, then four more, another eight, and orders kept coming.

He joined Sunday summer races in the Bois de Boulogne around the Hippodrome de Longchamp, a dirt horse track rolled smooth. His lack of speed mattered less than the reputation he garnered for making quality high-wheelers. In 1880 at a trade show in Le Mans, southwest of Paris, a jury of business executives awarded Clément a silver medal.[31] That stoked his entrepreneurial spirit. His demand as a locksmith remained even while orders for his bicycles were taking off. He had chucked his day job for a new career. Clément later told associates that he realized his trade—and its tools—were obsolete.[32] To inform street traffic that he made bicycles, he prevailed on a Chéret protégé to make a new sign to hang over his shop door. The sign depicted France's iconic rooster, head aloft, tail feathers spread, balanced atop a wheel.

Soon Clément employed a man and a shop boy.[33] He applied lessons from his hero Bayard, who had prepared for battles on behalf of French kings by conducting reconnaissance and espionage to learn as much as possible about the positions and plans of his enemies. Clément attended trade shows proliferating around France—in Nice, Tours, Epernay, and Alençon. His bicycles and tricycles won enough medals to fill a pirate's chest.[34] Then came a big order from France's Ministry of War for troops. He purchased additional lathes, drill presses, benches, and other machinery, and hired laborers and shop boys by the dozens.

In the mid-1880s, modern chain-drive bicycles burst on the scene, with both wheels the same size and a unique diamond frame.[35] These vehicles, again from artisans in Coventry, featured wheels about twenty-seven inches in diameter, comparable to today's adult bikes. Cyclists could set their feet conveniently on the ground and prevent falls, which led to the bicycles being referred to as safety bicycles. Clément realized their appeal was unlimited—especially to women. Safety bicycles made high-wheelers old-fashioned, similar to the 1980s when personal computers got the better of mainframe computers.

When the Exposition Universelle opened in May 1889 for the six-month-long world's fair, Clément served on the jury for the Palais des Arts Libéraux, a neoclassic stone building constructed to celebrate the liberal arts, including transportation. The Palais—near the Eiffel Tower on the Champs-de-Mars, an open greensward where Napoléon's army had marched and drilled—was among sixty thousand exhibits, from Buffalo Bill Cody's Wild West Show to a pavilion dedicated to France's champagne makers.[36] Clément and fellow jurors selected creations showcasing French merchandise that transported people and goods. Thirty million people from around the world entered the Exposition Universelle through the arch at the base of the Eiffel Tower. Clément could hold court in the Palais with distributors from cities around Europe to establish a network and pump up his company's sales.

More than anyone in France, Clément took a feverish interest in modern bicycles.[37] He saw that they would transform how everyone went places on public roads. Men and women were at liberty to hop on a bicycle and off they went—whenever or wherever they chose. For long distances, travelers could take their bicycles on the train as luggage; when they reached their station, they could pedal the rest of the way to where they were going. So when Clément came upon the Dunlop Pneumatic Tyre Company and the du Cros men at their table in the Stanley Show, he recognized that pneumatics were just what bicycles needed to appeal to the masses.

Clément and du Cros, father and son, hit it off, especially when Harvey du Cros said his family had descended from a French infantry captain—a Huguenot who had fled France in 1704 to escape religious prosecution.[38] Important to Clément, du Cros was an avid sportsman. He enjoyed recreation cycling, had won Irish boxing and fencing championships,[39] and had fathered six sons.[40] Clément and the du Cross men exclaimed that in the near future bicycles would become as great a necessity for getting around as a pair of boots.[41]

After the Stanley Show closed, Clément accompanied the du Cros men on a train rumbling across southern England to the west coast. They boarded a commuter ship crossing the Irish Sea to Dublin, home to an uncontested monopoly on pneumatic tires.

The elder du Cros informed Clément that the company founder was John Boyd Dunlop, a Scottish veterinarian who cared for farm animals near Belfast, in Northern Ireland. Dunlop neither owned a bicycle nor cared to learn how to ride one.[42] While the tires named for him were first used for cycling, he shrank from travel and avoided any kind of physical exertion,[43] a holdover from a childhood fear about his health. Dunlop, shambling around stoop-shouldered,[44] like he had recently recovered from an illness, moved slowly and in a deliberate manner,[45] and he spoke in a low-toned voice, as though he were an invalid. His ragged beard extended halfway down his chest, and his hair had gone completely white by the time he filed his patent at age forty-eight. He created the pneumatic tire in response to ten-year-old son Johnny complaining of the rough ride on his new bicycle's hard-rubber tires over Belfast's cobblestone streets.[46]

Dunlop devised pneumatic tires as a cushion, protected by a rubber tread. On October 31, 1888, John Boyd Dunlop submitted papers for his invention to the English Patent Office in London; he received a patent guaranteeing fifteen years of exclusive commercial rights.[47] The veterinarian turned over the operation to a group of executives. They incorporated the Dunlop Pneumatic Tyre Company and appointed William Harvey du Cros Sr., as chairman and executive director, based on his professional reputation.

Harvey du Cros gave Clément a tour of the facility. The only factory on the globe that made pneumatic tires occupied the floors above the Booth Brothers bike shop in a standard-issue four-story brick building.[48] The tiny company in the country best known for its potatoes and fiddle players could not have been more underwhelming. The company consisted of a half dozen sewing machines in the attic,[49] a few wooden racks, some scissors, and odds and ends.

Dunlop pneumatics, with the tube sewn inside the tire,[50] an inch and a half wide, with the Indian-rubber tread and a linen casing, were called "Mummy" tires (still popular worldwide as tubular tires). They fitted tightly over the steel rim and glued on. In case of puncture, the flat tire was pulled off and replaced by a fresh one, which could be neatly folded for convenient storage and inflated for the ride to continue. The factory may have been rudimentary, but Clément understood the power of an idea to motivate management and workers to make a business prosper.

Clément grew up with a peasant's frugality and spent only when unquestionably necessary. Investing in the Dunlop Pneumatic Tyre Company was risky. The product was untried—more of a prototype. It had no demand. The tires were wider than solid-rubber versions and required fashioning new steel rims, building different wheels, and modifying the diamond frame to fit the new wheels. Laborers had to learn new techniques. All the changes required time and capital, a dicey proposition for manufacturers that had recently converted from making high-wheelers to producing modern bicycles. Yet John Boyd Dunlop had exclusive patent protection—essential for spectacular potential. Clément personally liked the du Cros team of father and son. They had his confidence. The former locksmith wrote a check for 500 francs to buy one hundred

shares in the Dunlop Pneumatic Tyre Company, divided evenly between prefer-
ence, ordinary, and deferred shares.[51] He became the first stockholder outside
the British Isles.

Always seeking to leverage every deal for maximum possible payback,
Clément secured a license for exclusive manufacture of Dunlop tires in
France.[52] If the tires did as well as he thought, his investment would turn into
gold. Clément kept his regular product line to retain faithful customers. The
Dunlop Pneumatic Tyre Company would take a while to produce the tires and
ship an order to Clément in Paris. He planned how best to introduce the pneumatic tires on Clément Cycles.

Dunlop pneumatics faced a tough sell with a public forever wary about buying
a new product—only persuasive evidence would sway the public to accept
change. Clément could count on the rabid racing crowd, even back then, to
try *anything* racers *thought* could give a competitive edge. When his first order
of Dunlops came in time for the spring of 1891, Clément supplied special
new bicycles to the stable of racers he kept on retainer, among them Fernand
Charron, a professional he treated as a son—and would become his son-in-law.

Charron was short and wiry, with taut muscles—an ideal combination for
speed and stamina. His hairless face, trim mustache, and clothes like a fashion
plate signified him as one of the Moderns. In a country steeped in social rank-
ings, he was noted for being courteous to men and women of all classes. The
French press dubbed winners of five events with the honorific *l'as*, the ace.
Charron was an ace many times over. In Sunday races around the Longchamp
track in the Bois de Boulogne, his Dunlops rolled lightly over the dirt surface
while rivals on the thinner solid-rubber tires that bit into the sand had to fight
increased resistance. He could pull away from the competition at will, but,
mindful of keeping the race exciting for the paying audience, he avoided making
it look easy. Clément hawked Charron's triumphs by purchasing ads in journals,
touting his deeds on Clément Cycles, and promoting success on Dunlops.

Coinciding with the arrival of pneumatics, the arts and the march of capitalism came together to create an unparalleled mass-marketing medium—pic-

torial posters.[53] Clément's neighbor, Jules Chéret, had perfected an innovative printing method, which used chemicals for the first time.[54] From four basic color stones of red, yellow, blue, and black, his lithographic printing process made a nearly unlimited rainbow. Chéret's posters, typically four feet tall and three feet wide, advertised wine, perfume, soap, chocolates, paper for hand-rolling cigarettes, even chanteuses and dancing *femme fatales* frolicking in front of the stage footlights. The artist featured a smiling coquette using the array of products—his instantly recognizable Chérette. Jules Chéret, at fifty-four, was a rumpled little old gent in a smock mottled with paint smears, but his posters sold *joie de vivre*.

Clément commissioned Chéret's young understudies along with other artists to promote bicycles, tandems, and tricycles—and Dunlop tires. Advertisements flaunted Clément's name in large letters across the top. His address along the bottom was just as prominent: 20 rue Brunel, off the Avenue de la Grande Armée.

Posters brashly declared that Clément was the most important and the oldest bicycle manufacturer in France. His four-color advertisements stood out with France's national symbol, the rooster, balancing on a wheel. It was inevitable that Champion would ride for Clément, but not in the way either of them expected.

3

A BEAUTIFUL DEVIL

*THE FRENCH PEOPLE WERE LED TO HAVE GREAT
FAITH IN THE TYRE BY THE FACT THAT A
CELEBRATED RIDER NAMED JIEL-LAVAL, RIDING
WITH DUNLOP TYRES, EASILY BEAT THE FRENCH
CHAMPION, TERRONT, IN AN IMPORTANT RACE FROM
PARIS TO BREST.*
—*TO-DAY* (LONDON), JULY 18, 1896[1]

When Champion pedaled some twenty miles on the unicycle back and forth between his home on rue Debarcadere and Noisy-le-Sec, he passed an increasing number of vibrant four-color posters proliferating on walls and fences. The advertisements beckoned him like sirens, promising a better, smarter, sexier life. They cultivated his thirst for glamour and, of course, la gloire! He was feeling good about the money and attention he was pulling in from unicycle exhibitions.[2] In the summer of 1891, he learned of a bicycle race so radical it captured the fascination of Paris and changed his destiny.

An announcement of the race appeared on the front page of the June 11, 1891, edition of *Le Petit Journal*, a daily aimed at the working class.[3] The paper's correspondent Pierre Giffard, pudgy and partial to blowing smoke rings with cigars, had recently learned to ride a Clément cycle equipped with Dunlop pneumatics. He found the experience exhilarating and wrote articles about cycling as a social benefit, especially for *les petits*—the little people, workers toiling for low wages and never counting the long hours that bled them white. *Le Petit Journal* boasted one of the largest circulations in France, one million. Giffard had been a journalist long enough to realize the difficulty of impressing people to take advantage of something even when it was to their advantage. He concocted a preposterous idea calculated to grab the attention of les petits, and he astutely garnered support from the publisher.

Endurance races from one city to another far away were in vogue for newspapers to boost circulation. Advance articles glorified the event like carnival barkers in print. Prerace favorites were profiled, a map of the course was laid out, towns' unique attractions were listed, then race-day coverage transformed winners into heroes—all to pump up newsstand sales.

Giffard promoted his contest, which would require the racers to go from Paris west for 375 miles to the Atlantic coastal city of Brest, so far away it seemed outright beyond the capabilities of anyone on a bicycle, with the added fillip that contestants must double back. Ancient Bretons had considered Brest the end of the earth, which translates to the region's name, *Finistere*. The round trip of 750 miles was equivalent to fifteen days by a stagecoach pulled by four-horse teams, replaced with a fresh team every twenty miles.[4] *Le Petit Journal* promised an extravagant 2,000 francs to the winner, 1,000 francs for second, 500 for third, paying down to twenty-one places—the richest sports purse in France.[5] *Paris-Brest et retour* drew attention as being as outrageous—and as exclusively French as Eiffel's Tower.[6]

Over the twelve weeks leading to the start on Sunday, September 6, Giffard wrote a steady flow of articles extolling the social benefit of bicycles and touting his daring Paris-Brest-et-retour. He signed articles *Jean de Sans Terre*, translating to the everyman whose feet never touched the ground.[7] Paris-Brest-et-retour turned into the talk of the town. Giffard laid out the route from the *Journal*'s building on rue Lafayette in Montmartre west over rugged cobblestone and country dirt roads to the ocean. Science fiction author Jules Verne, famous for novels about space travel to the moon and exploring twenty thousand leagues under the sea, gave it his endorsement.[8]

To most folks, Paris-Brest-et-retour generated curiosity and wonder. To the sporting world, it posed the supreme test of character, intellect, and physical strength and endurance. To Adolph Clément, the contest presented a high-stakes bonanza. It pitted his Dunlop franchise against new tires from André and Edouard Michelin. The Michelin brothers had created a pneumatic tire after the recent disclosure that the original inventor was not John Boyd Dunlop.[9] After granting him a patent, the English Patent Office discovered it had overlooked a nearly identical patent it had issued in 1845 to Robert W. Thompson,[10] an engineer in Scotland. Thompson also had registered his patent in France and the United States. His patent had expired in 1860,[11] and he had died in 1873.[12] A surprise revelation was that the claims of both Thompson and Dunlop were nearly identical. Thompson had called for an improvement in *horse-drawn carriage* wheels,[13] whereas Dunlop intended his for wheels of *bicycles, tricycles or other road cars.*[14] Thompson's tires were so far ahead of their time that they disappeared in commercial failure. Dunlop's tires were a difficult sell, but some cyclists were beginning to accept them. Thompson had had the patent and no business while Dunlop had the business and no patent.

The abrupt loss of patent protection coincided with the Michelin brothers' struggle to save their late grandfather's rubber and agricultural equipment company in Clermont-Ferrand, in France's south-central region, from bankruptcy.[15] Neither knew anything about the business they had inherited. André was an engineer with a metal-framework company in Paris.[16] Younger Edouard had graduated from fine arts studies in Paris and had rented a studio in Montmartre to begin his career as a painter.[17] Nevertheless, they were passionate about preserving the company that had been in the family for three generations and moved to Clermont-Ferrand.

They had developed a pneumatic tire, and they were planning to market it when they learned about Paris-Brest-et-retour. The Michelins hailed the race as providential. They scurried back to Paris and hired French national champion many times over, Charles Terront, to ride their tires. Short with a bushy mustache, Terront in street clothes looked like nothing special, what Giffard might describe as *Jean Ordinaire*, a regular guy. On a bicycle, however, Terront had a deserved reputation as a giant, a pioneer pro athlete racing on dirt horse tracks and board-cycling ovals called vélodromes in every big city on the continent. Terront, now thirty-four, had even been invited in his youth to America in 1879 to tour with a vaudeville troupe—he rode high-wheel exhibitions on roller-skating rinks to demonstrate cycling to thousands in Chicago and Boston. The Michelins bet the future of their company on Terront.[18]

Clément was also competing against dozens of other French and English bicycle manufacturers to win Paris-Brest-et-retour. He had to contend with the Peugeot family—brothers Jules and Émile and their adult sons, Eugène and Armand. They followed generations of artisans who made practical household products—coffee grinders, sewing machines, winding mechanisms for clocks, whalebone corset stays, and umbrellas.[19] Since the nineteenth century the family trademark, the Peugeot lion, either rearing back on hind legs or striding on an arrow, had been familiar across Europe. Now from their plant in Valentigney, in eastern France, the Peugeot clan made bicycles adorned with their lion on the frame's head badge.

A recent challenger was Alexandre Darracq, who had converted his plant in northeast Paris from manufacturing sewing machines. Darracq did not put his name on bicycle frames like Clément and the Peugeots. In an appeal to the masses, Darracq invoked the Roman warriors who fought in arenas against great odds. He called his two-wheelers *Gladiator*.

There were arms manufacturers in France's eastern cities producing bicycles and muscling in for their share of the growing market, too. And British companies had established factories in Paris, among them Thomas Humber of the London Borough of Kingston-on-Thames.

Clément hired a greyhound of a man and rising young talent from the east-central wine-growing region of Burgundy, Pierre Jiel-Laval. When Frenchmen took pride in distinctive facial hair, Jiel-Laval wore a handlebar mustache, waxed to keep the ends flaring to the borders of his face. The day Jiel-Laval came to collect the Clément cycle he would race, the manufacturer hired a portrait photographer. Clément, in suit and cravat, stood next to Jiel-Laval, in shorts and jersey, behind the two-wheeler, a one-speed model; the frame with a sloping top tube anticipating contemporary mountain bikes.[20] They were flanked by Jiel-Laval's manager and support crew of nine men, selected to shield him from the wind—all showing off their Sunday finery.

Before the sun rose on Sunday, September 6, 1891, thousands of Parisians swarmed over rue Lafayette to witness the start of the momentous Paris-Brest-et-retour. Weeks of Giffard's journalism had roused them to engulf *Le Petit Journal*'s fortress-like stone building, draped in red-white-and-blue bunting. Gendarmes shouted above the hubbub to clear spectators from the street. Thousands lined deep on both sides of the road and created a tunnel of humanity nearly a mile long. In the dark some fifty pros lined up in rows on their cycles ahead of a throng of about 150 amateurs, contesting for trophies. The atmosphere was jubilant yet anxious. Nowhere in the world had there been such a sports extravaganza. There was no telling what would happen to the adventurers. Only Frenchmen were allowed—a point of national pride. Rules required contestants to finish on the same bicycle they started with. More than three hundred had signed up, but only two hundred came.[21]

At first light, a bugle blared. Thousands cheered, their voices echoing off adjacent buildings. Giffard led the rolling parade down the long street on its way to the Champs-Élysées and into the Bois de Boulogne for the seven o'clock rolling start.[22] Another bugle blast set the racers off to Brest.

Champion could have been a witness taking in the impact of this great adventure. He also could have followed the reporting by the pack of journalists following the race by train. Members of the Fourth Estate filed dispatches along the route by jumping off at station stops and telegraphing dispatches. News was chalked longhand onto a big slate sandwich board set on the sidewalk outside *Le Petite Journal*'s entrance.

The contest turned into a duel between sentimental favorite Charles Terront on an English Humber cycle equipped with untried French Michelin tires and the younger Pierre Jiel-Laval on a French machine and Irish Dunlops.

On Monday afternoon, after thirty-three hours and 375 miles of nonstop pedaling, Jiel-Laval encountered a massive throng of Bretons on the outskirts of Brest clapping and screaming *Allez Jiel-Laval!* A noisy mass of folks filled the road—at the last moment, they opened a narrow passage for him to glide through unharmed. In his wake, the patch of road he had just cleared at once filled with people jostling back in their places. Before automobiles and motorcycles could keep up with the race leaders for crowd protection, contestants went alone and were required to stop at a number of designated village squares where two or three officials sat at a table holding an inkstand and sign-in sheet. In village after village, Jiel-Laval had encountered similar loud, riotous welcomes. He hurried through the sea of people shouting his name and parting just in time to accommodate him on his way to Brest's rustic town square.

When he arrived there, dirt covered him from head to shoes. His face was haggard with fatigue. Yet his mustache retained its flared ends. It seemed every citizen in Brest shouted Jiel-Laval's name. He basked in la gloire! He barely had space to dismount in front of the table to write his name. He accepted a cup of beef soup and some pears.[23]

Jiel-Laval had won the race to Brest. It was the greatest moment of his life. Then he hopped back on his Clément cycle, waved to the crowd, and headed to Paris.

Fifty minutes later Terront, slowed by two punctures in the countryside, spun into view. He received a similar tumultuous reception.[24]

Late that night, Jiel-Laval's support crew heard from Terront's manager that Terront was distraught at being so far behind and had threatened to quit. Jiel-Laval's crew suggested he take time off for overdue bed rest in a hotel they had secured.

However, the information was a ruse. All's fair in love and war, and this was a commercial war. The formidable Terront kept pumping his legs straight through the night, with his support riders ahead pacing him. They had kerosene lamps hanging from their handlebars for guidance. In the dark, Terront stole the lead from the sleeping Jiel-Laval. Terront kept up his effort through the night, the next day, and the following night.

At sunrise Wednesday, ten thousand people milling around Porte Maillot in western Paris spotted Terront headed in their direction.[25] The morning stillness was shattered by ear-splitting cheers. Terront, coated entirely in dirt thrown up from tires, face streaked with snot and sweat, rolled over the finish line. He dismounted and stood on unstable legs. He straightened his back and waved an arm in every direction to fans shouting at the tops of their lungs. He wiped his forearm over his nose and mouth. Someone handed him a bottle of wine. He seized it by the neck and guzzled as though it were water.

André and Edouard Michelin stood in black morning coats, white shirts, and silk top hats in the enthusiastic mob filling the air with Terront's name. The Michelins made their way through the crush to embrace Terront like fathers welcoming their heroic son back from battle. Victory gave the Michelins a tidal wave of publicity in newspapers across the continent to launch their new tires. Their bet on Terront had paid off.

Champion, like all *Petit Journal* readers, learned that Terront had grown up in the cramped, congested slums of central Paris's Île de la Cité. A chord that must have struck Champion was that Terront came from nothing, a nobody, *vin ordinaire*. Yet through the force of willpower, keeping his wits under extreme physical demands that made Jiel-Lavel give in, and drawing on the strength of his body, Terront turned into a grand winner. Perhaps Jiel-Laval had more talent, which he showed as the first to reach Brest. Nevertheless, Terront had greater tenacity—and that difference made him the victor. Parisians cried out Terront's name with unreserved adulation. Such gloire! Champion could see he could do that, too.

Eight hours later, Jiel-Laval came in second, to a similar frothy ovation—a worthy opponent who had put up a spirited fight. Nearly a hundred finishers wobbled in for the next seven days. The other hundred starters had abandoned the race.

Terront's feat of going on his own means from Paris to Brest and back in less than three days (71 hours and 22 minutes), without any sleep whatsoever, evoked collective fascination. He had endured tire punctures, but after repairs he continued on his way. Pneumatic tires proved their worthiness.

Fulsome details of his exploit were published in *Petit Journal* and all the city's publications. An illustration depicting a refreshed Terront standing with his Humber cycle and Michelin tires covered an eight-page *Petit Journal* illustrated supplement. It sold one million copies.[26]

Michelin tires gained overnight fame.

Clément had orders pouring in from around France, Great Britain, and Europe.

Paris-Brest-et-retour fulfilled Giffard's goal of educating commoners about the social benefit of bicycles and he moved on to other projects. The French masses embraced bicycles for personal transportation and called the bicycle *la petite reine*—the little queen. She appealed to men and women across the social register, from chimney sweeps to aristocrats. The Bois de Boulogne soon filled with men and women cyclists spinning la petite reine through on its paths.

Solid-rubber tires faded from sight along with high-wheelers.

Pneumatic tires began their march to conquer the world.

Modern bicycles with pneumatic tires presented the first threat to the hegemony of horses on roads.

Giffard planned his event as a one-off, and he succeeded in making a big impression upon the general public regarding the social benefit of bicycles. His idea for a race across France impressed a law clerk who would take what Giffard had started to another level.

Champion realized he could have a future in cycling. He bought a top-of-the-line Clément racing bicycle with Dunlops.[27] It was a one-speed machine, built for riding on roads and banked-board vélodromes. Racing bicycles did not have a brake; riders slowed by using their legs to hold back the pedals propelled by "fixed gear," which did not coast. They were like toddler tricycles today. It's a measure of how much young Champion was earning that he helped support his mother and three brothers and paid about 700 francs for his cycle.[28]

He took a day to practice.[29] Feeling the cushion of pneumatic tires for the first time must have been sensational. Then he felt ready to win prizes in Sunday competitions in the Paris suburbs.[30] He took out a license from the French governing body. Thirteen-year-old Champion was among the youngest and smallest in the junior category, for boys under age eighteen. He joined packs of teenage hopefuls, backs bent low over dropped handlebars, legs pumping as fast as they could go through the streets in circuit races, known as criteriums. His legs were strong from so many miles on the unicycle, and he had developed impeccable balance, an invaluable asset to negotiate sharp corners at speed.

"From the first time he touched a racing bicycle, he rode like a beautiful devil," a journalist recalled. "His skill was extraordinary—he was a diabolical break-neck."[31]

Word about Albert Champion soon spread. A former racing celebrity, Henry Fol,[32] had retired to open a bike shop, Select-Cycle, on Avenue de Malakoff,[33] near where Champion lived, and he offered Champion a job as instructor.[34] Fol had won track titles as junior champion in his teens,[35] racing bicycles and tricycles on vélodromes in his hometown of Bordeaux. Fol, barely five feet tall, came to Paris as a pro and made his name as a sprinter. He paid Champion a decent wage and shared winning tricks of the trade.[36] When a tail-wind blew down the final straight to the finish line, sprint a long six hundred to eight hundred meters. Into a headwind, hold back the final spurt until the finish line is within one hundred meters. A dry surface is fastest, calling for a long sprint. A wet track requires a decisive move late in the game. Champion absorbed Fol's advice and shined in races.[37]

Champion was getting inculcated with a mix of sport and a life, shot through with an unrelenting exercise regime, a stern work ethic, pride, tradition, and ignorance. Old tales accepted as gospel prohibited swimming because water softened muscles.[38] Bathing in warm water opened pores and let in diseases. Getting a haircut carried the risk of catching a cold. A winner never washed his jersey or shorts to keep the good luck, a superstition that made generations of athletes adamant about wearing smelly, sweat-stained clothing, to the annoyance of their families.

He experimented with drafting—riding close behind the rear wheel of the cyclist ahead, whose front wheel, face, shoulders, and chest divided the air like the bow of a ship pushing through water. When the finish came in sight, followers had fresher legs and whipped ahead of the leader as though thrust by a slingshot. Racing was a confluence of fitness and tactical skills.

Clément continued to make news that impressed Champion. The manufacturer constructed an outdoor five-hundred-meter vélodrome with a big grandstand and bleachers the rest of the way around near rue de Courcelles, a stone's throw from the Seine in the northwest suburb of Levallois-Perret. The track opened in August 1893, christened as *Vélodrome de la Seine*.[39] Behind the cheap seats along the back straight stood a row of wooden cabins for racers to change clothes and store bicycles and equipment, along with the latest thing—a building offering cold showers.

London's *To-Day* called the vélodrome "a splendidly made cement track, and every Sunday the enclosure is thronged by ten to fifteen thousand persons, who assemble to witness the exciting contests. French, English, Dutch, German, and Belgian riders competed in the races, and the sport is of a truly international character."[40]

Near the vélodrome he added a plant to manufacture Dunlop tires. His new factory was powered by steam engines with five-hundred-horsepower (500-hp) capacity. A cafeteria offered ovens for employees to warm food they had brought.[41]

Yet Clément kept expanding his empire. Major railroad companies serving travelers from Paris to cities all the way south to the Riviera on the Mediterranean Sea contracted Clément to supply their legion of workers with cycles. He bought an abandoned factory in Tulle, the south-central city that gave its name to the stiff fabric used for veils and ballet costumes.[42] Clément converted the building into a division of his Paris operation to produce cycles. Depending on the season, his Tulle plant employed up to one thousand workers.[43]

In the spring of 1895, seventeen-year-old Champion gave up the job of instructing clients how to ride. He left Fol to present himself to Clément and Company on rue Brunel, conveniently close to where he lived.[44] It is likely he had passed many times past Clément's sign of the rooster on a wheel hanging over the front door.

The window on the street displayed new cycles with enameled finishes that glinted even in the grubby light of Paris's chronically overcast skies. Clément and Company had taken over the Saint Ferdinand Building, at 18 and 20 rue Brunel, after Jules Chéret had decamped with his atelier and print shop to a new venue a few blocks over. Champion may have been unaware the building was named in tribute to the thirteenth-century Spanish king sainted for taking care not to overburden his subjects with taxes, something that appealed to the sensibilities of Clément.

Champion stepped under the sign of the rooster and pushed open the door. He entered the factory intent on securing a job, oblivious to how it would become his school.

4

THE "HUMAN CATAPULT"

CLÉMENT IS A HOUSEHOLD WORD.
—WESTMINSTER BUDGET (LONDON),
OCTOBER 9, 1896[1]

Once inside the St. Ferdinand Building, Champion's nose was assailed by the pungent smells of oil, grease, lacquer, and acetylene laced with sweat and nicotine from about 150 laborers and artisans cutting steel, brazing frames together, and painting frames to produce finished *petits reins*. He heard the whirring and flapping sounds emanating from a forest of long leather belts, four or five inches wide and thick as fingers, connected to pulleys high overhead feeding power down to run machines at workstations on the concrete floor—the universal clatter of nineteenth-century steam-powered factories.[2] He encountered the floor manager, in a dark smock and flat wool cap, a cigarette burning in a corner of his mouth, and received his once-over.

It may have struck Champion that he stood where countless other candidates had, only for the majority to fail. As he began to present himself, mentioning his name, the floor manager raised a hand—no need to say anything more. It seemed his audition ended before he drew his first breath.

Instead, he found to his surprise that at Clément Cycles, they already knew Albert Champion.[3] They were looking for someone with his list of amateur victories—referred to as *palmarès*. He was offered a sponsorship to race as a pro for Clément Cycles the next spring season. The prize money was going to be his to keep, like a prizefighter on wheels.

He would have a new racing cycle—built with a modern diamond frame and lighter than the one he had bought, plus all the Dunlop tires he needed. Even better, Clément Cycles offered to provide a pair of three-seat triplets and six riders to pedal them for Champion to pace behind for faster workouts. He had the autumn and winter to get race ready. He would try out in the twenty-five-kilometer (15.6 miles) paced race serving as the new season opener on the first Sunday in April,[4] at the winter indoor vélodrome in the Palais des Arts Libéraux, a massive marble building near the Eiffel Tower. If he performed as expected, he would receive a Clément team jersey with the trademark rooster across his back and race full-time for Clément. Champion would be on his way to garnering honor, fame, riches, and la gloire!

The offer was bittersweet. For the next five months, when he wasn't training for his tryout, he would earn his keep by working as a bicycle courier, copying Clément's handwritten correspondence with a delicate letter-copying book process, and performing odd jobs—all for a weekly salary of 6 francs.[5] The pay was meager, a substantial cut in income. He still had to support himself and help provide for his mother and three younger brothers.

Champion, not inclined to ponder negative prospects, seized the positive, his opportunity to ride as a pro for Clément.

Guiding him into his new métier was Pierre Tournier, a wiry gent in his mid-thirties dressed like a banker, his swank felt hat tilted at a jaunty slant.[6] Tournier had a certain way of getting along with people of all types of personalities.[7] Clément put him in charge of sponsored riders to ensure they had the Dunlops and whatever supplies they needed—when they succeeded, so did the manufacturer. Tournier would have arranged for Champion to receive a new racing cycle, all steel except for a leather saddle and rubber Dunlops. The frame had modern straight lines of the diamond shape as well as curved handlebars clean of any attachments.

Pierre Tournier, far left in the back seat, enjoys a smoke, sitting next to American national cycling champion Harry Elkes (middle) and Arthur Zimmerman, world cycling champion and US champion many times over. Tournier shepherded them around Paris in 1900 to see the sights in a Clément-Talbot motorcar. *Photo by Jules Beau. From the collection of Lorne Shields, Thornhill, ON, Canada.*

Champion's new job involved learning how to ride the steeply banked indoor board track, a saucer ten laps to the mile, or 176 yards around, in the Palais des Arts Libéraux.[8] The vélodrome was surrounded by box seats at the start/finish line. A few tiers of seats surrounded the track. There was a judge's stand in the infield at the start/finish line and a bandstand in the middle of the infield. The vélodrome and stands took up only a small portion of the facility, languishing after the 1889 Paris Exhibition. The vélodrome's banked turns of thirty-eight degrees and straights of fifteen degrees looked daunting.

Tournier instructed Champion to follow experienced cyclists tacking a diagonal angle up the banking, moving as easily as dancers on a stage, to near the top edge's wooden rail, about twenty feet high, before diving down to build speed. To spectators, the precipitous banking appeared like a wall. One of the first things Champion learned about vélodromes, however, is that onlookers see a *trompe l'oeil*. Cyclists appeared to lean precariously as they flashed through the turns, when both rider and machine actually remained upright over the surface at all times, as though traveling straight on a flat street. The illusion added to track racing's mystique.

Champion became comfortable whizzing around laps before Tournier had him progress to pacing fast behind the triplets.[9] First Champion drafted with his front wheel close behind the rear wheel of his team on a three-seat machine, clocking off fast times on the lower end of the vélodrome while the second team cruised the upper rim. After three or four laps, the legs of the first team grew tired and the riders angled up the banking to recover as the second team, with fresh legs, descended for Champion to catch their draft for nonstop highballing.

Scarcely a week went by before the former unicyclist entertained himself by rubbing his front wheel against the rear wheel of his pacing machine in the turns, shaving the triplet's speed and disturbing its equilibrium.[10] It was a reckless yet fantastic stunt.[11] Pacing cyclists always guard their front wheel at all costs, like a boxer's arms and fists guard his face. Overlapping wheels were by far the most frequent cause of crashes. In the blink of an eye, the slightest false move could cause Champion and the triplet to topple over at the expense of torn clothes, abrasions, bruises, or worse. Speeding around the saucer called for a change of balance about every fifteen seconds, into and out of the next banked turn, then on the straight, for thirty-second laps. There were infinite opportunities to make a mistake. Yet he never fell down. He liked showing off.

"The game was not without danger, but Champion got a kick out of it," noted one observer. "He had extraordinary audacity."[12]

The press became alert to Champion's exceptional talent. Rubbing wheels was part of his debut preparation. In competition, there was no such thing as "good enough."[13] He was adding a skill of the trade to make him into a winner, like Charles Terront. He planned to win his try-out race in a handsome fashion.

Champion's workouts were usually in the mornings. The rest of the time, from Monday through Saturday, he arrived at the factory by six o'clock,[14] in time for the Angelus devotion, the triple-stroke bell ringing repeated three times in the ancient stone Saint-Pierre-de-Montmartre Church. He opened the heavy window curtains. He swept and dusted around numerous workstations with lathes, drill presses, milling machines, and the benches holding heavy vises and clamps.[15] He swept the back-room offices of the bookkeepers and dusted their leather-bound ledgers standing on shelves like financial soldiers at attention. He built the hearth fires to ward off morning chills, wound the wall clock, split kindling, and carried coal that ran steam-powered machinery. Sometimes he washed windows. When the laborers and office employees arrived at seven o'clock, they found everything ready. Then he was free to meet his pacers at the Palais for their practice sessions before he returned to the factory.

At twelve o'clock, the church bell rang the noon Angelus. Workers donned hats and lit cigarettes they hand-rolled. The factory emptied for traditional two-hour lunches by the ringing of the ninth bell. Champion grabbed his cap and beat it home for lunch with his mother, taking her customary break to return home with his brothers. By two o'clock he and others sauntered back to work.

At six o'clock the third Angelus rang, signaling the workday's conclusion. He closed the window curtains and left.

The only exception in the routine was Saturday afternoon. Champion joined shop boys lining up outside the bursar's office in the rear of the building. He received a pay packet of 6 francs. He carried his francs home at once to his mother, a welcomed addition to their slender family income, as he awaited his debut to earn 100 francs as the race winner.

More bicycle manufacturers and deeper economies of scale drove down prices and increased sales. Advertising took on an increased premium in the hurly-burly of escalating capitalism. The enormous success that Chéret's beguiling Chérettes wielded in retail sales impelled Clément to commission posters of carefree ingénues, naked or clad in diaphanous negligees, sitting atop their Clément cycles or flying like angels, holding his two-wheelers, over the Paris skyline. Flirtatious, bare-breasted beauties with fresh makeup implied the bicycles were light as air and easy to ride. To traditionalists objecting that women lost femininity when they indulged in physical activity, the posters shouted *au contraire*, cycling added to feminine allure.

Clément hired Paris's renowned artists such as Jean de Paléologue, who signed his posters *PAL*. His classical art studies in London and Paris had nurtured his flair for making women practically leap off the paper. He selected well-endowed models and depicted them as Greek goddesses in states of *déshabille*, frolicking in skimpy, sheer gowns. They exposed considerable flesh and sold great sex appeal. Another artist Clément relied on was Ferdinand Misti-Mifliez, who signed his work *Misti*. His brush strokes reflected Chéret's lightness.

Telephones were coming into use, but not with artists. Clément sent Champion as a courier carrying proposed designs back and forth between his office and artist ateliers.[16] On his courier runs Champion would have encountered de Paléologue and Misti in their ateliers, a shaft of brightness pouring through a skylight. Usually the object under the light was a young woman posing, either in the nude or déshabille, standing, or ensconced on a chair, surrounded with discarded clothing or gossip sheets *Echo de Paris* and *Psst!* Deft brush strokes transferred facial features, shoulders, hips, and breasts onto the canvas with playful, even magical, touches. On walls and kiosks all over the city, a blonde goddess of Paléologue in gossamer dress falling off her shoulders defied gravity and soared in the colorful dawn pastels over the Paris skyline. She brandished a laurel wreath of victory in one hand while her other gripped a Clément cycle.

As soon as the artists painted their posters, Clément ordered couriers to expedite them to printers. Shrewd about how he spent money, he took care not to rely on just one printer. He used several so as to get the best deal and quickest turnaround. Once off the presses, stacks of poster advertisements were distributed to a fleet of couriers, including Champion, armed with glue pots. They fanned out and plastered posters on surfaces all over Paris, a city of posters.

Adolphe Clément gave Champion pointers for advertising to promote products. Champion gained notice in America racing on Clément Cycles. *Image courtesy of Poster Photo Archives, Posters Please, Inc., New York.*

These activities kept Champion couriering throughout Paris, crossing its many bridges that spanned the meandering Seine, to deliver written or oral messages. In this way, he made personal contact with artists, business leaders, laborers, and government bureaucrats—getting comfortable with the people operating the business arena.

Champion had entered the urban workforce as the Second Industrial Revolution picked up tempo. Machinery and manufacturing surpassed the long-standing domination of the agrarian economy. He had the good fortune to work for Clément, who took pride in a paternal interest in his workers, as Bayard had cared for the well-being of his troops. All machines, including those cutting wood, were equipped with ventilators to remove dust and prevent damage to workers' health.[17] Champion had joined a new order.

Clément was exchanging letters with power brokers around France and across Europe, which led to Champion learning how to master the letter-copying book process.[18] A ubiquitous piece of nineteenth-century office equipment was the screw press—the copier machine of its day,[19] which made tissue-thin paper copies of correspondence that Clément wrote longhand. The screw press squatted on a table of its own in Clément's office in the back of the factory. It was a magnificent machine, made of cast-iron parts painted a uniform black lacquer and decorated with gold-leaf fleur-de-lis, the heraldic emblem of French kings, with stylized three-pedal iris flowers. The handle on the middle of the top spun a spiral shaft that lowered the upper plate onto the bottom flat plate for the paper to make an impression.[20] Turning the handle so the plate made soft contact with the paper made only a faint copy, or failed altogether; tightening it too hard made an illegible blob. Champion had to turn the handle to the proper tension to get it right.

He was instructed to begin the delicate procedure by dampening a sheet of imported Japanese rice paper, prized for its strength and ability to absorb ink, with water from a brush, or a blue cotton cloth with serrated edges soaked in water.[21] The acid-free sheets of rice paper were numbered in sequence up to a thousand folios in a leather-bound volume, containing an index. Champion inserted the letter intended for reproduction in the bound volume, insulated the wet page from adjacent dry pages with sheets of oiled paper, and set the volume on the bottom flat plate. Copies were made by turning the handle, which lowered the top plate.[22] To get the proper pressure without spoiling the original letter while making a clear copy required a knack. Copies stayed in the leather-bound volume; originals went into envelopes for posting. He had to practice before passing.

Champion came to appreciate his boss's fascination with the great knight Pierre Bayard. Clément likely had a painting displayed on a wall of Bayard in a suit of armor, visored helmet in the crook of his left arm, right hand gripping a lance. Bayard was killed in action in Italy in 1524 while leading troops for Francis I.[23] Bayard's body was returned to France and interred in Grenoble.[24] Clément would have mentioned a pilgrimage he had made to the knight's memorial and ancient family estate, Chateau Bayard.

When Clément sat at his desk to pore over the accounting ledger, he had occasions to instruct Champion about the intricacies of commerce. Payments received from the sale of bicycles, tandems, and tricycles to distributors as well as royalties from the Dunlop tires generated gross revenue. From that, Clément deducted the costs of material, labor (including Champion's paltry wage), and the building rent. The difference was his company's gross profit. Clément tallied all operating costs—from the purchase of firewood and coal to installation of electricity (which increasingly took over from steam power to operate machinery) to advertising expenses—and subtracted them from the gross revenue, which left Clément with a net profit.

Net profit supported him and Madame Celeste Clément, their two sons, the oldest also named Albert, the other Marius, daughters Jeanne and Angèl, and his staff of servants in a grand residence across town at 35 Avenue du Bois de Boulogne—an address with status.[25]

Like many Parisians, Clément and his wife had a passion for opera. To ensure access to tickets for opening nights of new productions of works by Georges Bizet, Jules Massenet, or revivals of Jacques Offenbach, Clément bought the land for construction of the new Paris Opera House—securing his place of importance not only as manufacturer but also as a patron of the arts.[26]

While Champion picked up information about his boss, he shared some of his background. Clément understood what it was like as a child to lose a parent, having lost his mother when he was seven. He assessed the youngster as deserving a chance to develop his talents. In Clément, Champion gained a tutor, albeit a rather driven man who put his work before family, which Champion came to assess as a consequence of constantly pushing his business ahead of the competition.

Clément subscribed to trade journals, some from England, to keep up with developments. He would have chortled with Gallic hubris, informing Champion that so many English words derived from French that Champion could easily get the essence of the articles. Since William the Conqueror of Normandy had overwhelmed English troops in 1066, everyone in the courts and wherever commerce took place spoke the language of the conquering French. So the trade press in England, Ireland, and the former colony in America relied on French vocabulary, such as *attention, courage, important, agent, surprise, plus, extra, minute, idiot, silence, urgent, problem,* and *solution.* The Irish, the English, and the Americans all spoke French now.

Robust sales of la petite reine stirred two Montmartre craftsmen to think up something radical. Réne Panhard, a graduate of the École Centrale des Arts et Manufactures,[27] and Émile Levassor, a businessman, co-owned a company that manufactured machines that cut and shaped metal.[28] Panhard had bought French rights from Gottlieb Daimler of Germany to make internal-combustion gas engines.[29] Daimler had fitted an engine under the driver's seat of a carriage, creating self-propulsion in 1885.[30] He turned the machine with a tiller that substituted for reins. Daimler saw his invention as a horseless carriage.

Panhard and Levassor improved on Daimler's design. The Frenchmen mounted the engine on the chassis front and replaced the standard leather-belt drive with a metal shaft-and-gear transmission, which included a clutch that allowed the driver to change speed ratios as the vehicle sped up or slowed down.[31] To cool the engine, Panhard and Levassor added a radiator.[32] They introduced a round steering wheel for making turns. In 1892 they introduced the archetype modern *automobile*.[33]

Clément had a historical perspective on the long competition between France, England, and Germany for leadership in the quest for self-propelled vehicles. During the early nineteenth century, adults and children alike in all three countries had rolled around on hobbyhorses with two wooden wheels under a board slab. Riders sat on the slab and moved by scooting feet on the ground. Paris coach maker Pierre Lallement in 1860 had attached pedals to cranks that fit to the front-wheel spindle of a hobbyhorse.[34] It had iron-rimmed wheels made of chunky wooden spokes and straight iron handlebars that turned the front wheel. Lallement's leather saddle attached to a steel spring fastened over the frame. He named his invention a *vélocipede*, the prototype bicycle. He had a stint producing vélocipedes with Pierre Michaux and son Ernest, builders of baby carriages in Paris. Then the Franco-Prussian War of 1870 had dealt vélocipedes a fatal blow.

Yet creative minds continued to mull over some kind of machine enabling people to get around on wheels. For years steel had been made from iron, but it was expensive and available only in limited quantities, measured in pounds, for making tool bits and swords. English engineers led by Henry Bessemer in Sheffield refined the iron-making process to produce cheap steel in quantities that sold by the ton for constructing bridges and buildings.[35] The advanced miracle steel enabled Eiffel to build his iconic tower and had applications for improving bicycles. English steel could be drawn, hollowed for lightness, and shaped while retaining its tensile strength.

Artisans in Coventry, in England's Midlands, took advantage of Lallement's concept and the advent of improved steel. In the early 1870s, they increased the size of the front wheel and fashioned long steel spokes with steel rims on a bicycle frame of lighter, hollow tubing. They created the high-wheel bicycles, which thrust England ahead as world leader in mechanical personal transportation.[36] Local artisans introduced more advancements, including the modern bicycle with a chain drive and both wheels the same size on a diamond frame. Bicycle manufacturing poured money into the Coventry's economy. The city that had been renowned for Lady Godiva once riding naked on a snow-white horse through the town at noon had a thriving business in transportation.

Then Panhard and Levassor initiated a critical advancement that made Clément's entrepreneurial juices run. He felt that the progression from vélocipedes to high-wheelers to safety bicycles to Daimler's horseless carriage culminated in the Panhard-Levassor automobile. Clément put his resources behind Panhard and Levassor to make certain they won the commercial war in personal transportation for France. Clément invested heavily in their company and made sure its autos were equipped with Dunlops.[37] He was appointed director of the corporate board.[38] Clément felt sure the future of individual transportation was in autos.

At some point Champion encountered twenty-nine-year-old Henri Desgrange, a former law clerk with writing aspirations, employed then writing ad copy and handling publicity for their boss, Clément. Desgrange came from money, and the security he drew from it conferred on him a religion of might. In photos a bearded young Desgrange stared defiantly into the lens, arms akimbo, chin jutting, demeanor brazen. "His motto could have been *Vae Victis* (woe to the vanquished)," observed journalist Roger Bastide.[39] When Desgrange stood near Clément, his employer came to his chin. Desgrange wrote in his office near the bookkeepers at the rear of the factory on rue Brunel, pen scratching across reams of paper, pausing only to dip his steel nib in an ink well. He dispatched Champion, as courier, to printers, artists, and journalists.

Desgrange had established the first world hour record (for distance pedaled over sixty minutes around a track).[40] He had good legs and pushed himself with focus, hard work, and audacity. Before anyone better, Desgrange had acted. Clément acknowledged him as a maverick. Desgrange became one of Champion's influential models for how a young man might change his life through cycling and realize grand ambitions.

Champion's courier runs on one of the house beater bikes inevitably had him cruising along Boulevard des Batignolles, bordering the southern edge of his neighborhood. Shops standing shoulder to shoulder catered to all the indulgences of Parisians and troops of tourists from around Europe, Great Britain, and America. Riding in the sun's glare, his reflection on the shop windows kept him company.

Boulevard des Batignolles exerted a lasting effect on Champion. A fashionable grocer at number 86 gratified epicurean palettes with a selection of wines as well as a delicatessen with fresh fruit and vegetables from the continent.[41] The shop was operated by Bernard and Marie Delpuech.[42] There one afternoon he encountered their daughter, Julie Elisa, counting change for customer purchases. Family and friends called this willowy, dark-haired *jeune fille*, Elise. She was tall, standing eye to eye with Albert, with fine features, a small chin, and eyebrows drawn sharp like a Modigliani model. She had long thin arms and legs and delicate fingers. Albert, dashing around Paris on his courier's cycle and stopping to swagger into the wine aisle with confidence rolling off him, attracted her interest. He began to court this daughter of the merchant class, a rung above his station. He found her chic—a catch.

Champion's career-making tryout in the race in the Palais des Arts Libéraux and his eighteenth birthday on April 5, 1896, fell on the same Sunday, as though he were bestowed a gift. Where the Palais had once held exhibits of the liberal arts for the 1889 world's fair, including medicine and surgery, theater, and transportation, it now held Champion's professional debut.

Pierre Tournier, as manager, fussed over Champion and the three-rider triplets to mollify their prerace jitters. The audience filling tiers of seats created a wall of voices. The announcer on his megaphone kept up a patter. A band in the middle of the infield filled the air with popular tunes. Riders were whizzing around the track in the preliminaries. Through the distractions, Tournier spoke calmly to his crew, methodically took care of the mundane tasks of pumping up all the tires, making sure everyone on the team had properly signed up with officials, and tying the competitor cloth numbers securely around their upper left arm for easy spotting. He kept Champion and his pacers attentive.

Champion would be tested. Win or lose, the outcome would determine his future. Expectations were high for him. Some journalists compared him with Jimmy Michael, the diminutive Welshman pace follower and world champion who drew crowds that packed every track in Paris and around Germany to standing room only.

The race was organized by Henri Desgrange.[43] He put on weekend events to realize his ambition of one day creating the world's greatest sports extravaganza.

"He's called Champion, a strangely prophetic name for his future battles," Desgrange wrote for Le Cycle under the nom de plume A Spectator of the Third Arrondissement, caricatured on the margin of the page as an aristocrat in top hat, frolicking on a bicycle, coattails flapping.[44] "It's a bit like the crowning of the winner coming before the event itself. Physically, the young rider is not very attractive. I would even go so far as to say that he's not very appealing."[45] He chided Champion for having a sultry expression and wearing an ill-fitting purple jersey: "Some riders show off their shape, show off their muscles and their suppleness, but Champion hides his spindly legs and pulls his jersey as low as possible to cover them up."

Champion and three rivals lined up next to one another along the breadth of the banking. The triplet teams waited behind them. Tournier bent low at the waist and with both hands held Champion steady on his Clément cycle. When the official in a silk top hat fired the starting pistol, Tournier gave Champion the traditional push off like a shot-putter. The triplets came around wide on the track for their riders to catch rear wheels and they were underway.

Champion charged to the front early. He had a fierce drive to *prendre le pouvoir*, to take supreme power, like Napoléon. Champion not only rode fast, but he added a showman's flair—he sat up straight, like the unicyclist he had been, and put on an intimidating exhibition of speed and bike handling.[46]

"He simply took his hands off the wheel and, by a skillful jerk of the knee, he regained the balance he had momentarily lost, all in the flash of an eye," a reporter cited.[47]

When he dropped back down and grabbed the drops of his handlebars, he made a graceful switch to catch his relief triplet.

"His mastery of pacing and competency in switching from one pace team to another exceeded his experience," claimed one account.[48]

As the number of laps wound down, Champion sped behind his triplet teams like a courier fearful of getting sacked for tardiness.

The ringing of a cowbell to announce the final lap roused the audience in the Palais to jump up and down and cheer Champion. The noise level created a wall of sound. It blocked out all his pain and made him spin his legs faster.

Approaching the finish line, he leaned deeper and faster into the turns to live up to his name. He whipped down the back straight to impress his *jeune fille* Elise. He zoomed around the final turn for extra cash to take home to his mother and brothers. He flew across the finish line for victory and la gloire!

"He turned in a masterpiece," a journalist wrote. "The rookie's victory was complete and convincing."[49]

On his victory lap, Champion waved the bouquet of flowers he received to show the audience his gratitude. The francs he won fit in his fist, a down payment on the fortune he needed—if he could follow his dream. He took the money home to his family. He kept la gloire for himself.

The next morning, Clément dispatched him to the studio of Jules Beau, a prominent portrait photographer. Taking his Clément cycle into the studio, Champion smelled the chemicals and eyed mysterious paraphernalia. Beau's apprentice, who signed his work as Bauenne, set up a camera on a tripod. Champion posed on his bicycle in profile for one image and then gripped the handlebar drops and glared at the lens as though to challenge the world.

A print of Champion ran with A Spectator's story in *Le Cycle*.[50] The magazine devoted a full page under the banner "Le Coureur Champion." The coverage was all about him, as though his opponents had failed to count: "He is a small rider on a small machine, with small legs which turn short cranks, but will achieve some great performances, because Champion only just began to find his voice in his race last Sunday. We will have to wait and see him begin to shine with the kind of brilliance that will perhaps put even Michael in the shade."[51]

At age eighteen in 1896, Champion's speed and riding skill prompted a reporter to write that he had extraordinary audacity and rode like a beautiful devil. *Photo by Jules Beau. Courtesy of Cherie Champion.*

Champion immediately nabbed the spotlight of the sports world. Bestowed with a Clément team jersey with a rooster on the back, which fit better, and a contract from the Roubaix Vélodrome, Champion raced as a regular in cycling-mad Roubaix, a textile city some 170 miles north of Paris, in northern France near the Belgian border.[52] Roubaixians, known to work hard six days a week in the mills, spent Sundays watching their favorite racers at the cement outdoor vélodrome. Roubaix had so many mills it was known as *la ville aux mille chemi-nées*, the town of a thousand chimneys.[53] Here Champion experienced the trial-and-error seasoning required of every young pro cyclist: defeats and victories.

Champion inhaled the cheers of the spectators, taking in their adulation like oxygen. "The kid was marvelous," a journalist wrote.[54] "He began to dominate right away. The little demon was soon tearing down the track like a torpedo behind triplets and quadruplets and no one could beat him. He knew only victory."[55]

He grew stronger with confidence and savvy. He was dubbed the "Human Catapult" by a journalist who wrote that he "didn't know his own strength and showed himself to be more and more a man of some class."[56]

Many in the press corps remarked on his superior handling skills. "At the old, almost flat, Buffalo [Vélodrome], he aroused general admiration by his impressive turns," a reporter noted.[57] "At the speed he went, his two wheels slid dangerously. He flew by anyway, fearing neither God nor the Devil."[58]

Racing was about making money for the dual compelling needs that invig-orated him. He gained financial support for his family and the ego endorse-ment enjoyed by entertainers and politicians. As his ego grew, he needed to impose himself on crowds of strangers and win their love. Each race he won was greeted immediately with audience approval followed by a bouquet of flowers, a victory lap, then a cash award. Champion also craved Elise's attention, and winning elevated him in class as a suitor for her hand.

As Champion soared like a comet, Clément directed construction of a massive factory in Mézièrs, an ancient fortified town on the Meuse River in northeast

France, with a bustling commercial center and network of railroads. He face-tiously named the facility *La Mercerienne*, a haberdasher's shop, to make custom spare parts for bicycles and Panhard-Levassor autos.[59] Clément selected Mézièrs for his new factory in homage to the heroic knight Pierre Bayard.[60] He erected a statute of the knight in front of La Mercerienne.[61]

Clément's fortunes were soaring. The one hundred shares of Dunlop stock he had purchased for 5 francs a share were now selling for 7,500 francs each.[62] He was an early advocate of the capitalist notion that the best way to deal with com-petitors is to make them an offer they cannot refuse and then buy their business. He advertised on posters that he had capital of 4,000,000 francs—letting the row of zeroes separated by commas scream his worth.[63] He negotiated with Alexandre Darracq to purchase Gladiator Cycles.[64] In turn, Darracq used the money to found the Darracq Motor Company.[65] Clément also bought Humber and another maker called Phebus (a synonym for the sun), and merged all three to create the largest bicycle production company in France, Clément Gladiators.[66] What better advertising for Clément than Champion riding a Gladiator with Dunlops?

Adolphe Clément bought out his business rival Gladiator Cycles and boldly promoted Gladiators with cheeky advertising. *Image courtesy of Poster Photo Archives, Posters Please, Inc., New York.*

On August 24 Clément sailed from the Normandy seaport of Le Havre on the English Channel, aboard the French liner *La Bretagne*, to New York.[67] His intention was to scout out the American scene, and he included a visit to Colonel Albert Pope at his corporate headquarters in Boston, Pope's huge bicycle manufacturing plant in Hartford, and other manufacturers.[68]

Prior to his shipping out, Clément received a visit from the English trainer, James "Choppy" Warburton, on the prowl for his next big star, a *vedette*. Warburton, impeccable in a swallowtail coat, a diamond stickpin in his silk scarf, and a bowler, had developed Jimmy Michael into a world champion pacer. But the two had had a falling out, and Michael sued him for doping his drink. Then Warburton sued Michael in London for libel. The Englishman, in search of a new Michael, had determined that of all the young prospects in Great Britain and France, Champion's talent stood out as the most glory-bound.

"I thought his form was good, so I made inquiries about him, and found out where he was working,"[69] Warburton explained in an interview. He saw young Champion as a complete package: an optimistic nature, sound teeth, and requisite square shoulders in a slight but sturdy build.[70] He brought other assets. Affiliation with Clément meant unlimited bicycles, Dunlop tires, and, of major importance, advertising opportunities. "I went and saw him while in the workshop, had a chat with him and his employer, and offered to take him in hand and make a man of him," Warburton said.[71]

Champion didn't see a need for the services of the Englishman, in his fifties—old in Champion's estimation. "I thought I had about accomplished all anybody ought to be expected to do,"[72] Champion recalled. "Then along came 'Choppy' Warburton, who said he wanted to train me. I asked him, 'What for?' I thought I was pretty good just as I was. I remember Warburton smiled and then he said, 'Well, you never can tell what for.'"

Warburton offered two axioms from his experience about competition that impressed Champion: No lead is too great to overcome, and you can't win unless you think you can.[73]

"The lad put me into communication with his mother. I explained matters to the old lady," said Warburton.[74] He proposed to train and manage Champion for paced racing the next year. Warburton sought to flee London and Paris because of the vile drug gossip enveloping him.[75] He had Germany in mind. Many cities touted large vélodromes with banking suited for *demi-fonds*—middle distances of twenty-five miles to one hundred kilometers (62.5 miles), pacing behind tandems, triplets, and quads.

Marie Champion, a widowed mother of forty-three, associated cycling with disaster. Her Albert sometimes came home with torn, dirt-smeared britches and jerseys from one fall or another on his courier runs. If streets were harsh, then tracks to her were clothes-tearing flesh-eaters. She had patched and mended his clothes. She had refused to visit a track to watch him race, fearful he would end at the bottom of a pileup with bones broken and blood spilled. Even so, she and his brothers had relied on his earnings.

In his best French, Warburton explained that he understood her concern.[76] He said that Champion had what it took to make it as a *vedette*, a star, like Jimmy Michael, one of the best-paid sportsmen in the world. Albert could provide a generous living for her and his brothers. The concept of earning money from bicycle racing baffled Marie Champion, as it still unnerves parents of an aspiring cyclist today. The widow knew only frugality, life's hard edges, no margin for protection.

Whether Warburton's campaign was reinforced by the assurance of Clément, himself the father of a son, or the pleadings from Champion, she acquiesced. She did, however, lay down stipulations. As long as Warburton paid all expenses, she would allow him to train her son.[77] He could take him out of Paris—but only for brief trips. This last caveat jeopardized his plan to take Champion on the German circuit.

"Of course, as he was under age, that was all I could do," Warburton admitted.[78] "I started work upon him at once." He devised a two-fold strategy: first, to train Champion and make him a world-class cyclist, and, second, to win the trust of Marie Champion.

Albert Champion followed Warburton to his second residence, at 19 Avenue Le Boucher, in the tree-lined west Paris suburb of Neuilly-sur-Seine, near the Bois de Boulogne. Warburton began by sizing up the Frenchman. In stocking feet, Champion measured 5 feet 7-1/2 inches.[79] He weighed, according to

Champion credited James "Choppy" Warburton with broadening his horizons. *Photo by Jules Beau. Courtesy of Cherie Champion.*

the English system, 8 stone 10 pounds—122 pounds.[80] Afterward, Warburton escorted him to a tailor for clothes suitable for a gentleman sportsman. The tailor needed a few days to make the garments. In the meantime, Warburton and Champion visited Jules Beau's studio. This time, Beau himself, rather than an assistant, took the photo. Champion, in his cycling jersey and shorts, posed with Warburton, holding Champion on his Gladiator. With the a new publicity photo, Champion had embarked on stardom.

James Edward Warburton earned his bona fides by grabbing each opportunity with both hands and exploiting all it could offer. He is remembered as a controversial figure, reviled by some historians but acknowledged for finding diamonds in the rough and polishing their talents to astound the world.

The eldest of thirteen children, he was born in the Lancashire village of Haslingden, thirty miles from the Irish Sea.[81] One day a boyhood companion had inquired about his father's business. Warburton replied that he captained a ship cruising the sea—a fanciful scenario based on his friend's awareness of how far they lived from the coast. The elder Warburton worked his whole adult life in the village. He managed a local beerhouse, the Wagon & Horses, favored by workers from a local wool mill.[82] Next young Warburton's gullible chum asked how his father's passage had been. Warburton played along and said, "Rather choppy." The story gained currency around the village. Thereafter he was nicknamed "Choppy."[83]

Locals agreed he was an inveterate joker. "Many of his funny stories were told in so serious a manner that one could hardly tell whether he was joking or not," one friend remarked.[84] Haslingden residents knew the Warburton family as members of the local regimental brass band—young Warburton played the trombone. "Every year on the first Sunday in May, starting about 4:30 in the morning," recalled an account in the *Haslingden Observer*, "we were awakened by the strains of 'Hail, Smiling Morn,' followed by hymns played by the whole family from the heights above their home."[85]

In 1860, at seventeen, he was a runner competing for the Haslingden Athletic Club.[86] Period accounts describe him as 5 feet 10 inches and whippet thin at just 110 pounds.[87] "Tall and lithe, with scarcely an ounce of a superfluous flesh upon him, but with a remarkably broad chest, indicative of plenty of lung power, he had a long steady stride," a neighbor remembered.[88]

He competed on cinder tracks, grass cricket grounds, and dirt paths of villages, towns, and cities up and down the length of England. His results led to invitations, a quarter-century before the modern Olympics were established (in 1896), to America for footraces up to twenty-five miles. He returned to England with tales of having toed start lines in venues from Buffalo to New York City and Newark, New Jersey, with red-skinned Indians, brown-skinned Africans, and pale faces from America and Canada—all of whom he outran.[89] Altogether, he was credited with an excess of astounding six hundred wins.[90] He collected 150 engraved cups of silver or tin and dozens of gold medals—some worth extra with a diamond chip. His 1870 national record for thirty miles in 2 hours, 58 minutes, 43 seconds[91] bettered the 2:58:50 of Greece's Spiridon Louis, winner of the 1896 Athens Olympics marathon of forty kilometers, or twenty-five miles.[92] (London's 1908 Olympics marathon introduced the standard distance: 26 miles and 385 yards.[93]) Other records included two miles in 9 minutes 49 seconds, and ten miles in 54 minutes 6-1/2 seconds.[94]

After Warburton had retired from competition in the 1880s, he worked as a full-time trainer at the Manchester Athletic Club before going to the London Athletic Club.[95] He had acquired the bartender's expertise of listening and holding someone's attention with facial expressions, gestures, and modulating his voice in a manner that put his athletes in the right frame of mind. He also picked up an athletic trainer's stock in trade of how to stimulate muscles. He concocted a mixture containing pungent witch hazel liniment, poured it on his hands, and gave his harriers' leg and torso muscles a light massage to get the blood circulating to perform at their utmost. After a competition, Warburton administered a deeper recovery massage. As he had done with hundreds of young athletes, Warburton, thirty-five years older than Champion, turned into his best friend.

Warburton also instructed Champion to jump rope to strengthen his calf muscles—and burn off teenage excess energy. Next, Warburton deployed pacers to lead Champion around the Vélodrome de la Seine and timed him with a stopwatch. Warburton fancied four-rider quads for pacing. They hugged turns tightly and went faster than triplets. When he observed that Champion lacked the power and endurance to keep up behind quads, Warburton put him on a strict regimen.

Champion was awakened at 8:30 a.m. He began with twenty minutes of jumping rope that left him panting with a light sweat.[96] Then he received a vigorous massage, followed by a light breakfast with *café au lait*. His morning workout consisted of pedaling nineteen to twenty-five miles in the Bois de Boulogne, or out on a country road, concluding by 11:30. Another massage followed. At one o'clock, he and Warburton lunched together.

Two hours later, Warburton directed him to the Velodrome d'Hiver, the Winter Track, referred to in the French penchant for contractions as Vel d'Hiv. The indoor track was identified for a half-century with bicycle racing in Paris as Fenway Park is to the Boston Red Sox. A few blocks from the Eiffel Tower on the Left Bank, it sat solid and square with a huge glass roof. There Champion pedaled fifteen brisk miles pacing behind triplets and quads.

On the Vel d'Hiver Champion practiced race starts. He did drills of jack-rabbiting off the line, as if he had stolen a loaf of bread and had to flee from the police. His pacers then would swing around from behind and he would chase to catch the slipstream of the rear wheel and the game was on. In open racing, trailing to let others lead and offer shelter is a reasoned tactic. But paced racing differs. The cyclist at all times follows a fresh team, and the lead team controls the inside lane—prime real estate. Warburton trained Champion to explode from the starter's gun and take possession of the rail.

Following his afternoon workout, Champion returned on foot to Warburton's residence by around 5:30. He washed up for dinner at six o'clock.[97] The Englishman paid attention to diet. "Good meat, well cooked, keeps up the heat of the body," he said to a journalist.[98] He served Champion—accustomed to horsemeat—beef, veal, and lamb. "And a man may drink ales and light wines in moderation." Warburton and Champion usually took an after-dinner stroll around the Bois de Boulogne. Sometimes they ran short bursts against each other. They returned to Warburton's digs by nine o'clock for another meal of cold meat and vegetables, this time with pale ale and stout beer. At ten, Champion read a newspaper or cycling journal for twenty minutes. Warburton gave him a deep massage. Then it was lights out.

On Sunday mornings, rain or shine, Champion attacked the foundation of his regime, one that he talked about with pride for the rest of his life. After a full English breakfast to fortify a farmer for a long and arduous day, Warburton gave his charge a bottle of tea and a couple of sandwiches and said, "Meet me in Orléans at one o'clock."[99]

He told Champion that Orléans was 101 miles away,[100] and Champion accepted the distance as gospel, although the cities are about seventy-five miles apart.[101] After he saw Champion leave, Warburton took the train to Orléans, the historical town on the Loire River where Joan of Arc had led French troops that fended off English invaders.[102] Failing to make the distance in the prescribed time would mean getting scolded, and Champion wanted to please Choppy. But the older man already had a good gauge of Champion's abilities and gave him a challenge he was capable of doing. The distance took a mail coach drawn by four horses some eight hours.[103] Champion pedaled it in under six hours.

"I wasn't permitted to have even a sou on the trips and I could buy nothing— not even food or transportation—so I simply had to pedal to reach my destination," Champion related.[104]

Warburton was waiting at the prescribed time at the Orléans train station with a luncheon of a baguette bulging with ham and cheese, some fruit, and plenty of milk to wash down all the food.[105] Champion devoured his lunch while they chatted. When the meal was over, Warburton would say, "Meet me back in Paris at eight o'clock."[106] Champion rode home—a round trip of 150 miles, most of it over France's best maintained roads, and he thought he had covered 200 miles.

"But Choppy was doing something—he was educating me to take punishment, and whenever I began to tire in a race, the grueling training I had would permit me to overcome the fatigue and come out victorious time and time again," Champion recounted.[107] "No matter what game a man is in, he is only as big as the amount of punishment he is able to take, so I feel today that Choppy did a lot for me, not only in that respect, but in educating me on the importance of physical training, for as the old saying goes, you cannot be mentally fit unless you are physically fit."[108]

Two months of the dedicated regimen of track workouts and the Sunday endurance jaunts—without cheering spectators, no bands performing music, and no letup from physical exertion—changed Champion physically and mentally. He had faster leg spin and greater stamina. He and his teams synchronized smooth transitions from a tired team to a fresh one. Never one for doubt, he had more confidence.

Champion's mother allowed him one overnight sortie with Warburton in mid-December, to Berlin for the Prussian capital's indoor track championships. Berlin was an important market for Clément. His Gladiators had won a gold medal there at the 1896 International Exhibition trade show.[109] Warburton took three triplet teams for Champion, who would be competing against the best German youths who showed promise to become future stars. Bicycles, triplets, and extra wheels were packed into wooden boxes for the train trip.[110]

In Berlin for the Sunday afternoon event of fifty kilometers around an indoor track similar to the Vel d'Hiv, Champion took command behind his pacers from the firing of the starter's gun. Surrounding the vélodrome were seats filled with men and women puffing tobacco, eating fried food, guzzling beer—and cheering at the top of their lungs. Champion spun behind his pacers, cutting through the overhanging nicotine haze, to victory. Warburton perceived in Champion's debut under his direction something unanticipated. Each time the triplet Champion paced behind swept up the banking and the new team dove down to take over, their finesse drew applause. Champion gained a kilometer or two per hour in extra speed just from audience reaction. He possessed Jimmy Michael's qualities, with something extra from the crowd. He lapped young local heroes, risky for a Frenchman in front of proud Prussians. Yet everyone loved him for his panache.

Defeating Berlin's stars of the future entitled Champion to wear the city flag around his waist.[111] He also took home a purse heavy with gold coins. He returned to Paris triumphant. The Englishman delivered Champion to his mother and brothers. The trainer, having showed himself worthy enough of Marie Blanche Champion's trust, invited her son to join him with his wife and son in London during the first week of January 1897. A new racing season beckoned.

In December, Clément came back from America with souvenirs: two large industrial Pratt and Whitney Company lathes, purchased from Colonel Pope.[112] Clément found Pope, a veteran Union Army officer who had fought in the Civil War, to be a progressive leader. Pope had directed a national movement to improve roads.[113] He also had founded a pair of successful magazines to advocate the pleasures of outdoor leisure, recreation, and cycling. One of the editors was S. S. McClure,[114] remembered for early investigative journalism into social and business misconduct. A young commercial artist Pope hired to design Columbia Bicycles posters was Maxfield Parrish,[115] on his way to shaping the course of early American visual arts. Pope planned to manufacture autos that ran on electric batteries. He forecast that there would be charging stations established from the Atlantic to the Pacific for drivers to pull in, power up batteries, and return to driving.[116]

Pope introduced Clément to the mass-production method perfected by New England arms manufacturers,[117] such as Samuel Colt in Hartford, inventor of the revolver handgun. Mass production relied on assembly lines manufacturing every part to specific, high-quality standards for interchangeable parts.[118] By contrast, Clément, like other French manufacturers, prided himself on craftsmanship. French artisans built bicycles one at a time, starting with the frame and then the wheels, before assembling the handlebars, chain, and other components.

After studying Pope's Boston business office and Hartford factory, Clément visited some of the three hundred other US bicycle companies. In Cleveland and Chicago, he came upon the innovation of machines stamping sheets of steel to produce crank arms, sprockets, and other parts.[119] Stamping turned out parts faster, and of higher quality, than parts made by hand. Under the influence of Americans and their creative methods, Clément returned to Paris and reorganized his factory in Levallois-Perret with production lines. He impressed upon Champion the need to keep abreast of the competition and never hesitate to innovate.

Warburton's managing of Champion was chronicled throughout the continent and across the Atlantic. In Chicago's weekly *Bearings*, an article with Champion in Bauenne's photo heralded: "Champion, 'Choppy' Warburton's Latest Find."[120]

In January 1897 Champion, as instructed, boarded a train from Paris to Boulogne-sur-Mer, embarked on a boat across the English Channel, and climbed into a train to London's Charring Cross. Warburton met him and took him to Wood Green in north London to meet his wife and son, James. Warburton took a sophisticated approach to managing Champion as a brand. He arranged for a portrait photographer on Chancery Lane to take a photo of Champion on his Clément Gladiator.[121] Warburton distributed fresh, glossy prints to the London press corps up and down Fleet Street. Clément bought ads in publications around Great Britain promoting Champion riding on Dunlops. Word of Warburton's new *poulain*, or pony, circulated around London.

Another poulain under Warburton's management was Amélie le Gall, a Parisienne who rode with the *nom de vélodrome* "Lisette." Attractive, with dark curly hair, Lisette had fast legs on the bicycle. Women's racing attracted high-spirited ingénues and bolstered ticket sales. Lisette won in Paris and other cities around Europe, and she toured the United States, from New York to Chicago, racing on velodromes against American and Canadian women.[122] Under Warburton's tutelage, she reigned as Paris's sprint queen. The Englishman's coaching her and other women drew notice on both sides of the channel. A Paris journal caricatured him on the cover: in his bowler and loud plaid jacket he pulled a cart overflowing with women dressed in bonnets and finery in a jumble of spare wheels, valises, and a big marching drum.[123] The cart was labeled "Rumpus Army."

England's governing body for cycling, the National Cycling Union, demanded Victorian primness in sports and sought to ban Warburton from all tracks in England. Though he intended Champion for paced racing in London, Warburton couldn't resist matching the young Frenchman against Paris's sprint queen to sell tickets.

Warburton knew how to game the system on a grand scale; he rented the Royal Aquarium, a two-story entertainment complex in central London. Its spires and stone facing in Westminster stood directly across from the towers of Westminster Abbey, where for centuries English monarchs have been crowned.

The Royal Aquarium's main hall was built to hold thirteen large tanks intended to display exotic ocean creatures, but the water system was expensive and created such operating problems that the empty tanks languished. Displaying a dead whale had failed to impress the public. For years the building, known as "The Tank," accommodated plays, art exhibitions, and performances by orchestras with up to four hundred performers. Warburton installed a board-cycling track and seating for some one thousand spectators. Natural light flowed from the roof made of glass and iron into the hall's palm trees and statutes. The Royal Aquarium track was exempt from control of the National Cycling Union. Warburton was free to stage women's racing and men racing against women as he pleased.

He put Champion on a daily regime of jumping rope, riding a unicycle, and pedaling behind pacers around the Royal Aquarium's board oval. One after-noon the Englishman, sensing that his protégé had a bright future, presented him with a leather-bound ledger to use as a scrapbook. Today these filled pages attest to Champion's gloire!

Champion took his scrapbook to a stationer, perhaps accompanied by War-burton. Albert Champion intended to grow up and become the next Adolphe Clément and had silver letters stamped on the cover: AC. The passing century has darkened the monogram, but it remains visible when the scrapbook is tilted at a certain angle and catches the light.

Reporters insisted on interviewing Champion. Uncomfortable speaking English, he deferred to Warburton. "He takes matters easily, and works just as he feels he will, although, naturally, I see that he is well looked after," the trainer said.[124] "I am just now putting him through his pacings, so to speak, and haven't really found out what are his best distances. Up to the present time, he has only ridden on cement and wood, but I shall have to try upon him other surfaces, just to see what he is made of."

In mid-January, Warburton issued a challenge through the press for any English pairs against Champion and Lisette on the Royal Aquarium track. He called for side bets of £100 for the winner, with the loser's team to pay the cost of the winner's pacers. No one responded, a sign that the murky drug allega-tions had tainted his reputation. Ever resourceful, he devised a special program of handicap races between his poulains. It drew spectators and the press.

The first Champion-Lisette match was twenty miles. He toyed with her, leading so she could draft. That lasted till he grew impatient and upped his speed. Albert pulled ahead so Lisette lost the protection from his rear wheel. He lapped her time after time to trounce her.[125] Warburton next devised a handicap twenty-miler. She had a head start of two miles and two laps. Champion, ferocious at heart, routed her. Proud, he clipped French newspapers and pasted accounts on the first page of his scrapbook, next to the Jules Beau photo of Warburton bracing him on his Clément Gladiator. Lisette managed to beat him in other handicap events, but he neglected to paste any of those clips in his scrapbook.

Champion received an invitation to compete on the final Sunday evening in January 1897 in *Les Gosses Blanc*, the Paris junior city championship, in the Vel d'Hiv. Among hundreds of young hopefuls, he was selected as one of four contenders. The fifty-kilometer race (approximately 31.1 miles) offered a purse of 2,400 francs—the princely sum of 1,000 francs to the winner and a special white jersey, *gosse blanc*, designating Paris's young city champion.[126] The program matched Albert Champion against the promising Marius Lartigue, Edouard Taylor, and another named Collomb. The foursome made up France's future cycling leaders and drew enormous publicity. Taylor had the most racing experience, beginning at age fifteen, and he'd come off a successful season in America. Warburton declared to the journalists he collected like lint that he had France's next great talent: "Champion's opponents might stick with him up through thirty-five kilometers, but after that Champion would leave them behind."[127]

The trainer's spirits were buoyed by Michael recently admitting to reporters that Warburton had given him only water to drink rather than dope. Michael had agreed to ship across the Atlantic and meet Warburton in Paris to settle their legal differences amicably. And Warburton had successfully persuaded Champion's mother to attend the Vel d'Hiver.

Marie Champion may have been inclined to scoff at having to go out on a freezing winter night. But the attention Warburton had lavished on her son, the money they had brought back from Berlin and London, and publicity surrounding the evening's event had softened her resistance. Even if she were illiterate and unable to read accounts, she recognized photos of her son. And the evening presented Champion with the opportunity to invite Elise to accompany his mother, her future mother-in-law, and brothers to watch him in action.

"In spite of a cold, biting wind and the snow which covered the approaches, an enormous crowd wended its way to the Winter Track," reported Chicago's *Bearings*, publishing a dispatch from a Paris correspondent.[128]

Electric lights hanging from the ceiling revealed to Marie Champion and her sons and Elise an indoor board oval with banked turns as steep as cliffs. The track looked to her more like a squirrel cage than something for cyclists to ride. Leading Louis, Prosper, Henri, and Elise to their seats in a tier of the grandstand over the start/finish line, Marie saw the infield, dense with men in top hats, women in elaborate broad-brimmed ones, everyone in overcoats, most flaunting fur. She and her boys and future daughter-in-law would have caught pungent whiffs of rubbing liniment and a mélange of perfume competing with the smell of damp wool, tobacco, and food seasoned with garlic. Customers filled chairs around tables covered with white linen; everyone else stood chatting with cigarettes and drinks at the long bar, or milled wherever they could wedge into a niche. Musicians in the bandbox played popular tunes. Riders flew around the vélodrome with apparent ease. Pacer teams with riders on triplets and quads, pedaling in perfect unison, must have appeared to Blanche like a scene from another world.

The evening program opened with a 920-meter handicap race. It drew a field of pros whose battles got the audience aroused. Next up, a one-lap race against the clock—the test of truth. Five riders went off, one at a time, for a solo lap at top speed. A former Warburton protégé, Edouard Nieuport, destined to be Champion's first business partner and to set three world aviation speed records, grimaced under his dandy's upturned mustache. Nieuport scored the fastest lap: 23-2/5 seconds.[129]

The audience was in full cry by the main event, *Les Gosses Blanc*. "A few minutes before the race, the track was taken possession of by a perfect army of pacemakers, each boy having five or six triplets and quads," *Bearings* told readers.[130] "'Choppy' busied himself with his young ward's pacing teams, and kept the spectators amused by his comical gestures and gesticulations."

An official in top hat and tails tossed a coin to determine the inside position—auspiciously, to Champion. Warburton steadied Champion's bicycle for him to sit on the saddle and grip his handlebars for the start. Lartigue, Taylor, and Collomb took their places up the banking with their trainers. Behind ranged their triplets. At the pop of the starter's pistol, Warburton put his upper body into shoving Champion away. The triplets chased and came around their charges. Champion was quickest to catch his. "After a few laps had been negotiated, it was clearly seen that the race would be a grand struggle between Champion and Lartigue," reported *Bearings*.[131]

Taylor, nicknamed *le gosse rouge*, the red kid, for his red silk jersey, was small and thin with a narrow chest and sharply cut facial features. He surprised the audience, as the fast pace forced him several times to sit upright and catch his breath in the first six miles.

Champion chatted and laughed with his pacers. Lartigue, five months older, kept trying to pass. But Champion each time counterattacked. He owned the night. "For the first half of the race, the fight between Lartigue and Champion was a sight worth witnessing," reported *Bearings*.[132] "The ease with which Champion followed his pacemakers was really remarkable." He kept lapping Collomb—ultimately ten times.

At nineteen miles, Choppy tipped his top hat to his protégé, signaling time to make a move. Champion shot ahead and gained ten lengths on Lartigue, who fought back gallantly, but the effort knocked him to pieces. Lartigue dropped back and caught his breath at twenty-two miles. His pause signaled Champion as nonpareil. Warburton let out a whoop, threw his hat in the air, and ran up and down the inside track apron, all the while yelling encouragement to Champion. Warburton gave the impression of a windmill with his long arms waving in the air.[133]

Taylor, profiting by Lartigue's pumped-out condition, regained a lap on him. Champion lapped them both twice more. In the first hour, Champion had pedaled 29.6 miles—a new national hour record.[134] He won Paris's city championship and set a new national record of 1:03:11-3/5—an average of nearly 30 mph.[135] He received a bouquet of flowers for his lap of honor to a rousing ovation. He was awarded the Gosse Blanc jersey to wear in future races. Champion and Warburton left the track to roaring applause.[136]

Reporters praised Champion for performing in a style that promised to make him the French Michael. Press accounts credited Warburton for accomplishing marvels with those he had trained. Michael was in the audience. That evening Warburton and Michael reconciled. Champion made a quick change of clothes to pull on a suit and overcoat while Jules Beau set up his camera. Warburton stood tall between Champion and Michael for the photo.[137]

Marie Champion, as every mother must, realized that her son had slayed his own dragons. He had earned 1,000 francs. Nearly half went to Warburton and the pacers. That still left Champion with a bounteous payday, a fortune in her estimation, and in just an evening's effort. She had a frisson that with her son as the family breadwinner she could retire from washing laundry. She had heard everyone in the audience yelling for him. The evening swayed her. She relented and put her faith in Warburton, granting him permission to take her son to race in Germany.

A NEW CENTURY, ANOTHER COUNTRY, A FRESH START

AUTOMOBILES ARE SOMEWHAT OF A NOVELTY JUST AT PRESENT, BUT IN A HUNDRED YEARS FROM NOW THEY WILL BE PART OF EVERYBODY'S HOUSEHOLD ECONOMY, OR AT LEAST SO IT IS SAID.
—MONTREAL DAILY STAR, AUGUST 5, 1899[1]

Drafting behind human pacers prepared Champion for switching to following tandems powered by the latest internal-combustion gas engines, which would change his life. A recent technology leap in aluminum processing led to smaller and lighter engines than those made of iron parts. Aluminum is an abundant metal but lies underground combined with other minerals. A process to extract aluminum from surrounding minerals had been introduced at the 1855 Paris Exposition.[2] Yet the pure metal was costly to produce and available in such scant supply that aluminum was more expensive than gold, which made it prized in fine jewelry. With the advent of electricity, Frenchman Paul-Louis-Toussaint Héroult and American Charles Martin Hall had simultaneously invented a method to produce the metal in bulk for little cost.[3] Around 1890 the value of aluminum jewelry plummeted. Yet other applications came to light.

Paris engineer Georges Bouton enjoyed boating on the Seine with one-cylinder, gas-combustion engines. He replaced the cast-iron crankcase—housing the crankshaft, connecting rods, and related parts—with aluminum.[4] That reduced engine weight and size. Jules-Félix-Philippe-Albert De Dion, a marquis in Montmartre, was awestruck with the magic of internal-combustion engines.[5] Friends dubbed him Count Mechanic. He saw that Bouton's lighter crankcase improved the ratio of weight to speed. With his progressive attitude toward technology he took to internal-combustion engines with his heart, soul, and check book.

The count and the engineer formed the De Dion-Bouton Motorette Company to produce small autos—for driver and a passenger—and engines.[6] The engine piston chuffed and delivered two-horsepower—the muscle of eight competitive cyclists. De Dion-Bouton engines fit onto the back of tricycle frames, between the rear wheels. De Dion and Bouton then allied with Clément to manufacture motor-tricycles. De Dion modeled in jacket and tie, relaxing with a cigarette on a new motor-tricycle, marking him as a trendsetter. An advertisement for a De Dion-Bouton motor-tricycle asserted an antiestablishment attitude, depicting a smiling coquette, in a frilly nightgown revealing cleavage, driving her boyfriend, in a harlequin costume standing behind on the rear-wheel axle and thumbing his nose to mock a pursuing gendarme pedaling a bicycle and a military officer chasing on horseback. In 1895 Clément, De Dion, Bouton, and other devotees of engines cofounded *L'Automobile-Club de France* to spread information about the proper care for gas-combustion vehicles and encourage auto racing.[7] De Dion was elected its first president.

When Champion investigated the motor-tricycles Clément made at the Levallois factory he discovered the engines had a life of their own, a unique smell, a distinct sound. He saw how the engines operated. Gasoline mixed with air in the combustion chamber enclosing the piston. A magneto coil, consisting of a magnet embedded in a flywheel, generated electric current. The current fired the spark plug end, which screwed into the combustion chamber and ignited the mixture of gasoline and air, driving the piston down to convert chemical energy into mechanical energy. That turned the crankshaft, which propelled the rear wheels to drive the vehicle. These were the basics.

Champion was taught to jump start the engine by pedaling (like a latter-day moped) until he heard its *put-put-put*, steady as a metronome as the engine took over; then he rested his feet on the pedals. When the air-cooled engine had burned all its oil,[8] it ran irregularly until the cast-iron parts heated, expanded, and locked up. Overheated parts had to cool and return to normal size, which took about twenty minutes. Then insertion of an oil-soaked cloth allowed the ride to resume. He inspected the cylindrical brass gas tank, twenty inches wide and five inches deep, fitted on the rear seat stays of the two back wheels, dripping gas by gravity to the engine. He measured the amount of gas in the tank by unscrewing the cap and dipping a stick inside. Motor-tricycles could go more than a hundred miles on a gallon of gas. A brass cup two inches in diameter held an oil-soaked cloth that dribbled oil down into the crankcase. He received instructions to experiment with the oil-gas mixture to make the exhaust burn clear. Dark blue smoke meant too much oil; light blue smoke was acceptable, as it would soon burn clearly.

It wasn't long before Champion examined spark plugs stamped with the De Dion-Bouton trademark, fundamentally the same construction as spark plugs today. The De Dion-Bouton Company was the first to use spark plugs successfully. Champion scrutinized the electrode on the center top of the plug that ran the length of it and carried the electric current. The spark plug bottom held a small J-shaped piece of metal, and the gap at the end determined the size of the spark that fired in the chamber. The gap had to be the proper size—too wide and the spark could not leap to ignite the fuel-air mix; too narrow and the spark was so weakened that it would not ignite the mixture. Analyzing how the spark plug worked gave Champion entry into the world of internal-combustion gas engines.

One wintry day he pulled on leather gloves, stuffed newspaper broadsheets under layers of clothes over the front of his chest to ward off the wind's chill, and drove a motor-tricycle out of the Levallois factory to the Bois de Boulogne to test the novel machine. Next he persuaded one of Clément's mechanics, called Broc, to motorpace him around the Vélodrome de la Seine. Now, instead of collecting four riders pedaling a quad to pace him, Champion needed only Broc on a motor-tricycle. Broc took pride in driving. He wore the motor fraternity's special regalia—a long duster coat to shield him from dirt roads, leather gauntlets extending halfway up his forearm, a big cap, and enormous spectacles to protect his eyes. The outfit made Broc resemble a deep-sea diver.[9] Pedaling behind Broc, Champion inserted his front wheel between the tricycle's rear wheels to follow, protected in the sweet spot. The youths exuberantly slalomed through horse-drawn traffic across Paris to the Bois de Boulogne. There they made the dirt fly.

When Champion and Broc felt like getting a special thirst quencher, they dropped in on the *Brasserie de l'Espérance*, Bar of Good Hope, on the edge of the

Bois de Boulogne at Porte Maillot. The brasserie was a hangout for cyclists, bookies, betting coves, reporters, fans, groupie *jeune filles*, and riffraff prowling for the latest hearsay. The brasserie was well known for an annual spring professional road race that started outside its front door. Pros ventured north 170 miles to Roubaix. Champion heard incredible stories about the Paris-Roubaix race, but he did not care about racing through the countryside on rough roads.

Champion's accomplishments in early 1897 under Warburton's tutelage generated coverage beyond France. Chicago was home to the cycling weekly *Bearings*, as smart a title as *Wired* is today for the tech savvy. *Bearings* hawked "Champion Rides Like a Demon."[10] He had no way of knowing about his press attention in America.

In England, however, Warburton's prominence had thrust him under the glare of the National Cycling Union, the governing body adamant in opposing professional cycling. The NCU believed that competing for money sullied the sport of gentlemen amateurs. His biggest offense, according to the judgment of NCU officers, was coaching pros, including Lisette—an especially outrageous breach because, like men, she wore leg tights.

The NCU so ardently disapproved of cash prizes that it accused John Boyd Dunlop of supplying his company's pneumatics to pros.[11] The NCU barred the white-haired, fifty-five-year-old veterinarian from amateur racing and extended the injunction against the entire board of gray-beard trustees.[12] Dunlop walked with a shuffle and had never sat on a bicycle. But the gentle man became enraged. He prevailed on son Johnny to teach him how to ride in defiance of the NCU bullies.[13] The elder Dunlop suggested that he just might one day show up on the start line against athletes in their prime if he felt the urge to take a break from his veterinary practice.

Warburton faced the menace of a one-year NCU ban from every track in Great Britain, thereby depriving him of his livelihood in England, Wales, and Scotland. But the ban had no effect across the channel. He met with Champion in Paris and organized a cadre of pacers to lead him on Clément Gladiator triplets and quads. He took Champion and pacers to his tailor to outfit them as successful sportsmen. In late February they decamped together to Germany for a campaign on the winter indoor vélodrome circuit.[14] Champion raced as Warburton had trained him, to blast from the starter's pistol, claim the inside lane behind his pacer, and lay down the law. In Berlin, Dresden, Hanover, Leipzig, Cologne, Hamburg, Frankfurt, and other cities he won enough prize money for the team to travel first class by train and stay in fine hotels. Opponents included Fritz Opel, who would later join his brothers in a business making autos.

Champion and Warburton returned to Paris for a March 28 match of one hundred kilometers in the Vel d'Hiver, pitting Champion against Constant Huret,[15] a former baker turned cycling star. Huret wore a flattop haircut way ahead of its time. He was Champion's height and packed twenty pounds more muscle. Artist Henri Toulouse-Lautrec immortalized him, crouching with his back low behind a tandem, in a poster advertising La Chaîne Simpson, plastered all over the city. In the Champion-Huret match, both paced behind motor-tricycles, all the rage among the Paris elite. The match meant that Champion was a recognized pro. The contest was hyped as a clash between the young challenger and the established star, eight years more mature. Ten thousand devotees filled the Vel d'Hiver. Champion was impatient to show off.

Artist Henri Toulouse-Lautrec captured Constant Huret in action. Huret arrived to have dinner with Champion on October 26, 1927, only to learn his friend had died an hour before. *Image courtesy of Poster Photo Archives, Posters Please, Inc., New York.*

The contest started out fast, with Huret and his driver setting an aggressive pace, topping 35 mph. Champion kept close behind, biding his time, waiting to see what the big guy had in store. The cheering crowd rocked the building. After seven miles, however, the engine conked out on Huret's pacer.[16] Huret swung around the stalled machine while his driver dismounted on the apron inside the track to make repairs. Champion caught Huret and, as one account he pasted in his scrapbook put it, "passed him like an arrow."

Champion shot into the lead. While Huret soloed as best he could, Champion took advantage of tucking behind his motor-tricycle to lap him several times. Thousands in the grandstands and gallery seats grew angry over Champion's unfair gain. They jeered, whistled, and threw balled-up programs at him. He was so mad he shook his fist at the tiers of spectators. They yelled even louder at him and turned hostile.

"The public found Champion guilty of a breach of etiquette so he was booed," wrote journalist Victor Breyer of *Le Vélo*.[17] "The crowd wasn't with Champion. Then young Champion stopped finally when he saw their reaction, and he didn't get back on his bicycle until he saw Huret got going again."

Victor Breyer, one of France's leading sportswriters, had watched Albert Champion's meteoric ascent and described him as a gifted athlete but impulsive. *Photo courtesy of Alain Pernot.*

Champion, a sophomoric eighteen-year-old, could not conceal his resentment at having to stop, even for Huret. He turned an angry face at the tiers of humanity and glared. To his astonishment, the people who had cheered him continued to rebuke him. They had paid to watch, and they expected either heroics or gallantry. Huret did his best to limit the damage. He kept going like a bulldog. Ticket holders had expected Champion to assess the state of affairs and make a *beau geste* toward his unlucky adversary. Instead, he trounced Huret like a ruffian.

"Never in my life have I raced in front of such an unfair and cruel crowd of spectators," Champion declared.[18] "Undeserved whistling cuts into your legs more than a series of sputtering engine kicks. What's so bad about the sharp little stones they throw at you is that they hit your thighs. Then they toss programs weighted with coins that slash across your face. The crowd wanted me to wait up for my opponent. But could I reasonably be expected to imitate his every movement, dismount the same as he, slow down when he slows down, drink when he drinks? No, that would be even worse! And what would racing become? If a match must be stopped by the occurrence of an accident that puts one of the competitors in any kind of inferior position, then let's not have any matches at all. It's quite simple. Racers themselves, made victims like I was on Sunday and subjected to verbal abuses from a delirious crowd, will be the first to agree."

Victor Breyer had observed Champion over the past year and caught signs of pride, brusqueness, and a streak of childishness.[19] The youngster's outburst before the audience demonstrated hot-headedness. Breyer, born in London to an English mother and French father, had grown up in Paris and lived in Champion's arrondissement of Batignolles.[20] A small man of twenty-nine with narrow shoulders, he had tried racing high-wheelers. Competing as a club mate of Marius Renault from the French automobile family, Breyer lacked the fortitude and turned to journalism to cover the "cracks," an English term for those with superior talents. He maintained an open curiosity about the personalities, training methods, and strategies of those he deemed as cracks, seeking insights into what made them excel. Athletes felt relaxed talking to the courteous journalist with a mustache, cravat, and bowler. He wrote with ironic distance about Champion's match with Huret, describing him in the affectionate patois as a young *Parigot*. Breyer had heard reports around Batignolles about his pressing money, unsolicited, into the hands of neighbors so they could buy food and firewood to get them through the winter.[21] This Parigot supported three younger brothers and provided enough that his widowed mother retired from working as a washerwoman. Breyer assessed him as a gifted cyclist, well intended, but with a complex personality. Cycling was a pastime for Breyer and multitudes of others, but Champion treated it as a profession—he was the family breadwinner.

The Champion-Huret rematch was inevitable.[22] Both men had full racing calendars and could not meet until May 30 in Roubaix, on the outdoor cement vélodrome that Champion knew so well. The highly anticipated match filled the stands. This time, Champion's pacing machine engine faltered and quit on the twelfth lap. He kept pedaling as Huret kept lapping him. Champion expected his driver would fix the engine, but the driver gave up. They did not have a spare machine. Champion withdrew. This time it was he who pleaded for a rematch.

On June 7 the second rematch took place, a fifty-miler in Paris at the Buffalo Vélodrome. Huret had been logging long, hard miles prepping to defend his *Bol d'Or*, the coveted Golden Bowl, a twenty-four-hour competition in three weeks at the same venue. Huret's workouts required extraordinary stamina for the round-the-clock contest, at the expense of dulling his high-end speed. In their rematch, Champion tore away from the start and opened a big lead. Huret felt Champion was too full of hubris and pulled out before the second lap.[23] If Champion had restrained himself to make the competition look even, Huret would have kept going. Champion had tried too hard, desperate to prove himself. He had to learn about giving spectators a show for their money.

On the weekend of June 26 and 27, Huret won his third twenty-four-hour Bol d'Or,[24] pedaling 518 miles behind pacers, yet another world record. The press called Huret *King of the Long Distance*. He left Champion feeling perplexed. The surest way to gain an opponent's respect is to beat him. But the sport, like life, had more dimensions. Huret taught him about character, self-confidence, and a professional's obligation to his audience.

In 1897, Englishman H. O. Duncan published a book in Paris offering his perspective on the sport: *Twenty Years of Practical Cycling*.[25] Duncan, a pioneer pro in the high-wheel era, remained a close observer of the game. His book's twenty years stretched back to 1876, the dawn of high-wheel racing on both sides of the channel. In a section dedicated to cycling as a lifestyle, he recommended an extensive list of French wines, champagne, German and English beers, and

Caribbean rum for their health benefits when taken in moderation. He saw Champion as full of promise and explained his training regimen under Warburton. Duncan published the Bauenne publicity photo of Champion on his bicycle and line art of him and Warburton running in the Bois de Boulogne. He identified Warburton as an early proponent of cross-training, and Champion as destined to mature into one of France's greats.

"Choppy" Warburton, left, manager-trainer of Champion, right, was an early advocate of cross-training for cyclists. They ran together in Paris's popular Bois de Boulogne. *From H. O. Duncan's* Vingt Ans de Cyclisme Pratique *(Paris, 1896).*

Champion needed constant reassurance. When Warburton became distracted with other matters and his family, Champion sulked that his trainer ignored him.[26] Champion threatened to leave. However, Warburton knew how to soothe him. They kept together through the season. October brought the season to an end—and a break from racing. They parted company and planned to continue together for the next season. Then the fates intervened.

Champion spent time at home with his mother and Prosper, Henri, and Louis. He came out of the spring and summer more fit, his competitive skills honed, and with a new appreciation of the show-biz aspect of his métier. He and Warburton managed expenses against race winnings and appearance fees. Champion had picked up some English and a smattering of German.

His luggage was festooned with colorful travel stickers advertising railroad companies and hotels. Porters and bellhops had slapped them on as souvenirs beckoning his return. Champion could point to each artistic oval, square, and rectangle label to regale Marie and his brothers with stories about the travel, accommodations, and meals he had experienced on trains and in hotels and restaurants.

Warburton returned to his house in London's Wood Green. Every day when he rose and buttoned his tattersall vest and reached for his bowler to go outside, he could anticipate being persecuted by whispers and rumors of drug accusations. He was fifty-three and anxious that the National Cycling Union might ban him for another year. While shaving on the morning of December 17, he collapsed to the floor, still clutching a hand towel.[27] Warburton had suffered a fatal heart attack.

National Cycling Union officials went to Wood Green Town Hall and demanded an inquest. The findings of the coroner who performed the autopsy noted that Warburton's heart had been double the normal size.[28] The jury returned a verdict of death from natural causes.

Publications across Europe churned out recollections of Warburton's practical jokes and knack for spotting potential in Michael, Lisette, and Champion. Champion and Clément sent wreaths for Warburton's funeral in Wood Green and donated money for a headstone.[29] Its engraving testifies: *Tombstone erected to his memory by sorrowing English, Scotch, and French friends.*[30] For the rest of his life, Champion described his manager as crucial to taking him out of Paris and expanding his outlook.

A pro at pursuing motor-tricycles, Champion focused his attention on another pursuit. He wanted Elise Delpuech as his sweetheart. She had graduated from high school—well educated in his perspective. Her wine-merchant parents had given her and a younger sister and brother more comfort than Champion and his brothers had known. Elise knew about his rise from unicycle performer to courier and racer. Nobody in her family had been cited in journals or in a book like Champion had. She watched him flashing around on his Clément Gladiator, all energy and ambition. She liked his handsome face and gray eyes. Elise couldn't miss seeing his rough edges, the fiery temper. But he made up for those faults in the way he supported his brothers and liberated his mother, so petite yet strong, from having to wash clothes for a living. Now Marie Champion stayed at home to care for her other sons.

He fell under the spell of Elise's intelligence and her brown eyes that scrutinized his. A daughter of shopkeepers,[31] she could glance at a pile of coins of different denominations on the counter and announce in a heartbeat exactly how much they totaled. She could transform from demure ingénue into flirting minx. She wore her dark hair long down her back, sometimes in a chignon, and she had a penchant for white blouses with high lacey collars. Chic scarves and artistic earrings displayed her refined taste. For time together away from the stares of relatives and neighbors, Champion and Elise escaped to the city's center. At sidewalk cafés, they indulged in coffee and pastries.

In April 1898 he turned twenty. Elise, already twenty-one and thus an adult capable of making her own decisions, pledged herself to him. Champion promised himself to her but put his career first. Winning meant not just crossing the line ahead of his rivals and earning more francs but also thrusting himself into the center of attention with the public and the press. To be the focal point of others stroked his ego.

Now, assured he had won Elise, he turned his attention to the intoxicating addiction of winning races.

In May 1898 a new outdoor track, the *Parc des Princes*, named in honor of the Bourbon royals, opened near the Bois de Boulogne. Built to accommodate paced racing, Parc des Princes was more than twice the size of the recently closed Buffalo Vélodrome. With long straights and wide turns, it measured 666 meters around.[32] Its grandstand and bleachers seated thirty thousand—one of the largest sports arenas in Europe. There Champion upset France's two-time paced titleholder Emile Bouhours, descended from Normans who had defeated the English at the Battle of Hastings. Race programs with Champion, Huret, and Bouhours ensured that the stands at the Parc des Princes—as well as Clément's Vélodrome de la Seine—were filled with fashionable society and the press. Their cheering for Champion nurtured his lust for la gloire!

Despite their struggles against one another, Champion and Huret developed a friendship, which endured right up to Champion's final hour. Huret considered him a younger brother in need of assurance, fast on the track but slow to acquire humility. Huret recommended his own trainer-manager, Dudley Marks, an Englishman who knew his way around the world. Champion looked up to Marks. In November 1896, Marks had shepherded the Irish endurance rider Teddy Hale across the Atlantic for the international individual go-as-you-please six-day endurance grind in New York City's Madison Square Garden.[33] Marks kept Hale fed and motivated to pedal 1,910 miles around the indoor board track to victory.[34] Hale filled his hat with $2,000 in gold coins, worth four years of wages. Such a payday indicated to Champion that racers could make a decent living in America.

Champion asked Marks to deal with promoters offering him contracts. They typically paid travel expenses plus an appearance fee as sweetener in addition to a chance at the prize money. The press puffed up the matches, wrote profiles, dished gossip. Spectators turned out in droves. Champion—with Marks as manager, publicist, and motor-tricycle pacer—boarded northbound trains to Amiens,[35] which was notable for its historic three-tier gothic cathedral. They went southwest to competitions in Agen,[36] where plums grew on trees the crusaders had brought from the Middle East. Champion and Marks commuted to Berlin for races against Huret and German stars. Without fail, Champion shared the prize money he earned with his family. As usual, he clipped journal accounts of his exploits for his flourishing scrapbook.

His home vélodrome became Parc des Princes. He paired with Bouhours, who had moved to Paris from a farm village in Normandy, against Welshman Tom Linton and an Englishman named Armstrong. They competed in team matches billed as France versus the United Kingdom. The matches were reported in Desgrange's sports newspaper L'Auto-Vélo and throughout the continent and America. At the Parc des Princes in a Sunday program on September

22, 1898, Champion scored a career highlight. Barreling behind a tandem, he tore across the start line at full speed and flew around the oval to set a paced world record for the flying kilometer,[37] two-thirds of a mile. He covered the showcase distance in fifty-six seconds flat—a leg-burning 60 kph or 37 mph. Thousands of spectators filled the air with unrestrained vocal adulation as Champion claimed the honor of the world's fastest man in the kilometer.

The Paris press corps was hyping the premier season opener for 1899—a road race for pros on Easter Sunday, starting near the Bois de Boulogne and finishing on the Roubaix Vélodrome, a distance of 167 miles. Paris-Roubaix offered a hefty purse, put up by two wool mill owners, and extensive coverage from the sponsoring newspaper *Le Vélo*,[38] published by Pierre Giffard.

Today Paris-Roubaix, a World Cup race, stands out as the most important one-day event on the international pro cycling calendar. It is widely regarded as Queen of the Classics—cycling's crown jewel among venerable events, ranking in stature alongside the Boston Marathon in running or Wimbledon in tennis, with a roll of winners celebrated as legends. Paris-Roubaix still includes the same rutted dirt thoroughfares, ancient paths cutting through farm fields that disintegrate to muck in the rain, and some three dozen stretches of cobblestones the size of large bread loaves—northern France's notorious *pavé*, now protected as part of France's heritage and open to car traffic only on race day.

Champion had trained often on roads, but he had not raced on them since he turned pro. For the 1899 event, organizers were so enthralled by engines that they encouraged cyclists to pace behind their choice of motor-tandems, motor-tricycles, or automobiles.[39] The 167 miles was more than twice the distance of any of his other races. In addition to a motorized pacer, another incentive was 1,000 francs to the winner.[40] Foremost in his mind was finishing on the Roubaix Vélodrome. He respected road racers for their stamina and perseverance, but he felt smug about having superior speed. Road racers earned his respect as rugged, but, like workhorses, they were pluggers. The unforeseen opportunity to motorpace Paris-Roubaix intrigued him. With this in mind, he was willing to go the extraordinary distance, give up the smooth, level track surfaces to which he was accustomed, and brave the rough roads and daunting pavé so he could win on the Roubaix Vélodrome.

Champion discussed Paris-Roubaix with Marks, who protested that the pavé would tear them both apart. Marks refused to drive. Champion turned to Broc, a cheerful friend and an intrepid driver. Broc regarded the race as an adventure and agreed to pace him over the pavé with a Clément motor-tricycle. Paris-Roubaix demanded as much physical training as careful planning. Champion, puffed about his chances, prepared to win.

The first Paris-Roubaix in April 1896 had taken place in the same week as the revival of the modern Olympics. Josef Fischer, a big-boned man from Munich, remembered as Germany's first great road rider, had triumphed in the debut Paris-Roubaix. He finished in 9 hours and 17 minutes, astounding everyone by pedaling an average of 19 mph.[41] Fisher's stature on the continent stamped the race with cachet. Marius Garin, operator of a cycle shop in central Roubaix, had worn the city's colors and finished third, which made him a national hero.[42]

The 1899 event was scheduled for April 2, 1899.[43] The night before the race, the Brasserie de l'Espérance on the edge of the Bois de Boulogne stayed opened late for everyone wanting the latest rumors. Champion and Broc— swanning in his unbuttoned duster coat—mingled in the hubbub. They had devised a two-part strategy.[44] First, because Paris-Roubaix went so much farther than Champion's range, he determined to ride as though it ended in Amiens, the midpoint at eighty-six miles. If he signed in at the control table at the Café Odelin in Amiens ahead of the others, he figured he could make it unchallenged to Roubaix. In a contest so punishing, the first half wore everybody down. Just to finish, they relied on reserve energy and sheer willpower. Champion would be just as fatigued, but he would have a big psychological advantage and rivals would concentrate on surviving rather than catching him.

Second, race organizers had announced that pace vehicles would stage in front of the cyclists.[45] Champion and Broc expected a traffic jam of heavy, smelly autos belching smoke exhaust for miles before the caravan thinned out in the countryside. They agreed Broc should wait nineteen miles up the road near the village of Hérouville.[46] Champion would dash away at the starter's gun and weave, courier-style on his one-speed Gladiator, through traffic to meet Broc.

Opening the event to motorpacing also drew other fortune-hunting vélo-drome stars. Among them Bouhours, eight years older than Champion and more experienced, and the durable pro Paul Bor, a Parigot Champion's age. Could these track specialists go the distance? Could they survive northern France's diabolical cobblestone sections against toughened road racers? Bookies thought not and favored the previous winners: Garin and Fischer.

"The local favorite is always Garin," wrote *Le Vélo* reporter Victor Breyer.[47] Breyer's recent book on France's top racers made him a national authority; he devoted a section to Huret, including the Huret-Champion matches. Garin, born an underdog, came from a large Italian family. The story that followed Garin as close as the hair on the back of his neck was that his father had traded him as a child to a chimney sweep for a wheel of cheese.[48] Racing bicycles had enabled Garin to give up toiling inside sooty chimneys. Even fully grown, he remained small. But he was physically nimble and mentally hard as steel. He won twenty-four hour tests on tracks in Paris and Liège, Belgium.[49] Victories polished his reputation for stubbornness. Desgrange had designated him, "the little chimney sweep." Garin had settled in Roubaix and become a naturalized French citizen. He had won the 1897 Paris-Roubaix by two meters.[50] The next year he triumphed by twenty minutes.[51] Roubaixians proudly called themselves Garinistes.[52]

The bookmaker at the Brasserie de l'Espérance offered Garin and Fischer odds of two to one to win, acknowledging that, as previous winners, they knew the course best.[53] Wagers on Bouhours went for three to one. The bookie rated Champion at five to one. Paul Bor had odds of eight to one.

Paris's police chief decreed the city had too much traffic already and moved the start to the western suburb of Chatou.[54] On race morning, a photographer near the sign-in table on the sidewalk of a Chatou café, serving as race head-quarters, captured Champion sporting a fresh haircut and a new wool cap as he bent at the waist to pen his name at seven o'clock on the start sheet.[55] On Champion's upper left arm he wore a white cloth brassard bearing his com-petitive number, eleven. An official in a trimmed beard and mustache seated at the table opposite gazed through his pince-nez at the camera. Broc fixed his brassard over the bulky sleeve of his long coat, worn to offer Champion a tad more shield from the wind. Then Broc drove his motor-tricycle off to their rendezvous.

Garin flouted the rules by wrapping his brassard around his left thigh. Younger brother Ambrose Garin also signed in. Frenchmen dominated the field. Only two Belgians entered. The lone German, Fischer, sought to reclaim victory—including the bonus basket holding a dozen bottles of champagne. "Asked what special motor would pace him, Fischer refused to answer so as not to give his opponents any helpful information," noted the *Journal de Roubaix*.[56]

Champion lined up with thirty-one other pros spanning Route 47 de St. German, in front of the Chatou café, for the start.[57] Three-quarters of them would give their all for nothing but sore muscles and ravenous appetites. Every entrant was highly regarded, noted Breyer, adding that vélodrome stars Champion, Bouhours, and Bor heightened the public's fascination. Patches of blue sky poked through the clouds on a day in the low fifties (Fahrenheit). At 8 a.m. the official starter in a silk top hat stood before the contestants. Ahead of them awaited a cavalcade of cars, motor-tandems, and motor-tricycles suitable to any modern-city rush hour.

At the starter's pistol shot, Garin, Fisher, and others rushed to their waiting cars and disappeared in a swirl of dust. Champion dashed away clean ahead of everyone and slalomed through traffic-clogged roads, fleeing like a fox before the hounds.

"Paris-Roubaix provoked a tremendous enthusiasm in the villages the race went through," the *Journal* declared.[58] "People filled the crossroads and almost interfered with the race." In the era before officials cleared the path with their motorcade and prior to barriers protecting racers from crowds of spectators, Paris-Roubaix racers and their pacers fended for themselves—even from cattle, sheep, and goats that farmers herded across roads between barns and grazing fields.

Officials at eight designated villages along the route set up tables with ink stands outside cafés in central squares for racers to sign control sheets.[59] The first came at four miles, the Café François on rue de la Surintendance in Saint-Germain. When Champion pulled up as the leader, a mass of spectators let him squeeze through. He scratched his signature and galloped away.

Champion sped past folks standing two and three deep and shouting encouragement along the undulating dirt roads at the villages of Conflans, Pontoise, and Ennery, which led to Hérouville, where he joined Broc. Together they sped to the lyrically named village of Vallangoujard, at twenty-three miles. Breyer traveled by train and stopped to scamper off at the Vallangoujard station long enough to telegraph his first dispatch: "Ten o'clock. A springy, light vehicle torpedoed along, topped by a man who looked like a diver with big goggles. It was Broc, sweeping the little Champion, his white jersey and pants coated in dust."[60]

Two minutes later came Paul Bor, Fischer, and Bouhours drafting behind automobiles. At Vallangoujard, Garin's car coughed to a halt.[61] Two riding mechanics, his insurance against mechanical failures, endeavored to revive the engine. "Finally, he felt he had waited too long and announced he had quit," the *Journal* reported. "Despite pleas of his mechanics and automobile pacers, he pedaled off to the train station."[62] (Garin would score immortality four years later by winning the first Tour de France.) Meanwhile, Ambrose Garin and Fischer tried, and failed, to catch Champion by the second control point in Beauvais, at forty-seven miles. After Beauvais, Bouhours tucked behind his car and overtook Fischer and Ambrose Garin so fast that he looked sure to do the same to Champion. By the third control, in the Village of Breteuil, sixty-six miles, Bouhours chased Champion like a cop after a fugitive.[63]

The roads were bordered by multitudes. They cheered Broc and Champion, flying through villages at short distances from one another, the villages like stepping stones leading to their mid-race goal of Amiens. In one village, Broc had to turn his motor-tricycle sharply to avoid striking pedestrians. The sudden move knocked Champion over.[64] He promptly remounted and kept going. Shortly before 11:30, Broc and Champion pulled into Amiens, its cathedral spires looming over the treetops. Champion zoomed to the esplanade Saint-Roch, where a pair of officials sat outside the Café Odelin with the fourth control sheet. He signed in to a rousing reception. Then to perilous sections of pavé.

Minutes later, Bouhours sped into Amiens. A seasoned pro with more world records to his credit than he could remember, Bouhours had the potential to vanquish Champion. When Bouhours left the city, his driver swerved to avoid hitting a pedestrian crossing the road, but he bowled him over anyway. Bouhours smacked into the vehicle and fell to the road.[65] An injured elbow forced him to abandon the race and seek medical help. Fischer endured a similar accident that ended his bid. (Bouhours returned the next year to win, when the race dropped motorpacing.)

Champion and Broc received applause and cheers through villages that led to the fifth control at Doullens, 104 miles. On the grimy road to the sixth control at Arras, 128 miles, Champion confronted his first section of pavé. His wheels dropped into the fissures at the end of every stone, rounded like the top of a skull, and smacked into the next. Bumping over the cobbles beat up his arms, back, and legs. Witnesses watched the world record holder of the flying kilometer straining over each cobble at a pedestrian pace.

After Arras, he and Broc reached the craggiest pavé, en route to the ancient Gaulic-Roman town of Séclin. The cobblestones had shifted willy-nilly over two centuries since Louis XIV's order to upgrade dirt roads for farmers to take their harvest to markets. Champion battled to keep his balance as tires slipped on the rounded edges. Again and again he toppled over and smacked onto the stones.[66]

"The struggle took everything Champion had," Breyer asserted.[67] Champion labored two hours to cover the twenty-three miles from Arras to Séclin.

In Séclin, some thirty-one miles from Roubaix, an enormous population greeted Champion as he signed the seventh control sheet. From Séclin to the vélodrome, there were two hedgerows of spectators lining both sides of the roads.[68] "Police had a difficult time holding back the crowds," the *Journal* noted. "They confirmed the race's popularity."[69]

As the first to reach Roubaix and write his signature on the final control sheet at the Café Leon on the Boulevard de Paris, Champion earned a bonus of fifty francs from the Roubaix cycling club.[70] He continued pacing behind Broc across town to the Roubaix Vélodrome, where Broc peeled off to the track's infield and left Champion to finish alone.

"There was not an empty space anywhere," the *Journal* stated.[71] When the Union of the Trumpets of Roubaix blared Champion's arrival, some twelve thousand people packed into the stadium and infield let out a roar. "Everyone expected to greet Garin winning his third Paris-Roubaix," observed the *Journal*. "But it was Champion who dashed onto the track. The crowd was disillusioned."[72]

Yet the partisan audience quickly recalled his earlier races as a young pro on the track. "When he appeared at the entrance to the vélodrome, they gave him an ovation," said the *Journal*. "He was covered with dust and mud. His jersey looked like he had several falls. He had fallen seven times! But he still pedaled like he was fresh."[73]

As winner of the 1899 edition of Paris-Roubaix, the spring classic of bicycle road racing, which ranks in prestige with the Boston Marathon in running and Wimbledon in tennis, Champion was honored on the cover of *Vélo* as one of the kings of cycling. His victory led to a contract to race in America. *From* Le Vélo, *April 1899.*

On the infield, the Musical Society of the Vélodrome performed lively tunes urging him on his ceremonial six laps to complete the distance. Champion won in 8 hours, 22 minutes, 53 seconds. Eighteen minutes passed before Paul Bor took second place for 500 francs. Champion received a bouquet of flowers for his deserved lap of honor. Then he steered onto the infield. Roubaixians created a narrow path for him to squeeze through to join Broc. A photographer waited with his camera on a tripod. Officials surrounded Champion. Held by the smiling Broc, he set his flowers across his handlebars. To the lens, he turned a weary face.

News of his feat flashed around the continent, the United Kingdom, and the United States. *Le Vélo* published his portrait in a jacket and cravat. Text proclaimed him "Les Roi du Cycle," asserting he had joined the sport's pantheon. (The honor represented a grace note from the publisher, Giffard, who had sued *L'Auto-Vélo* over its name and won, forcing Desgrange to rename his publication *L'Auto*.) Chicago-based *Cycle Age and Trade Review* (successor to *Bearings*) reported, "Champion surprises everybody by winning great event on his debut."[74]

"He had entered Paris-Roubaix as a youngster,"[75] Breyer wrote. "Now he is a man."

Champion impressed Breyer because he had moved up in class to claim victory in a major road race, enduring the worst roads in northern France and beating established road racers at their game. Winning Paris-Roubaix put Champion into France's pantheon of *Les Grands*.

Indeed, Champion's draft board in Batignolles treated him like a man. All able-bodied young Frenchmen were required under the law to serve two years in the military. France's empire ranked second only to England's, with colonies in Africa, the Pacific, South America, and Southeast Asia. A few weeks later, after he had turned twenty-one on April 5, he received orders to report in November for compulsory boot camp. This threatened to upend his life. He was headed into the ranks of *les poilus*, foot soldiers, for wages notoriously beggarly. He would no longer be able to support his brothers and mother. She would go back to work hauling water buckets from a well and doing laundry. In an army uniform, he would lose his individuality. Two years of duty would disrupt the career he had built. How could he win the hand of Elise? Worst of all, would he forfeit la gloire?

A solution arrived in a trans-Atlantic cable from Charles Herman Metz, manufacturer of Orient Cycles in the Boston suburb of Waltham. The American offered a one-year contract to race, with a salary of $25 a week,[76] a solid middle-class income or better when the average Yank earned $9. Motor-pace races paid winners $250,[77] and the prize money would be all his.

Such a sparkling opportunity tempted Champion, yet it forced him into a dilemma. Ignoring his draft summons meant arrest and imprisonment, possibly on Devil's Island off the coast of French Guiana in South America, whether he remained in France or fled to Boston and later attempted to return home. How could he even get to America? Trying to leave France by taking a ship from any French port required eluding gendarmes with hawk eyes for spotting draft-eligible men attempting to shirk their duty. If he avoided detection and sailed to Boston, he would live alone there, and he spoke hardly any English. The specter of a bad crash—an occupational hazard—could leave him stranded, drained of income, cursed. He felt overwhelmed and turned to Dudley Marks, who had visited America, for advice. Marks, a bachelor, loved to travel. He agreed to accompany him. They could make their way to England without raising suspicion and ship out of Liverpool.

That strategy tipped the scales for Champion. But he needed more assistance. He asked Breyer, fluent in French and English, to act as his agent dealing with Metz. Breyer understood that what Champion requested could get him into trouble. Breyer had performed his duty at Champion's age, as a rifleman in a cycling regiment.[78] He sympathized with Champion's plight. He reflected that Metz's offer was extraordinary, the *deus ex machina* from a Greek play. Breyer brokered the deal with Metz for Champion and Marks to sail from Liverpool.[79] Champion seized Metz's offer and chose a backdoor scarper. It was the biggest decision of his life.

Champion packed several of the latest De Dion-Bouton engines, prized in America. De Dion-Bouton Motorette Company ruled as the world's biggest carmaker, with annual production of 400 autos and 3,200 engines.[80] Champion also took his unicycle and other accoutrements in wooden crates. Everything was sent by rail freight from Paris to the White Star Line office in Liverpool. He promised his mother and Prosper, Henri, and Louis that he would mail money home. To Elise, he vowed that he would send for her to join him in Boston.

He boarded HMS *Majestic* of the White Star Line to escape conscription.[81] Instead of reporting for duty in the French Army on November 15, he sailed to America. Seven days later, the *Majestic* steamed into New York harbor. At the dock he and Marks were met by Metz.

Charles Herman Metz was Clément's American counterpart in creativity and enterprise. He made bicycles designated Orient to reflect the vogue of the Far East's ancient mystery and perfect porcelain vases.[82] Metz's business, the Waltham Manufacturing Company, was near the Waltham Bicycle Park. The park had a track with long straights and tight turns, famous for world records. Its bleachers and grandstand accommodated ten thousand spectators, more than double what the Boston Red Sox considered a profitable turnout. Journalists filed race accounts over a state-of-the-art telegraph. Telegraph poles, including one near turn three, took the lines over the track into Waltham—and the rest of the world. Metz retailed Orients through John Wanamaker,[83] who had introduced the United States to department stores in Philadelphia and New York City. Metz also advertised widely. He commissioned posters from the artist Edward Penfield,[84] whose introspective figures were compared to those of Toulouse-Lautrec.

In 1896 for publicity, Metz had built the longest bicycle in the world—a special ten-seater, puckishly dubbed Oriten.[85] (It's on display today at the Henry Ford Museum in Dearborn, Michigan.) Orient racing models weighed only twenty pounds, but the Oriten tipped the scales at 305 pounds.[86] Twenty-three feet and nine inches long,[87] the length of four bicycles, it boasted a carrying capacity of 2,500 pounds—the weight of two full-sized horses. Metz and nine employees had set a world record for the mile on the board track in Charles River Park: 2 minutes 12 seconds.[88] His Oriten, however, was so long that its front wheel carved deep into a turn while the rear remained on the straight. That forced the ten-seater wide around turns on standard velodromes—a disadvantage against shorter triplets or quads hugging the inside. Metz had taken human-powered pacing to its natural limit.

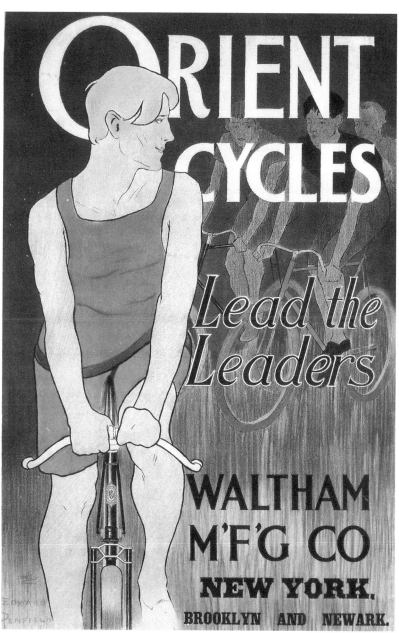

American posters were staid compared with what was popular in Paris, yet Edward Penfield had a flair for depicting a rider on Orient Cycles with poise decades before it was called cool. *Image courtesy of Poster Photo Archives, Posters Please, Inc., New York.*

Charles Herman Metz, at the front of his ten-seat Orient, took human pace to its limit. He imported small French motors to put on tandems then brought Champion from Paris for motorpace races. *Used by permission of the Waltham Museum, Waltham, MA.*

Then Metz read in the trade press about De Dion-Bouton engines on Clément tricycles and tandems. He wrote to Count Mechanic and secured North American rights to import his engines.[89] In 1898 Metz had fitted them on Orient tandems and tricycles. The metronome *put-put*, the smell of gasoline, and the sensation of cruising 25 mph without any physical exertion prompted him to order Waltham's dirt oval track surfaced with concrete—for less rolling resistance and more speed.

Other business chiefs fascinated with motor transportation were General Electric Company president Charles A. Coffin, in neighboring Lynn, and Lynn Gas and Electric Company president M. P. Clough. General Electric, the product of a recent merger of utilities, had headquarters in Schenectady, New York, although Coffin remained in Lynn. General Electric powered Boston's metropolitan trolley system. Coffin and Clough had deemed that automobiles with electric motors trumped gas-combustion engines. Electric vehicles ran on lead-acid batteries, one of the nineteenth century's technical triumphs, and they could be recharged at home (like plug-in hybrid electric vehicles today) or in charging stations, which, they foresaw, could be built around the country.

New electric autos, some manufactured by Pope from capital flowing from his Columbia Bicycle Company, allowed the driver to start them by pushing a button on the dashboard. That made for a convenient selling point over gas-combustion engines, which required that the driver go to the front of the vehicle, insert a hand crank, and turn it over to engage the engine, which required muscle. Steam-powered cars needed up to twenty minutes for water to heat up and make steam before they could be driven. Coffin and Clough ordered their companies to buy stock in Metz's business and encouraged him to make electric-powered tricycles and autos.[90]

Gas-powered engines aroused suspicions at the *Boston Globe*, which disparaged motor-tandems as "devil catchers."[91] After Champion's Paris-Roubaix victory, two events impelled Metz to take unprecedented action.

The first event occurred on June 30. Charles M. Murphy of Brooklyn, New York, pedaled on a special board surface laid between rails and paced behind a train car pulled by a locomotive on Long Island, near Hampstead Plains. Murphy, in cycling tights as the wind ruffled the hair on his bare head, had astounded Metz, and the world, by riding a mile in 57-4/5 seconds—the first person ever, on two wheels or four, to cover a mile in less than a minute.[92] Murphy had proved that with a locomotive providing protection from air resistance a cyclist could pedal in the protected sweet spot and keep up, even at speeds topping 60 mph. Witnessing his feat were fifty New York journalists aboard the pace car. They filed dispatches published in newspapers across America and worldwide.

Press attention ignited discussions about changing prevailing technological assumptions. "Lesson of Murphy's Ride: May Prove Means of Saving Millions in Transportation,"[93] decreed *Cycle Age and Trade Review*. The editors called for designing wedge-shaped locomotives: "It is strange that with all of our earnest effort to reduce fuel expenses and increase the hauling power of our locomotives by improving the track, compounding the cylinders, enlarging the boiler and so on, we have not taken one of the obvious and simple precautions by which the greatest of all train resistances might be overcome."

The second event happened in mid-August at the weeklong world cycling championships in Montreal. Organizers had held a twenty-mile exhibition race with five autos on the track in Queen's Park. The *Montreal Daily Star* noted: "Automobiles are somewhat of a novelty just at present, but in a hundred years from now they will be part of everybody's household economy, or at least so it is said." Johnny Nelson, a diminutive Swedish immigrant from Chicago, put in a performance that indicated autos were coming much sooner. He followed an Orient motor-tandem around the track and thrilled twelve thousand spectators in the 100-kilometer (62.5 miles) amateur paced race. He hit a steady 31 mph—exceeding Montreal's speed limit of 10 mph. He caused a sensation by lapping rivals on human-powered tandems and smashing world records every mile.[94] A throng of jubilant fans carried him on their shoulders around the track.[95] In the professional event, the winner paced by a regular tandem took ten minutes longer—time enough for Nelson to have gone five more miles.

Metz's lesson from Montreal was that the approaching century would open the way to dramatic changes. The United States in 1899 had a population of 75 million.[96] Among them, they owned 10 million bicycles.[97] The market had reached saturation with oversupply that set off frantic price competition. In an attempt to control supply of products and limit a price war, the American Bicycle Company,[98] a holding company directed by Pope, was established to merge seventy-five brands.

Around Massachusetts prototype horseless carriages, built with a tiller that the driver held like reins to steer, began venturing onto roads. The Stanley twins in Watertown produced steam-powered Stanley Steamers.[99] Charles Duryea downstate in Springfield drove gas-combustion vehicles he made with an obsolete socket on the dashboard for buggy whips to appease traditionalists.[100] Pope offered electric cars,[101] which he favored for running silently and without spewing out black smoke from burning oil. Few motor enthusiasts and tinkerers dared to take to the streets dominated by horses. For every automobile running on steam, gasoline, or electricity there were 3,600 horses and mules. Motor carriages powered by gasoline were noisy before mufflers were introduced, and they reeked of gas and oil. Steam-powered autos hissed. They spooked horses and caused disasters when animals ran out of control. Ransom Olds in Lansing, Michigan, affixed a replica horse's head on the front of his early gas-combustion Oldsmobiles in an effort to prevent frightening the real equines.[102]

Metz's friends and customers who earlier had rhapsodized about the joys of cycling now raved about driving autos and other diversions, such as photography and golf. The United States was undergoing a cultural makeover. People in greater numbers were moving from the countryside to jobs in cities. With increased social and economic mobility, a new middle class was emerging. Just as bicycles had usurped business from horse-drawn carriages in the 1880s and 1890s, it appeared to Metz that autos would do the same to bicycles. Then Metz received a large injection of cash from General Electric and the Lynn Gas and Electric Company buying stock in his Waltham Manufacturing Company to encourage Metz to expand his company.[103] He invested the extra money to hire Champion.[104] As if on cue, HMS *Majestic* docked in New York and Champion walked down the gangway.

When Champion first met Metz, he saw a thin man of thirty-five, his size, who appeared capable of challenging him in a race. Metz trimmed his mustache precisely. Like Marks, he wore a bowler. Champion, clean-shaven, favored the flat wool hats of his proletariat class, also popular with American boys waving newspapers for sale on street corners. Champion had grown up with his family and Elise calling him Albert when, to everyone else, he went by Champion. Warburton and Marks had shortened his first name, in the British manner, to Bert, sometimes rounded out to Bertie. Charles Herman Metz called him Al. Metz asked Al Champion to call him by his initials: C. H.[105] So it was that Al and C. H. shook hands.

Metz had hired the Frenchman to race for him and to aid in his plan to shift from manufacturing bicycles to manufacturing autos. He also planned to prevail on Champion's experience with De Dion-Bouton engines as part of his effort to narrow France's lead in engine technology. One of their first conversation topics on the train ride from New York to Boston revolved around crafting a gas-combustion engine small enough to fit on a bicycle: *voilà*, the motorcycle, still awaiting development in America.

Champion and Marks moved into a boarding house that Metz had booked for them, a triple-decker Victorian with bay windows on a tree-lined street in Cambridge. Champion's new digs at 19 Cottage Street were near the outdoor Charles River Park with its outdoor board track, and they were a short bicycle commute to Metz's factory along the Charles.[106] Assertive about promoting both his business and Al Champion, C. H. had committed his newcomer to a twenty-five mile paced match race in three weeks behind motor-tricycles in New York's palace of play, Madison Square Garden.

C. H. showed Al and Dudley around his factory, a wooden building on Rumford Avenue.[107] He introduced them to general manager John C. Robbins, a disciple of Metz since their youth in Utica, in upstate New York.[108] Utica cycling pals had included Charles Stewart Mott, a second-generation wheel and axle maker and future General Motors director. Robbins, a self-taught engineer, at twenty-eight, directed some 150 skilled machinists,[109] mechanics, craftsmen, and laborers. They took pride in calling themselves the Men of Metz.

Metz came to own his company through an eclectic route consistent with many ambitious men of his generation. His father had immigrated, from Germany at fifteen and apprenticed as a carpenter in Utica.[110] Young Metz had quit school after the sixth grade to apprentice to his father.[111] He had an avid sense of curiosity and bought a set of the *Encyclopedia Britannica*.[112] By the time he had read all the volumes from A to Z, studying famous people and the wonders of mechanical power transforming the nineteenth century, he had learned how to work with tools, build houses, and manage a business. His eclectic education made him restless. He left carpentry to operate a men's clothing shop, followed by a stint as clerk in an insurance company until he was about twenty, in 1883, and discovered high-wheel bicycles.[113] He enjoyed cycling and had no trouble landing a job as a sales rep in Utica for Pope's Columbia Bicycles.[114] In 1885 Metz won the New York State one-mile championship.[115] He made his own bicycle accessories. By 1889 he had moved to Boston for a job as a designer for a bicycle company.[116] He married Elizabeth Humphrey and the two had a son.

Following the arrival of the chain-drive on a diamond frame from England, Metz founded his company with two financial backers.[117] He bought land in Waltham on the Charles River. Waltham was home to skilled workers in iron and brass foundries, textile factories, and paper mills. Waltham had a history of advances. Early in the 1800s, a Waltham company had produced sulfuric acid, essential for making iron and steel in vast quantities.[118] Dentist Dr. Francis F. Field had invented the process for making chalk crayons, and he had founded the American Crayon Company.[119] The Waltham Watch Company had innovated mass production, relying on interchangeable parts to make jeweled pocket watches.[120] In 1855 Waltham's Tar Factory produced the first clear white Kerosene from coal oil, replacing whale oil for lighting and heating.[121] After the Panic of 1893, brought on by railroads overbuilding with dubious funding, fifteen thousand companies failed, five hundred banks folded, and the economy cartwheeled into depression.[122] One of the few bright spots was the bicycle

industry. In October 1893 Metz and partners incorporated the Waltham Manufacturing Company with $100,000 capital to make Orient bicycles, with Metz
as president.[123]

During the progressive 1890s, men and women on bicycles filled urban
parks on summer evenings and cycled on weekends to explore the countryside for fitness and sightseeing. Cycling had become America's first coast-to-
coast craze. Poems and songs were composed to celebrate cycling, such as
"Bicycle Built for Two." Racing rivaled baseball and horseracing as America's
most popular spectator sports. Most cities supported at least one velodrome.
Racers dominated as America's best-paid athletes. National champion Tom
Cooper, who would fund Henry Ford in 1903, earned more than $15,000 a
year,[124] while major league baseball team owners tethered greats like Honus
Wagner, the Pittsburgh Pirates shortstop commemorated today as the subject
of the most valuable baseball card in existence, to contracts of around $5,000
per year.[125] Basketball had only started to catch on in Northeast colleges. Football moldered as a raffish underworld diversion. Boxing had a red-light-district
reputation and was outlawed in many states.

In 1897 Metz's company produced fifteen thousand Orient bicycles, tandems,
and tricycles.[126] (In 2014 that would amount to operating revenue of about $40
million.) He kept making innovations and received twenty-two patents, including
one for a sturdy fork crown holding the front wheel to the frame, a design still in
use worldwide. He promoted Orients with famous riders, including the Columbia
University cycling team, and advertised their victories. At the 1899 Montreal
world championships, Marshall "Major" Taylor of Indianapolis, the first African-
American to leap over the color line in pro sports, made history by winning the
world professional sprint championship on an Orient. C. H. hired Al Champion
to help his company shift to motor vehicles.

6

"PACEMAKERS KILLED"

*THE SHADOW OF DEATH, WHICH MANY FOLLOWERS OF
CYCLE RACING HAVE MAINTAINED HOVERED OVER
THE HEADS OF MOTOR CYCLISTS, AT WALTHAM
YESTERDAY BECAME A REALITY.*

—JOHN J. DONOVAN,
BOSTON GLOBE, MAY 31, 1900[1]

Bostonians were cycling crazy. Even after autumn freezes, punctuated by bucketing rains and wind gusts, had stripped trees bare and made everyone seek refuge indoors, Boston offered what Champion needed. He rode on the board velodrome of the Park Square Coliseum,[2] which was housed inside a wooden building owned by the Boston and Providence Railroad at Park Square and Boylston Street. Boston's dynamic, big-city controlled chaos made him feel comfortable. Paris operated as the head for the body of France—its national capital, heart of banking, focal point of fashion, and, at the time, the epicenter of France's bicycle and auto milieus. Champion discovered that Boston served much the same function as the Bay State capital, business hub for Massachusetts and the five surrounding New England states, which together were comparable in size to France. And Boston was the center for bicycle and auto enterprises.

The coliseum offered a shabby but genteel version of the Vel d'Hiv while functioning as the center for cyclists compulsive about keeping their edge. Sunday afternoon programs attracted decent attendance and offered prize money. Champion joined an army of amateurs and pros from around the United States, Canada, Europe, even Australia.

When he was not training, Champion was assigned by Metz the task of fitting the latest De Dion-Bouton engines he had brought from France onto Orient tricycles for his twenty-five-mile paced match race in Madison Square Garden. Champion was to compete against another Orient pro, Harry Elkes of Glens Falls, New York, America's first national paced champion, for Champion's introduction to America.

Champion easily spotted Elkes, a six-footer—unusual among pro cyclists and exceptional for one who specialized in pacing. His ears stuck out like jug handles under dark hair parted on the left side rather than down the center, which was in vogue. Toothpick arms, shoulders narrow as a greyhound's, and long scissor-like legs added up to his nickname "Lanky." He was known for his calm disposition, which vanished when he raced aggressively and screwed his face into a grimace, what the press termed a "bicycle face."[3] In 1898 he had turned twenty and shot into national prominence by breaking one national record after another while becoming America's inaugural national pacing champion, entitled to wearing the stars and stripes around his waist in competitions.[4] The next year in Philadelphia, Lanky Elkes set a new world hour record of 36.7 miles,[5] pedaling behind a relay of four Orient motor-tandems. He had broken the record of Champion's rival Edouard Taylor, set months earlier in Paris, by a full mile.

As soon as Champion and Elkes met, they became friends. The American pleaded for Champion's help to race in Paris. Both men were the same age—Elkes just four months younger—and Champion obliged by contacting Clément and Pierre Tournier, who arranged contracts in Paris. Clément served as president of the French Board of Trade and Automobile Makers and was happy to have an American national champion racing on his Gladiator Cycles.[6]

In the weeks before he shipped out, Elkes followed motor-tandems steered by Frank Gately, a sardonic man in his mid-twenties. Gately preferred driving the motors and gave up racing bicycles. He appreciated the better pay—earning at least ten percent of Elkes's winnings. Gately's duties involved keeping the engine in top running condition. Elkes endured enough falls and injuries to half-joke that he was saving his prize money to attend college and become a doctor.[7] He often praised Gately for steering through traffic congestion in motor-tandem paced events, extolling Gately's nerves of iron, sound judgment, and sense of tactics. He called him "King" Gately.

Champion trained in the coliseum behind Marks on a motor-tricycle. Elkes worked out following King Gately. Reporters from the eight dailies on Newspaper Row, downtown on Washington Street,[8] reported on the Sunday international races. To sharpen his skills, Champion competed in different events.

His limited English curbed rapport with journalists unless Marks showed up and translated. Champion resumed pedaling the unicycle around the flat inside perimeter, which would remind him of Paris and Warburton and their days together. He took advantage of riding without hands on the handlebars to wave to spectators in the stands. The unicycle captivated the *Globe*'s John J. Donovan. He described Champion as "famous as one of the best Continentals on a unicycle—a single-wheel contraption which required the skill and dexterity of a tightrope walker to manipulate."[9]

On the evening of December 2, 1899, Albert Champion strode along New York's Madison Avenue with Elkes, Marks, Gately, and Metz. They trooped into Madison Square Garden—an oversized Moorish castle designed by the famous architect and leader of New York's artistic renaissance Stanford White. Champion's gang led porters pushing handcarts with motor-tricycles and bicycles packed in wooden crates into the main hall. Madison Square Garden's length of 350 feet, width of 200 feet,[10] and height soaring eighty feet led to the claim that it was the largest hall in the world. In the middle of the hall stood a new board velodrome ringed by seats filled with spectators.

"The Garden seats 5,500 but more than 8,000 people were on hand to give a royal Yankee welcome to the best foreign aggregation that ever crossed the pond," observed *Cycle Age*.[11] "The Elkes-Champion match was billed as the feature of the card."

Their match race was part of a program that culminated one minute after midnight with the introduction of a new sports lollapalooza. The impresario behind the night was William A. Brady, who had strutted and grinned his way into the hearts of audiences from New York to San Francisco. Brady had managed world heavyweight boxing champion Jim Corbett,[12] brought cyclist Jimmy Michael to America, and presented lion acts, marquee theater actors, cakewalkers,[13] and even flooded the garden to fill it with miniature battleships to reenact the 1898 sinking of the U.S.S. *Maine*, which set off the Spanish-American War. "After all it was just showmanship in one form or another," he said with typical bravado in his 1937 memoir *Showman*.

Since 1895, Brady had presided over the garden's annual six-day bicycle endurance challenges. Every December, cyclists had pedaled solo around the clock, beginning at 12:01 a.m. Monday to avoid competing on the Sabbath, circling the treadmill of a track for 142 hours to see who could put in the most miles. Cartoonists from the city's fifteen newspapers sketched fans with necks wound up like rubber bands from head turning to count laps. Riders were on their own for eating, sleeping, and making any calls of nature. Charles Miller, a beefy twenty-three-year old grocer from Chicago, had won the 1898 event after riding 1,962 miles,[14] a distance that would have taken him from the garden to Albuquerque, New Mexico. Miller even took a half-hour break to marry his fiancée on the track infield.[15]

After the 1898 six-day, Governor Theodore Roosevelt had signed a law that barred anyone from competing more than twelve hours a day.[16] To circumvent the law, Brady created two-rider teams. He put up $4,000 (worth $116,000 in 2014) for the winning two-rider team,[17] and he signed up nineteen pairs from ten nations, in an appeal to sell tickets to the city's diverse ethnic groups. The *New York Times* reported: "It is seldom that so many champions of international fame are assembled on the same track."[18]

Brady stocked early events with amateur racers and star pro sprinters from the United States and Europe. Metz took advantage of Brady's perpetual quest for something exotic and proposed an exclusive motor-tricycle race of twenty-five miles between US national champion Elkes and French ace Champion. Brady seized Metz's offer.

Champion and his crew led porters to the track infield where they assembled their machines. As part of the entertainment, a band on another part of the infield performed jaunty show tunes. Swarms of cyclists careened around the boards in the preliminary events. Now and then a tire would explode after being jabbed by a splinter from the pine boards.

The garden's great hall had turned into a frenetic beehive. Brady stood with his chest out, thumbs hooked in his vest, preening by the start-finish line like a bantam rooster. Brady chatted with Corbett, who brandished a revolver as the celebrity starter. The promoter, in his late thirties and balding, reached only to Corbett's shoulders, his head so full of hair that the press nicknamed him "Pompadour Jim." Brady removed his cigar and exhaled a plume of smoke that disappeared into the garden's general nicotine cloud.

At eight o'clock sharp, Brady stepped onto the boards. He waved his hands and the cigar he was holding and ordered the track cleared. Champion's manager, Marks, took to the track with his motor-tricycle, and Gately did as well on his machine. Marks and King Gately both wore suits and ties, Marks topped by a bowler while King Gately pulled his flat wool hat on tight. They lined up, side by side, on the banking behind Champion and Elkes, in their cycling black shorts and long-sleeved jerseys emblazoned with *Orient* across the front and back. Elkes wore an American flag tied around his waist as national champion, while Albert Champion wore the French tricolor. Metz stood on the inside lane holding the bicycle of Champion, who stared straight ahead, gripping the drops of his handlebars, back straight, feet jammed into steel toe clips, while Elkes was held by another man next to Champion.

When Corbett fired his pistol, Champion and Elkes charged into the first turn as King Gately and Marks drove up the banking to overtake them. Unlike bicycles that lean with their riders into turns, tricycles follow different forces. The pull of gravity on the forty-five-degree banking forced King Gately's machine to slip[19] and bowl over Elkes, who knocked down Champion. Corbett fired his handgun, this time twice in quick succession—signaling a false start, which required the competitors to return to the start immediately.[20]

After the restart, Champion could not pedal properly—the crash had bent the seat post of his bicycle.[21] He lost several laps to Elkes before he stopped and exchanged it for a fresh bicycle. He chased to regain the laps until the engine of Marks's motor-tricycle gave out at eleven miles. Marks had to pull off the track, stop, and snatch a replacement before continuing.

Despite the disruptions, Champion put up a feisty chase. In the thirteenth mile, the crowd cheered as he overtook Elkes. The Yankee and Frenchman traded the lead until more mechanical difficulties again slowed both Marks and Champion at nineteen miles.

In the end, Elkes won by seven laps. Champion and Elkes wheeled off the track to the band's merry music as the six-day riders rolled onto the boards with their trainers for the 12:01 a.m. Monday start. Surprisingly, more than half of the audience stampeded out the exits, protesting the end of individual six-days.[22] Only three thousand spectators stayed to watch the new event.

Despite their inauspicious debut, Brady's two-rider cycling track races worked their way into the language of cycling, and even today around the world these events are known as *Madisons*. In the Olympics and annual world championship track programs, Madisons are medal events. For his part in this new category, Champion had performed as the opening act.

If he'd been interviewed about losing, Champion would have explained that he much preferred pacing on the track behind motor-tandems, which flowed better through the banked turns. Motor-trikes were best suited to roads. In fact, he'd propelled to trans-Atlantic fame after pacing behind a motor-trike in the only road race of his career, the grueling Paris-Roubaix classic. He would have shrugged his shoulders. He might have added that since Metz had already introduced motor-tandems, the motor-trikes were a novelty that the American audience would prefer. Then he would have shrugged once more in acknowledgment that he and Elkes, his professional teammate, had only been giving an exhibition. They'd had nothing at stake. He was aware of how sport approaches religion, as the devoted keep trying to do better. He still had ample opportunities to win races and thrill audiences.

Following the Madison Square Garden excursion, Champion returned to Boston. He rode his bicycle with Elkes and other pros on the board velodrome of the Park Square Coliseum to practice for his first race in Waltham on Memorial Day, May 30.

After morning training sessions and before his afternoon sessions, Champion worked in a corner of Metz's Orient bicycle factory on Rumford Avenue, near Waltham Bicycle Park and close to the Charles River. Champion fitted horse buggies with the latest engines he had brought over from Paris. Some engines were one-cylinder De Dion-Boutons, which generated 2 hp, equivalent to eight cyclists pedaling together. Other engines were Asters, which were new water-cooled engines. Aster engines featured two forward speeds and an innovative option: reverse. All French engines, batteries, and magnetos (metal coils around a magnet embedded in a flywheel) were mounted American-style under the chassis and steered with a tiller.

That spring Metz, Champion, and Marks often drove these engine-powered buggies, dubbed Runabouts, over the dirt roads of Waltham and Cambridge. Sometimes they were joined by Metz's general manager John C. Robbins. They careened along at 25 mph in defiance of 10 mph speed limits. Their Runabouts whipped up dirt clouds and frightened horses that ruled public roads. Boston's newspapers reported that alarmed drivers of horse teams grumbled to police about wild troublemakers disturbing the peace.

When he wasn't terrorizing the locals, Champion took advantage of the milder weather to train in Cambridge's Charles River Park to take advantage of its wooden oval, which ran six laps to the mile with banked turns. He preferred it to Waltham's concrete velodrome, which was only three laps to the mile, and where he had to ease off before each tight turn before picking up speed on the next straightaway. Before motorpacing came along, the Waltham track's longer straights had helped riders build speed. But cyclists pacing behind quicker motor-tricycles and motor-tandems complained that Waltham's velodrome, eight years old, was out of date.

On sunny days, a thousand spectators showed up to watch and yell encouragement to Champion and others working out behind motor-tandems. After Elkes shipped out for Paris, King Gately took over steering the motor-tandems for Champion while Marks would sit on the motor-tandem's rear seat over the engine as the "stoker," continually reaching down to manipulate the throttle lever that fed or reduced the flow of gasoline. Marks also doubled as a windscreen for Champion. Wearing a jacket gave Marks extra bulk to provide Champion added wind protection. Champion would bark commands to speed up, hold steady, or slow down. When the three men and their engine synchronized, Champion would jab his front wheel within inches of the tandem's rear and they would click off laps for mile times well inside of two minutes—often topping 30 mph.

They were prepping for Champion's racing premier in Waltham on Memorial Day, a twenty-mile motor-tandem paced event. Motor-pace races paid top dollar: $250 to win ($7,150 in 2014), $125 to place, and $100 to show.[23] That exceeded the $100 first prize for the marquee sprinters—or the $6 that textile workers earned for toiling fifty-six hours a week in noisy brick factories.

They practiced at race pace, ten to twenty brisk miles every morning, sixteen to twenty miles in the afternoon. *Boston Globe* reporter John J. Donovan often mingled with spectators and wrote of Champion:

At times he would lose his pace, as did all paced followers, but the comparison stopped there. Opponents losing their pace carefully controlled their bicycles at the high speed until they slowed down. The Frenchman, however, gave American spectators "heart failure," for he would be whipped from behind his motorcycle and in his anger would not be content to shout at his pace-makers but would take his hands off the handlebars and gesticulate, and it would seem as if he must be thrown, but he rarely fell, though others did.[24]

In the boarding house where Champion and Marks lived, Eliza Holaway and Mary E. Watling were employed as servants.[25] Both twenty-five and from French-speaking Canada, they were obvious targets for the men to ply their continental charm, kissing the backs of the women's hands, murmuring *en Français*. The four soon formed pairs, even though Champion's intended was still back home in Paris.

One afternoon in late April, Champion encountered Jimmy Michael on the Charles River Track. Michael pedaled onto the velodrome and received a welcome as warm as the sunshine from fans who recognized the former star. Since the Welshman's retirement at age twenty-two to a gentleman's life of leisure, Champion had heard and read accounts about Michael's purchase of a stable of horses in New Orleans.[26] Michael had decamped to London and bankrolled American ex-pat Ted Sloan, the jockey who had led a revolution in horse racing with short stirrups that had the riders hunkering low on the horse's neck—the "monkey crouch."[27] Sloan had run into trouble for betting on his own mounts. Michael had flunked as a jockey and chucked it as hopeless.[28] In 1900, twenty-four and broke, he accepted a hefty contract from a US tire company and a smaller one from Metz to ride Orient Cycles.

On May 13, at the Charles River Track, Champion was practicing behind King Gately and Marks while Michael spun onto the track behind a motor-tandem. Champion lapped the Welshman and taunted him.[29] To Champion, Michael had slandered Warburton with false accusations and abused his own talent. Champion kept taunting Michael until the engine on the motor-tandem Champion paced behind faltered and he almost ran into the rear wheel. The team pulled into the infield to fix the problem. Meanwhile, Eliza Holaway, who frequently came to watch the practices, left the bleachers to see what had happened.

Upon inspection, the problem lay with the spark plug. Champion had become well versed in De Dion-Bouton spark plugs and their loosening from engine vibrations,[30] which in turn caused misfires. The De Dion-Bouton spark plug's center pole was cemented in place.[31] Other brands had an outer locking ring that screwed into the outer conductor pole for better stability.

Marks needed time to find a replacement plug and adjust the spark. Champion, ever impatient, did not want to stand around, sweating. He instructed Marks to give Eliza the stopwatch so she could call out his times from trackside as he clicked off laps.[32] He pedaled so fast for ten miles that many riders tacked onto his rear wheel to draft, like a locomotive pulling train cars.

Donovan, under the spell of his recent honeymoon and confused about Champion's relationship with Eliza, reported: "An interested spectator was his wife, a handsome and vivacious French woman, who scored his laps and told him at intervals the distance he had traveled."[33] When Champion rode cool-down laps, he berated Michael. Donovan saw the kerfuffle and tactfully said Michael "will train at Waltham for the season as he thinks the air is better there."

Memorial Day 1900 fell on a Wednesday. As the holiday approached, veterans from around the Commonwealth of Massachusetts and adjacent states converged on Boston. Generals delivered speeches in theaters filled with cheering audiences waving hand-held flags,[34] and citizens upheld the tradition, established in 1868 as Decoration Day,[35] of putting flowers on the graves of Civil War dead. Champion's arrival coincided with the national holiday extending to those who had fallen in the Spanish-American War in Cuba.

Newspapers, which Champion read to improve his English, recounted the historic Battle of Gettysburg in July 1863. The Commonwealth of Massachusetts had suffered the loss of 1,537 men in the three-day fight—some under the command of Colonel Pope.[36] Boston broadsheets published old lists of casualties from the two-dozen Union infantry, light artillery, and cavalry regiments—killed, wounded, and missing.[37] Drawings depicted stone monuments in Gettysburg commemorating regiments from Massachusetts. The bloodiest battle of the four-year Civil War marked the war's turning point and the rise of the Union. Champion would have noted that Bostonians remembered Gettysburg with the fervor of Parisians commemorating the Franco-Prussian War.

Waltham's business community regarded the Memorial Day cycling program as the city's signature event, like Boston's annual marathon the previous month on Patriot's Day. It was the rare occasion when the Waltham Watch Company and a cotton mill nearby shut their doors. Storefronts and residential porches showed off red-white-and-blue bunting. Flags, numerous as flowers, flew everywhere.

At ten o'clock, the League of American Wheelmen paraded down Main Street in military-style wool uniforms on bicycles. The parade concluded with a picnic on the Charles River bank and music by the Waltham Watch Company brass band. Then everyone sauntered to the bicycle park for the race program, which commenced at 2:30 p.m.

The *Globe* predicted, "Memorial Day Races Promise to Play Havoc with Records." It published a woodcut of Champion, favored among four contestants to win the twenty-mile motor-pace competition.[38] He clipped out the article with his image and pasted it in his scrapbook. Michael, embarking on his comeback in a five-mile paced demonstration, rated sentimental press but a smaller woodcut. Champion ignored it.

Racers came from far and wide for the event. When Oscar Hedstrom and Charles Henshaw from Brooklyn arrived in Waltham with their team, their pacing machine attracted considerable attention. Hedstrom, a Swedish immigrant, had built his own engine and carburetor for the motor-tandem. It was so powerful, he claimed, that he named it Typhoon.[39]

Hedstrom, and his business partner Henshaw, who came from a wealthy merchant family in Brooklyn, had arrived to pace Everett Ryan, Waltham's native son. Ryan was a spindly twenty-year-old with coat-hanger shoulders. He had a devoted following among the Irish, who turned out in big numbers to cheer. "Those who have been watching the lean Waltham ex-amateur, Ryan, in training say he will have a fighting chance," noted the *Globe*.[40]

Another racer was Canadian national champion Archie MacEachern, who came to Waltham after a victory that Saturday in Philadelphia. Reporters called him Champion's strongest challenger.[41] MacEachern, a well-built six feet tall and 185 pounds, was quick to smile. He had devotees among the mill girls and nurses, although he had a wife and baby son home in Toronto.[42] Joining him was the New York City motor-pace team of Fred Kent and John Ruel.

The final motor-pace team was led by twenty-one-year-old Harry Miles, steering for the first time professionally,[43] with stoker Will Stafford of Cambridgeport. Miles, a machinist at General Electric,[44] was engaged to his high school darling, May Nolan,[45] and the couple had set June 13 as their wedding day.[46] Miles was racing to earn extra money for their honeymoon. His partner, Stafford, twenty-four, had racing experience—in fact, Stafford had recently recovered from a motor-pace crash in Nashville. Full of bravado, he told John J. Donovan, "I have come through the battle of San Juan Hill, but I'll get killed at this game yet."[47]

Miles and Stafford were on hand to pace Billy Stinson of Cambridge, an eighteen-year-old with a contract to ride for the Chicago-based Rambler Cycles, predecessor to the Rambler Motor Company. Superstitious reporters noted the team armbands that Stafford, Miles, and Stinson each tied on: unlucky Number 13.[48]

More than ten thousand spectators—almost half of Waltham's population—streamed into Bicycle Park, the largest crowd since opening day in 1892.[49] Half of the spectators were women—many from textile mills and a school for nurses. Wearing white dresses with leg-of-mutton sleeves that were all the rage, they had donned broad-brimmed hats trimmed with dried flowers. Most of the men sported new straw boaters for the season; some wore derbies.

The spectators crammed the cheap bleacher seats around the oval, while those who could afford it took seats in the cavernous grandstand, sheltered from the sun by a high, slanted roof. The stadium and cheap seats burbled with excited voices. Behind the bleachers stood a row of wooden cabins that riders used as their quarters.[50] Racers and trainers milled around the cabins on the dirt service road, pungent with rubbing liniment, gasoline fumes, and sour sweaty clothing.

On the infield, straight above the start-finish line, loomed a wooden tower for officials and timers. Next to it sat the press table for reporters and illustrators. A pack of newshounds from Boston's eight newspapers and other trade publications lounged on chairs as they traded gossip and shoptalk, smoked, and hoped for world records so their stories would get more attention.

At 2:30 on the dot, announcer Fletcher Hayvee stepped up to a huge megaphone supported by a steel stand jammed into the grassy infield near the start/

finish line. A portly man, Hayvee dabbed sweat from his forehead with a hand-kerchief. He wore all white—from his boater, linen jacket, shirt, and duck trousers down to his shoes. His handlebar mustache danced in front of the metal rim of the megaphone as he introduced the first race.

The program's first act featured a one-lap competition for sixty novices.[51] The hopefuls competed in heats of a dozen contenders, with the winners advancing to the next round. In one of the early heats, a rider's chain broke and set off the day's first big spill.[52] Riders limped away, leaving their hides on the concrete.

Ultimately, finalists vied in the runoff for a gold watch.[53] They set such a hot pace that the audience stood and cheered. Then followed a half-miler and additional events. A handicap tandem contest finished so close that the crowd sprang to its feet again and hollered with excitement.

During these preliminary races, Champion warmed up outside a training cabin, pedaling on wooden rollers set on the grassy lawn off the service road. He worked up a sweat, listening to the roar of the crowd, while Gately and Marks made a final inspection of their motor-tandem. Marks squatted beside the engine and discovered the spark plug needed replacing. From somewhere in his battered tool chest he dug up a spare. He inserted the replacement plug and later mentioned to Champion that it did not fit well but it was the best he had.[54]

Michael wheeled onto the track behind a motor-tandem for his five-mile celebrity exhibition ride, his first public appearance in two years. "As the little fellow entered the stretch riding alone, a cheer went up from the crowd, which fully attested the everlasting popularity of the Welsh midget, the idol of the women and the bleacher fans," wrote John J. Donovan in the *Globe*.[55] "Lap after lap the little fellow reeled off, following in his old-time manner, head erect and body perfectly immobile, and occasionally displaying the wonderful control he has over a machine by affectionately rubbing his tire against the rear tire of his pacing machine."

His stunt of rubbing wheels drew gasps from the audience, sophisticated about the danger he invited. Hayvee boomed out Michael's lap times. Michael showed he still had the chops—and he entertained.

Finally, it was time for the main event: the twenty-mile motor-pace race. Champion yearned to control his Waltham debut from start to finish, earn a generous payday in about forty minutes of riding, and grab his fix of la gloire!

As he rolled onto the cement oval behind King Gately and Marks, announcer Fletcher Hayvee directed his megaphone at the grandstand and boomed introductions. Champion had a name perfectly suited for Hayvee: *Al-bear Champ-eee-on! Champ-eee-on! All the way from Pair-eee, France!*

Cheers and applause greeted Albert. The mill girls and nursing students all shook white linen handkerchiefs at him.[56] He acknowledged them with a wave and a broad smile.

Gately and Marks, togged up in black wool shorts and white jerseys matching Champion's outfit, pulled alongside their man and accelerated for a few practice laps. Albert caught their draft and increased the speed to 30 mph. After they finished, Gately aimed for the black start-finish line painted across the cement in front of the grandstand. There the Typhoon and the two other motor-tandems waited, engines *put-putting*. Champion and his rivals dismounted as officials conferred, a scrum in white suits and straw boaters.

Official starter Lon Peck was scolding Typhoon pacers Hedstrom and Kent for the trousers they wore, claiming they gave more shield for Waltham's Everett Ryan.[57] Champion, in his broken English, took Peck's side and looked ready to take a swing at Hedstrom as they squabbled. Peck ordered Hedstrom and Kent to leave and come back wearing regulation shorts like the other teams.

Despite the dustup, when it was time to go to the start line, Peck gave local favorite Ryan the inside lane. Champion, MacEachern, and Stinson sidled up alongside Ryan. Metz and three other men stepped from the infield to grasp the bicycles of their riders, who jammed the fronts of their shoes into the steel toe clips and gripped bare hands around the handlebar drops.

Behind them, the motor-tandems idled with metronomic *put-puts*. Peck pointed his pistol to the sky while Hayvee intoned: "Get Ready . . . Get Set . . ."

Then Peck's pistol boomed.

Once around the track the motors went, whirring back over the start-finish line. Then the cyclists were pushed on their way, muscling the one-speed bicycles that had been fitted with a gear bigger than regular bicycles so they could ride faster behind the motors.

Ryan, eager to prove himself, caught his motor-tandem first, on the back straight.[58] Next, Champion dove behind his team and urged Marks to fly after Ryan. Down the homestretch after the first lap, Marks opened the throttle; King

Gately guided Champion past Ryan and the Typhoon with finesse that evoked applause from an audience well attuned to the nuances of motorpace racing. Ryan and his Typhoon chased, pursued by MacEachern and Stinson. At the end of the first mile, the order stayed the same, with Champion leading by twenty feet.[59]

During the second mile, Stinson and his pacers attacked with a sharp acceleration.[60] Miles aimed the machine wide, while stoker Stafford gave the engine more gas. Stinson pedaled hard to overtake Champion on the approach to the top of the bank on turn three. Abruptly, however, the engine of Champion's pacing machine skipped and the tandem of King Gately and Marks slowed.[61] Champion's front wheel, traveling 30 mph, punched the rear wheel of the tandem. Champion fell to the track as his steel bicycle clattered on the concrete.[62]

At this point, all four teams had spread out in an echelon across the track. To avoid driving over the fallen Champion, Miles aimed his tandem through a hole between the tandem of Kent and Ruel and the outside perimeter.[63]

Then came the unforeseen. As John J. Donovan reported in the *Globe*:

> Critics say that an expert could have done it, but be that as it may, Miles steered the tandem straight up to the top of the bank. But he could not have seen that he was steering straight toward a big telegraph pole at the top of the bank. With a crash and a thud that was heard across the oval, tandem and riders were hurled upon the pole. With a roar that was partly a scream, 10,000 persons rose to their feet in time to see the tandem, after recovering from the recoil, leap over the bank and land on the picket fence separating the track from the entrance. After Miles crashed into the pole, his body dropped down, while Stafford was thrown to the right and he shot through the air like a human catapult, his head and shoulders being driven through the fence.[64]

Hundreds stumbled down the stands and ran to the disaster.[65] Blood poured from the mouths and ears of both Miles and Stafford, their clothing torn to shreds. Miles's fiancée, May Nolan, who had been watching from the stands, went into shock and fainted.[66] Friends gathered around to comfort her.

Miles and Stafford were carried to the training quarters and placed on cots. The collision had also injured two spectators standing near the telegraph pole. One man had both hips broken; another man's leg was fractured.[67] Long minutes passed before horse-drawn ambulances hauled all four to the Waltham hospital, atop a hill over the track.

Albert Champion is shown here lying on his stomach after falling from a crash that caused two men to die, the worst accident at the time in American sports. *From the* Boston Globe, *May 31, 1900.*

Miles was dead on arrival.[68] Hours later, Stafford was lifeless.[69]

Incredibly, the competitors on the track were ignorant of the horrific accident and kept on as usual. Ryan and MacEachern capitalized on Champion's spill by yelling at their stokers to go faster.[70] Ryan stole the lead, MacEachern trailed by thirty feet, and even Stinson kept chasing though his motor-tandem had disappeared into eternity.

As quickly as he had fallen, Champion had scrambled to his feet.[71] He slapped the dirt and grass from scrapes and cuts as a group of onlookers and some reporters ran to offer help. He exclaimed, "What do you think—I know not how to fall, hey?"[72] He grabbed his Orient and pedaled away.

When Gately and Marks swung past on the home straight, Champion caught the draft but threw both arms in the air and bellowed at them to go faster. He did not grip the handlebars again until Marks reached the speed he demanded.

Champion had lost two laps to Ryan and MacEachern, flying behind their motor-tandems, and the lone Stinson, who would soon be pulled from the race by officials.[73] Champion kept up with their speed until the five-mile mark. Then, once again, the engine of his pacing machine popped with one misfire after another.[74] Gately slowed down and Albert swung to the side to avoid more trouble while Marks reached down and made adjustments on the fly.[75]

Champion lost another half lap before he resumed full flight. By ten miles, he had made up the half lap—although he was still two laps down, two-thirds of a mile behind—and he pushed MacEachern into the back straight's far turn, forcing the Canadian outside. For a lap they rode neck and neck,[76] backs low, legs pumping like pistons.

On the home straight, the Canadian overtook the Frenchman.[77] MacEachern kept up his momentum and by fifteen miles he had gained a lap on Ryan. As MacEachern usurped the lead, Champion, whether suffering trauma from his fall at 30 mph on the cement or pain from abrasions, lost two more laps on MacEachern and Ryan.

At the end of twenty miles, MacEachern was the winner. Ryan came in second. Champion placed third.

"Although defeated, Champion must be given credit," reported John J. Donovan in the *Globe*.[78] "Had he not met with accidents, he would probably have won." Donovan added that Champion had lost about a square foot of skin from hip and thigh, with more scraped from his knees, elbows, and shoulders.[79]

As soon as Champion veered into the infield, reporters engulfed him. They accused him of causing the tragedy by looking around and not paying attention.[80] Champion, sweat pouring, his dark-blond hair wild, barely had time to recover his breath and dismount.

Fortunately, King Gately barged his motor-tandem into the pack of press and defended Champion: "A motorcycle pacer must take every chance and risk his neck. A careful rider will never make any money."[81]

Meanwhile, Marks—coated in grease and oil up to his forearms—told the *Boston Post* that someone may have tampered with the engine. "If any oil had been put into the gasoline tanks, it could have spread over the surface, thus preventing the gasoline from vaporizing rapidly enough to furnish the required volume of gas. If a little water had been placed in the carburetor, where the gas and air are mixed, the moisture would have kept the mixture from exploding as it should have done."[82]

Stubby pencils scratched across writing pads. Then the news hawks fled to rush their stories into the next edition. Champion had created what *Cycle Age* called "the most terrible accident ever known in cycling annals."[83]

The accident, which at the time was actually the worst disaster in American sports, not just cycling, dominated page one of all the dailies along Boston's newspaper row, pushing aside news from Pretoria, South Africa, of the Boer War. The *Globe*'s headline blared: "Pacemakers Killed,"[84] while the *Herald* roared: "Death Race."[85] Lurid block-print illustrations depicted Miles and Stafford flying headfirst toward the telegraph pole.

Champion was so upset by the accident that for the first time since he had swung a leg over a bicycle frame as a courier in Paris, he did not care to ride. Over the next couple of weeks, he entered local events but opponents gave him a thrashing. He had never before experienced such failure. Humbled, he declared to John J. Donovan that he had retired from the racing game for the year.[86] Marks and Gately proclaimed themselves freelancers and went to work for other riders.

In Paris, Pierre Tournier read accounts and wrote to Champion. Not long afterward, Tournier sailed to Boston.[87] There he paced Champion and got him into a training routine that raised his spirits, even if his former protégé did not want to race again that summer. Tournier intended to restore Champion's confidence to come back the next season and fulfill his potential. Then Tournier sailed back home. Champion appreciated his friend's devotion and clipped an account that Donovan had written about their training together and put it in his scrapbook.

Metz had received more funding from General Electric president Charles A. Coffin and M. P. Clough of the Lynn Gas and Electric Company to encourage him to develop electric-powered tandems and tricycles as a bridge to producing electric cars.[88] From the perspective of Coffin and Clough, if the pacing machines had been battery powered, Waltham's tragic motor-pace accident would have been prevented.

Metz personally favored gas-powered engines because a gallon of gas would propel them much farther than a charged-up electric battery. But he had to placate stockholders Coffin and Clough. Champion, now retired for the season, was no longer tied to his regimen of twice-daily workouts, and he was still paid $25 a week, enabling him to send money back to Paris for his family. He and Metz conferred about what the racer should do next.

Going home to France was out of the question—Champion would be arrested by gendarmes at the port of entry and jailed for his failure to report for compulsory military duty. But Metz saw potential for an Orient Motorcycle that the working class could afford. So he put Champion in charge of designing a single-seat gas-combustion Orient Motorcycle.

And, as fate would have it, the motorcycle, rather than cycling, would redeem Champion and thrust him fully into the auto industry and his place in its nascent history.

In 1900, individual transportation in America relied on hitching or saddling one of the 18 million horses and mules, pedaling one of the 10 million bicycles in circulation, or driving one of the country's eight thousand automobiles. Cheap bikes cost as little as $50, and there was the convenience of taking them aboard trains for free, like any other luggage.[89] But by 1900 more people seemed ready for mechanical transport. At the same time, prices for autos—running on gasoline, electric, or steam propulsion—were steep, ranging from $280 to $4,000, compared with annual household incomes averaging $500.

Metz saw potential for introducing an Orient Motorcycle selling retail for around $250.[90] He decided to work on the electric motor designs himself to placate Coffin and Clough. But, at the same time, he put Champion in charge of designing a single-seat gas-combustion Orient Motorcycle.

In his corner of the Orient factory, Champion dismantled De Dion-Bouton and Aster engines and spread the parts on a table. He measured the diameter of the piston chamber, the length of the piston and its stroke, the flywheel, and other engine components. When he finished, he sat at a desk to sketch plans for a bicycle and the engine parts that would fit on it. Over the following weeks, Champion and general manager Robbins put gas engines and electric motors on tricycles, four-wheeled Runabouts, and one simple box-like four-wheeler called an Autogo. Champion, Metz, sometimes Robbins, too, tested them in intramural races on local streets.

Soon enough, this personal research and development led them to Harvard College.

"Probably the Harvard automobilists get more real fun out of their machines than any other set of enthusiasts around Boston," suggested *Automobile Magazine*.[91] "They go speeding about in them at all hours of the day or night, rain or shine." The magazine noted, "Only a month or two ago one member nearly smashed himself and carriage into unrecognizable fragments by collision with a tree while racing in the dark on a crooked street."[92]

Champion and Metz kept up with reports of Harvard Automobile Club members, who often timed their jaunts for bragging rights. Some students owned Wintons, made in Cleveland, while others had Locomobiles from nearby Newton. By the time Champion's abrasions from the Waltham race had healed, club members had agreed that the swiftest machines were Locomobiles. Members ordered an out-and-back race on a five-mile stretch of Newton Boulevard, beginning near the Chestnut Hill Reservoir, to settle the question of whose car was the fastest.[93]

Wanting in, Champion and Metz visited the club and pleaded to be allowed to join the race. In the spirit of automobile camaraderie, members agreed to include them. They set the start time for 6 a.m. Monday, June 16. They hoped the early hour would help them elude the Newton police.

The auto enthusiasts congregated before dawn by the reservoir. Competing against the Locomobiles of Warwick Greene and Charles Boyden were Champion and Metz on motor-tricycles and Robbins on a Runabout. Francis Edgar Stanley, who made steam-powered cars in Newton, volunteered as starter. A Cambridge doctor held the stopwatch.[94]

At first light, Francis Edgar Stanley gave the start command. Little did they know that about a mile away, around a sharp bend, a squad of uniformed police waited, concealed behind trees beside the road. When the cops heard

the engines coming, they fanned out across Newton Boulevard. The motorists rounded the bend and were confronted with a line of blue uniforms and
nightsticks.[95]

Metz was the fastest away and in the lead when the police came into view.
He swerved off the road into a vacant field to evade the officers before regaining
the road and escaping.[96] Greene and Robbins careened to the opposite side of the
road and executed a similar dodge.[97] But Champion and Boyden were caught.[98]

Police packed their scofflaws into a horse-drawn paddy wagon and took them
straightaway to the Newton police station. Champion and Boyden waited two
hours behind bars in a jail cell before a bailiff led them before a Suffolk County
judge.[99] Metz and a classmate of Boyden's paid the fines of $5 each for speeding.[100]

The arrests quashed the urge to race at Harvard, at least temporarily. But
Metz and Champion remained as determined as ever to keep driving fast.

After the Harvard bust, Champion's solo test drives subjected him to a succession of arrests in Boston, Waltham, and Cambridge.[101] It got so bad that one
morning, as he drove a motor-tricycle from his Cambridge boarding house to
Waltham, policemen held him up at every corner.[102] Each officer told him in
the same rehearsed speech to go slowly. His usual seventeen-minute commute
stretched to ninety minutes. He arrived to work tardy and furious about being
harassed.

The *Globe*'s John J. Donovan spent evenings with Champion and Marks,
tavern-crawling for pints of Boston Club Lager or Van Nostrand's Ale. Champion and the reporter were twenty-one, Catholic, and shared the same work
dedication. Donovan, a second-generation Irishman, shaved his face clean every
day and put on a freshly starched collar before fastening his necktie with a four-
in-hand knot. He was a native of South Boston.[103] After graduation from Boston
English High School,[104] Donovan had worked as a compositor—setting type by
hand in wooden composing sticks—for *Donahue's Magazine* on Newspaper Row.
After a couple years, he moved to the *Globe* as compositor.[105] Devoted to the
new leisure-time activity of candlepin bowling, he landed a job on the sports
staff, a promotion that enabled him to marry his fiancée, Mary McCarry.[106]

Donovan turned Champion's speeding arrests into copy for the *Globe*. Each time Champion was apprehended, Marks represented him as counsel and interpreter.[107] Marks was not an attorney, but that did not stop him from preparing a mock brief, which he carried in blank and pulled from the inside pocket of his jacket to fill out at the first sign of trouble.[108] The brief cited that Champion spoke only French, a stranger in a strange land, unaccustomed to the ways of the country.[109]

"Marks says that he will shortly apply for admission to the bar," Donovan informed *Globe* readers in a light-hearted manner.[110] "His eloquence has won the judges over to the small fines and also for taking a ride with Champion at times, after which they have sworn that no more will they fine men for going only as fast as the electric [trolley] car. Champion gauges his speed by the electric cars and gets arrested." One officer testified he had timed Champion for a 300-yard block. "He swore that Champion was going twenty miles an hour, which was, of course, out of the question," Donovan wrote. "At the time, Champion was merely keeping up with the car."[111]

In the meantime, Metz was busy importing Aster engines, which generated 12 hp—four times more powerful than either he or Champion had ever seen. Champion and Robbins fitted a pair of Aster engines on a tricycle. It weighed 385 pounds.[112] One evening during a program of bicycle races on the dirt track of the Readville Trotting Park, in what is now the city's Hyde Park neighborhood, Champion gave a demonstration ride. His upper body was pulled by centrifugal force and he dangled his torso off the side. He clocked 1 minute 14 seconds for the mile—closing in on 50 mph, a speed that made some in the audience take in a sudden deep breath.

"As he lay over when approaching the turns like an accomplished horseman stooping to pick up a handkerchief on the fly, he was greeted with cheers from the crowd," Donovan reported. "The trick made Champion a favorite again."[113]

Champion was in full flight when a rear wheel clipped the fence and the vehicle threw him to the ground.[114] He broke both bones of his left forearm—

surprisingly it was his first fracture. He was treated at City Hospital and his arm was immobilized in a plaster cast. His bicycle racing season was officially over.

When he recovered enough to return to work in Metz's factory, Champion groused that on a bigger track he could ride a mile under a minute, long considered a major benchmark. Metz suggested the Empire City Race Track, a horse track two-thirds of a mile around in Yonkers, outside New York City. It also happened to be one of William Brady's enterprises. Brady liked the idea and hired Champion to perform a motor-tricycle exhibition for a Sunday bicycle-race program.

So it was that on Saturday morning, July 14, 1900, Champion loaded his motor-tricycle on a train bound for Yonkers.[115] To Champion, July 14 meant Bastille Day, a national day of celebration in France. After Champion arrived in Yonkers and checked into a hotel, he decided to commemorate the French holiday by taking his motor-tricycle out for a trial run on the road to Mount Vernon.

"I was speeding along the road [back] toward Yonkers at a pace which must have been at least 70 mph when the left axle of my tricycle broke," he told John J. Donovan, who published Champion's account in the *Globe*.[116] "The break happened just as I was about to 'lie over' in order to make a slight turn in the road. Naturally enough, I was leaning toward the right side, and found myself going on at the frightful pace on two wheels. I closed my eyes as I found the machine racing into a telegraph pole, feeling that I must be dashed to death."

He missed the pole, but he crashed into a pile of rocks beside the road. When he finally extracted himself from his mangled machine, he walked, bleeding from head to foot, to the first house he saw.[117] A physician made a house call there and closed Albert's gashes from eye to chin with sutures made of silk thread, each stitch tied in a square knot. The dark lines of thread resembled tiny railroad ties.

That crash broke Champion's right hand.[118] He was forced to visit a hospital to have the broken bone treated, and he left wearing another plaster cast.

When Champion returned from his ill-fated trip, he was at last greeted with some good news after months of troubles. The Men of Metz had installed a one-cylinder Aster engine that produced 3-1/4 hp, equivalent to a dozen men pedaling together. It was fitted onto a modified Orient bicycle frame. Starting with the standard diamond-shaped steel bicycle frame, Metz and Robbins had designed a down-tube that curved like a swayback horse, which set the motorcycle standard for decades to come.[119] The engine, exhaust pipe, battery, and other components were fitted on the down-tube.

With the gas tank filled, the prototype Orient Motorcycle weighed 105 pounds.[120] A speed lever was fastened on the front of the top tube for Champion's easy reach. He started it by pedaling. After the motor engaged, a coaster clutch allowed him to rest his feet on the pedals and the engine took over.

It was a stunning achievement, and it marked an enormous advancement in motor-powered individual transportation. Now Metz and Champion had to introduce this archetype Orient Motorcycle to the public and the press. The manager of the Charles River Track offered a time slot for an exhibition during a race program.

On Tuesday evening, July 31, Champion dressed in his bedroom for the newspaper photographers who would attend his pioneering ride. He stepped into creased plus-fours and knotted a silk tie around an Eaton collar. Then he pulled a jacket over his cast and donned a cap. He strode outside to his one-off Orient Motorcycle and drove to the Charles River Track.

"Eighteen thousand packed themselves like sardines into the grandstand and bleachers, and 2,000 more stood inside the oval," reported the *Boston Post*.[121] They had come to attend a program of races that culminated in a twenty-mile paced match between two world champion pros: Jimmy Michael and the younger Johnny Nelson, a Swedish immigrant even shorter than Michael.

First prize paid $4,000 ($114,000 in 2014), sufficient to buy a three-bedroom house. Michael was so favored that bets of five-to-four on Nelson went begging. Nevertheless, once the race began, from start to finish Nelson ruled the track. Then Champion piloted his Orient Motorcycle onto the track boards.

After a few practice laps, he pulled up by the start-finish line. Announcer Fletcher Hayvee informed the crowd through his megaphone that Champion would give a five-mile demonstration of his original motorcycle made in Waltham.

The audience gave him a thunderous applause. Lon Peck fired the starting pistol.

"When Champion turned his machine loose," observed the *Post*, "one pretty girl behind the press box swore as she said, 'Look at him *go!*' She did not know she used profanity, and the recording angel, looking on, probably did not score it up against her, but she simply gave way to lack of language to express her feelings."[122]

Hayvee boomed through his megaphone that Champion clicked off his first mile in 1 minute, 26-3/5 seconds—topping 35 mph.[123] By the end, Champion had covered five miles in 7 minutes, 16-1/4 seconds. Jerry Hatfield, in *American Racing Motorcycles*, his 1989 book on motorcycle history, cites Champion's ride as the first-ever United States motorcycle record.[124]

All of the Newspaper Row dailies covered the Michael-Nelson match and mentioned Champion's exhibition ride as well, listing each mile time. The *Post* published a photo of Albert looking sedate on the prototype motorcycle and reported that he drove five miles without moving his feet. Some accounts claimed that Champion had driven the first American-built motorcycle, though purists later pointed out that the engine, spark plug, spark coil, and battery all were imported from France.

Nevertheless, Champion's motorcycle ride became the talk of the town. On Sunday, the *Globe* committed greater coverage to the motorcycle's introduction, including an illustration of Champion on his ride.

Accordingly, Metz ordered Robbins to prepare his factory for motorcycle production. Metz planned to have Orient Motorcycles available for purchase in time for the New York Automobile Show in November in Madison Square Garden.

As for Champion, the acclaim and attention inspired him to vow he could drive a motorcycle under a minute for the mile. Better yet, his motorcycle exhibition stirred him to get back on a bicycle and start training again for the next year.

7

AMERICA'S FASTEST
MAN ON WHEELS

THE DIFFICULTY LIES NOT IN THE NEW IDEAS,
BUT IN ESCAPING FROM THE OLD ONES.
—JOHN MAYNARD KEYNES, THE GENERAL THEORY
OF EMPLOYMENT, INTEREST, AND MONEY[1]

In the late summer of 1900, Champion swayed in a train rumbling west to Chicago. He had packed an Orient motor-tricycle and a spare engine to compete in the Windy City's first auto exhibition and race meet, organized by the Chicago Automobile Club.[2] The four-day affair in Washington Park,[3] on the south side, featured one of America's foremost automakers, Alexander Winton.[4] The event attracted the postmasters of Chicago, Milwaukee, and Indianapolis, who served on the US Post Master General's national committee studying companies for the one best suited to the federal government's move away from horses pulling mail wagons.[5]

Washington Park offered a one-mile dirt horse track rolled firm, a sanctuary from the city's deplorable streets, a troubling condition nationwide. In all forty-five states combined, America had some two hundred miles of hard-surfaced roads beyond urban areas.[6] Chicago property owners and the business community were angry about sinkholes,[7] which opened up without warning and then swallowed load after load of broken bricks dumped in to fill the holes,[8] only for the bricks to disappear later under sludge as traffic rolled over. Everyone was incensed by ruts from wheel tracks left after rain. Motorists cursed tire-slashing rocks.[9] Yet citizens kept tight-lipped for fear of repercussions from city bureaucrats protecting their jobs.[10]

The *Chicago Tribune* took up the public's cause. On September 1, the *Tribune* hawked a front-page story: "Michigan Street, Near Rush, Where Trucks Sink To

Hubs In Mud."[11] A photo, among the paper's earliest, showed a driver holding the reins of a brace of horses on one of the main commuter arteries, the wheel bottoms lost in muck.

On September 19 the *Tribune* reported, perhaps with relief, that on the previous day the drivers and the thousand people attending the Chicago Automobile Club races had found the track to their liking.[12] "To those accustomed to see gasoline, electric, and steam vehicles on the streets of the city, the sight of untrammeled action was a revelation. Around and around the broad stretch of track sped the little machines with a whirring sound that acted as a warning to all to stand clear."[13]

Spectator turnout was light despite Chicago being the country's second-largest city, with nearly 1.7 million residents.[14] *Motor Vehicle Review* observed that "the program of track events did not arouse a great deal of enthusiasm." Yet the Chicago Automobile Club was determined to show the magnificence of the machines. Steam-propelled autos puffed and snorted like horses. An electric omnibus made by the local Hewitt-Lindstrom Motor Company took the gold medal for carrying the greatest number of seated passengers—twenty-two persons.[15] A women's two-mile electric-car race was won by thirteen-year-old Jeanette Lindstrom.[16] She had an operator's license after having two weeks earlier passed an examination administered by the Chicago city electrician.[17]

Tuesday's opening day main event was an international ten miler pitting Albert Champion against Alexander Winton and another rival. Winton, a forty-year-old immigrant from Scotland, retained an athlete's slimness and was clean-shaven except for a neat mustache, flecked with white. He had given up making bicycles in Cleveland for early internal-combustion engines.[18] Winton was convinced that autos were more than a passing fad.[19] In 1898 he had taken the unprecedented step of advertising his Winton Motor Carriage Company in *Scientific American*: "Dispense with a horse and save the expense and anxiety of keeping it."[20] He scored the first commercial sale of a US car,[21] and he went on to sell twenty-two, priced at $1,000 to $1,250.[22] They were equipped with B. F. Goodrich pneumatic tires made in Akron. In 1899, auto sales had passed one hundred, catapulting Winton to the status of America's biggest seller of gasoline-powered cars,[23] commanding more than ten percent of that market.

One customer, James Ward Packard, scoffed that he could make one better.[24] Winton dared him to try—a retort that altered Packard's career and would later endanger Champion.[25]

Champion piloted his Orient motor-tricycle to the start line next to Winton's car, which had no windshield or top. Joining them was Kenneth A. Skinner of Boston on his motor-tricycle. John J. Donovan of the *Boston Globe* reported that Skinner had recently returned from France with the latest De Dion-Bouton engine, ballyhooed as the most powerful in America: "He had brought it from Europe expressly to defeat Champion with it."[26]

The drivers wore ties and suits with plus-four trousers, snugged up by buttons running up the sides below the knee. To protect their eyes from flying dirt, they donned green goggles.

Champion on an Orient tricycle holding a French engine that was state of the art in 1900. *Photo courtesy of Buck Peacock.*

When the start pistol boomed, Champion flew ahead. Skinner had boasted that his engine was bigger than Champion's Aster 4-hp. Yet Champion had departed Waltham with a second engine.[27] After he'd unpacked in Chicago, he had fitted the second engine to his Orient frame below the saddle, which doubled his horsepower. In the first race, Champion appeared to have victory locked up at the mid-point, five miles, when an engine conked out.[28] He was passed by Winton and Skinner, who then dueled until Winton won.

For an extra attraction, Winton competed in a five-eighths-mile contest against a jockey on a horse named In Debt.[29] Winton's vehicle was given a mile lap to build speed for a flying start. The horse won by two hundred yards.[30]

The next day rain converted Washington Park into an expanse of glistening mud. Chilly downpours cancelled the races, but some fifteen hundred hardy fans trudged through the elements to visit the exhibit booths assembled under the grandstand. They checked out modern motor-transport styles. Champion, aided by a French expat to translate, spent the day explaining how the new-fangled machines worked.[31] Champion promised the *Tribune*'s correspondent he would drive a mile in one minute,[32] a blazing benchmark around a circular track. Humans could ride 50 mph on turf on a quarter horse bred for speed.[33] But driving a mile faster than a minute in the early twentieth century represented an epic challenge for man and machine.

On Thursday, September 20, the sun shined bright and wind gusted from Lake Michigan. Some two thousand folks converged on Washington Park by the afternoon. The dirt oval had dried enough to hold competitions, although the *Chicago Daily News* observed, "The track was bad at the pole and all hell to the center."[34]

The crowd cheered the international fifty-mile motor-tricycle race with Champion against Skinner and Charles G. Wridgeway, a New Yorker on a motor-tricycle made in England. Champion dashed to the front, his engines running in sync. He edged wider each lap until he was hugging the outside rim by the time he won, with a quarter-mile margin over Skinner, who was in turn ahead of Wridgeway. "Seated on the small, rakish looking trikes, this trio made a hard bunch when speed was required," reported the *Boston Globe*'s John J. Donovan.[35]

On the final day, Friday, two thousand Chicagoans flocked to the park.[36] A light breeze wafted and the ground was again dry for fast conditions. The program was devoted to speed trials timed against the stopwatches. In a fifty-mile exhibition, Winton drove solo around the circular track. When he roared across the finish line, three official timers jammed their thumbs down on their watches. Winton had set an American record for fifty miles on a circular track, in 1 hour 17 minutes 50 seconds, an average of 38 mph.[37] He was awarded the Chicago Auto Club Challenge Cup,[38] valued at $500—about what a typical worker could expect to earn that year.

Then Champion mounted his Orient motor-tricycle and cut Winton's time by almost two minutes, to 1:15:51.[39] Most important, the Frenchman became the first in America to drive a motor vehicle an average of 40 mph.[40]

Driving headfirst into history as the first in America to hit forty miles per hour, Champion's average for fifty miles in 1900 around the Washington Park horse track in Chicago. *Photo courtesy of Cherie Champion.*

"It can be seen that had the Frenchman been allowed to go against Winton, he might have defeated him," John J. Donovan speculated in the *Globe*.[41]

The meet concluded with Champion and Wridgeway in a five-mile match. Champion won by breaking his record from Charles River Park in Cambridge. His time of 6:50-3/5 averaged 45 mph.[42]

The records reported in Chicago newspapers were unofficial, but they had credibility on a track certified by the governing body for turf racing. Champion had displayed the capabilities of motorized three-wheelers. And he'd scooped up $500 in cash prizes.[43] His announced goal of breaking the minute for the mile remained in the future.

Champion lingered in the Windy City long enough to experience the local specialty of Wrigley juicy fruit chewing gum and possibly to ride on the brand-new El—the elevated train line radiating from downtown into the neighborhoods. He returned to Boston for a week before leaving with his Orient motor-tricycle to compete against Kenneth A. Skinner at the Great St. Louis Fair.[44]

On October 5, the *St. Louis Globe-Democrat* estimated that close to one hundred thousand people ambled through the fairground gates on Big Thursday.[45] Champion's excursion into America's heartland coincided with the throwing of confetti, as practiced in New Orleans during Mardi Gras—sprinkling little patches of red, white, blue, and yellow paper over the gowns of women and jackets of men strolling the fairgrounds.[46] The contests Champion chose to ride at the mile-long dirt horse track, with its majestic grandstand, were a sideshow. St. Louis, America's fourth-largest city, fulfilled its role as the nation's gateway to the West.[47] Famed pace horse Joe Patchen came with Coney, acclaimed as the next harness wonder.[48] Even the equines had to vie for attention against exhibits of pigs, cattle, fowls, textiles, and embroidery along with steam-powered farm equipment for threshing and collecting hay. One man dug a well for every person who would watch.[49] Barkers emphasized the advantages of their hog traps and cattle-loading platforms. In the amphitheater were vaudeville and circus acts. One performer delighted the audience when he jumped from a pole 110 feet tall onto a ten-foot net stretched above the ground.[50]

Unruffled by the clamor of all the diversions, Champion stepped onto the track under the glaring sun, aware that the crowd was watching him as the prerace favorite. He won a pair of ten-mile motor-tricycle matches against his would-be nemesis Kenneth A. Skinner. An anonymous *Globe-Democrat* journalist was moved to write, "These machines can beat any race horse."[51]

The next month Champion boarded another train from Boston, in the company of Charles Herman Metz, bound for New York. Metz directed porters to load crates of Orient motor-tricycles with De Dion-Bouton engines, motor-buckboards, the prototype Orient Motorcycle, even bicycles for what was ambitiously advertised as the First Annual Automobile Show,[52] November 3 through November 10. The title's bravado suited Madison Square Garden and the nation's premier city, with 3.4 million people.[53] The sponsor was the Automobile Club of America, formed a year earlier by auto manufacturers and owners demanding decent roads.

Metz's Waltham Manufacturing Company joined thirty-four businesses exhibiting motor vehicles,[54] the majority of them open-topped two- and four-passenger autos with leather upholstered bench seats like those common in horse carriages. Also among the exhibitors were seventeen parts-and-accessories firms in the garden's great hall. Alexander Winton had exhibition space displaying Winton Motor Carriage Company vehicles near the exhibit of a one-year-old company from Warren, Ohio, offering an auto called Ohio Model A. It had a one-cylinder gas engine and a tiller for steering, and it was sold without a top or windshield. The Ohio Model A was made by James Ward Packard.

At some point Champion and Packard likely met at the show. Packard, thirty-seven, wore rimless spectacles, a bow tie, and a fresh, white collar. He exuded self-assurance from operating the thriving Packard Electric Company. It produced electric light bulbs, transformers, and cables. James Ward Packard earned millions in profits, which he deployed as capital for his auto company.[55]

James Ward Packard was a mechanical engineer from Lehigh University. He had researched Panhard-Levassor auto bodies, which were built with steel, as opposed to American autos, which relied on wood. He would have sought from Champion personal anecdotes about the men behind the Panhard-Levassor Motor Company. Packard even had a ready conversation icebreaker—he had founded the Lehigh University Bicycle Club.[56] Albert, for his part, was under the influence of what he saw, and he contemplated how to find his way into the auto industry.

Nineteen companies in the garden's great hall displayed automobiles that used gas-combustion engines, seven companies displayed autos powered by steam, two hawked autos with engines that used a combination of gasoline and electric (forerunners to today's hybrids), and six companies exhibited engines that were electric, running on lead-acid batteries.[57] Prices ranged from $250 for an Orient motor-tricycle to $10,000 for a Columbia- Electric Vehicle Company automobile.[58] The Columbia-Electric Vehicle Company of Hartford stood out as America's biggest auto company—in 1899 it had manufactured 2,092 vehicles, accounting for half the cars made that year.[59] Hartford was ready to become synonymous with automobile manufacturing in the twentieth century.

America in 1900 had more electric than steam-powered autos; gasoline-fueled autos were the minority.[60] Each technology had strengths and weaknesses. The technology that overcame its weaknesses would rule the industry.

Electrics had a range approximating forty miles, were capable of a speedy 30 mph, and easily conquered hills.[61] Urban women favored electrics, which started by pushing the ignition button, and the motor ran smooth and silent. However, lead-acid batteries were heavy—the Columbia-Electric Vehicle Company battery weighed twelve hundred pounds,[62] the weight of a big workhorse. Electricity to charge batteries was exclusive to metropolitan communities; rural America, then home to most of the nation's population, lacked power into the 1940s.[63] Thomas Edison, illustrious for inventing the first electric light bulb, the phonograph, and other modern wonders, announced from his research and development laboratory in Menlo Park, New Jersey, that he planned to make a game-changer nickel-iron battery that would store extra energy and have a longer life.[64] The wizard of Menlo Park raised expectations for electrics to win the automobile war.

Steam-powered autos, called "steamers," were promoted for the virtues of simple steam power over complex internal-combustion engines, derided by steamer manufacturers as relying on a sinister "internal-explosion."[65] The Stanley Steamer used only thirteen moving parts in its two-cylinder motor—eliminating the need for a transmission or gearshift.[66] However, owners of steamers complained that up to twenty minutes were required to heat the boilers before the vehicles could move, and once underway they needed frequent stops to add water.

The first American to build a steam automobile may have been Ransom Eli Olds in Lansing, Michigan, in 1894, although in two years Olds had switched to making autos running on gasoline, which he offered at the 1900 New York show. Olds, Winton, and other automakers with internal-combustion engines used primitive fuels such as coal oil (a form of which was trademarked as Kerosene), ethanol, benzene, alcohol, naphtha (a flammable liquid distilled from petroleum, coal tar, and natural gas), and gasoline.[67]

Of all the fuels, gasoline was the Cinderella. It was long regarded as an unwanted byproduct of Kerosene until around the 1890s and the advent of electric lights, which weakened Kerosene's commercial beauty while gasoline was found—by trial and error—to boost combustion-engine horsepower. Winton advertised that driving his motor carriages cost the attractive price of a half-cent per mile. Gasoline sold for fifteen cents a gallon,[68] although it was available only in limited quantities. The engines fired up by inserting a hand crank into the front of the vehicle and turning the crank, a process requiring muscle.

At the First Annual Automobile Show, the New York host club sought to win the public's confidence by constructing a wooden track twenty feet wide to show customers how to drive and maneuver around barrels, placed as decorator barriers.[69] The board oval surrounded the rows and columns of 160 different vehicles parked on display—allowing drivers to commute from the exhibit floor onto the smooth track and prove the vehicles ran as advertised.

Companies selling accessories had stalls in the great hall's balcony. One stall was taken by the Hyatt Roller Bearing Company of Newark, manufacturer of tapered, flexible roller bearings made of celluloid, an early plastic that featured a spring-like quality that yielded to irregularities caused by poor manufacture.[70] Hyatt's general manager was Alfred P. Sloan Jr. He and his sales director were watching the cars go through their paces around the track like show horses when a tall man, slender as a reed, stopped by the counter and lifted his bowler to wipe his forehead. Sloan's sales director invited the man to step past Hyatt's front counter to the rear of the stall by the gallery's railing and offered a chair, like sharing a box seat. Sloan was introduced to Henry Ford,[71] then building a racing car in Detroit with Hyatt roller bearings. Ford tilted back in a chair,[72] heels locked in the topmost rung, knees even with the level of his chin. The three talked for hours, innocent that Ford, a self-taught mechanic, would make an auto that would dominate the industry, and that Sloan, a recent MIT graduate with an engineering degree, would overtake Ford with a greater enterprise.

The Mobile Company of America, manufacturer of steamers in the New York suburb of Tarrytown, had missed the display-space deadline, but the company annexed a zone of its own with a dizzying publicity stunt. Madison Square Garden soared 320 feet above the sidewalk and featured a roof-garden restaurant crowned by a tower supporting a statute. Peaking at 485 feet, the Greek Goddess Diana was mounted on ball bearings so her bow and arrow continually pointed into the wind. The Mobile Company of America rented the roof garden and built an outdoor board ramp two hundred feet long with a wooden "hill"[73] ascending fifty-three feet, the height of five stories, to demonstrate the steamer's climbing and braking powers.[74] A driver titillated audiences looking up from the street by motoring twenty times a day up the ramp toward Diana, then turning around to go back down. On each descent, the driver halted on two or three occasions to show off the grabbing and holding efficiency of the brakes—to the awe of pedestrians down below.

The eight-day show averaged six thousand daily spectators handing over fifty cents admission,[75] a modest draw compared with the garden's six-day bicycle races, Buffalo Bill Cody's Wild West Show, and other extravaganzas. Automotive journalist Chris Sinsabaugh would later recall that the show amounted to "something like a morgue as to attendance, for in those days there were many people who had never seen a gas car."[76] Those venturing into the aisles could welcome motor vehicles as a way to reduce the 450,000 tons of horse manure and 15,000 horse carcasses removed from the city's streets each year.[77]

Hardly any of the automobile companies survived long enough to display at later shows. Among the first to vanish was the Mobile Company of America, one of some fifteen hundred US auto companies that would form and dissolve between 1895 and 1930.[78]

A ghost of the First Annual Automobile Show still flutters every Memorial Day weekend in the Midwest. Twenty-six-year-old Carl Graham Fisher had locked the front door of his Indianapolis bicycle shop and climbed aboard a train to New York to see what he had only read about in trade publications or heard from friends who had visited Cleveland or Chicago, noted for their car companies. Fisher located the Waltham Manufacturing Company exhibit. He strolled around with a roll of cash the size of his fist and nonchalantly pulled it out from a trouser pocket as though he wondered what to do with it.[79] Impressed with the

Orient motor-tricycle, he bought one.[80] Champion would have instructed him in the care of the De Dion-Bouton engine and how to drive the machine. Fisher took it back home. He zipped around on his motor-trike to flaunt it, spellbound with the engine's sound and smell. In a flash of inspiration, he wheeled toward the future of Indianapolis as a motor city.

In 1900, Champion's first year in America, nearly 4,200 automobiles—1,681 steamers, 1,575 electrics, and 936 powered by gasoline—were manufactured.[81] That doubled the number built between 1895, the year of his adopted country's first-ever car race, in Chicago, and 1900.[82] Thus, the United States entered the twentieth century with approximately eight thousand autos[83] for 75 million people.[84] Most vehicle owners lived in metropolitan areas. Albert had every reason to join enthusiasts expecting that by the next decade autos would outnumber horses in US cities.

Business commitments and travels didn't slow down Champion from exchanging letters with Elise Delpuech in Paris. He was free to cavort with local girlfriends like Eliza Holaway, but Elise knew where he came from and was knowledgeable about his brothers Louis, Henri, and Prosper. Elise remained his tie to their Batignolles neighborhood, unique for quirky serpentine cobblestone streets and window boxes growing flowers. His first love, she owned a piece of his heart.

Champion, with his chronic urge to work and earn money, craved attention and could inundate Elise with letters bulging with newspaper clips mentioning him from cities she might consider exotic. Mail between Paris and Boston took seven to ten days. By early 1901, Albert and Elise made plans for her to join him.

Elise turned twenty-four in December 1900 and, as an adult, was entitled to make her own decisions.[85] France was not large enough for her Albert. He had greater prospects in America. In addition, if he tried to return to France, he would be arrested. She had to cross the Atlantic for him. She was willing, but it was up to him to provide her with passage.

Albert was still sending a portion of his salary to his family. To bring Elise over, he required more money. He had to have a successful season racing in 1901—or he would lose Elise.

Winter weather forced Champion indoors to train again in the Park Square Coliseum with Orient teammates—tall, lanky Harry Elkes and short Johnny Nelson, of Chicago's Swedish community, who had to stand on tip toes to reach the height of five feet. Nelson was twenty and competed with fierceness that made him more successful than his older brother, pro cyclist Joe Nelson. Newspaper artists and photographers depicted Johnny Nelson in profile on the bike, back arched like an attacking cat.

Champion, Elkes, and Johnny Nelson used special Orient aero-pacing bicycles, fitted with a smaller front wheel, eighteen inches in diameter, than the standard twenty-seven-inch rear wheel. The innovation lowered the cyclists' center of gravity and put his chest and shoulders—the greatest source of wind resistance—closer to the pacing machine to improve drafting and balance.

The aero pacing bike prompted Champion to update his publicity photo. Around Boston, Elmer Chickering was distinguished for portraits of athletes, theater actors, politicians, and public figures. Chickering had taken the vintage photo of heavyweight boxing champion James J. Corbett—chest bared, arms cocked, wielding the fists that pulverized John L. Sullivan, the Boston Strong Boy, for the world title. When Champion visited Chickering's studio at 21 West Street in central Boston to make an appointment, he met Chickering, in his early forties, a flower in the lapel of his jacket over a crisp white shirt, a bow tie, thin hair submitting to a crossover, and the intent eyes of an avid listener. Chickering scheduled Champion to come back with his bicycle, shorts, jersey, and shoes. Champion returned, freshly barbered. Chickering posed him on the saddle, hands gripping the handlebar drops—as spectators would see him. Albert ordered prints in cardboard frames for his family and Elise in Paris and extras to hand out to the press.

Champion posed for noted Boston society photographer Elmer Chickering on his aero motor-pace bicycle, with the front wheel smaller than the rear wheel to lower his center of gravity for better pacing behind motor-powered tandems. Champion gave out dozens of copies to the press for publicity along the Eastern Seaboard racing circuit. Photo by Elmer Chickering. *From the collection of Lorne Shields, Thornhill, ON, Canada.*

Champion put his 1901 season in jeopardy on a Sunday afternoon program with a disastrous crash before Christmas at the Park Square Coliseum, racing a motor-tricycle against compatriot Henri Fournier. Champion could hardly pass up the opportunity to drive against Fournier, seven years his senior. With a barrel chest, bold mustache, and an insouciant attitude, Fournier personi-fied Gallic swagger. In Paris Fournier had been chauffeur to Mistinguett,[86] the husky-voiced cabaret singer whose smile beamed from hundreds of posters plastered around the City of Light. He also rode in the shotgun seat as mechanic for Fernand Charron in ultra-long auto races between cities across France—forerunners of Grand Prix auto racing—before he set his own world records. One of Fournier's American marks of distinction, in late 1898, was that he was the first to drive a motor-tricycle around Madison Square Garden, a one-mile demonstration pacing a US cyclist to the garden's fastest mile.

Around the track at the Park Square Coliseum, Champion and Fournier drove at full speed when their machines went airborne off a tight turn.[87] Both Frenchmen crashed hard into unforgiving wooden seats and spectators and were knocked out cold.[88] A horse-drawn ambulance took them to Massachusetts General Hospital.

"I wake up and see that I am in a hospital,"[89] Albert later reminisced. "I lie still for a while and then look around me. In the next cot, I see my friend Fournier. He looked at me and I see him wink.

"'Henri,' I say. 'Where am I?'

"'In Boston,' says Henri.

"'Boston,' I say. 'Where is Boston?'"

Champion was treated for a broken arm and walked out of Massachusetts General Hospital wearing a plaster cast.[90] He was still wearing the cast on January 4, 1901, when he pedaled in his white silk jersey behind a motorcycle around the same small track in a fast one-mile motorpace demonstration during a race program. He blitzed the mile in 1 minute and 37 seconds—approaching 40 mph—to break Harry Elkes's national record.[91] The audience gave Champion a rousing ovation.

Champion's arm healed in time for him to make up for lost time in the 1901 season. From May to September, he entered forty motorpace races on the outdoor velodrome Eastern Seaboard pro circuit, from Boston, Providence, and New York west to Pittsburgh and south to Newark, Baltimore, Washington, DC, and Atlanta.[92] He competed three times a week for fourteen weeks, most often in middle distances of ten miles to twenty-five miles, against one to three opponents. They pedaled behind motor-tandems. Because engines misbehaved, Champion's team traveled with an extra motor-tandem. All racing accoutrement were packed in wooden cases with *Entertainer* painted in large black letters on the sides so that baggage handlers would rush them, in the tradition that the show must go on, straightaway to the destinations indicated by their tags.[93]

He won twenty-nine races.[94] Each win paid $250, which would have generated prize money totaling $7,250. He also earned approximately another $1,000 from other races, paying $150 to place and $50 to show. His contract with the Waltham Manufacturing Company was for $25 a week, covering the off-season of eight months, or thirty-two weeks, for about another $800. A rough estimate of his winnings and salary came to $9,050 ($256,000 in 2014). Compared with major league baseball hall of famer Cy Young, earning a salary of $3,500 ($99,000 in 2014) pitching for the Boston Americans and leading the American league in wins that year, Champion was one of America's best-paid athletes.[95]

Champion's travel expenses were likely offset by his share of the gate. As pro cycling had evolved after the mid-1890s, promoters offered marquee cyclists a portion of receipts, usually up to 40 percent, to ensure they would compete in their programs, encourage audiences to watch, and induce the press to write previews and then cover the events. Owners of major league baseball teams considered five thousand fans seated in their ballpark a profitable day; Charles River Park was selling tickets of twenty-five cents to $1.50 each to ten thousand or more spectators. After every race, the promoters—local businessmen who organized and advertised their events—doled out the prize money. The era was unfettered by taxes. Dollar bills were longer and wider than today; $250 in ones and fives, with a twenty on top, rolled up to the size of a fist.

The biggest earner in sports was the cyclist Major Taylor. An African-American from Indianapolis, Taylor was a pure sprinter, capable of churning his legs in one sharp acceleration after another to decimate opponents in their surge to the finish line. He had made history as the first athlete to cross the color line in professional sports when he won the 1899 world pro sprint championship in Montreal—a decade before Jack Johnson won the heavyweight boxing title. In 1901, a Paris promoter lured Taylor with a $10,000 appearance fee ($283,000 in 2014) to compete in short races over six weeks in Paris with forays to London, Berlin, and Brussels.[96] Taylor beat all of Europe's national champions and pulled in $1,000 a race. That year his income topped $25,000 ($707,000) from appearance fees, victories, and product endorsements.

On August 7, Champion faced Taylor in Charles River Park for a five-mile match behind motor-tandems. Both men had been born the same year, and they stood eye to eye and had similar builds of taut, light muscles. Their duel filled the stadium and cheap seats and packed the infield to standing room only with more than twelve thousand spectators. Champion and Taylor had a few laps to build speed behind their pacing machines for a flying start. At the crack of the start gun, Champion set a swift first mile in 1:29-4/5, a combative 45 mph.[97] Taylor, however, quit after the first mile. It was a hollow victory for Champion, although he broke the US record held by Jimmy Michael.

Faster motors on tandems kept audiences leaping to their feet and cheering. Upping the speed also boosted the dangers. On September 4, Johnny Nelson battled in a fifteen-miler against Jimmy Michael in Madison Square Garden. In the third mile, the engine of Nelson's Orient motor-tandem broke down as he was flying into a banked turn. The motor-tandem of Michael banged into Nelson from behind, throwing Nelson under the machine.[98] Its chain, slathered in oil and churning like a buzz saw, ripped his left leg calf muscle to the bone.[99] Nelson's pacers and Michael's pacers crashed into Nelson. His wound showered blood onto the pile of men. Michael swerved away, unscathed. Nelson was taken by horse-drawn ambulance to Bellevue Hospital. His leg developed gangrene, prompting doctors to amputate the infected leg above the knee in an attempt to save him.[100] Four days after his accident, he died.[101]

The garden's management of James Kennedy and Patrick T. Powers barred motor-tandems from the track and ordered them replaced with "singles," or one-seat motorcycles.

Neither Johnny Nelson's surviving brother, Joe Nelson, nor Champion,

Harry Elkes, or any other pace followers voiced any intention to quit. They refused even to wear a helmet like football players because, so the rationale went, matadors in the bullring never wear breastplates.[102]

Champion's other Orient teammate Elkes, one of the tallest pros in the game, had been struggling to regain his form after a hard fall on Memorial Day. Lanky Elkes had crashed on the boards of the new open-air Revere Beach velodrome, which replaced the now-closed Waltham Bicycle Park oval a few miles to the south. Revere Beach's track was eight laps to the mile with forty-degree banks on the turns. His fractured left collarbone left him without full use of his arm.[103]

Nevertheless, Elkes managed to round himself into form by the end of the season to face the steadily-improving Bobby Walthour of Atlanta in a twenty-five-mile motorpace contest in Charles River Park for the motorpacing national championship. Walthour had come up from the Southern circuit with a skein of victories. Almost six feet tall, he had haystack-blond hair, blue eyes, and an outgoing personality that drew hordes of fans.

Frank "King" Gately on a motorcycle drove pace for Elkes as he put the challenger Walthour away and thus claimed a third national motorpace championship. Yet Elkes conceded that his falls were taking a toll. He began talking about retiring from the sport,[104] possibly going to college to study medicine after spending so much time in hospitals.[105]

At last Champion had saved enough winnings to send for Elise. He arranged her ship's passage to Boston and scouted for a residence in Cambridge. In November, she arrived.[106] It was a measure of her commitment to him. Elise and Albert moved into a three-story Victorian house at 63 Highland Avenue,[107] on the other side of Massachusetts Avenue from his boarding house on Cottage Street. She had to cope with a different language, an unfamiliar currency, and all manner of American customs. However, she and Albert were living together, although in the eyes of the Catholic Church, as unmarried Catholics, they were living in sin.

Having come off a successful season, Champion could devote time to showing her around Boston. They would have time together before he had to go back to his itinerant schedule in the spring.

Elise immigrated around the time Charles Herman Metz was pondering what to do about escalating interference from General Electric president Coffin and M. P. Clough of Lynn Gas and Electric Company. Metz's investors kept buying more stock in the Waltham Manufacturing Company and forcing their ideas on him to build electric cars.[108]

With sales of steam-powered autos in a downward spiral and Thomas Edison pledging the resources of his lab in Menlo Park, New Jersey, to invent a breakthrough nickel-iron battery, the prospects for electrics looked bright. But Metz was committed to internal-combustion engines. He considered that the dazzling increase in the supply of gasoline from recently discovered East Texas oil fields since 1901 would meet unlimited future demand. Metz had to decide what he should do.

December brought the annual six-day in Madison Square Garden. The 1901 edition, December 7 to 14, was directed by William A. Brady's understudies— James C. Kennedy, the bespectacled and wiry retired cyclist turned promoter, and rotund Patrick T. Powers, former manager of the New York Giants baseball team,[109] predecessor to the San Francisco Giants, and the founding president the National Association of Professional Baseball Leagues,[110] composed of all minor-league teams. Between baseball and cycling, Powers continually operated sports enterprises.

The sixes caught the eye of newspaper magnate Joseph Pulitzer. He was transforming publishing from his office in the tallest skyscraper in New York, the Pulitzer Building. Born in Hungary,[111] Pulitzer had learned English as a common laborer in St. Louis and turned to a career there in journalism, writing for a German-language paper, which over time he purchased. He moved to New

York, the portal for migrants pouring into America by the shiploads. Pulitzer saw class conflict as an unpleasant truth and bought the *World* to tell about the plight of the poor.[112] He made headlines bigger, enlarged typefaces, and used drawings and photos to get his message across even to illiterates.[113] Pulitzer paid attention to sports for their mass following. He created the sports section,[114] a force behind the *World* ballooning to the largest circulation of New York's fifteen dailies. The *World* promoted the December six-day and announced an exclusive. Jimmy Michael would report on it—or at least the *World* would publish Jimmy's byline, a privilege reserved for star journalists. The *World* ran a photo of him posing with a Jack Russell terrier named Trixy.[115]

James C. Kennedy and Patrick T. Powers hired Michael and Champion to give daily motorpace demonstrations that would entertain audiences and provide the six-day contestants a deserved break. Champion was to drive an Orient Motorcycle for Michael to pace behind in matinees. They would have the track to themselves while one rider from each of the thirteen two-rider teams pedaled at a casual pace along the inside apron, out of the way but still rolling under the six-day rules of round the clock riding.

Whatever grudge Champion harbored for Michael's false accusations about their mutual trainer Choppy Warburton, he had acquiesced to a détente. He and Michael would each be paid $200 a day, plus expenses, for pace exhibitions of two to five miles. Champion talked Kennedy and Powers into letting him drive a one-mile motorcycle demonstration on the final afternoon to test how fast he could make his new 2-1/4 hp Orient Motorcycle zoom around the track.

Pacing Michael also afforded Champion the opportunity to hone his cornering technique. Some pacemakers entered the banking high and wide and dropped down for gravity to give them a boost in speed while others went into the turn close to the edge and then swept up higher before dropping down. Such a series of swerves increased the risk of a crash or losing the pacing cyclist. Champion learned that the most direct way to take the banked turns was to enter and leave at the same angle.

Day after day, ten thousand men and women bought tickets and crammed into the garden, yelling for favorites.[116] The team of Bobby Walthour and Archie MacEachern of Toronto took turns charging around the wooden bowl, reeling off hundreds of miles daily to lead the other teams. On the final afternoon, Saturday, December 14, Champion drove a one-mile exhibition, ten laps. The six-day riders took a breather—one from each team soft-pedaled around the apron on the inside perimeter. In the crowd was Champion's agent, Victor Breyer, from Paris to report for *La Vie au Grand Air*.[117]

Champion flattened over his machine and zipped through the half mile at 40 mph, leaning over so far on the banking that everyone in the garden stood up and cheered.

"Mon Dieu!" exclaimed Breyer,[118] standing with an anonymous scribe from the *World*. "Champion will kill himself! He is going too fast for such a track."

The words escaped Breyer's mouth as Albert was rounding the high, steep curve on turn three. His motorcycle shot up the bank and crashed into box seat number 13, shattering the wooden railing into matchsticks.[119] He fell off his machine and plunged down the smooth boards.

"Champion lay stunned, and an ambulance was summoned," the *World* reported.[120] "The cyclist, however, finally sprang to his feet, shook himself, and amid the deafening cheers of the crowd, limped off to his quarters. He sustained a compound dislocation of two fingers of his right hand and sprained his right side from shoulder to foot."

Champion was bundled into a horse-drawn ambulance for emergency treatment at Bellevue Hospital, but he was able to make it back to the garden and witness the ten o'clock finish.

"The excitement of the surging crowd was strained almost to the bursting point," observed the *World*.[121] "Men stood on chairs and railings and mounted on each other's shoulders."[122]

At the end of 142 hours and a new record of 2,555 miles,[123] far enough to take the riders from the garden to Phoenix, Arizona, the pack in vibrant silk jerseys rocketed like a meteorite. Bobby Walthour bent almost double over the handlebars and heaved to the front for the final 176-yard lap. A former Atlanta bicycle courier accustomed to traffic pressing from behind while he sped to make deliveries, Walthour whooshed to victory. A swarm of humanity quickly engulfed around him and his partner Archie MacEachern, shouldered them, and carried them to the judge's stand so the winners could claim the $1,500 first prize ($42,400 in 2014).[124]

Champion, his broken fingers immobilized in a splint, recognized the qualities under pressure that made Walthour a world-class athlete.

In early 1902, Metz asked GE president Charles Coffin and M. P. Clough of Lynn Gas and Electric Company to buy him out of the Waltham Manufacturing Company, which they did.[125] Metz severed his ties with the company he had founded and moved to New York to serve as technical editor of *Cycling and Automobile Trade Journal*.[126]

The Waltham Manufacturing Company hired a new director and introduced Orient Motorcycles equipped with engines of its own manufacture with 2 hp, 3 hp, and 4 hp. Orients introduced the two-cylinder engine, called V-Twin for the v-shape created by the orientation of the two cylinders in the crankcase.[127]

Champion remained under contract with the Waltham Manufacturing Company, which supplied him with Orient bicycles, motorcycles, and Dunlop tires. Motorcycle sales would become more important as bicycle sales took a nosedive.

Albert joined the Madison Square Garden syndicate of James C. Kennedy and Patrick T. Powers for race contracts.[128] That put him in a select stable of pros along with Elkes and an amiable Englishman named Tommy Hall. Kennedy told Champion that Hall, five feet tall with wide, expressive eyes,[129] was a better cyclist and instructed Champion to drive the pace motorcycle for Hall. However, Champion was too proud. His broken fingers and body bruises had healed, and he was ready for another racing season. He liked driving pace when it suited him, to practice driving fast, unrestrained on oval tracks from the nuisance of police arresting him for speeding on public roads, but he was not about to drive pace for Hall when he had come to America to race. He had an idea how to outfox Kennedy and upstage Hall.

In February 1902, Albert took Elise to live in a French community in Brooklyn while he decamped to Washington, DC to train[130] in the milder Southern climate around the outdoor board oval, the Coliseum on Capitol Hill[131] at Fourteenth and East Capitol Streets in northeast Washington. On the track, he could see through bare branches of oak and maple trees the brilliant white Capitol dome towering like a snow-capped mountain.

He rented a room in a boarding house near the Coliseum and stayed in the nation's capital in March and April. Albert and Elise, separated even though she came to America to be with him, could keep in touch with letters and, now, perhaps the occasional long-distance telephone call.

Determined to prove himself to James C. Kennedy, he exercised with dedication at the Coliseum. Sometimes he would pedal down Capitol Hill and into the Maryland countryside, with its brick roads and some sharp hills, to improve leg power. By the time he and Elise reunited in May, Albert was ready to fly.

During the corporate restructuring in Waltham, Elkes had shipped out again to France with contracts for races in Paris on Clément Gladiators. Elkes returned in late May 1902 to Boston, accompanied by seventeen-and-a-half-year-old Basil De Guichard.[132] That spring at the Parc des Princes outdoor cement vélodrome, De Guichard had showed bright prospects by setting a long-distance world record in a motorcycle race. He drove 875 miles in seventy-three hours on a 1-1/4 hp Clément stock motorcycle, averaging 12 mph, including all stops for gasoline and rest.[133]

De Guichard had blue eyes and brown hair,[134] the cherub cheeks of adolescence, a low forehead, and a square jaw. His calm disposition and suave manner made it easy to make friends with strangers. He also was fluent in English. De Guichard had been born in Denver to English parents.[135] The family returned to England when he was a child, then moved to Paris, where he grew up and received his education.[136] Like many youths, he took up cycling, which drew him to work at Clément Cycles. He would have heard stories from Adolph Clément, Pierre Tournier, and laborers who had watched Champion's arc from unicyclist to bike racer, French cycling *vedette*, and American star.

Upon meeting Champion, De Guichard was ready to report that Clément was making heftier motorcycles in his Levallois-Perret plant for motorpacing competitions with bigger De Dion-Bouton engines for ever-faster speeds around the Parc des Princes cement oval, about two-thirds of a mile around. Thirty thousand spectators on a regular basis filled the stadium and bleacher seats to yell above the thunderous engines and urge the motor-pacers. There seemed no limit to how fast the pacing cyclists could go.

It was natural that De Guichard would join Champion, Lanky Elkes, and other pros for track workouts. De Guichard seemed a natural for pacing as he stood five feet five inches,[137] and had developed superior handling expertise that enabled him to highball around turns and straights. He bought a pro license. The Orient Team roster was full, and with Metz gone, Champion lost influence with management to put his compatriot on the payroll. Instead, De Guichard opted to sign with one of the other top-tier pro squads,[138] Rambler bicycles, made in Chicago. Joining this team signified an extraordinary coincidence. The bicycle company would later reorganize as the Rambler Motor Company. De Guichard was destined in his thirties to marry the daughter of that company's president.

Right away De Guichard garnered press attention. His name was touted in trade journal ads with Champion, Tommy Hall, and Bobby Walthour.

Champion's priming in Washington paid off. He set more than one hundred US records, which the Fourth Estate often proclaimed as world records. "Champion is following pace to-day faster than any other man in the game," exclaimed the *Washington Star*.[139]

The Washington Star, then the capital's most influential paper, published the Chickering portrait of Champion in a story that said, "The Frenchman was never in better form than at present."[140] The *Star* added insightful commentary: "As Champion was somewhat nettled by the knowledge of Kennedy's intention, he pitched in and worked like ten men. Soon he was able to laugh at Hall and eventually he turned the tables completely on the midget and his manager, and Champion himself became and remains the star of the Kennedy-Powers team."[141]

The article indicated that he played as hard as he raced.[142] "On the other hand, the Frenchman exists upon admiration, and is what is called a 'grandstand rider.' Some of his rivals call him a 'ladies' man.'"[143] "Nevertheless," it continued, "he rides with terrible speed and dogged purpose to win. His pace following is simply beautiful to behold. He seems inseparable from the motor tandem pacing him."[144]

This reportage carried the understated reference to Champion's promiscuity. The gentlemen sports writers avoided any direct references about the misbehavior of newsmakers as long as no arrest was made. Yet it was apparent that Albert was cutting a wide swath among the Potomac debutantes.

On July 15, 1902, in Pittsburgh, Champion raced against Basil De Guichard and set forty-four national records en route to the US hour-paced record of 43 miles and 293 yards, obliterating all existing records at every mile along the way.[145] De Guichard, trailing close behind, had beaten the prevailing times. Both men averaged a breakneck 43 mph. That afternoon cemented their friendship and began their intertwined careers, which would exceed what either could ever have imagined.

Albert continued to set other motorpace records up to ten miles in Boston, Baltimore, and Washington, DC. He earned $500 for thirty-five minutes of riding in a twenty-five-mile challenge against a rookie pro, endowed with a farm boy's muscle and much taller than Champion.[146] His opponent, from New Hampshire and nicknamed the Manchester Giant, had lost to him in August in Charles River Park. Later, the Manchester Giant put up $500 for a winner-take-all match in Providence. At that match, Champion lapped him twelve times to win by two miles.

Champion's ride on September 1 in a twenty-five-mile race against Orient teammate Harry Elkes in Charles River Park earned him a shot at the US middle-distance title on September 6 at Charles River Park against Bobby Walthour. Their twenty-five-mile match would close the 1902 season. The contest set off debate about whether a foreigner could win the American championship—and the right to wear the stars and stripes around his waist for the next season.

Walthour had remarked that his motor-tandem, which cost him $750, was so sweet he had named it *Candy*.[147] He started behind Candy from the tape in front of the grandstand while Champion and his Orient team began on the back straight.

At the beginning, the Georgian and the Frenchman reeled off laps without either making any appreciable gain. Twelve thousand fans were yelling for their favorites. After four miles, Walthour forged a margin, which he stretched to pass Champion at fifteen miles. Champion's pacemakers even pedaled as hard as they could to supplement their tandem motor. In the closing miles, Candy's engine skipped, putting Walthour's one-lap advantage in jeopardy. Just in time, however, Walthour's stoker on the back seat somehow fixed the engine. Walthour kept close to Champion to defeat him for the national title.[148]

Champion wrapped up the 1902 season with forty-eight victories in the fifty-three events he had entered.[149] His wins alone amounted to $12,000—a princely income compared with earnings of major league baseball players.

Champion's triumphs led to a full-page photograph on his aero bicycle in the *Police Gazette*, an influential national tabloid popular for its coverage of sports, murders, and racy pictures of scantily clad burlesque dancers: "Albert Champion—Speedy French Bicyclist Who Has Been Breaking Records in This Country."

From Police Gazette, *no. 1313, October 18, 1902.*

With savings in the bank, his contract extended for 1903, and press attention going his way, Albert and Elise agreed it was time to marry. He was twenty-
four, Elise twenty-five. A traditional wedding in Paris was out of the question.
Under his exile, she could be with him only in America.

October 31, 1902, was a sun-splashed Friday. Trees were shedding golden
and crimson leaves along the sidewalk. The couple strolled after lunch from
their residence on Highland Avenue to the marbled corridors and dark-wood
trim of Cambridge City Hall, where they were married by a justice of the peace,
Julius Meyers.[150] They were the only couple married that day.

In the Marriage Registration, Elise wrote her occupation: "at home."[151]
Albert listed his as "automobile,"[152] indicating the direction he saw his career
going.

Albert's teenage sweetheart and first wife, Elise Delpuech Champion,
on a chilly November day in 1920, sightseeing outside Dallas, Texas.
Photo courtesy of Kerry Champion Williams.

Despite Champion's robust 1902 season, the craze for two-wheelers had fizzled. His employer planned to cease bicycle production in the summer of 1903 and terminate his contract. After a decade and more than one hundred thousand Orient bicycles,[153] including their offspring tandems, triplets, quads, and the famous ten-seat Oriten, the Waltham Manufacturing Company set its future on small-engine motorcycles and four-cylinder cars.[154]

Champion looked to 1903 and determined his new challenge would be racing cars, a career leap easier to discuss than to realize. Unlike France, where motorists like Henri Fournier competed on public roads between cities hundreds of kilometers apart in contests fraught with spectacular accidents and narrow escapes, auto racing in the United States was confined to horse tracks. Every city, town, and most backwater crossroad communities took pride in the local fairground ovals and permanent grandstands. Ambitious promoters put on programs for the thundering machines to churn up dust clouds thick as forest-fire smoke. Paying audiences filled the stadiums and marveled at the noise, the dirt flying, especially how fast the roaring dirt-track devils could go. To ensure that most drivers would finish before their cars crapped out, events were limited to five miles—often just one mile.

Car racing was an exclusive gentleman's game, like golf, but precipitously more expensive. However, a growing number of carmakers valued press coverage that winners generated, and the idea of driving a mile in a minute had captured the public imagination. Motoring a mile a minute was discussed around dinner tables and especially in saloons and barbershops. Mile-a-minute fever was in the air.

Since Champion had introduced the Orient Motorcycle three years earlier, motorcycles were becoming fashionable in New York. Members of the New York Motorcycle Club would charter the Federation of American Motorcyclists in their Brooklyn clubhouse that autumn to assist the good-roads movement and regulate motorcycle racing.[155] Members rode Orients from Waltham, Indian Motorcycles produced downstate in Springfield, and a model Charles Herman Metz introduced from his C. H. Metz Company on Staten Island. They all had one- or two-cylinder engines generating up to 5-hp and weighed about one hundred pounds. Some cruised about 40 mph. That was good enough for the New York City Police Department to supply motorcycles to a squad that chased down speeding autos and issued traffic tickets.[156]

Champion required a more powerful machine than anything made on these shores. He looked to Paris, to Adolphe Clément's Gladiators, and obtained a brochure about the French machine. It weighed a muscular 350 pounds.[157] The Gladiator packed a brawny four-cylinder engine,[158] called a V-twin after the shape made by the double sets of compact cylinders joined at the base. The V-twin fastened in the triangle section of the steel diamond-shaped frame, near the ground for a low center of gravity. Its mighty 14-hp engine harnessed the power of a herd of fourteen horses. Champion could afford a Gladiator. With his Gaulic hubris, he naturally reckoned that he could pilot the motorcycle 60 mph around a velodrome. And, of course, he expected that the ensuing publicity would impress an auto company enough to hire him to race cars. It was a gamble. Because he could not afford to buy his own auto, this was his only chance. He sent Clément a bank draft for $1,500 to import a Gladiator.[159]

The 1903 US motorpace season commenced on Memorial Day, May 30, a Saturday. Single-seat motorcycles took over from motor-tandems, ushering in a new era. After renovations, Charles River Park reopened for the holiday. Its track featured an enlarged grandstand to sit eight thousand viewers,[160] cheap bleacher seats to accommodate six thousand folks, and an infield capable of accommodating two thousand standing spectators. The oval's distance had been shortened to five laps for a mile from the old six-lap template,[161] and it had steeper banks of thirty-eight degrees on the turns.[162] The hardwood surface was twenty-five feet wide—five feet broader to give motorpace teams extra room to pass. State-of-the-art, the track was built for national-record speeds.

As tempting as Charles River Park was to Champion, he climbed aboard a train bound for New York a couple weeks earlier with Elise. That was unthinkable to his motorpace confreres. More often than not, they persisted in entering every event they could reach out of gnawing insecurity that their capabilities would somehow diminish, or that they would be forgotten by promoters, the press, and fans. But Albert, with his unreserved faith in his abilities, pursued his new passion to drive racecars.

At the US Customs warehouse on the harbor dock, he claimed his Clément

Gladiator. Word about the machine and its innovative V-twin got out to connoisseurs who were intrigued to see it unpacked from its wooden crate A photographer came with tripod and set up his camera. Albert obliged by driving on the wooden floor around a vacant area, the engine making the brick walls and low ceiling vibrate.

Champion test driving a new two-cylinder Clément Gladiator motorcycle inside the US Customs warehouse in New York after the machine arrived by ship from Paris. The square box on the motorcycle, between the front wheel and the engine, is the gas tank. Note the four-wheel horseless carriage parked in the background. *Photo courtesy of Gary McCoy.*

Then he took his Gladiator to the Empire City Race Track in Yonkers. It was three laps to the mile, made for trotters pulling sulkies. The American Automobile Association, recently formed by auto associations in New York, Chicago, and eight other cities, leased it for a Memorial Day program of motor races. The AAA's Racing Committee had copied rules from the Automobile Club of France, derived from the regulation of horseracing, and had created a comprehensive code for US autos.[163] Several clubs had approved the new rulebook, from competitor weight divisions to rules governing leaders and challengers. The Memorial Day events marked the first program to be sanctioned by the AAA.[164]

Champion registered to compete in one-mile time trials open to all gasoline, electric, and steam machines weighing less than a thousand pounds,[165] whether they had two wheels, three, or four. The time trials made up one of six undercard events, with loving cups valued at $100 each to winners,[166] culminating in a five-mile match between two big autos. He faced a daunting task to master the bulky Gladiator in time for his race.

Daily trains delivered dozens of vehicles and drivers and crews. At the track Champion witnessed a beast of a machine with an engine roaring like Niagara Falls and veering through turns like it protested against going anywhere but straight ahead. In the practice laps, the first thing everyone took in was a driver, a tall, husky guy in a suit and tie and goggles. He crouched on the ungainly car, which had no transmission—a triumph of brute force over anything approaching finesse.[167] The wind mussed his mat of dark hair. He steered with both hands wrapped around grips protruding from a straight steel rod resembling bicycle handlebars. He stared ahead in stolid concentration. His name was Barney Oldfield.

Oldfield was promised 25 percent of the gate and a chance at the winner's purse of $500 to drive in the main event, the best of three five-mile matches.[168] His opponent was Charles G. Ridgeway, a New Yorker steering a Peerless Greyhound. Unlike the skeletal 999, the Greyhound had a hood of pressed steel, painted black. Ridgeway sat on an upholstered leather seat wide enough to accommodate a passenger. He had a few years of motor experience. Oldfield had been at it only since October and had already established himself in Detroit for defeating Alexander Winton, the pioneer auto manufacturer and racecar driver.

A week before Memorial Day, the *New York Times* assured readers, "Mile-a-minute automobile racing is anticipated at the Empire City track."[169]

Memorial Day brought six thousand spectators flocking to the grandstand,[170] equal to the attendance of the eight-day First Annual Automobile Show in 1900 in Madison Square Garden. The unmuffled gas-combustion engines detonated such ear-splitting racket that track officials, in suit and ties and their heads topped with fresh straw boater for the summer season, communicated by waving handheld flags. Yonkers's Mayor Walsh held a solid green flag overhead and made a downward chopping motion to begin the first race at 2:30 p.m.

First was a three-miler with four cars that featured an assistant in each serving as postilion, harking back to horse-drawn mail coaches, when a coachman sat on one of the pairs pulling in the traces. Postilions were necessary on the Empire City Race Track for domestic cars with the steering wheel mounted on the right side, imitating the European style for driving on the left side of the road.[171] Circling the turf track counterclockwise required a driver's assistant to hold onto the opposite side of the car and lean as a counterweight through turns to prevent "capsizing." The awkwardness hastened American carmakers to move the steering wheel to the left side.

Then, in the one-mile speed trial, Champion hunkered down over his Gladiator like a jockey. He spun around a lap to hit the start line at full speed. The entire audience jumped to its feet in unison to cheer him on his three-lap mission. The tumult persisted as he leaned so far on turns that it looked like he might fall over. Somehow he shot through the turns and popped back upright down the straights. It kept up like that until he blazed over the finish line. An official on the line near the grandstand waved a checked flag.

Three timers, required under AAA rules, squeezed their watches to click off. Silence fell on the stadium. The timers consulted with the announcer. When he grabbed his megaphone, it was to declare a new world record: 1 minute 4-1/5 seconds,[172] an impressive 55 mph. The quiet in the grandstand split with everyone erupting into cheers and applause.

A perfectionist, Champion made a second run and clocked 1:03 flat.[173] He was knocking on the edge of the one-minute barrier. He was awarded a silver loving cup valued at $100.[174] With a little more horsepower, he could hit 60 mph.

The five-mile main event was a pursuit race—both drivers began on opposite sides of the track to chase one another, ensuring one of the wild chariots dashed past the grandstand about every twenty seconds. Oldfield started 999 in front of the grandstand while Ridgeway in his Peerless Greyhound began on the back straight.

When Mayor Walsh waved the green flag, Oldfield depressed the gas pedal all the way down to the floor and held it there like his life depended on it. Around every turn, 999 looked as though it would fly out of control, but somehow Oldfield pulled it out in time to cut in again on the straights. Ridgeway piloted the Greyhound through the turns with more finesse, its chassis as high as a wagon, with him ensconced atop a cushy seat on an island of leather.

Oldfield and 999 survived to win the first heat by a decisive ten seconds, in 7 minutes and 2/5 seconds, an average of 56 mph.

In the next heat, Oldfield was timed through the second mile in 1 minute 1-3/5 seconds,[175] 59 mph. The announcer bellowed through a megaphone that Oldfield had set a world one-mile record around an elliptical track.[176] He lapped Ridgeway twice and won with a new five-mile record: 5 minutes 31 seconds.[177]

Two straight matches gave Oldfield victory. He collected $1,300 and received a silver trophy for scoring the meet's fastest mile.[178] He split his prize money with the owner of 999 and his manager-publicist.[179] That left him with $650,[180] a substantial payday compared with a factory laborer's wage of $2 a day. Oldfield bought a train ticket home to Toledo. At the station, his father waited with a horse-drawn wagon as the younger Oldfield waved his wad of dollar bills in the air. He proclaimed that the money was to pay off the mortgage so his parents would not worry about losing their house.[181] His father had tears in his eyes when he embraced his son.

Special dispatches ran nationwide over newspaper syndicate wires. The *Boston Herald* reported, "World's track records were broken by 'Barney' Oldfield in an automobile and Albert Champion on a motorcycle."[182]

Boston's dailies covered a local Memorial Day auto race meet at the Readville Trotting Park, under the auspices of the Massachusetts Automobile Club. Twelve thousand attended. The main event was a one-miler. A car called the Red Bath Tub won in 1 minute and 2-4/5 seconds,[183] two seconds ahead of the Aluminum Flyer.

Other cities also held auto races. Oldfield led the automobile mile-a-minute chase for automobiles. Champion's closest competitor in the motorcycle game lived in England.

Also on Memorial Day, in Charles River Park, lanky Harry Elkes had a fresh approach to the new season. He had trained like a Spartan over the winter in an effort to overcome the hoodoo he had felt the holiday held for him. Now he was back at the top of his game, tucked over his handlebars behind his world-famous German motorcycle pacer Franz Hoffmann. Elkes pedaled behind Hoffmann on the fastest ride of his life in the featured event, the twenty-mile motorpace. "He had broken the world's records behind motorpacing for five, ten, and fifteen miles at the new Charles River Park track," reported the *New York Times*.[184]

John J. Donovan wrote in the *Globe*, "More than 15,000 persons filled every available seat and inch of standing room for the record-breaking race."[185]

At sixteen miles, Elkes led Bobby Walthour and two more rivals hurling at more than 50 mph down the backstretch. The tires were *choooo*-ing crisply on the boards. The engines made regular popping noises.

Then the chain of Elkes's bicycle snapped apart and the sounds changed.[186] Coasting, he slowed as his pacing motorcycle shot ahead. The broken chain tangled in the spokes of his rear wheel and flipped him high into the air. He somersaulted over the handlebars and landed on his back with a thud.[187] His disabled bicycle clattered onto the boards. A motorcycle behind Elkes whammed into his prostrate body and cracked his skull open like a walnut.[188] The motorcycle, its driver Frank "King" Gately, and the rider Gately was pacing, Will Stinson, whose motorpace driver and stoker had been killed on Memorial Day three years earlier at Waltham when they'd struck a telegraph pole, cannonballed into Elkes.

Now came a moment of horrified silence.

Elkes, King Gately, and Will Stinson were lying inert on the smooth board surface. Blood poured from the wounds of all three.

Elkes's clothing was torn to ribbons and he looked as though he had been struck by a locomotive.[189]

Stinson pressed a hand to stanch the bleeding from a gash on his face,[190] and to keep an eye from falling out of its socket.[191]

"Women fainted and men acted like crazy beings, shouting and yelling," reported John J. Donovan of the *Globe*.[192] Hundreds of spectators jumped from the bleachers onto the back stretch and rushed across the track to give assistance to the casualties.

Ambulance horses galloped the injured men to Massachusetts General Hospital. Elkes was dead on arrival.[193] Surgeons struggled to save Stinson's eye.[194] Gately and Stinson were hospitalized for days before being released.[195]

Someone at the hospital told Gately he'd been lucky to survive. He retorted: "Lucky nothing! Do you call it lucky when you see the money in sight to come down like I did? I may have escaped serious injury, but I cannot see where the luck comes in."[196]

Elkes's body was returned to his hometown of Glens Falls,[197] near Syracuse, New York. In Boston the Harry D. Elkes Memorial Fund was established to buy a headstone.[198] Steel collection boxes were distributed at tracks and shops around New England and New York.

Champion learned about the tragedy of Elkes from scruffy newsboys on street corners hawking their stacks of the latest editions. Elkes became the sixth US cycling fatality in three years.[199] Champion packed his Gladiator and caught a train with Elise back to Cambridge. He rented Charles River Park velodrome to practice steering through the banked turns, getting the hang of changing his balance every six seconds in and out of each steep, curved turn. The turns exerted a gravity force three times his body weight—what jet pilots in coming decades would refer to as "3-Gs." He upped his speed and concentrated on keeping his tires on the pole line, the black strip around the inside lane where distances are measured. The Cambridge oval served as his research facility.

In addition to honing his technical agility, Champion needed to nudge up the Gladiator's horsepower. He was an early advocate of boosting the capability of the engine—essentially an air pump—by increasing the air volume moved by the long, smooth pistons stroking up and down inside the cylinder holes. Boring out cylinder holes even a little enhanced engine displacement and bolstered the horsepower on stroke three, the power stroke in the four-stroke cycle. For this he had Waltham Manufacturing Company machine tools at his disposal.

Champion was getting ready for his assault on the mile when news flashed from coast to coast that Oldfield had blazed into auto history on June 20 at the horse track at the Indiana State Fairgrounds in Indianapolis. Oldfield drove a mile in 59-3/5 seconds, a scorching 60 mph.[200] Oldfield had achieved the holy grail of speed.

Born Berna Eli Oldfield in a log cabin on a farm west of Toledo, Ohio,[201] he left a one-room brick schoolhouse at fourteen to work full-time in the kitchen of a Toledo mental institution[202] before crossing town for a job as hotel bellhop.[203] One frantic afternoon in the hotel, the bell captain, an older teenager, called him Barney and dispatched him on an errand.[204] Oldfield, in his wool uniform with shiny brass buttons and a pillbox hat, corrected the bell captain, saying his name was Berna.[205] Oldfield's father, Henry Clay Oldfield, had christened him after a fellow soldier the elder Oldfield had served with in the Union Army during the Civil War. The bell captain snapped that Berna was a sissy's name and commanded him to get cracking.[206] In the heartbeat it took to flinch from the insult to family honor, Oldfield had to weigh following an order or quitting on the spot. He acquiesced to Barney.[207] Afterward he moved to another hotel to operate an elevator and his pay packet read *Barney*.[208] When his parents and older sister,[209] Bertha, learned about what had happened, even they called him Barney.

By 1894 he'd purchased a bicycle and begun racing. In Ohio's amateur state championship, he scored a silver medal,[210] showing promise as a sixteen-year-old. After gaining more experience, Barney turned pro for the Stearns Bicycle Company of Syracuse. For the next six years he rubbed wheels and bumped shoulders in packs with cycling's elite. Rude strength helped him win provincial races, but his legs lacked the snap to make it to the top tier. At the 1899 Montreal world championships in Queen's Park, which attracted national champions from a dozen countries, he was eliminated in every first heat. He idolized the quicker Tom Cooper,[211] a star to Oldfield's supporting role. They buddied up and took trains together to tracks from Omaha to New York's circus maximus, Madison Square Garden.

Cooper's clean-shaven face and pleasant waspy features coordinated with his tuxedo and silk top hat. At twenty-two in 1895, he had been a registered pharmacist,[212] dapper in a striped bow tie and short-cropped hair parted precisely down the center, employed by the Michigan Drug Company in Detroit. That

Tom Cooper retired as national professional cycling champion and funded Henry Ford to design their racing car called 999. Cooper brought in Barney Oldfield to join them. *Photo courtesy of Janet E. Brown and Roy H. Drinkwater.*

summer he won his first bicycle race, in Pontiac, and then more than a dozen more on ovals from Toronto to Washington, DC. His meteoric rise had earned him the nickname "the Phenomenon of '95."[213] A Chicago bicycle company and a New York tire company put him under contract and took out ads promoting his name and image. The next year he chucked his day job for the lucrative pro circuit, from San Francisco to New York, and racked up a dozen national titles at various distances, including the coveted mile. "Cooper heads the list in the race for championship honors,"[214] remarked the *Chicago Tribune*. It was not unusual for him to pocket $1,000 in prize money in one day. Cigarette packs carried cards with his visage, like the cards of musical-comedy stars and baseball heroes.[215] He bought houses in Detroit for his parents and married sister.[216] When the Detroit Telephone Company was forming, he became a prominent investor.[217] He accepted the invitation from a Paris syndicate to compete for the 1901 season,[218] and he returned to Detroit with a souvenir motor-tandem.[219]

In October 1901 Tom suggested to Barney that they take the motor-tandem to the horse track in Grosse Pointe,[220] a community of summer mansions on Lake Michigan outside Detroit, and ride an exhibition prior to a scheduled auto race. They expected the motor-tandem to enchant folks in the stands. Instead, the audience was enraptured by the contest between Alexander Winton, the grand old man of autos, and an unknown tinkerer from Detroit driving an auto he had made, Henry Ford.[221]

Barney dismissed cars as a fad,[222] a popular belief at the time. Tom said he was excited watching the spindly underdog Ford beat the celebrated Winton.[223] He told Barney, five years younger, that he was quitting the cycling game. He wanted to do something different and had bought a coal mine in southern Colorado.[224] He invited Oldfield along to dig for coal. After months of backbreaking labor through the winter in the Cow Creek Coal Mine, the two men netted about $1,000.[225] Cooper told his friend to kick him for suggesting the mining idea.[226] He insisted that Oldfield take all the money. *Bicycling World* estimated that Cooper's worth exceeded $100,000 ($2.7 million in 2014).[227] He had decided to go back to Detroit and have Ford build him a racecar for his next career.[228]

Oldfield called for splitting their earnings.[229] He asked to take Tom's motor-tandem to compete in Salt Lake City, on the velodrome near the Salt Palace, with its glistening dome made of rock salt.[230] Then they went their separate ways.

By May 1902 Cooper and Ford had formed the Cooper-Ford Racing Team to build two racecars.[231] Cooper put up most of the capital,[232] and Ford designed the vehicles and selected the materials.[233] They set up a shop at 81 Park Place,[234] employing a chief mechanic, Edward "Spider" Huff, along with a draftsman. After a while, Cooper and Ford decided they needed another mechanic.[235] Cooper suggested Oldfield as a man who lived for speed.[236] He wrote a letter to invite his friend in Salt Lake City.

In late September, Oldfield hired into the Cooper-Ford Racing Team.[237] He found the racecars so stripped to save weight that he complained they looked like ugly bed frames on wheels. Cooper explained that they were built for function, not looks. Each auto had four cylinders with cast-iron cylinder walls. One, 999, was painted red.[238] The other, dubbed "the Arrow," was yellow and had a round steering wheel.[239] Cooper and Ford entered 999 in the Grosse Pointe track's five-mile Manufacturers' Challenge Cup against Winton.[240]

After Cooper drove practice laps at Grosse Pointe, Ford told Cooper, Spider Huff, and Oldfield that he was discouraged with 999's engine, and he declined to have his name associated with what he saw as a probable failure.[241] Ford, thirty-nine, may have been looking for an excuse to quit because his wife, Clara, detested Cooper's prowling nightclubs and roadhouses accompanied by women. On October 13, Cooper bought out Ford's interest in the business and both autos for $800.[242]

The day before, Cooper and Spider Huff took turns doing practice laps and complained that 999's steering bar was strenuous to handle. Cooper grumbled that at top speed 999 could be death on wheels.[243] Oldfield asked for a turn—likely his first opportunity to drive a four-wheeler.[244] Cooper warned that he could break his neck.[245] Oldfield retorted, with characteristic bravado, that it would be his own neck and he had not come from Salt Lake City just to squirt an oilcan.[246] He tore around the mile-long oval in the fastest time, 1 minute 6 seconds. Cooper was impressed with his friend's skill at sliding through the turns without crashing into the stout wooden fence bordering the track.[247] He and Huff agreed that Oldfield would drive.[248]

On a cold and cloudy Saturday afternoon race day, October 25, 1902, Cooper had been registered to drive in the Manufacturers' Challenge Cup race, but he gave up his seat for Oldfield.[249] Barney Oldfield buttoned up his jacket, stepped into 999's bucket seat, fastened goggles over his eyes, and gripped the steering bar.

The contest, the fifth on a card of six, pitted 999 against three cars, all made in Cleveland. The event also tested gas-combustion engines against steam power. One entrant was a Geneva Steamer. With four black boilers and a tall exhaust stack, it resembled a small locomotive. Trackside wagers favored the Geneva Steamer to defeat the admired Alexander Winton, who was driving his Bullet.[250] A second Bullet, dubbed "Pup," was driven by Charles B. Shank of Cleveland. The fourth entry was Thomas White in his White Steamer.

Rolling up the straight toward the grandstand, Oldfield joined them. His opponents may have disregarded him as a country rube. They were unaware he was a veteran of hundreds of starts. Oldfield focused on getting 999 to the first turn as though it were his final destination. The wheels of 999 skidded around the turn, throwing up a dirt shroud. He never let up on the gas and lapped the Geneva Steamer, then the White Steamer, and finally Shanks in the Winton "Pup." In the last mile, Alexander Winton pulled out with engine trouble.

As soon as Oldfield stopped in front of the grandstand, he "was carried from his machine to the judges' stand on the shoulders of admirers who rushed on the track by hundreds," reported the *Cleveland Plain Dealer*.[251] It pronounced the contest "the most exciting event at the Grosse Pointe automobile races today."

Henry Ford watched from the grandstand.[252] When Oldfield returned to 999, still parked on the horse track by the grandstand, Ford marched over and congratulated him and Cooper. Ford, bundled in an overcoat and a bowler, posed with Oldfield in his bucket seat for a photograph.[253] Then Ford left to call on newspaper offices and claim credit as 999's designer. This publicity helped secure him financial backing to found the present-day Ford Motor Company.

Oldfield would comment in later interviews that he reaped more press for that victory than he did over his entire eight-year cycling career. He and Cooper bounced on trains around southern Michigan to drum up attention for five-mile auto races on horse tracks—Oldfield in 999 against Cooper at the wheel of the Arrow, repainted red and renamed Red Devil.[254] These were some of the first auto races people in Michigan ever saw.

Barney Oldfield, left, on 999, the racecar designed by Henry Ford, standing. Oldfield and Champion shared a friendly rivalry about driving the fastest mile around a track. *From the collections of The Henry Ford.*

Oldfield's Memorial Day triumph at the Empire City Race Track thrilled Carl Graham Fisher in Indianapolis. Since Fisher had purchased an Orient motor-trike at the 1900 auto show in Madison Square Garden, he had converted his downtown bicycle shop into an auto dealership,[255] the city's first. In addition, he had begun to organize races. On June 20, 1903, he held a program sanctioned by the AAA at the Indiana State Fairgrounds, near the state capitol.[256] He served up three preliminaries and featured a five-mile match race, best of three, between Oldfield and Cooper.[257] Fisher offered $1,000 to the winner plus a $250 bonus to break the minute for a mile.[258] The sunny Saturday drew five thousand people. Society notables swanned in the box seats. Mayor Bookwaiter officiated as a timer with two civic leaders lending gravitas to record authenticity.

The occasion represented a career highlight for twenty-nine-year-old Fisher. As a child half-blind with an astigmatism,[259] he had stumbled and fell so often that other kids called him "Crip," for cripple.[260] Unable to see writing on the chalkboard, he was the class dunce until one day at age twelve he stormed away from school for good. He took a job as a vendor on inter-city trains,[261] walking the aisles brandishing a wooden tray—supported by a leather strap around his neck—to hawk peanuts, magazines, and books. The enterprise nurtured salesmanship. Eventually, he visited an eye doctor. The fuzzy world Fisher grew up in finally sharpened into focus with his prescription pince-nez. By seventeen in 1891 he opened a bicycle repair shop.[262] He exerted considerable energy in building his business, and also to campaign for Indianapolis to become synonymous with auto racing.

Now, on that June race day, Fisher ordered Cooper to drive slowly away from the grandstand, and after the car rounded turn two, Fisher barked to Oldfield in his famous Ford to cruise to the line in front of the grandstand. Once the cars were a half-mile apart, Fisher waved the green flag.[263]

Mayor Bookwaiter and other timers in the judges' stand on the infield by the finish line gripped a stopwatch in each hand—one for each driver. For the next five minutes, spectators practically held their breath, expecting at any moment that a driver might crash into eternity.

Cooper's Red Devil clocked the faster first mile,[264] at 1 minute 4 seconds. But Oldfield sped up and won by a tight seven-second margin.[265]

The second match made motorsport history. "Oldfield's machine was fairly flying through the air," reported *Automobile*. "He rounded the turns with a recklessness which did not characterize the driving of Cooper."[266]

Oldfield's 999 sprinted through the first mile in 59-3/5 seconds—clipping two seconds from his world record.[267] The judges announced the news to the grandstand.

"Every eye was on Oldfield, for the crowd felt that indescribable thrill of anticipation that another world's record was to be broken before the race was ended," noted *Automobile*.[268]

He burst across the finish of the clay oval in a new five-mile world record, 5 minutes 4-3/5 seconds.

"Hundreds of spectators left their places in the boxes and rushed to the track, where they surrounded Oldfield and overwhelmed him with congratulations," said *Automobile*. "Then the champion, who had surpassed himself, was led to the judges' stand and introduced to the crowd. Hats were thrown in the air and the fairgrounds echoed and re-echoed with cheers for Oldfield. Then Cooper was introduced and greeted warmly for his part in the race."[269]

Oldfield became America's first man to drive a gas-powered auto a mile around an elliptical track faster than a minute. He had changed car racing forever.

With that race and Oldfield's record, Fisher's Indianapolis starred on the map as a motor city.

Champion continued practicing laps on his Gladiator in Charles River Park until he could follow the pole line at 60 mph all the way around and hold it, lap after lap. At last, he arranged for an exhibition. He engaged the requisite official timers and alerted Boston's Newspaper Row, along Washington Street, that he would drive the mile in under a minute.[270]

John J. Donovan of the *Globe* assigned a photographer to stage the Frenchman on his Gladiator in Charles River Park.

When the Charles River Park held the matinee races, Elise sat among the unusually small crowd in the searing heat (multitudes had escaped for the cool Atlantic beach). Albert, a chauvinist, as a rule prohibited her from watching him race, concerned that he might get entangled in a horrific crash, an occupational hazard. He was more lenient when his solo effort gave him more control. "When running against time, I always feel safer—perhaps because I am an experienced mechanician and have confidence in my skill as a driver," he explained.[271]

Such a severe heat wave gripped the Northeast on Sunday, July 12, that the *Globe* would run the headline, "Many Died from Fearful Heat."[272]

Thus, Elise joined the audience witnessing a closely contested fifteen-mile motor-pace race in which national champion Bobby Walthour of Atlanta fought off challenges from Basil De Guichard and two Americans. Twenty-five amateurs battled in a ten-mile open. Between the events, Albert roared onto the boards.

On July 12, 1903,
Albert Champion
drove a mile on the
Clément Gladiator
motorcycle he had
imported from Paris in
58-4/5 seconds—the
first-ever mile in less
than a minute on a
motorcycle—around
a board cycling
track in Cambridge,
Massachusetts, on
what is now part
of the MIT campus.
*Photo by Elmer
Chickering. Courtesy
of Cherie Champion.*

Contrary to the staged photo published on page one in the next day's *Globe*, he wore a leather winter hat with earflaps. Only those fanning themselves for relief under the slanting stadium roof and in the exposed cheap bleacher seats in the blazing sun saw that Albert was attired in heavy corduroy trousers. He had pulled on so many wool sweaters that he looked like the Michelin man.

Hundreds of faces swiveled as one to watch Champion zoom around the velodrome to build speed, wheels tight on the black pole line for one lap. Two laps. The next time around, he nodded to the starter, standing like a sentry by the start/finish line in front of the grandstand.[273] A pistol fired. Champion set off on his wild ride.

Boston society photographer Elmer Chickering sensed history in the making and had set up his tripod and camera on the infield of the finishing straight to capture Champion at full speed.

Donovan wrote in the *Globe*:

> Lying flat on the long racing machine, as not to offer any resistance to the wind as he cut through the air, he was a picture of dare-devil nerve. He shot down the stretch and hit the first turn. True to his training as a motorcyclist, and the good lines of the track, he shot over so far that his body was in a horizontal position as he whizzed around the steep bank.
>
> Spectators held their breath and many persons on the front row drew back and did not lean over the edge of the railing as they have in the past at races. With a master touch he steered the machine, which was moving like a projectile. He followed the pole line as if he was glued to it, and even on the steep banks did not deviate more than a few inches from it. His control was magnificent, and experts saw that he was out to get a record.
>
> Lap after lap he shot around the track while women turned their heads away and more than one man got nervous. It was all over very quickly, for the gun was fired for the finish and the chronograph club, the timers' organization, announced that the Gaul had covered the distance in 58-4/5 s.[274]

Champion, first in America to drive a motorcycle under a minute for the mile, now boasted that he would beat Oldfield's world record.[275]

Days later, Champion was in Washington, DC, guiding his Gladiator to pace George Leander, a strapping six-foot rookie pro from Chicago, in a sunrise workout on the boards of the Coliseum on Capitol Hill.[276] They peeled off five fast miles and left the track to allow three other teams to prep for that evening's race. Champion leaned his motorcycle against a line of boxes on the south side of the track and went with Leander to the training quarters for their rubdown.[277]

Next to practice on the track was national champion Bobby Walthour. His pace driver had not arrived, so, alone, he pedaled some laps, then stopped to sit on a box next to Champion's motorcycle. Waiting for his pacer, Walthour grew impatient. Bored, he jumped on Champion's motorcycle, turned the speed lever, and zoomed away at a swift clip.

Champion heard the *choooo*-ing of his motorcycle tires on the boards and hurried, half dressed, from the training quarters.[278] As Walthour flew by, Champion shouted at him to stop.[279]

"Walthour laughed at the fiery Frenchman and, believing that he was the master of the machine, he turned on more speed, and the big single went around the bowl at a gait that made Walthour look like a squirrel in a cage," reported *Bicycling World*.[280]

Others joined Champion in yelling at Walthour. Everyone realized the star from Atlanta was going too fast. Walthour became conscious that he had no idea how to slow or stop the machine. The lever he thought controlled the speed failed to respond to his touch. Laps flew by before Champion and bystanders comprehended that Walthour was hanging on for his life.

"Hold on tight!" Champion hollered as Walthour went by, blond hair flying in the wind.[281]

Champion ran back to the training quarters and grabbed a pacing motorcycle that was ready. He was bare-chested as he hurried that machine onto the track and chased. His Gladiator had gas to keep going until Walthour became dizzy and fell. Champion wanted to prevent him from getting hurt, and he also wanted to protect his motorcycle.

Around went Walthour, gone pale with fear, followed by Champion, grim and determined as he gauged the speed of both motorcycles. Champion accelerated to close the gap separating him from Walthour. After circling the velodrome, Albert pulled up alongside Bobby. They rode side by side for some laps[282] before Albert dared to get close enough down a straight to lean over and press the correct lever of the motorcycle Bobby rode.[283] At once the roar of the motor quieted, grew more and more subdued, and after a half-dozen laps the Gladiator coasted to a safe stop.[284] Walthour was helped off. He declared he was finished driving motorcycles.

Witnesses congratulated Champion for averting disaster and demonstrating presence of mind and courage.[285] Bobby admitted he was nervous, on the verge of being rattled, until Albert pulled up to rescue him.

Champion, quick-tempered as usual, grew disgusted with motor-pacer colleagues he saw riding with caution rather than daring. He returned to the Eastern Seaboard circuit with his resolute confidence and paced in the slipstream behind George Leander driving an Orient Motorcycle. There, Champion won six out of eight events.[286] Three times he defeated the ginger-haired Bobby Walthour,[287] distinguished by the national champion's stars and stripes tied around his waist. Albert admired Bobby as America's greatest talent. He told Bobby, "I will race you any time for fun, money, or marbles but I am going to beat you and beat you badly."[288]

He may have stayed longer on the circuit to race Walthour more, but something else changed his mind. On July 26 Barney Oldfield created national news on the Empire City Race Track. Oldfield opened an afternoon program early with a one-mile time trial in 999 to take advantage of the day's smoothest turf surface. "He cut the corners so closely that at each turn his rear wheels skidded across the track, throwing up great clouds of dust, and it looked from the stand as if he surely would overturn," observed the *New York Times*.[289] "But no accident occurred and he came down the home stretch with such a burst of speed that a cry of 'Record! Record!' went up from the spectators."[290]

Oldfield scored a new record: 55-4/5 seconds, a new hallmark speed of 65 mph. The *New York Times* called him America's automobile racing champion.[291] Champion felt the compulsion to drive his motorcycle faster than Oldfield's record.

Some Charles River Park programs were fundraisers to raise money for the purchase of a gravestone for Harry Elkes. For the September 3 Harry Elkes Memorial Meet, several marquee names had signed contracts to compete but cancelled to take better offers. Albert Champion purchased new batteries for his Gladiator and skipped a couple of meals while he tuned up his engine and readied his motorcycle.[292]

John J. Donovan of the *Globe* informed him that many of the fifteen thousand spectators attending that Thursday afternoon program were saying that on his own Albert could not do anything remarkable.[293] That galvanized the Frenchman. He stood on the start-finish line and spoke through a megaphone: "I am going to try, and try hard. I am here for business, and I intend to do as I always do, whether in a race or not—do the best I can and risk my neck to the limit in order to get the best results."[294]

The audience watched him swing a leg over his Gladiator. Fifteen thousand heads turned as one to follow his preliminary laps before he turned the machine loose. Only his percussive engine broke the silence. Everyone saw him whirl around the banks, entering and leaving each turn at the same angle, to shoot down the straights.

He felt his tires slip on the pole line as the Back Bay mist made the boards damp.[295] But he kept in control and whizzed through five laps.

When his time was announced, the crowd cheered so loud that voices echoed. Fifty-six seconds flat.[296]

"Albert Champion Cuts His Record on a Motor Cycle," declared the *Globe*.[297]

The meet receipts totaled $772.[298] The summer-long fund raising bought a headstone carved with Harry D. Elkes's name arcing over a winged wheel for his grave in Syracuse.[299]

On Monday, September 7, Champion participated in the Charles River Park motorpacing season finale. Despite a damp, chilly afternoon, all the seats and the infield were filled. Champion dominated a twenty-mile motor-paced race against two adversaries.[300] Then everyone watched him dismount his Orient bicycle and hop onto the Gladiator to drive an exhibition.

Moisture in the air interfered with the carburetor's vaporized fuel-air mixture for combustion, causing his engine to misfire.[301] Nevertheless, he managed fifty-six seconds flat.

Champion adjusted the carburetor.[302] It was late afternoon. The slanting sun cast long, exaggerated shadows for his last chance for the season to beat Oldfield's record.

"Like a meteor, he dashed around the track, the motor throwing out sparks, and with the lights and shadows playing on the 'speed demon' it was a picture spectacular enough to hold the most blasé case of 'speeditis' enthralled," John J. Donovan told *Globe* readers. "A mighty cheer greeted Champion at the finish, the vast crowd finding a vent for its pent-up feelings."[303]

Champion leaned low and aerodynamic as he steered his motorcycle to lower his world-record time for the mile to fifty-six seconds flat, again on the board track in Cambridge, witnessed by fifteen thousand spectators. *From the* Boston Globe, *1903.*

Champion drove the mile in 55-2/5 seconds.[304]

He had eclipsed Oldfield's latest mark by two-fifths of a second. The Frenchman was now the fastest driver in America around a circular track, on two wheels or four.

The automobile trade press buzzed about a French engineer at the Packard Motor Company in Warren, Ohio, renowned for high-priced luxury cars. The engineer had designed a one-off racecar, the Gray Wolf.[305] It was so sleek and close to the ground that it looked fast even when it was parked. The front tapered to a slim nose like its furry four-legged namesake. Packard's new general manager, Henry Joy, a Detroit businessman, was shaking things up. He had formed a group of investors that purchased the company from the founder, James Ward Packard. Henry Joy hired the French designer and commissioned the Gray Wolf as a gift to the eponymous Packard before moving the enterprise into a modern factory in Detroit.

Champion received a cable inviting him to meet Packard sales manager Sidney Waldon, contract driver Harry Cunningham, and a couple of mechanics a few days before auto races on the mile-long Brighton Beach horse track in Brooklyn.[306] Waldon and Cunningham wanted to discuss his possible role as Cunningham's backup for the Gray Wolf.[307] But first Champion was to face off with Walthour in Atlanta for the US national motorpace championship.

8

"NEARLY KILLED
AT BRIGHTON!"

RACING OBVIOUSLY IS MADNESS.
—GRIFFITH BORGESON,
*THE GOLDEN AGE OF THE
AMERICAN RACING CAR*[1]

Bobby Walthour, winner of thirty-seven motorpace races over the 1903 season, ranked at the top of some twenty-five professional motor-pacers.[2] The northeastern press gushed about the Georgian and had dubbed him the "Dixie Flier." By early September, he had claimed his second national pace title and returned home to Atlanta. Champion had competed in only eight races, with six wins. He claimed that by defeating Walthour three times, he considered himself to be national champion. Nevertheless, the governing body and a promoter in Atlanta decreed that Champion and Walthour must battle on Thursday, September 17, in a best-of-three series of five-mile matches to settle the American national paced title.[3]

This Atlanta event was to be held at the Piedmont Coliseum, built by Jack Prince,[4] a bantam-sized English expat with a squeaky yet loud voice that could cut through the din of any crowd like a saber.[5] Forty-two-year-old Prince at all times presented himself freshly barbered, in a suit with a diamond pin winking in his cravat, the ends of his bushy mustache waxed, and he donned a bowler before he stepped outside. He was known for courtly Victorian manners,[6] and answered to Jack. He had been England's national champion in the 1880s on high-wheelers with hard-rubber tires.[7] When safety bicycles became available with pneumatics in the early 1890s, he was racing in Boston. Prince valued the new tires, inflated to high pressure, for their easy rolling along a hardwood surface, like bowling balls down an alley. This motivated him to launch a new career constructing board-cycling tracks that were banked and lightning fast.[8]

A self-taught engineer, Jack Prince built his tracks without a blueprint to safeguard anyone usurping his franchise. Instead, he carried in his head the exact number of ten-penny nails and two-inch-wide boards needed to construct his ovals,[9] complete with seating for thirty-five hundred to twelve thousand spectators, depending on the local population. He hired carpenters by the dozens and directed them early in the week to complete the tracks in just five days so he could fire the start gun for races on Saturdays. He kept on the move through the 1890s, erecting coliseums, as he called them,[10] from Havana to Omaha, and from Philadelphia to Los Angeles. Atlanta's Piedmont Coliseum, ten laps to the mile, provided triple-pivot banking through the curved turns, forty-eight degrees at the top and sloping down to fifteen degrees on the straights. Prince drummed up press coverage by handing out bottles of four-star brandy or boxes of cigars to reporters to get their attention before selling them on the entertainment value of his upcoming program.

Prince hustled across Atlanta to sign Bobby Walthour to a contract. Bobby was a dream star—his name sold tickets and filled the stands. Walthour was born on New Year's Day of 1878, four months Champion's senior. The Walthour family had been well off, but lost everything in the Civil War, a predicament common across the South. Bobby's grandfather, George Washington Walthour, had owned a sprawling cotton plantation and slaves.[11] The plantation lent its name to Walthourville, near Savannah. Bobby's father, William Walthour, was a lawyer in 1861 when Georgia and ten other states withdrew from the Union over the issue of slavery and formed the Confederate States of America.[12] William joined the Confederate Army as an officer. He suffered a serious neck wound during a battle and bore permanent scars.[13] His house was burned to the ground by Union general William Sherman's troops on their march to destroy everything in their path from Atlanta to Savannah. After the Confederacy surrendered in 1865, the state government seized the Walthour property for back taxes.[14]

Bobby and twin brother James were the ninth and tenth sons of William Walthour, who died when the twins were twelve. Four years afterward, the boys moved to Atlanta to work full-time as couriers for an older brother's bicycle shop. Bobby started racing at seventeen.

The sport's fervent expansion had taken Bobby around Georgia. At eighteen he was five feet ten and 155 pounds with striking blue eyes.[15] He had turned pro and joined the Southern Circuit on coliseums built by Jack Prince in Memphis, Nashville, Chattanooga, Birmingham, and Montgomery. Racing also had taken Bobby north to Michigan, Illinois, and Wisconsin, then east. Experience with packs of riders bumping shoulders and throwing elbows and knees for better position had toughened him and taught him tactics. Every time he had crashed, which was often, he got up and charged right back into the action. What kept him going was pocketing decent prize money. The amounts grew bigger after he won the 1901 Madison Square Garden six-day partnered with Canadian Archie MacEachern. The next year he took up motorpace races, and he eventually dethroned the formidable Harry Elkes.

Wherever Bobby traveled, he still called Atlanta his home. He was Georgia's first national-class sports hero. Fellow Georgian Ty Cobb was eight years younger and just entering baseball, and Bobby Jones was too young yet to swing a golf club. Walthour's triumphs raised the morale of Georgians, recovering from what they referred to as the "War against Northern Aggression."

Yet another incentive kept Bobby racing to win. At nineteen in 1897, he had eloped with his fifteen-year-old fiancée, Blanche Cooledge.[16] They had pedaled a tandem to a justice of the peace in suburban Decatur. Now Bobby and his wife had two daughters and a son.

Prince also considered Albert Champion a big star. Prince climbed aboard a train to Boston to sign up the Frenchman. The $1,000 purse meant the winner would have a $600 payday and a new American flag to tie around his waist for the next season's races. Like the previous year, when Albert and Bobby contested the championship, controversy swirled over whether a foreign rider could claim the American title. That heightened the pressure on Bobby.

Atlanta, Georgia's largest city and the state capital, was home to 90,000 residents,[17] as well as Coca-Cola, which was sold nationwide. Champion considered the Dixie Flyer his only worthy American rival and had agreed with Prince to climb aboard a train and travel 1,100 miles to Atlanta to race against him in the season finale. Prince knew Bobby was fast, and that he would force Albert to ride his best. They would compete in Bobby's home town.

A week before the match, Champion boarded a train from Boston with a sleeping car for the thirty-hour trip to Atlanta. He joined Jack Prince and Jed Newkirk, whom Champion had hired to drive his Orient pacing motorcycle around the Piedmont Coliseum. Newkirk, a twenty-year-old of medium height, clean-shaven, with dark hair, had showed potential as a sprinter but had switched to driving the motors for more money. Albert christened his motorcycle "Fleur de Lis."[18] The machine had long handlebars sweeping back so Newkirk could hunker down over the rear wheel to shield Albert.

The *Atlanta Journal*'s sports writer, Grantland Rice, announced Champion's arrival in the newspaper and called him the "Demon Devil" for his recent motorcycle records.[19] Rice had graduated Phi Beta Kappa from Vanderbilt University with a degree in Greek and Latin.[20] He coined immortal designations that contributed to his ascending to the dean of America's sportswriters. He would nickname Notre Dame's football backfield the Four Horsemen of the Apocalypse[21] and refer to the sensational University of Illinois running back Harold "Red" Grange as the Galloping Ghost of the Gridiron.[22] Rice captured the excitement he felt watching Champion take risks at speed behind motor-pacers by calling the Frenchman a "Dare-Devil."

Walthour's former pacing motorcycle, Candy, had burned up in a crash on the Revere track in Boston, after gasoline spilled and caught fire from sparks flickering out the exhaust pipe. The Dixie Flyer had purchased a replacement, which he named "Candy Junior." Driving it was Gussie Lawson, an eighteen-year-old Swedish immigrant out of Chicago. Lawson's deft handling of the hulking machines, with their noisy, temperamental engines, around triple-pivot banked turns while sheltering his cyclist put him in demand as a master motorman.[23] Attired in a leather jacket, pants, football helmet, and boots, he proved an original advocate of motorcycle leathers.[24]

The new pacing machines were equipped with special roller bars fastened to a bracket hanging over the back of the rear tire.[25] When the cyclist's front tire touched the roller bar, the roller turned to serve as a light brake for the bicycle. This simple device could have prevented Champion's tragic accident on Memorial Day 1900 in Waltham.

Every day leading up to the Thursday evening race, Grantland Rice wrote stories promoting the match. Champion had departed Boston with a new portrait photo by Elmer Chickering. The Frenchman's photo showed him in a suit, tattersall vest, and tie like a society figure. On the day before the match race,

Rice splashed Champion's visage across the *Atlanta Journal*'s sports page. The headline proclaimed: "Cycle Kings to Settle Title."[26]

The sports writer told readers that "in Albert Champion there could not possibly be a better rider to meet Bobby Walthour." He added:

> It is Champion who has proven the hard nut for the cracks to go against last year, and this season he seems to have at times speed and endurance beyond conception, and when it looks as if he has been ridden off his feet he comes back so strong that he wins. As a pace follower he is the equal of any rider in this country, and in Champion Walthour meets the only rider in the game he really fears. It is a well known fact that Walthour is more afraid of Champion than he was of Harry Elkes or any other rider who follows pace.[27]

Ticket sales were brisk for the Piedmont Coliseum, within sight of Atlanta's skyline. On the evening of the race, Champion pulled on his white jersey, the *maillot blanc* of the Paris city champion, a *beau geste* lost on Rice, who complained he looked plain. "Walthour, on the contrary, was decked out with the American flag like a Labor Day float."[28]

More than four thousand men, women, and children filled the Piedmont Coliseum to capacity. The building had poor ventilation and right away filled with a gray tobacco cloud. Smoky halos glowed from incandescent light bulbs hanging from the curved ceiling. Yet nothing distracted the raucous audience, excited to cheer its hometown hero in his battle against the Frenchman.

Jack Prince stood in the infield near the band and the cyclists and their motorcycle drivers. At seven o'clock sharp, he waved both arms to get everyone's attention and the band stopped playing "Dixie." He raised the megaphone—nearly as long as he was tall—to his lips. His Queen's English sounded quaint to the audience accustomed to a Southern drawl as he boomed out Albert Champion's introduction.

Without delay, Albert spun onto the track. The audience gave him a standing ovation for his lap of honor. He waved and flashed his showboater smile. When he stopped on the start/finish line, a woman handed him a wreath of flowers.[29] He looked bashful and took the wreath into the sawdust arena and set it on his bicycle crate.

Prince's attempt to introduce Bobby was drowned out by the mass of admirers. Bobby rolled onto the track, an arm wrapped in bandages from a recent spill.[30] The partisan audience rocked the building with applause.

Next the pace drivers, Jed Newkirk and Gussie Lawson, thrilled the audience on their lap by revving their noisy engines, unrestrained by mufflers.

Only when the two teams lined up at the start/finish line did the spectators hush. Prince hoisted his megaphone to announce that Champion had insisted on following the National Cycling Association rules. That meant that after the riders had completed the first mile, no accident or mechanical failure could suspend the race, unlike the coliseum's house rule that an accident at any time meant a restart.

Then Prince, his bowler askew, fired the starting gun. The throng yelled and stomped. Near the end of the first mile, Champion's front tire tore away from the wheel and threw him onto the track at 40 mph.[31] He slid down into sawdust. He hopped back up, slapped sawdust off, ignored a bleeding cut on his forearm, and got back on his bike for the restart.

When they set off again, Walthour dashed ahead and gained one-third of a lap. For a mile, Champion held him even, then closed the gap to catch Walthour in the fourth mile.

"It was an anxious moment for the thousands of Walthourites on the seats, although the performance of the game foreigner was applauded," Rice reported. "Perhaps Walthour took the applause to himself. At any rate, he let out a kink in his legs and slowly took the lead again, getting in forty yards to the good in a last mile that made the pacing machines grunt like razor-back hogs with the hounds after them."[32]

To the foot stamping and yelling that made the coliseum walls vibrate, Walthour won the first match, in 7 minutes and 25 seconds, an average of 40 mph.

In the second match, Albert and Bobby rode shoulder to shoulder for two miles, their backs low, shoulders steady, legs spinning in a fluid motion so close to the roller bars of their motorcycle pacers they looked attached. Both teams swooped up and down the banking to get an advantage. The Frenchman yelled at his driver to speed up. Newkirk obliged and Champion followed Fleur de Lis as they pulled ahead.

"At the end of the third mile, Jed Newkirk's chariot of fire was close upon

Bobby's hind wheel and it looked surely as if Bobby was going to be lapped," recounted Grantland Rice.[33]

Gussie Lawson gave Candy Junior more gas. The audience leaped up in unison as Walthour pedaled smoothly to circle around behind Champion and make the race even.

"But the lilies of France were destined to whither," wrote Rice. "Bobby ruthlessly mowed them down, winning by a much narrower margin than the first heat."[34]

Bobby won by fifty yards. He crossed the line in 7 minutes 17 seconds, breaking his own coliseum record by three seconds and clocking 41 mph. He captured the match in two straight victories to win his second national motorpace title and once again fend off the foreigner.

Over the line, Bobby slowed down and Albert pulled alongside. "The Frenchman reached out and gave the American a hearty handshake, congratulating him on his victory," a reporter for the *Atlanta Constitution* observed.[35] "The act did not escape the spectators. Immediately Champion was greeted with a hearty round of applause. He had shown by his action that he was a true sportsman and the crowd showed its appreciation."

Jack Prince took in the boisterous scene—everyone standing and yelling, men throwing hats in the air, women waving white handkerchiefs, people hugging one another. Putting on more matches would be like printing money. He moved his show to the Savannah Coliseum for another race.

The act could have lasted longer. However, Albert, seeking a new route to glory, chose to debut as a car racer up north in Brighton Beach, Brooklyn.

Champion ventured by train in late October to Brooklyn, at the southwest end of Long Island, and its Brighton Beach resort on Sheepshead Bay. The resort boasted of a lavish hotel and a horse track with a mammoth stadium. The Long Island Automobile Club was holding its second annual racing program, which drew American drivers and cars like Packard and Cadillac as well as a French contingent including Renault, De Dion, and Darracq.

Champion had been invited to Brighton Beach by officials of the Packard Motor Car Company, who had wooed him to drive their first-of-its-kind racecar, the Packard Gray Wolf.[36] The company's general manager, Henry Bourne Joy, sought Champion for his star power, the cachet of his name, and his audacity to drive a motorcycle faster than the mark of Barney Oldfield with 999. Oldfield now was employed by Alexander Winton to drive Bullet II.[37] Henry Joy wanted a standout name associated with the Gray Wolf, and he picked Champion.

Albert strolled to the track's stadium and mingled among mechanics, with grease to their elbows, who were working on parked racecars, preening owners, swanning drivers, and loitering reporters. Everyone was eager to shake his hand and praise his motorcycle record. He had the opportunity to speak French with youthful compatriot Marius G. Bernin, a wiry athlete who would drive a Renault to three victories on race day and turn into the star. A photographer for *Automobile* posed Champion, looking pensive in a tie and bulky sweater, his cap pulled snug to keep offshore gusts from blowing it away.

Champion easily found the Packard Gray Wolf, on display for public inspection under the grandstand. The Gray Wolf, having been cited in trade journals, was causing a stir. Most auto chiefs marshaled their limited resources to build passenger roadsters with lackluster names for the consumer market. Only a small number felt obliged to turn out a singular racing car that broadcast blazing swiftness. Alexander Winton produced Bullets. Henry Ford had his 999. Ransom Olds called his racecar "the Pirate." Walter C. Baker created the electric Torpedo Kid. James Ward Packard wanted a fast car to grab attention for his Ohio Automobile Company of Warren, Ohio. It produced a limited number of pricey Packard models named methodically from the alphabet.

The Gray Wolf was the first car built by the company for the sole purpose of speed. Trade journals had introduced it in photos taken back on September 5 at the Cleveland race meet. Its designer, Frenchman Charles Schmidt, sat on the bucket seat. He gripped the steering wheel and peered over the body, crouching like the vehicle was impatient to spring.

Schmidt was small and trim like a gymnast, with a clipped mustache and intense dark eyes. He had graduated from the École des Arts et Métiers in Angers and had worked in the late 1890s for Mors automobiles in Paris.[38] He had a hand in designing Mors cars, which he drove in races. In 1901 he had immigrated to the United States to apply his talents at the Mors factory in Brooklyn. He was a supervisor and came to the attention of Henry Joy,[39] then shopping for talent.

Henry Bourne Joy had bought a Packard Model C in 1901 on a visit to the New York auto show. Impressed with the car's reliability, he took a train to Warren, in northeast Ohio, near Youngstown, and suggested that James Ward Packard make more of his luxury cars. While popular Oldsmobile Runabouts cost $650, Packard autos started at $2,600. They had gained a following among the wealthy. Packard told Henry Joy that boosting output required greater capital. Joy, a slim, aristocratic Yale man, looked through his pince-nez and saw his future.

Henry Joy, thirty-eight, a year younger than Packard, had come prepared to deal. He was born into one of Detroit's wealthiest and most socially-connected families, the son of a railroad magnate.[40] In early 1902 Joy formed a group of investors. The investment group pumped money into the Ohio Automobile Company and took over majority ownership. One of the first things Joy did was recruit Schmidt in April 1902 as his handpicked chief engineer to design a fast car for James Ward Packard. In October the investors renamed the business the Packard Motor Company.[41] The eponymous James Ward Packard continued with the title of president while Joy, as general manager, called all the shots and planned to move everything to Detroit.

Manufacturing racing autos was in its infancy. That original generation was all about speed. Racing tested designs and materials, and pushing the limits of man and machine made for good advertising. Like Ford's 999, early racing cars allowed the driver to step into the side or rear, drop onto the bucket seat, and stretch his legs out—like sitting in a kayak—to set a foot on the gas or brake pedals. Drivers were on their own to make the vehicle hold the turns around fairground tracks and reach the finish line. Nobody considered the advantage of a windshield, a roll bar to protect the driver in case the car flipped over, or a seat belt. Safety protections came much later, always in response to deaths from horrific accidents.

In 1903 Schmidt, a fanatic about saving weight, built the Gray Wolf's frame with light pressed steel instead of the standard steel-plate-and-wood construction.[42] He deployed the minimum of aluminum required for the chassis and the hood, painted gray, to cover the engine like a skin. Its wheels were weight-saving wire rather than wooden-artillery wheels.[43] The rear wheels were equipped with drum brakes. The Gray Wolf's four-cylinder 25-hp engine and transmission, with two forward speeds and one for reverse, unleashed a ripping top end of 75 mph.

This machine cost $10,000—double Schmidt's salary.[44] The vehicle, loaded with a full six-gallon gas tank, water, and oil, tipped the scales at 1,310 pounds.[45] That saved almost a thousand pounds compared with a similar passenger car, the four-cylinder open Model K roadster, which Schmidt also designed in 1903. However, Henry Joy despised the Model K, one of the most expensive vehicles in America, as too complex. Almost immediately, Schmidt simplified it with the Model L, which was also pricey, but it proved a commercial success. Model L introduced a new design for the front water-cooled radiator, a headstone shape that became Packard's signature and endured for the rest of the company's life.[46]

Only Schmidt drove his Gray Wolf. At the early September meet in Cleveland when he had posed for photos in his car on the track, he drove practice laps. He had been going at least 40 mph when he veered into the bordering white picket fence,[47] tearing out twenty feet of pickets and a half-dozen posts before he was flipped out like a rag doll onto the grassy infield. He scrambled back up to his feet but complained of acute chest pain. Three ribs were cracked and the car's radiator was wrecked. The Gray Wolf failed to get to the start line that day. It was an ominous introduction.

Damages were soon repaired. However, sales manager Sidney Waldon realized Schmidt was too valuable a designer to lose in an accident and looked around for a contract driver. Waldon heard about Harry L. Cunningham, a Detroiter gaining a reputation as an expert racecar driver. Cunningham had schooled himself in techniques by listening to experienced veterans dispensing advice.[48] Slim with a thin face and a strong jaw line, he was suited for the Gray Wolf. Waldon tempted him away from driving 999 to take the wheel of the Gray Wolf for a meet three days later at the Grosse Pointe track. There Cunningham was driving the Gray Wolf on the inside lane alongside Oldfield, steering Winton's Bullet II, when Oldfield followed his custom of swinging wide on the outside bank and then attempted to crowd back onto the inside lane. Cunningham held his place and kept ahead of hard-charging Oldfield.[49] Cunningham earned glowing press for fending off the intimidating Oldfield.

However, in another event that day, the Gray Wolf blew a tire coming out of a turn. The car crashed through the inside fence, breaking off a front wheel. Cunningham came through unscathed. He estimated the car's weight was balanced on the right side,[50] the driver's side.

When Schmidt first learned Cunningham was contracted to drive, he declared his ribs had improved and took the Gray Wolf to a program at Narragansett, Rhode Island. Schmidt placed in the money in a couple races and won the five-mile time trial.

At the following meet on the Empire City Race Track in Yonkers, sales manager Waldon showed up with Cunningham. Waldon tactfully suggested to Schmidt that with the company moving all the factory machinery and office furniture from Warren, Ohio, to a much bigger, modern factory on East Grand Boulevard in Detroit, the chief engineer might want to leave the racing to Cunningham. Schmidt acquiesced to relinquish the Gray Wolf only after Waldon reminded him that his office furniture was waiting for him that Saturday to unpack.[51]

When Schmidt at last had departed for Detroit, Waldon and Cunningham took the Gray Wolf with a couple mechanics to the concluding star event of the racing season, at Brighton Beach.

At the Brighton Beach stadium, amid the car-talk hubbub, Champion met Waldon, Cunningham, Packard mechanic Jack Lavin, and another mechanic called Densmore. Cunningham agreed to let Champion drive the car for practice as an emergency man in case Cunningham could not run it or if anything happened to him.[52]

"So on Thursday and Friday last we went down to Brighton Beach, and Champion drove the car, I should say, between forty and fifty miles, which is quite as much as I ever did with the same car," Cunningham said.[53] Such was typical training for the racing fraternity, accustomed to on-the-job learning.

The 1903 racing season's last hurrah, on Saturday, October 31, was chilly and overcast. A field of thirty-five contestants turned out with their support crews. Most of the thirty-five hundred men and women spectators, in long wool overcoats as protection against the raw offshore winds, arrived by train. Some three hundred drove autos and parked them in the paddock between the judges' stand and the grandstand. *Automobile* sniffed that "the football game between Columbia and Yale drew 30,000 people and kept thousands away from the automobile races without a doubt."[54]

Albert Champion at the wheel of the Packard Gray Wolf, shortly before his disastrous crash in a race that snapped his femur. *Photo from* Motor Age *magazine, October 1901.*

The program opened with a five-miler. Cunningham drove the Gray Wolf and discovered the track's back corners were mushy as oatmeal. Heavier cars navigated through the loose dirt, their tires sinking deeper to get a purchase on the hard surface beneath, but the lighter Gray Wolf slid.[55] He reported to Waldon and the mechanics that he regarded the turns as treacherous for his car, too light and too powerful for the turf's condition.

Cunningham said the rear-wheel disk brakes—the vehicle's only brakes— were dragging and asked the mechanics to loosen them. In the fifteen-mile free for all open to all weight classes, both brakes in the Gray Wolf failed by three miles.[56] The stationary rods connecting the brakes to the frame's rear end had dropped out and dangled under the car, making a noise that Cunningham heard over the unmuffled engine. For the next eleven miles, he drove defensively. He experimented with slowing the car around the back turns by shutting off the engine to coast through, then restarting the engine on the home straight. He still had a problem on the last turn's slight incline to the left.

Marius G. Bernin of France in his Renault lapped Cunningham twice en route to victory.

At fourteen miles, Cunningham coasted to a halt on the home straight. The Packard mechanics jogged out to push the Gray Wolf back to the paddock by the stadium. Cunningham climbed out and declared that he refused to drive the car any more on a course he considered hazardous.[57]

It was still early in the day. The Gray Wolf was registered for more events. Its race bib, a white cloth with the imperious number one painted broad and two feet tall, was tied to each side of the body for race officials, photographers, and spectators to spot. The Gray Wolf was still fueled up and ready to race.

"Thereupon Champion was asked to take the car," Cunningham said to *Automobile Topics Illustrated*. He cautioned: "'If you take it, Albert, be careful. Mind you, it has no brakes and you must not forget how to shut off the engine before making the ugly turn.' He answered me, as well as I can remember, 'I won't shut off the engine for any turns.' I said, 'All right. I have told you what to do. Jack Lavin and myself will go around to the turn to see you go through the fence.'"[58]

Champion was primed to drive. A perennial publicity hound, he took advantage of a photographer from *Motor Age* who was on the scene. He looked through goggles at the camera, which was placed in front of the car, on the driver's right side, capturing his white shirt and tie over the steering wheel, behind the number one.

In his new career debut, the ten-mile open for cars under 1,800 pounds, Champion placed third out of three entrants, averaging 50 mph.[59] The reporter for *Automobile* called him a clever and daring driver. "Given a heavier car he certainly would have starred in his first automobile race, as he was unafraid and sent the rakish little machine at the best speed its light weight would warrant, and he held the turns perfectly. Harry Cunningham, the regular driver of the same car, did not drive it nearly so fast."[60]

Next, in the five-mile open, awarding points toward the Manufacturers' Challenge Cup, Champion scored second place among four starters.[61]

Then he entered the unlimited Class A free-for-all pursuit race. It would change his life.

Champion and two opponents began at different positions on the oval and chased each other—the first to catch his opponents would win. His compatriot, Marius Bernin, in a Renault with a body that slanted elegantly down between the front wheels to slice through the air, began on the start/finish line as scratch. Frederic A. LaRoche, in a blunt-nosed, boxy Darracq, started from the quarter pole. Champion had the three-quarter pole. At the dropping of the green flag, all three roared away in pursuit of each other.

Champion flew through his first mile at 52 mph,[62] based on lap time. He was into the third turn when it happened.

The Gray Wolf turned sharply and plowed through the heavy timbers of the inside rail fence, demolishing them as though they were thin slats.[63] Two fence posts were ripped out; the middle board, twenty feet long, vanished.[64]

"Champion was moving at terrific speed," reported the New York Times.[65] "The wheels skidded and the car swerved and plunged through the fence on the inside of the track. Apparently Champion had his wits about him, for he ducked his head and threw up a protecting arm. The car cut through the fence, leaving the top rail intact. It turned over in the ditch next to the turf course, and Champion was thrown twenty feet."[66]

Later Champion told a New York Tribune reporter that he was still conscious when he landed on the infield grass but had no time to tuck into a ball to evade the onrushing Gray Wolf: "She roll over me and my legs go numb."[67]

He lost consciousness before Marius Bernin in his Renault blew past him and caught Frederic A. LaRoche in the Darracq on the home stretch to win. Bernin, unaware he had won, kept going and was forced to dodge the hundreds of spectators all of a sudden fleeing the grandstand, climbing over two fences, and running across the broad track toward the infield to reach Champion. An official waved the checkered flag at Bernin to signal the race was over. He drove straight to Champion's accident.

"It was with difficulty that the police could hold the crowd back while the doctors worked over the injured man," the *New York Tribune* reported.[68]

Cunningham and mechanic Jack Levin had watched on the back turns, the only eyewitnesses to the accident. They saw Champion struggle with the steering wheel to keep the car away from the fence, but the machine slid sideways through the fence into the infield.[69] They looked at the Gray Wolf stranded on the grass—its hood knocked cockeyed, the front wheels torn from their axles.

"Only the motor remained in perfect condition, and that was still working when Cunningham reached the car," noted the *Times*.[70]

Champion's right arm was lacerated and almost torn from its socket. Blood poured from a head gash. Worst of all, his left femur—the longest bone, the heaviest and the strongest in the human skeleton—was snapped in a jagged-edged compound fracture.[71] White broken bone shoved through bleeding flesh. Blood soaked his hip and both legs.[72] Physicians from among the spectators stanched the bleeding of his head and mangled leg flesh and fastened makeshift emergency splints on the broken leg. According to Cunningham, Champion was unconscious for twenty minutes.[73]

There was a delay getting a horse-drawn ambulance. "Finally one came from the Kings County Hospital, and before it arrived Champion had recovered consciousness, although he was in great agony," said the *Times*.[74]

While this drama unfolded, the next events were held. *Automobile* remarked: "Champion's accident, speaking in a cold-blooded way, was what they looked for. In Mexico, the people cheer the men for killing the bull or the bull for killing the man, and Americans are just as cold-blooded."[75]

Frederic A. LaRoche leaped from his Darracq on the turf near the stadium. He operated a business in New York importing Darracqs from Paris. He had won sixteen loving cup trophies over the season and asserted in high dudgeon to reporters that drivers should be trained to handle their vehicles before being allowed to race.

Automobile added, "Champion is king of the motorcycle riders with a record of :55 on a five-lap track to his credit, but there are yet many things for the great Champion to learn."[76]

Automobile Topics Illustrated took up Champion's defense, calling the accident "hard luck on poor Champion, holding himself in reserve all the season, when nervy racing men have been at a premium, and then at the eleventh hour to have his hopes and ambitions wrecked."[77]

Newspapers capitalized on his disaster for their Sunday editions, the week's highest daily circulation.

The *New York World* screamed, "Racing Autoist Nearly Killed at Brighton!"[78] A photo across the broadsheet showed the crippled Gray Wolf, surrounded by a scrum of journalists and race officials.

The *New York Times* declared, "Albert Champion Hurled from His Machine at Brighton Beach."[79]

The *Boston Globe* ran the Elmer Chickering society portrait of Champion on page one with a stack of staccato heads down the front: "Champion Hurt. Hurled from a Racing Motor Car. Going at Terrific Rate of Speed at Time. Vehicle Swerved, Going through Fence. Frenchman Seriously Injured on Arm, Head and Leg."[80]

The *Boston Herald* bellowed: "Champion in Smash."[81]

A furious Charles Schmidt ordered Waldon to return his Gray Wolf to Detroit for repair by Monday.[82]

Unlike the car, restored in a workday, Champion was fighting for his life. As soon as the ambulance took him to Kings County Hospital in Brooklyn, doctors X-rayed his broken left leg and operated. Standard medical practice was for doctors to insert bare hands into the wound and feel along the bone to identify and set the fracture.[83] A piece of crushed femur was sawed off to fit the broken ends together. The muscle wounds were closed with gut thread, which would dissolve on its own, and the skin opened from knee to hip was closed with silk thread. To reduce the shortening of the broken femur, his leg was put in trac- tion—a weight attached to a rope and tied to the end of the foot for constant pulling tension. A typical traction weight was ten to twelve pounds, but with his highly developed quadriceps, shaped like wine casks, doctors doubled the weight to twenty-five pounds.

It is unknown whether Champion was the first patient operated on that day or where he may have been in the surgical order. Doctors in this era wore the same raven-black smock for their entire shift, regardless of how much blood and other fluids splattered on them during the course of their rounds. The chance of infecting a patient soared over the course of a day spent treating other patients. Home births were safer than the 50 percent mortality rate of hospitals. Within days, Champion's wounds became septic. He was threatened with blood poisoning. Doctors considered amputating the leg to save his life, an expeditious option for compound fractures. Period slang for doctors and surgeons was "sawbones." With a sharp saw, a practiced doctor could completely sever a limb in just three minutes. As the *Boston Globe* remarked, "It didn't look like he would survive anyway so he was left alone."[84]

In the era before penicillin or broad-spectrum antibiotics were available to fight infection, his septic wound was washed often with water and he was fed a diet heavy in meat for protein and potatoes or rice for carbohydrates. Doctors left broken bones to heal on their own.

Early twentieth-century hospitals resembled warehouses. Beds were pushed against opposite walls along the length of the ward, and patients rested their heads on pillows near the wall. Beds were spaced for physicians and nurses on their rounds to have access to patients. For privacy, curtains were strung up between patient beds.

Elise was rarely referred to in news accounts of Champion, but she was reported to be attending him in the hospital.[85] With his usual itinerant life on hold, Albert was now all hers.

Publications speculated whether Champion would be permanently maimed. Some opined that his cycling was over probably his automobile racing, too.

He wrote a letter to *Boston Globe* reporter John J. Donovan to let the public know his condition and future plans. In a *Globe* story, "Albert Champion Still Undaunted," he said, "I have been here for nine days, and I have not yet had a night's sleep. I have never suffered so much in my life."[86] His back hurt the most. "Yet I must lie on it on account of my leg. When I struck the fence, the terrible shock threw me back against the back of the small racing seat, and I am a lucky fellow that I did not break my back." He continued, "My leg has a twenty-five pound weight tied to it, so that it will not be short when I get up. It will be eight weeks anyway before I leave my bed." He loathed staying in bed for so long. "When that thought comes to my mind, it makes me crazy, and I try to forget it." Despite his pain and prolonged convalescence, he remained characteristically optimistic. He said that after he healed he planned to stay with the Packard Motor Company, either as a testing expert or racecar driver. He closed his letter with a colloquial fillip, asking Donovan to send his regards "to all the Boston boys."[87]

Elise's care of Albert, the continual washing with water of his wound, the high-protein and carbohydrate diet, and his resilient constitution beat back the infection in two weeks. He was moved for better care from Kings County Hospital to the Flower Fifth-Avenue Hospital at 106th Street, near Fifth Avenue.[88] Arrangements were made by Colonel K. C. Pardee, a local race official and the New York branch manager of the Packard Motor Company, which paid his medical expenses.[89] Champion was packed, in traction with the twenty-five-pound weight, into a horse-drawn ambulance for the cross-town trip.

The editor of the New York magazine *Motor* commissioned a first-person account from Champion for the December 1903 issue. He was tasked with describing his feelings about fast driving and its dangers. At twenty-five, he was recovering from a compound fracture in addition to a previous broken arm, fractured hand, broken fingers, and numerous deep bruises, cuts, and gashes. Yet he expected to keep putting his life at risk in the name of speed.

The article, "Piloting Motor Driven Racers," ran as a full page, illustrated with Elmer Chickering's photo of Albert bent jockey-style over his Clément Gladiator on his first sub-minute mile in Charles River Park. Albert's commentary offered rare introspection on his obsession for speed and its constant potential for disaster.

Up till then, only a trifling number of people, chiefly urban, among the 75 million US population had ever ridden in any kind of automobile. Even fewer had been on a motorcycle. Only Champion, Oldfield, and a small group of others—so limited they could sit around a dining-room table—had felt the wind on their face driving 60 mph. Champion wrote that it was difficult to explain what it felt like to drive so fast to another person who may never have ridden on such a machine, even the privileged folks who experienced tolerable low speeds.

> I forget to be afraid of being killed, although I know it is very possible that I may be, and I am most conscious that my living—my reputation as a racing man—is at stake, so, though fully aware that death may reward my efforts, I always find myself thoroughly able, with a philosophy that is perhaps calloused by experience, to carry the performance through with every nerve alert to make it successful and avoid its dangers.
>
> There is no question but what my calling is dangerous. I recognize this to the extent of never having my wife witness a race in which I am entered.[90]

Whether barreling at 40 mph or 60 mph, it felt the same to him:

> I crouch low and make myself as small as possible to lessen the wind resistance, the hum of the engine, and the air rushing past becomes a roar; and then it seems as if the machine stood in the same place and the track spun beneath it like an immense disk—its center away over in the infield and the grandstand on the outer edge, coming around at regular intervals; I feel as if the whole earth were spinning like a top and nothing but perfect coolness and attention on my part will keep it from ending in disaster.
>
> If the track is right, the movement, tremendously rapid, is smooth. The least unevenness, however, is felt, and even a smooth rise and a fall of an inch in a hundred feet passes under the machine with a sharp jar—for if the machine is lifted and lowered an inch in a hundred feet, it means that it jolts an inch up and down in a second."[91]

Eleven weeks and three more operations went by before Champion's leg healed sufficiently so that doctors could remove it from traction.[92] Out of bed on his own for the first time in nearly three months, he depended on crutches to get around.[93] He finally left the Flower Fifth-Avenue Hospital, accompanied by Elise, in mid-January, stabbing the ground with the end of the crutches and swinging his legs through. He was too weak to travel to south Florida for the speed carnival he'd planned to attend.

Instead, he visited the New York Automobile Show in Madison Square

Garden, which opened January 19, 1904.[94] The *Boston Traveler* hired him as a correspondent, honoring him with a byline. Seeing friends must have served as welcome medicine.

His dispatch, "All Kinds of Machines at the Auto Show," offered a tour d'horizon of the exhibits. His former Paris employer Adolphe Clément had a booth offering autos and motorcycles for sale in New York. Several other French auto manufacturers attended. They joined the burgeoning number of American automakers and suppliers. The French presence reflected America's growing demand for motor-powered vehicles in the growing trans-Atlantic auto industry.

Making the rounds of daytime exhibit booths and evening restaurant dinners, Champion inspired a feature in the *New York Sun*, "Thrilling Accidents and Narrow Escapes." The account ran a large illustration of him on his first racing bicycle and summarized his Brighton Beach brush with death. He said, "I do not care to come any closer to the Great Reaper than I did at Brighton."[95]

The article also featured a line drawing of Henri Fournier at the wheel of a Mors auto. "Escapes from death by a hair's breadth are plentiful everywhere," rationalized Fournier, popular with American audiences for his courage and the press corps for his fluency in English. "Only yesterday I read in a New York newspaper of a veritable hair-breadth escape on Broad Street—a brick from the top of a new skyscraper fell so close to the back of a man's head that it made a red streak down the back of his coat, then crumbled in a puff of dust on the sidewalk. If that man had been one-twentieth of a second slower in his stride he would have been blotted out of life. It is as close as that many a time in automobiling. You come within a few millimeters or within an infinitesimal fraction of a second of a frightful death—and after a few quick breaths you are placidly wondering what you shall have for luncheon."[96]

In Fournier's view, if you act quickly, you are safe. "If not, the coroner gets you."

Champion had acted quickly and survived. But he required several weeks after leaving the hospital before he and Elise boarded a train west to Detroit and the Packard Motor Company.

Packard's plant on forty acres along East Grand Boulevard on the city's east side boasted the most modern automobile manufacturing factory in the world. It introduced extensive use of reinforced concrete in walls, supports, and roofs—a departure from traditional wood and offering better fire protection. The architecture also provided a larger unobstructed interior space than conventional buildings and more windows for letting in natural light. When Albert arrived, he found the Packard factory was energized with craftsmen practicing dozens of trades. They were turning out the new Packard Model N, which would set the industry standard for engineering and luxury.

The factory represented a vast improvement over the alley garages of early carmakers, like the workshop in which Henry Ford had made 999. Behind the architecture was the youthful German immigrant Albert Kahn. Henry Ford was impressed with the Packard factory and commissioned Kahn to design a similar plant for his new startup, the Ford Motor Company.

The Packard Motor Car Company was among the first automakers to test products.[97] Its acreage had a road made of loose gravel with a steep hill to put cars through grueling drives.

Henry Joy furnished Champion with an office of his own to begin plans for racing the Packard Gray Wolf in the upcoming season.

The Frenchman wrote letters to friends in Boston. "I am lame, and will be, but that will not prevent me from running my car and making new records," he told John J. Donovan of the *Boston Globe*. "As soon as I get going, Barney Oldfield and Mr. [William K.] Vanderbilt and others had better look out, for I will smash all their records."[98]

Donovan, in an article for the *Globe*, described how Albert sometimes in fits of enthusiasm tossed aside his cane to hobble and limp around his office with the aid of benches and chairs.[99]

By April, Champion was approaching six months since his accident, and he felt his usual vigor returning. After fully healing, his left leg was a couple inches shorter than his right.[100] But he could put weight on the leg to walk without assistance and, as soon as he could, he put away the cane.

He wrote a letter to a friend in Boston to send for one of the bicycles he'd left behind there. Then he initiated light exercise on a bicycle he mounted on his training rollers, the rear wheel spinning over a roller and the frame held up by a mechanical support he rigged up where he and Elise were living. It was simple to insert a longer crank arm on his bicycle for his shorter leg to compensate for the length difference. More tricky was crafting a custom pedal to accommodate the foot of his healed leg, now turned permanently slightly outward. He fashioned a special pedal, built up with wood on top of the steel base like a version of a clubfoot,[101] and he had to experiment to perfect the angle. His aero bicycle's one-speed fixed gear, popular today among urban cyclists as a "fixie," helped his damaged leg to recover. The chain connected straight to the rear-wheel sprocket, without a coasting mechanism; when the wheels turned, so did the pedals, in cadence matching the turning wheels. He practiced accelerating from a slow speed to a brisk pace. Once up to speed, the fixed gear took on characteristics of a flywheel to sustain momentum. Both legs rolled in a synchronized motion, which prevented him from favoring his weak leg. He gradually recovered his usual fluid pedal strokes. Strengthening his injured leg also improved his walking.

Never inclined to sit back or drift on his past achievements, Champion got in touch with other drivers and race officials about the 1904 racing circuit. He gathered information about registration deadlines and fees, train schedules for transporting the Gray Wolf, and what hotels and restaurants were recommended. To drive the Gray Wolf, however, would depend on cooperation from Charles Schmidt. The older Frenchman wielded the upper hand.

Henry Joy may have tolerated Schmidt's attitude in order to placate him. The Gray Wolf induced him to stay when other companies like Peerless in Cleveland were offering higher pay for his talent.

Schmidt could have felt responsible for Champion's injuries. Schmidt also may have been peeved about something else. On January 2 and 3, 1904, at Ormond-Daytona Beach, he had driven the Gray Wolf in a straight line along firm coastline sands connecting the two cities and set a new national one-mile record of 46-2/5 seconds, clocking 77 mph. He also set national records for the kilometer and five miles. But what mattered most was the mile—the gold standard for achievement. Only a week later, Henry Ford drove his latest racing car a mile in forty seconds flat on the ice of Lake St. Clair in Michigan, a world record of 91.37 mph.[102] On January 25, William K. Vanderbilt Jr. drove a Mercedes a mile in thirty-nine seconds for the world's land-speed record, an astounding 92.3 mph.[103] Schmidt was in no mood to allow anyone to use his Gray Wolf. He focused on supervising production of his latest design, Packard Model N.

Henry Joy must have felt like George Washington with two headstrong Lafayettes. He had higher priorities and disparate demands on his time. James Ward Packard had stayed in Warren, Ohio, and left expansion of the company's operations up to him.

Champion deliberated about his future. He could take up what he knew best, as he was assured of good money motorpacing.[104] Over the previous nine years, April had been the month he dedicated to training in earnest for the next season. His leg discrepancy was easily compensated for by riding with one longer crank arm and a built-up pedal. Spectators watching him ride would see he was back to normal.

He had been pining for Paris. In September in Atlanta, Champion had mentioned to reporters that he had been planning to return home after the racing season to take advantage of the French government's amnesty for draft dodgers and deserters. Now with a limp and X-rays of his broken leg bone to show the draft board, he could go home without fear of arrest at the port of entry. He missed his mother and brothers Louis, Henri, and Prosper. Elise also longed to see her parents, Marie and Bernard Sr., sister Gabrielle, and brother Bernard Jr. Albert's Brighton Beach accident had wiped out that plan. Now he could follow through.

His stint in Detroit exposed him to the phenomenal importance of the gas-combustion autos to the city. Over a bottle of the local Vernors ginger ale conversations buzzed about the city of 285,000 residents in 1900 growing at a rate sufficient to nearly double its population in a decade due to job openings in the proliferating auto factories.

Packard had been in town less than a year and Henry Joy already had hired architect Albert Kahn to add additional factory buildings through 1911, which would expand the plant to 3,500,000 square feet. Detroit's Oldsmobile dominated as America's biggest-selling automaker in 1903, with sales of 4,000. Mass-produced, gas-powered Oldsmobiles outsold all the electric and steam-powered vehicles combined for the first time, signaling a tipping point for gas-combustion engines. Another thriving Detroit company was Cadillac, which trailed Oldsmobile in sales. Horace and John Dodge had a booming business making engine components and chassis parts for Oldsmobiles and for Henry Ford's new company.

Champion felt the onus to create his own business to serve America's mushrooming auto production. He considered forming a company, taking advantage of his name recognition, to import French auto parts, especially spark plugs and magnetos to generate current for the spark plug's ignition of internal-combustion engines. He had contacts in Paris. However, he lacked capital.

Sometime in April, Champion made up his mind to dive back into motorpace racing, hit the East Coast circuit for May and June, then return to Paris for a final racing campaign. He wanted a shot at winning the French national motorpace championship. Paris and Berlin offered bigger tracks for faster speeds, larger audiences, and more lucrative purses. He could raise the capital he needed on tracks and later return to Boston, a city he'd grown to regard as his second home, to start his own company.

Albert informed Henry Joy of his plan. Henry invited him to have their photo taken together in the latest Packard, a souvenir in appreciation for his service to the company.

On a bright, chilly day in late April, Henry Joy drove an open Packard Model N, a de luxe tonneau—with upholstered seats in the back for family members—out of the factory with Albert on the passenger seat. Henry parked next to the curb. The auto was regarded as one of the finest luxury vehicles made in America. The Model N had a four-cylinder engine and a transmission equipped with an H-slot gearshift pattern for three forward speeds and one for reverse—a pattern used universally for decades until the advent of automatic transmissions. Packards boasted the slogan: *Ask the Man Who Owns One.*[105]

Some Packard employees in their Sunday best looked on from the other side of the sidewalk. They watched the photographer set up the tripod and camera in the street to capture Champion and Joy in profile while showing off the graceful lines of the car and the shine of the polished hood reflecting the front wheel. Albert adjusted his bowler, unusual for him, as he preferred a wool flat hat. He checked his collar and the knot of his bowtie one last time before turning to look directly ahead.

Champion, left, sat next to Henry Joy in a new Packard in Detroit before he passed up Joy's offer to drive racecars for 1904. He returned to France to race bicycles and used his prize money to go into the auto industry. *Photo courtesy of Cherie Champion.*

Henry Joy removed his pince nez and put the spectacles in a waistcoat pocket. He placed his hands on his lap and gazed ahead, as though the car could drive itself. He would serve as president of the company and chairman of the board. In the next decade, he would take the helm as president of the Lincoln Highway Association, which built a paved highway from San Francisco to New York—America's first cross-country road.

Albert pasted this photo in his scrapbook with his career highlights.

On the first of May, Albert and Elise boarded an eastbound train to Boston. He had to prepare for the Memorial Day season opener in Charles River Park. Albert required world-class fitness by the end of June—and to be in Paris.

9

NATIONAL CHAMPION
OF FRANCE

While Champion hobbled around Boston with his gimp leg and splay-foot renewing acquaintances, *Globe* reporter John J. Donovan told readers, "Champion Is Back in Town." Albert pasted the article in his scrapbook, penciling in the date, May 5, as he was keeping track of the days while he weighed his opportunities and preferences. "He has almost entirely recovered from his injury," Donovan wrote, "and, with a little preparation, should be in his old-time condition."[2]

The odds against fulfilling the upbeat forecast were enormous, yet Champion was undaunted. Fractured legs were pitiless in the way they destroyed all manner of sports careers. His Paris friend Constant Huret had been forced to retire after breaking an ankle in a crash racing on the Parc des Princes.[3] Determined, Champion defied his fate.

The Memorial Day season opener loomed in only a few weeks. Yet picking up where he had left off before his accident had turned even more complex. The bicycle industry spiraled in freefall. Former cycling enthusiasts bought Brownie Box Cameras, made by the Kodak Company, for as little as a dollar. The cameras had George Eastman's ingenious flexible rolls of film for taking pictures. People carried the cameras around in a pocket and pursued photography as the new national hobby. In cities that boasted wheelmen by the battalions, golf courses also proliferated, with memberships swelling from converts swapping two-wheelers for bags of golf clubs. Men and women frequented downtown venues with novel roller-skating rinks and bowling alleys. As cycle sales languished, dozens of manufacturers merged and formed the American Bicycle Company,[4] a Chicago consortium, to control supply and limit competition. The new consortium slashed prices even when it meant sacrificing quality.

The early twentieth century saw autos increasing on urban streets. Motorists had to thread their way in traffic dominated by horses and manure piles. Drivers endured a chorus of righteous jokers on the side of the road singing out, "Get a horse!"

Many bicycle company owners were cashing out to make autos that retained their brand name, following earlier auto pioneers Alexander Winton, Colonel Albert Pope, and Charles and Frank Duryea. Thomas B. Jeffery, founder of Rambler bicycles, made in Chicago and once a dominant marque, sold the business and decamped north to Kenosha, Wisconsin, to found the Rambler Motor Company.[5] George Pierce in Buffalo, New York, was a master of entrepreneurial versatility.[6] He had made wire birdcages, then spokes for bicycle wheels, then complete bicycles. His Pierce Bicycle Company became well known for its logo of an arrow with a chipped flint arrowhead shot straight through the name Pierce. From that came the Pierce-Arrow Motor Company.

In such an effervescent climate, Champion discussed retiring from paced racing or reconsidering Henry Joy's still-open, flattering contract offer to drive the Packard Gray Wolf.[7] In Paris, the International Commission representing automobile clubs on two continents decided to allow professional drivers in the upcoming international James Gordon Bennett Cup Race in Hamburg, Germany.[8] The commission cited Champion, Barney Oldfield, and three others as possible drivers to make up a team driving US autos.

While he mulled over his next move, Champion turned his attention to building up his atrophied leg muscles. This pushed him to workouts at Revere Beach and Charles River Park. Champion signed a contract to ride for the Imperial Bicycle Company, which had formed in Buffalo before relocating under new ownership to Chicago.[9] Imperial's logo featured its name in diamond-style capital letters over an arrow shooting up at a diagonal to distinguish Imperial from the Pierce company. He practiced behind Billy Saunders, a disciple of the Gillette safety razor who shaved all facial hair.[10] Champion and Saunders wore jerseys with *Imperial* inscribed across their front and back.

Champion (left) in his final season stands with his aerodynamic motorpace bicycle made by Imperial, one of the last brands to survive the era when America had more than three hundred bicycle manufacturers and only a handful of automakers. *Photo from US Bicycling Hall of Fame.*

The Frenchman trained twice daily up to two hours each session, with the characteristic intensity the *Washington Star* had once described as pitching in like ten men. He grew stronger and steadily built up muscle mass. Cycling since he was eleven had endowed him with a base of strength and endurance to hasten his recovery. He tipped the scales at a robust 150 pounds.[11]

Barney Oldfield came by train to Boston in late May for an auto race at the Readville Trotting Park, sponsored by the *Boston Herald*. Oldfield visited the Revere Beach velodrome and spent an afternoon chatting with Champion and the men Oldfield had raced against in his cycling days, like an alumnus returning to those from whose ranks he had graduated.[12] America's fastest racecar driver volunteered to serve as official starter for the track's Memorial Day cycling program. He was employed by Alexander Winton to drive Bullet II. His illustrious 999 was still making the circuit rounds, piloted by Jed Newkirk,[13] Champion's former pacer.

"Albert Champion is particularly anxious to drive here as he desires to have his name engraved on *The Boston Herald* trophy," a scribe for the *Herald* asserted, "and he thinks that with the 'Grey Wolf' this will be possible."[14]

Perhaps he was thinking of something else even more. Gas-combustion automobiles were noisy, smelly, and prone to breakdowns. But after a medical doctor from Burlington, Vermont, had driven a two-cylinder Winton from coast to coast in seven weeks to win a $50 bet in 1903, the potential for motor vehicles appeared boundless compared to electric or steam vehicles. The oil gushing from Spindletop, and additional discoveries of northeast Texas wells, indicated that plenty of fuel would be available. Champion's former boss, Adolphe Clément, president of France's National Automobile Syndicate, had been invited to America that summer to serve on the jury of the World's Fair in St. Louis, Missouri.[15] The World's Fair commemorated the centenary of President Thomas Jefferson's Louisiana Purchase, buying from France the broad swath of land from the Canadian border to the Gulf of Mexico.

Since the turn of the century, US auto sales had swelled too fast for accurate accounting. *Automobile* complained that industry figures were so conflicting and confusing that accurate measures were unavailable. All anybody knew for sure was that the growth over the preceding half-dozen years had been tremendous. Autos had developed from a plaything for the very rich, like a fad of the hour. The magazine acknowledged, "Then very little capital was invested in automobile factories; now over twenty millions of dollars are employed in the business."[16]

From garages with dreamers and tinkerers and two or three small factories making a handful of early autos, which the automakers also had to sell on their own, the industry had escalated to about fifty large factories equipped with machinery and staffed by skilled workers. In five years annual production had jumped from four thousand to twenty-five thousand.[17]

Detroit was home to Ransom Olds and his Olds Motor Works, manufacturing one-cylinder Oldsmobiles.[18] Oldsmobiles were America's first auto produced in big quantities—600 in 1901, 2,500 the next year, and 4,000 in 1903.[19] Ransom Olds produced cars with an assembly line adapted from New England arms manufacturers. Oldsmobiles were light, made of wood, styled after open-topped horse buggies, and steered with a tiller. They sold for $650,[20] compared with about $250 for a horse carriage. Oldsmobiles were noted as the first commercially successful autos. They inspired the cheerful song, "In My Merry Oldsmobile,"[21] made popular from sales of sheet music propped up on pianos in drawing rooms for family sing-alongs and parties. The ascending vehicle production rate pointed to the United States surpassing France in a couple of years as leader of all the nations producing autos. Jokey get-a-horse cries were going the way of beards.

Champion, looking ahead, sought a way to enter the auto market. The prospect of supplying motor vehicles to America's 75 million people (less than one-quarter of today's population), suggested limitless opportunity—and wealth.[22] To get in the business, he needed capital. To acquire the needed capital, he would have to win frequently in his ninth and final season as a pro cyclist. He determined to go all out for one last campaign—not in America, but in France.[23] The purses were much bigger there, and he could win the money he'd need in order to establish his own business. He made up his mind to crown his career with the French national championship. Albert staked his ambitious future on capturing the title en route to raising the money to create his place in the nascent US auto industry.

France's reigning national motorpace champion, Henri Contenet,[24] two years older than Champion, had paid his dues toiling in the motorpace ranks. In 1903, Contenet transformed into a winner under the guidance of Marius Thé, a former road-racing star now driving the motors for him.[25] Champion knew Marius Thé and wrote a letter to request his skills when he returned to Paris in the early summer. Thé accepted.[26] Likely he was persuaded by Champion's panache and convenient access to Adolph Clément, the Midas of French industry. Thus Champion acquired one of the best drivers in the game at an adversary's expense—predicated on his making it back to Paris without arrest for evading military service.

Although the French military had announced a general amnesty for draft dodgers,[27] Champion mailed his draft board packets of medical records and X-rays of his broken leg to make sure he could go home to France without arrest at the border. In the meantime, he would race in the United States.

Rain had cancelled the traditional Memorial Day season opener,[28] but on June 5 Champion made his 1904 debut in a twenty-five-mile paced event at the

Charles River Park.[29] Tucked close to the rear wheel of Billy Saunders's motorcycle, he skimmed over the board track, back low, elbows pressed against his sides, and seemed to glide while his legs spun almost to a blur. He averaged 40 mph to win by a lap. The *Globe*'s John J. Donovan praised his remarkable form.

Four days later, he needed less than thirty minutes to win a twenty-miler in New York at Manhattan Beach Track.[30] He rode against his doctor's advice and ignored muscle soreness. "The Frenchman had abscesses in both legs, reminders of his almost fatal automobile accident last fall," said *Bicycling World*.[31]

His Paris draft board issued a letter granting amnesty. The *Washington Post* reported, "Permission having been granted him to return to France, Albert Champion, the French bicycle rider, will sail for Europe on June 23."[32]

Champion encouraged twenty-one-year-old George Leander to go with him. They had formed a friendship in Boston and Champion saw he could mature to succeed Bobby Walthour. The son of a Chicago printer,[33] Leander came from a family of nine and had an easy-going personality. He was tall and handsome in a wholesome way, beefier in the arms, chest, and legs than Champion. Stretched across his bicycle, Leander looked intimidating. He had tried to make a living as a pure sprinter. Early in his career he had packed on weight in the off season, inspiring *Boston Globe* reporter Donovan to dub him "Windy City Fat Boy."[34]

Stung by the nickname, Leander thereafter stayed active over the indoor six-day circuit during the winter. In a run-off contest to determine the outcome of the Boston six-day in the Park Square Coliseum, he was nipped over the final yards by an older, taller veteran. After they dismounted, the victor punched Leander, and Leander fought back, setting off a brawl that escalated to two hundred other riders, mechanics, masseurs, and bystanders.[35] Police swinging billy clubs finally broke up the melee. Leander gained the reputation of never backing down. In the December 1902 Madison Square Garden six-day, he won the final pack sprint to clinch victory. The next year he joined the better-paying motorpace circuit. Champion gave him pointers for improvement and put him in touch with his agent Victor Breyer for contracts in Paris.[36]

Another accompanying Champion, Elise, and Leander to Paris was Basil De Guichard. The group booked first-class passage on the French liner *La Savoie*, sailing out of New York for Le Havre. At 580 feet in length, *La Savoie* was one of the largest ships under the French flag.

Before sailing, however, Champion went down to Atlanta to compete against Bobby Walthour, recently back as the conquering hero from a spring campaign in Paris and Berlin. A Paris syndicate paid the Georgian an appearance fee of $5,000 ($125,000 in 2014).[37] Walthour, as American national motorpace champion, had defeated his counterpart, Henri Contenet, and other continental stars, in matches before standing-room only crowds.[38] The French press raved: "*Toujours* Walthour."

For each of his eleven victories in twelve starts, Walthour raked in an average of about $1,000—four times the prize money paid in America.[39] Endorsements to ride a French bicycle, a brand of saddle, and tires pushed his earnings from two months on the continent to about $15,000 ($373,000).[40]

Champion wanted Walthour to share the latest gossip and tell him how much promoters were paying. Champion and his pacer Saunders climbed aboard a train to Atlanta for the five-mile matches on June 15 around promoter Jack Prince's outdoor board track in Piedmont Park.

"The race was the most exciting ever seen in Atlanta," judged the *Atlanta Constitution*. "Champion was determined to win from Walthour and pushed the Atlantan from the very start as Bobby had never been pushed before either in America or in Europe. Champion was riding faster and better than he did before he received the serious injury last year."[41]

From the bang of the starter's pistol, Champion and Saunders bolted away and seized the lead. They reeled off swift 45 mph laps and opened up a half-lap lead, about 150 yards. Through the first four miles, Champion broke stadium records. The sight of both cyclists flying tight behind the roaring motors aroused the throng of a thousand to jump to its feet and cheer.

Orbiting into the last mile, Walthour perked up. "Lap after lap showed Walthour slowly gaining, though Champion responded to Walthour's increased speed with a great spurt," said the *Constitution*. "The curves were rounded in a reckless manner, but both men followed the big motors with all ease."

Walthour followed a French motorcycle with greater horsepower than Champion's motorpacer. The Georgian's machine carried a souvenir from his trip, a rectangular windshield over the rear wheel for extra slipstream shelter.

Champion accelerated to a scorching 51 mph. The crowd screamed louder. Walthour kept narrowing the gap. His driver pulled up snug behind Champion. The men and their machines whirled around the oval like a thundering dragon.

Off the final turn, Walthour's driver went wide on the run up to the finish in front of the grandstand and sling-shotted past team Champion. Walthour edged the Frenchman to clinch the first heat by a fraction of a second, what sports writers called a ding-dong finish.

Just past the line, Champion's tires slipped. He fell and barrel-rolled down the track to the inside apron. His pedal gouged the pine boards.

"He was badly shaken up and received a bad cut over the left eye," reported the *Constitution*. "Besides this, he picked up a number of splinters as he rolled down the track. One of these penetrated his stomach and an operation was performed at the Grady Hospital last night to remove it."

Surgery to remove the splinters delayed his planned departure from Atlanta. The tumble also reinjured his mended leg; he ignored medical advice for surgery.[42] Champion strode out of the downtown hospital with a neat row of square-knotted silk stitches that closed the laceration over his eye. The shirt he wore covered another row on his abdomen. A surgeon aboard the ship would remove the stitches at sea.

Alighting from a train on Thursday, June 30,[43] Champion's first day back in Paris, he headed straight to the office of the sports daily, *L'Auto*, at 10 rue Faubourg-Montmartre, in the Ninth Arrondissement on the Right Bank of the Seine. Passing along the Ninth's grand boulevards, adorned with grandiose architecture and chic shops, must have stirred his Gallic pride. He visited his friend Henri Desgrange, *L'Auto*'s editor and director.

Desgrange had shaved off his beard, revealing a rectangular face and a square jaw. Despite pushing forty, he maintained a youthful appearance, encouraged by rigorous daily exercise and thick, jet-black hair. He was basking in credit for pulling off one of the publishing world's most flamboyant coups—of such magnitude that it still demands global attention every July.

Like Champion, the newspaper had survived hard blows. Since its founding on October 16, 1900, as *L'Auto-Vélo*,[44] it had battled a nemesis, *Le Vélo*, the city's older sports journal. *Le Vélo* was edited by Pierre Giffard, the visionary who had created Paris-Brest-Paris as the ultimate cycling endurance contest. He had ignited the circulation war when France teetered on the lip of civil war over the guilt or innocence of an army captain named Alfred Dreyfus, falsely alleged to have given military secrets to the Germans. Most in France were paranoid about the prospect of another German invasion. Dreyfus, a Jew in a country dominated by the Roman Catholic Church, was sentenced to Devil's Island off the coast of French Guiana near northeastern South America. Between his imprisonment in 1894 and the retrial five years later that exonerated him, all of France had boiled. Giffard had mixed sports coverage with political commentary and had defended Dreyfus.[45] The editor had used his paper to denounce Clément, André and Edouard Michelin, and Jules-Albert de Dion as anti-Dreyfus industrialists.

Another protesting Dreyfus's innocence was the literary lion Emile Zola. He had written an open letter to the French president published on the front page of a Paris daily with the audacious headline, "J'accuse." Zola had accused military leaders of obstructing justice and of anti-Semitism. His bold charges and literary prominence had made him the most reviled of Dreyfus's defenders.

Clément and associates fumed.[46] They pulled their ads from Giffard's paper and founded *L'Auto-Vélo* with a considerable investment. *L'Auto-Vélo* marked the only time autos and bicycles shared equality in a masthead. Clément appointed Desgrange as editor.[47]

In the first issue, Desgrange had pledged that under his direction the paper would never mention politics. (He kept his word until the eve of World War I.) He picked yellow newsprint for *L'Auto-Vélo* to stand out on newsstands and kiosks against *Le Vélo*'s green pages.[48] Only one color and one newspaper would survive. Giffard had further angered Desgrange and his backers when Giffard won a legal decision over the similarity of their names. On January 16, 1903, Desgrange and Clément complied with the court order and renamed the paper. They called it *L'Auto* to reflect their enthusiasm for car racing as the sport of the future.

By then the legal fees and steady hemorrhaging of money since the first issue had pushed the paper's co-owners to the point where they were ready to cut their losses and close down the operation. In a desperate scheme, *L'Auto* had announced on January 19, 1903, in a front-page headline, that it had created a three-week bicycle road race around the inside perimeter of the nation, about the size of Texas.[49] The event would transform France into a huge vélodrome, the athletic equivalent of the Eiffel Tower. The founders opened their wallets to put up lavish prizes and bonuses guaranteed to draw two-wheeled fortune hunters. Desgrange named his event after the traditional tradesmen's journeymanship, the *Tour de France*.

On July 2, 1903, *L'Auto*'s inaugural Tour de France began on a road on the edge of Paris with seventy-three swashbucklers from four countries. They took off in a cloud of dust for Lyon, 291 miles away. The gambit paid off. *L'Auto*'s presses rolled off one special edition after another. Readers wanted to learn more about this unprecedented and extraordinary event. The circulation jumped from a money-losing 25,000 copies sold daily to a profitable 65,000— robbing a big chunk of sales from *Le Vélo*. The Tour de France finished 1,518 miles later on July 23 on the Parc des Princes. The winner was Champion's former adversary Marius Garin, the Little Chimneysweep. When Champion sauntered into *L'Auto*'s offices, Desgrange was bracing for the second annual tour, destined to deal his nemesis a knock-down punch.

Champion needed publicity. He had come to offer an exclusive on his adventures in America. Desgrange also directed the Parc des Princes in western Paris and organized Sunday race programs. He assigned nicknames to people so readers could conveniently identify them, like theater props. A tall man, he dubbed anyone shorter as *petit*. He introduced Champion to *L'Auto*'s staff on the first floor as *Le Petit Prodige*, "The Little Wonder."[50] Desgrange, mindful of his duties, left Le Petit Prodige with a reporter assigned to do the interview. Desgrange jogged upstairs to his office. His heart was more writer than political diehard. Under his hand, *L'Auto* read in the passionate style of his literary hero, Emile Zola.[51]

Champion also went to see Victor Breyer,[52] now director of the Buffalo Vélodrome, a going concern relocated from Porte Maillot at the city's northwest end to suburban Neuilly. Breyer had a grand prix scheduled for Sunday, July 10. He signed Champion to a match against national motorpace champion Henri Contenet. The bout would challenge both men, guarantee ticket sales, and entertain Breyer's audience.

Breyer's passions for sports and journalism united his professional and private lives. The gentleman scribe with a soft smile worked a day job as editor of the sports weekly *La Vie au Grand Air*, popular for generous photo layouts. Breyer wrote about the American exodus to Europe. He had cited the gossip about Champion's military desertion and present mentoring of young George Leander. A photo of Champion in a pin-striped suit, cuffs showing discretely, ran with the subhead, "Long Time No See." The article touted his debut at the Buffalo Vélodrome.[53]

The French auto industry's patron, too much of a workaholic to make the grade for sainthood, was Adolphe Clément.[54] French autos were exported all over the world, supported by France's colonial empire. For his role as a force behind the auto industry, he was invited by President Émile Loubet to the presidential palace for a promotion from Chevalier of the Légion d'Honneur to Officer of the Légion d'Honneur.[55]

Réne Panhard, the Renault brothers, the Peugeots, and other captains of industry in France's National Automobile Syndicate had re-elected Adolphe Clément to the organization's presidency.[56] The former locksmith, now portly, employed approximately twenty-five hundred workers in factories making bicycles, motorcycles, automobiles, and dirigibles. Clément still served as board president of Panhard Motor Company (Émile Levassor had died in 1897 in a car race), was president of the board of the French Textile Manufacturers, and carried the title of honorary president of France's Bicycle and Automobile Insurance Industry. He even performed a stint as juror for the Alcohol Exhibition in Vienna.

Clément's eminence led to a novel Anglo-French collaboration.[57] For a year, he had a term as vice president on the board at the Clément-Talbot Motor Works in London. He recently had left the English company, renamed Talbot Motor Works, to launch his own auto business in France. He had legally changed his surname to Clément-Bayard, after the medieval knight Pierre Bayard, and he christened the company as Clément-Bayard Automobiles. Like the old knight, he wore a beard shot through with gray. His vehicles were manufactured in a pair of sprawling plants in Mézièrs, to the north in the Ardennes. It was natural that a statute of the knight stood sentry on the factory grounds.

When Champion returned to Paris, Clément-Bayard was abroad at the St. Louis World's Fair. Champion would have dealt with Pierre Tournier, manager of operations. Tournier signed him up for contracts to ride Gladiator Cycles equipped with Dunlop tires, and for Marius Thé to drive Gladiator motorcycles with Dunlops. Both Champion and Marius Thé received an inventory of bikes, tires, and motorcycles—enough to leave two or three extra two-wheelers in storage at the Buffalo Vélodrome and Parc des Princes. Before every race, Champion hired a support crew to have a replacement bike and back-up motorcycle at the ready on the track infield across from the grandstand. In keeping with the trend in motorpacing on the continent, the Gladiator motorcycles were equipped with a rectangular windscreen over the rear wheel for a little extra shelter.

On Champion's second day in Paris, *L'Auto* proclaimed, "Le Retour de Champion." Staff writer François Mercier noted that the twenty-six-year-old Little Wonder had returned after five years in America, thanks to his amnesty. The article mentioned that he was a married man and that he had trained with Choppy Warburton. Mercier noted that Champion's adventures abroad were marked by horrific falls that "put him on his road to Damascus."[58]

Mercier told readers that Champion had come back to Paris to embark on a new métier in autos—that Champion intended to settle in Boston to take advantage of his business connections in America. His idea was to link up with a French auto company looking to sell cars in the growing US market. To raise money, Champion intended to compete on tracks behind a motorcycle driven by Marius Thé. When he wasn't on the track, he planned to relax with old friends.

French historian Pierre Chany in his 1975 *La Fabuleuse Histoire du Cyclisme*, a French-centric tour d'horizon of the sport's first century, conceded that the draft board would have granted Champion amnesty for his limp to avoid disgracing the military uniform. Competing against French pros to raise capital, however, evoked skepticism, if not outright scorn. Back in 1904, memories were still fresh about what had happened in September 1902 to the admired Constant Huret after he broke an ankle in a collision with Jimmy Michael in a motor-pace race at Parc des Princes. Chany cites old-timers recalling Champion's declaration:

"I'm back in France to get the dough I'll need back there," he told friends.

"Not a chance, Albert. Banks aren't very generous right now."

"Who's talking about banks? I'm going to earn some cash on the track."

"With your leg?"

"Yes, with my leg! I'll just use one crank shorter than the other, that's all."[59]

Whatever others thought, Champion remained undeterred. He and Marius Thé practiced at race pace, cruising at 40 mph around the reconstituted Buffalo Vélodrome, three laps for one kilometer, or nearly 350 yards around. The track in Neuilly was a worthy homage to legendary American frontier showman Buffalo Bill Cody, remembered for his Wild West show at the 1889 world's fair. The facility accommodated fifteen thousand spectators seated in comfort behind the cream-colored railing or standing on the infield's manicured lawn. Painted in tall letters across the top of the grandstand, visible everywhere on the grounds, was: *Clément Cycles*.[60]

Marius Thé had a dark swarthy mustache and a characteristic Parisian's debonair manner. He sat upright on the Gladiator motorcycle and held handlebars sweeping the length of the machine all the way back to his seat, over the edge of the rear wheel. He was Champion's size and served as a windscreen. The smooth way Marius steered in and out of the banked curves and down the straights kept his friend sheltered at speed.

Rival papers *L'Auto* and *Le Vélo* both promoted the Champion-versus-Contenet match. The Sunday afternoon card also featured a pride of headliner pro sprinters from France, Germany, and Italy to dazzle the audience with tactics, drama, and speed. In addition, the program offered a ten-kilometer motorcycle race with four entrants.

"We applaud Albert Champion who, after five years in America, is making his return to paced racing in Paris after only eight days of training since he crossed the Atlantic," wrote *L'Auto*'s Géorge Lefèvre.[61] "We have seen with our own eyes he has excellent style and is in form."

Lefèvre, a year older than Champion,[62] was short and slight. On his own time, he played soccer and enjoyed cycling with his brother, Victor. Desgrange referred to them as Petit Géo and Petit Victor. Desgrange was forever indebted to Géo, whom he'd hired away, along with Victor, from the rival paper. At *L'Auto*'s darkest moment,[63] in October 1902, when it was circling the drain financially and Desgrange assembled the staff in a meeting to plead for someone to come up with a scheme to rescue the paper from having to surrender the circulation fight to *Le Vélo*, Petit Géo had suggested the idea of the Tour de France. He recommended a format of six days of racing an average of 253 miles per stage (some 130 miles farther than contemporary tour stages), based on existing classic races that tested character, fortitude, and physical strength. Each day's stage of racing would be augmented by two or three rest days, over three weeks. Now Lefèvre ran the entire show. He started every stage by firing his revolver, judged the finish, and tallied elapsed times for every rider counting toward overall standing. Motor transport still being unreliable, he traveled to the designated cities by express trains. Then he wrote dispatches for each stage and telegraphed his copy to Desgrange in Paris. His coverage pumped up the images of cyclists as national heroes. Lefèvre's Tour de France, free to the public, introduced a new paradigm into the sport.

A committed journalist, Lefèvre praised Contenet for courage and pacing expertise. Contenet, though dutifully neat and sporting a business-like haircut, had a dogged career, which had fallen short of landing him a nickname from the press. Even so, one journalist praised his form as so smooth, with shoulders steady, that he made his racing look effortless. He had attained his first big success at twenty-seven, scoring second in the 1902 national motorpace championship. The next year he had his best season. He had set three world paced records at the Parc des Princes,[64] stretching the celebrated hour record to 48 miles and 1,222 yards. In Germany had he won eight grand-prix events. He capped the 1903 season by capturing the French title. However, in a match in early spring 1904 against Bobby Walthour, Contenet was lapped twice.[65] He had pulled to the side and quit, blaming a cold. Otherwise, he had posted strong results. On the Sunday before his match against Champion, he had triumphed in a three-corner match against two tough opponents at the Parc des Princes.

"All these qualities will make this match a true test as long as the motors don't behave capriciously," Lefèvre forecast.[66]

The Buffalo Vélodrome matinee on Sunday, July 10, began punctually at three o'clock. Women holding parasols and men swinging silver-topped swagger sticks sauntered in their finery to fill the grandstand and surrounding cheap seats. Excited chattering voices punctuated by peals of laughter created a wall of bubbly anticipation—the same liveliness actors hear backstage before the curtain goes up on a show that everyone looks forward to seeing.

The Champion-Contenet matches followed Breyer's format: a ten-kilometer contest followed by another of thirty kilometers, with a runoff of thirty kilometers, if necessary. Champion wore a fresh white jersey in tribute to his days as Paris city champion. Contenet donned the tricolor of France's top motorpacer.

When Champion spun onto the track for his welcome-home introduction, the audience burst into clapping and cheering. His warm reception erased the stigma of his draft evasion and gave him a clean slate.[67] Contenet received a hardy greeting. After their introductory laps, they stopped at the start-finish line across from the grandstand. Officials stepped onto the track to hold the men on their cycles. The motorcycles waited behind in silence for the race commissar to give last-minute instructions to the riders and check with the timers.

At a nod from the official starter on the line, the motorcycle engines combusted to life and the starter shot his pistol.[68] Contenet blasted away.[69] His motorcycle hastened past Champion, pulled in front of Contenet, and the pair soon opened a fifty-meter lead. It stretched to one hundred meters. Champion prudently rallied with Marius Thé to reduce the gap until only ten meters separated the two teams. They whirled off laps regular as a metronome.

Spectators sat hushed on the edge of their seats to see if Contenet could control the race from start to finish. He and Champion bent low behind their motors, skimming over the boards. On the home straight heading into three laps to go for the final kilometer, two-thirds of a mile, Champion with Marius Thé caught his opponent on the outside lane and leapfrogged ahead to take possession of the inside rail. Team Champion leaned through the turn and shot down the straight then into the next turn, all so fast they lapped team Contenet. Champion charged around and was about to lap Contenet again when the finish line came up.

Champion averaged better than a kilometer per minute, a rapid 41 mph. "The winner, very satisfied, received hardy acclaim," reported Lefèvre.

Then the motor-pacers cleared the track to make way for the sprinters, the sport's aristocracy, in elimination heats. While the sprinters monopolized the track, Champion and Contenet repaired to the infield for a light massage from their trainers to speed up recovery. Drinking water to replace the fluids they'd lost to sweating, however, was avoided, as period wisdom held that drinking anything filled the stomach and interfered with food digestion.

In the second match, Champion high-tailed it off the line and put on a display of drafting skill behind Marius Thé that Lefèvre called remarkable. To the surprise of the audience, he lapped Contenet early.[70] He poured it on and lapped the national title holder again and again. Spectators watched him leaning over through the turns and popping upright on the straights, like a fish flicking its body in the current. He piled up a lead of ten laps—a distance of three miles—by the time he won.[71] He averaged 42 mph. He had ridden the legs off Contenet.

Champion, center, with his head swathed in gauze after a recent fall on the Buffalo Vélodrome, was celebrated on the cover of the magazine *La Vie Au Grand Air* for his return to Paris after four years of self-imposed exile in America. Looking at him on the right is French national champion Henri Contenet. *From* La Vie Au Grand Air, *July 14, 1904.*

Le Vélo correspondent Charles Ravaud remarked, "The former Little Wonder clearly dominated our champion of France."[72]

Contenet apologized out loud for having been trounced so badly. He had to choke back his frustration. "He failed so badly yesterday that he has decided to take a few days off to rest until he's recovered to get back to the unbeatable Contenet of 1903," Ravaud wrote in *Le Vélo*.[73]

Champion was awarded a bouquet of flowers for his lap of honor.[74] While the infield band beat out a performance of "La Marseillaise" to accompany him, he waved flowers and smiled to the applauding audience. He could take time to pause and present his flowers to Elise in the grandstand with his mother and three younger brothers.

Victory made Champion a contender among the elite motorpacers for the national middle-distance championship coming up September 18 at Parc des Princes. Champion informed officials of the sport's governing body, L'Union Vélocipedique de France, which sanctioned the program, that they should select him to wear the country's colors for the world's championships in London,[75] in early September, on the grounds of Crystal Palace, a modern spectacle of glass and steel. Bobby Walthour was going to compete for America. And Champion certainly wanted to race him for the world title.

Later that afternoon, when the sprinters had finished and the motorcycles had their race, Champion was riding cool-down laps and chatting with Contenet when he fell. Champion struck his head on the cement. Cuts to his scalp and left ear required wrapping his head in yards of gauze down to his eyebrows like a pirate.[76] A photographer for *La Vie Au Grand Air* posed him standing alongside Contenet at the mouth of the stadium tunnel. Champion radiates swagger, arms akimbo, grinning. Contenet only gazes at him.

The photo ran on the cover of the July 14, Bastille Day, issue: "The Return of Champion." The photo depicts his right leg straight, the left bent, foot splayed. Editor Victor Breyer ran a two-page photo essay depicting the legs of sixteen marquee stars, all clean-shaven for masseurs to knead muscles. Champion's photo has the caption, "Deformed after an accident, but working well all the same."[77] Adjacent is a comparable image of Contenet's gams: "Not elegant but solid."

Success led to another contract the following Sunday for a fifty-kilometer race at the Buffalo Vélodrome against his compatriot César Simar, a protégé of Constant Huret, and two others—George Leander and Welshman Jimmy Michael.[78] Then fate intervened. Champion faced a crisis. The strain of his performance aggravated the deep thigh-muscle tissue of his injured leg. Infection set in.[79] By the middle of the week, he came down with a fever and checked into the Hôtel-Dieu Hospital. Doctor Lucas Championniere drained the abscess.[80] His incision caused Champion to lose an enormous quantity of blood. In the absence of antibiotics, the infected wound required frequent irrigation. The physician considered operating on the leg. He ordered an X-ray of the bone and confined Champion to a hospital bed for lavage treatment and complete rest.[81]

"Poor Champion!" decreed Victor Lefèvre in *L'Auto*. "Yes, poor Champion, because he was looking for an encore, but now is sentenced to rest for long days on a bed in a hospital."

The destiny of his summer was hanging in mid-air, yet he was in no state to protest. He already had gone through four operations in New York.[82] Doctor Championniere considered a possible fifth. If the infection worsened, his leg would be amputated to save his life. The longer he stayed in the hospital bed, the more competitive edge he would lose.

Elise came to his side to take care of him. George Leander, Marius Thé, Champion's mother, his three brothers, and a platoon of friends paraded in to visit. After a week, he pulled through. "Champion won't be operated on," reported *L'Auto*. "All is well, according to his latest appraisal. After a serious examination, probing the abscess at the break, and an X-ray, the general idea is that the fears were unjustified that he would need to be operated on for the fifth time. All's well that ends well. Champion is radiant today. We will see him figure brilliantly on our tracks. He will be a big attraction because he has proved he ranks among the best."[83]

Champion walked out of the hospital revved up to make the most of what he had left of the summer. He resumed light workouts to test his leg, then he progressed to hard sessions twice daily.[84] He dedicated himself to a Spartan regime.

L'Auto journalist Edouard de Perrodil had been paying attention to Champion going back to Champion's childhood performing unicycle exhibitions.[85] De Perrodil, a recreational cyclist renowned for pedaling 930 miles in 1895 from Paris to Milan, Italy, in six days,[86] found Champion a rare combination of name and achievements. He wrote a feature describing with rare insight the arc of Champion's meteoric rise: "Champion! Has there ever been in the world of sports a name so predestined?"

The feature turned into a brochure, which *L'Auto* published and sold separately, *Albert Champion: His Victories, His Adventures, His Voyage to America*. De Perrodil declared, "Champion is his name and a champion he has been in every sense of the word, for his series of victories is unheard of and unique, including every kind of genre: unicycle, bicycle, tricycle, motorcycle, and even automobile."

At the end of July Champion returned to the Buffalo Vélodrome for an evening program.[87] In a fifty-kilometer event counting in the Grand Prix of Summer series, he lined up against César Simar, a pro with ten years' experience, and Paul Guignard, the Frenchman who had challenged Walthour. Simar took an early lead, followed by Guignard. A hundred meters behind lagged Champion. After a few kilometers, Champion found his rhythm. He caught Guignard, who put up a magnificent defense for several laps before Champion dropped him. Champion caught Simar by ten kilometers. After that, he surged ahead and owned the race. Guignard's motorcycle problems cost him fourteen laps. Simar's pacer developed mechanical difficulties that required changing his motorcycle. He lost twenty-one laps. "Champion was all alone," reported Géorge Lefèvre.[88]

Champion was awarded another bouquet of flowers for his lap of honor to the accompaniment of the infield band playing "La Marseillaise." And he basked in la gloire!

July segued into August. Champion kept busy racing and training, alternating between the Buffalo Vélodrome and Parc des Princes. He won more bouquets and rode more laps of honor to "La Marseillaise." He was raking in money and fattening his bank account. The press kept his name circulating. Reporters referred to him as the ex-pony of the trainer Choppy Warburton,[89] the former Paris city champion,[90] and one of the heroes of the Vélodrome d'Hiver.[91] He continued mentoring Leander in racing tactics.[92] On the track, the American stood out in a sleeveless black jersey, the stars and stripes tied around his waist. Leander and Champion had become nearly inseparable.[93]

Stress from pushing the limits of men on machines caused breakdowns and kept drivers and cyclists always wary. In one race, the chain on Champion's aero bicycle broke in the closing miles, too late for him to fetch his replacement bike.[94] This deprived him of a chance for victory. He and cohorts paced behind ever more powerful, bulkier motorcycles. The engines throbbed with the might of a team of twenty-six horses. Windscreens over the rear wheel of pacing motorcycles upped the speed on the 666-meter Parc des Princes track—with its long straights and wide, sweeping turns—to an astounding 60 mph. The loud-firing engines, cyclists doubled over behind pacers, and the swiftness of it all dazzled audiences. At all times, disaster lurked. Champion said he had to stay alert at all times not only for where his adversaries were in the prize-money chase but also for the sounds of combusting engines: "The slightest miss not only made the motor very unsteady but consequently was very hard on the bicycle rider to follow, and it was dangerous."[95]

Like all pro athletes, he had to go to work despite feeling pain. In early August, he finished last in a three-up ninety-kilometer race (fifty-six miles) at the Parc des Princes.[96] Leander won, ahead of France's rising star Eugenio Bruni. Yet, as journalists Géorge Lefèvre in *L'Auto* and Franz Reichel in the weekly *La Vie Illustrée* saw it, Champion was the moral winner.[97] He had competed with a boil on his butt and finished despite a tire blowout, which required him to stop, change bikes, and get back in the action. "Champion, as usual, shows implausible courage. In spite of enduring an abscessed leg and now suffering a boil, he put up a good fight," wrote Lefèvre. "Champion is faster than ever."[98]

Leander had scored six victories to establish himself in major-league motor-pacing.[99] One win had come at the expense of Bobby Walthour, fresh off the ship for another campaign on the continent. Leander wrote a friend back home that he had banked $2,000 and had contracts to ride in Germany and Belgium.[100] After he fulfilled his obligations by the end of the summer, he planned to go home to Chicago and prepare for the six-day in Madison Square Garden.

Champion recovered from his boil, but the left leg became infected again, even as he accepted an invitation to compete in the Berlin Grand Prix at the Friedenau Sportpark. It drew stars from around the continent and America. He checked into the Potsdamer Platz Hotel and befriended a young German professional sprinter, Walter Rutt, staying in the next room.[101]

"I knew Champion already had a good reputation because he had won the Paris-Roubaix road race," recalled Rutt, a future world pro sprint champion, in his unpublished memoir. "One evening he asked me to provide him with the latest sports newspapers from Berlin. When I came back, he sat on his bed and showed me a deep wound on his left thigh. He complained that the wound was festering and not healing. I saw pieces of cloth from his racing trousers in the wound and thought of acetate of aluminia [a topical medication for temporary relief of skin irritations]. I went out to a nearby drugstore and bought a bottle for twenty pennies and went back to his room. Champion was wondering about the low price. He said, 'If this stuff does not help, the werewolf shall get you.'"[102]

Young Rutt followed directions on the bottle to water down the solution. He helped Champion apply a bandage. "When I entered his room the next morning, Champion received me with a cry of joy. He showed me the pieces of cloth from his racing trousers that had come out of the wound. 'What is this stuff called?' I could only answer with the name written on the bottle. He pleaded [with] me to provide him with a big bottle of this wound water."[103]

An extreme heat wave had closed down the Friedenau Sportpark for several days.[104] The temperature finally became bearable by Sunday, August 21. When the gate opened, some forty thousand spectators stampeded in to fill the grandstand and bleacher seats surrounding the five-hundred-meter velodrome. Built in 1897, before motorpacing had come on the scene, the cement track had a rough surface and shallow banking. Winter freezes caused cracks, which were patched into bumps. The track was notorious for causing accidents. A year before, Jimmy Michael was nearly killed on it.[105] His face was torn from mouth to ear and he suffered a concussion. His recovery in a Berlin hospital had taken six months.

Champion rode in a four-up 100-kilometer paced race against Thaddhaus Robl of Munich, Germany's most prolific motorpace winner and twice a world champion, German Bruno Demke, and Englishman Tommy Hall. "Champion and Hall were ill at ease on this track, which had already claimed its share of victims," according to a French report. "The Germans knew it much better and took greater risks. The race lacked any battles, which eliminated any spectator interest, although Robl covered a blazing forty-six miles in the first hour."[106]

Champion returned by train to Paris and discovered the city was mourning Leander's death.[107] About the time Champion had bumped around the Friedenau Sportpark, his protégé had suffered a violent crash on the Parc des Princes. The American had been racing against Walthour and Eugenio Bruni, tearing around a banked turn at 55 mph behind his motorpacer, when he slipped from the slipstream. A wall of dirty air promptly rose up and filled the space between him and his disappearing pacer. Leander's handlebars all of a sudden wobbled beyond his control and he catapulted sixty feet through the air. Twenty thousand spectators saw him land headfirst. His inert body bounced over the cement before coming to a rest. He died in Beaujon Hospital of brain hemorrhaging without regaining conscious.

Champion and the motorpacer corps attended the fallen hero's memorial service at the Temple de L'Avenue de la Grande-Armée.[108] Leander's body was taken to a train station for the first leg of its journey to Chicago for burial.

In response to the American's fatal accident, L'Union Vélocipedique de France barred windshields from pacing motorcycles and required pace drivers to wear tight-fitting jackets.[109]

Champion and Bobby Walthour decided to break from the code of never wearing helmets. Champion and Walthour donned thick leather headgear styled after American football players.[110]

Champion's request to represent France at the London world championships on September 3 was rejected by the French governing body because he had shirked his military duty.[111] The organization instead chose César Simar for the 100-kilometer motorpacing event. Simar finished second to Walthour.

The governing body's sports commission announced the professional fields for France's annual championships set for September 18 at the Parc des Princes. Champion and six others were selected for the twenty-ninth middle-distance race of 100 kilometers. For the national sprint championship, about two dozen of the swiftest luminaries were picked.

Champion made the cut based on consistent results and his hard-fought victory at the prestigious Grand Prix de Paris on the Parc des Princes.[112] He had raced against the aggressive Bruni, national champion Contenet, Louis Darragon, a recent revelation who would win world motorpace titles two years in a row, and Welshman Tom Linton, holder of the world hour record.

First place paid $1,600 ($43,200 in 2014).[113] When the starter fired his pistol, Bruni and Linton roared ahead like it would be just a two-man race. After ten kilometers, Darragon, a former auto mechanic, caught them and usurped the lead. The audience jumped to its feet and screamed. Darragon was back in form after breaking an arm the year before. In the final ten kilometers, Champion came from behind to catch Darragon. Lap after lap, the two men battled, to the audience's delight. With five kilometers left, Champion pulled ahead and extended his lead until he lapped Darragon. Then he kept speeding as insurance in case of mechanical failure. He lapped Darragon a second time, difficult to do on a large track, to win by about a mile. Darragon maintained a margin of thirty meters on Linton. Contenet finished four laps down and fended off Bruni by a hundred meters.

"It was an admirable fight," Charles Ravaud wrote in *Le Vélo*. "Champion snatched victory from Darragon."[114]

Yet again, Champion received a bouquet of flowers for his victory lap and again the band played "La Marseillaise."

Champion's season, and his entire career, culminated at the French national championships. More important than capturing la gloire, greater than hearing thousands cheering and applauding, more gratifying than listening to the national anthem performed for the lap of honor, and more rewarding than receiving a check valued at about $1,000, the winners would have their names written into the record books alongside immortals. Such characters had carried around their own weather, commanding all the light and relegating others to dwell in their shadows.

The middle-distance title Champion sought went back to 1885.[115] Winning times reflected technology advances.[116] Early victor, Baron Frédérick de Civry,

on a high-wheeler, had required more than four hours to ride 100 kilometers. Charles Terront on his modern bicycle with both wheels the same size,
chopped off almost an hour. Constant Huret, behind human pacers in tandem
relays, won in under three hours. Emile Bouhours, following a motor-tandem,
needed only an hour and thirty-eight minutes—less than half the time of the
early high-wheelers.

The older sprint championships,[117] which began in 1881, shimmered with
dramatic personalities. Four-time-winner Paul Médinger had his name on
Cycles Médinger,[118] made on rue Brunel a few doors from where Champion
would work for Clément, until Médinger was fatally shot through the heart in a
jealous rage by his wife, who then killed herself.[119]

Hosting the championships at the Parc des Princes, the largest vélodrome
on the continent, suited its director and owner Henri Desgrange. French vélodromes then represented churches for racing, and Parc des Princes loomed
like a cathedral. For centuries the grounds had been only for monarchs. Louis
XIV, who transformed France into a modern nation,[120] frolicked there as a
prince before he strutted around the palace in Versailles on his beloved red
high heels.[121] French royalty was honored by the grandeur of the name, Park of
Princes. Desgrange had the track surfaced with pink concrete to commemorate
the charismatic Sun King and his beloved red high heels. Desgrange's Tour de
France finished there, an annual tradition that survived him by decades. The
track's inside perimeter walls generated revenue from selling ad space hawking
wines, chocolates, tires, and autos. The grassy infield abutting the pink cement,
riders leaning into a turn, and the signage inspired a thousand posters.

"The wind was terrible, a veritable tempest," Géorge Lefèvre wrote of that
chilly Sunday afternoon.[122] The program opened with the sprint championship. Small packs of men battled in a series of five lively heats over two laps, a
little more than a mile. For about two minutes, these aristocrats of the wheel
sport sparred with their wits and legs to gain the best position as the tempo
accelerated until the tight scrum veered around the final turn. Up the finishing
straight they dipped their heads down, hair blowing back, and tried to outkick
the others until the winner zipped over the finish line. Only the fastest of each
heat advanced to semifinals and the final.

A jaunty twenty-one-year-old from Lyon named Emile Friol proved himself as the most brilliant. Tall and wiry, he dethroned the defending champion in the first heat—dealing the old guard a shock. Friol's mustache spread across his chiseled face when he smiled. Unlike Champion, carrying the character stain for dodging his military duty, Friol had fulfilled his service before he mustered out and turned to pure sprinting.[123] His brothers had a business making tires.[124] On family tires, Friol won the sprint crown final by a gallant three-length margin—his first victory of any importance.

Friol pulled on his national champion tricolor jersey and accepted his bouquet of flowers. He made his lap of honor with the band playing "La Marseillaise." The audience cheered the rising young athlete.

After the silent aristocrats came the loud motorcycles. Champion donned a long-sleeved white jersey with a black brassard bearing the number three on his right arm for those in the grandstand to see at a glance.[125] He strapped on a leather helmet and threw a leg over his aero bike.[126] An official gripped the frame in both hands. Champion jammed his feet into steel toe clips, bent his back low, and grasped the handlebar drops. He was about to race his longest and most important track event.

He and six others fanned shoulder to shoulder across the black start-finish line on the pink cement before the grandstand. All had a good chance.[127] Emile Bouhours had won it three times and owned twenty-four world track records.[128] The fair-haired, blue-eyed Norman had received thousands of letters from women. Now thirty-four, he was the oldest contender, the sentimental favorite. Defending champion Henri Contenet was determined to fight to retain his title and the tricolor jersey. Paul Guignard, short with a bushy mustache that ruled his face, was two years older than Champion. Guignard had worked as a cook until he won a major road race that established him as a national-class rider.[129] In one season, he had scored eighty-seven wins. He took up motorpacing for bigger purses. Eugenio Bruni had had some excellent results but was inconsistent.[130] Louis Darragon, the youngest, at twenty-one, was improving fast.[131] Charles Brécy, a thirty-three-year-old Parisian with a waxed handlebar mustache, had given up sprinting for motorpacing to better support his wife and three children.[132] He treated the national championship as preparation for his plan to set a new paced-track world hour record.

About fifty yards behind waited the motors.[133]

Thirty thousand spectators packed the grandstand seats, standing ten deep around the perimeter fence and spilling into the spacious infield.

Under a new rule, the cyclists were pushed off by handlers to ride a neutral lap.[134] All seven stood over their pedals and muscled big gears up to speed for the next minute and a half. Motorcycle pacers pulled around to shelter their charges. Once the phalanx of teams sped over the line, a pistol fired.

Bruni, in a long-sleeved jersey with thick vertical stripes, dashed ahead.[135] He led through ten kilometers, followed by Contenet, Brécy, Champion, and Darragon in single file. Guignard trailed by 150 meters. Bouhours, who had set the standard for years and scored a silver medal for France at the 1902 Berlin World Championships in motorpace, lagged and had already been lapped a few times.[136]

Whipping along the finishing straight after about fifteen kilometers, Champion's chain snapped apart.[137] All of a sudden, he found he was coasting on a disabled bike. His pacer zoomed away, but Champion refused to accept his fate. Recently, his leg wound had flared up again with an abscess; his only concession had been to schedule an appointment for surgery at Boucicaut Hospital after the race. He had anticipated mechanical failures and stationed a spare aero bike and a replacement motorcycle with a support crew waiting on the infield facing the grandstand—just in case.

Momentum carried him to his crew. They saw he was in trouble and ran out to catch him, since he had no brake to halt. He popped off his broken bike, grabbed a replacement, hopped on, and jumped back in the game. By the time he caught Marius Thé's draft, he had lost two laps on everyone but Bouhours.[138] Champion, down to sixth place, pursued the others scattered around the pink road. In this, the 150-lap race, he had time to make up lost ground.

The bullying wind intruded. Blustery air battered him around every turn. Champion kept adjusting his front wheel placement for drafting. He followed a pace faster than race-leader Bruni. Kilometer after kilometer, Champion reeled in those ahead, lapping them one by one. He drew encouragement—la gloire—from the wind-blown slurry of cheers and applause. At fifty kilometers (thirty-one miles), he lapped Bruni for the second time—now the score was even. Then Champion surged ahead, the new leader at sixty kilometers.

Relentless wind and high speed wore down the field. Bouhours lost so many laps that officials stopped counting, but they allowed the old lion to keep going. The first ever to win the French motorpacing title in under two hours, four years previous, Bouhours now persisted as an also-ran. Brécy had over-trained. His body taxed, he dropped off the pace and lost so many laps that he hung his head low in humility, pulled off to the side, and quit as Champion took over. Bruni, despite his splendid start, struggled with a stomachache and leg cramps and lost places.

At the one-hour mark, an official's pistol fired.[139] The announcer bellowed through his megaphone that Champion had covered sixty-six kilometers, forty-one miles, at an average speed of 41 mph. The race belonged to him. He went on to lap Guignard four times, a distance of more than two miles.[140] Defending champion Contenet lost five laps, with Darragon nine laps in arrears. Bruni abandoned at eighty kilometers.

Champion had annihilated the competition. He won in 1 hour, 31 minutes, 10 seconds, with an average speed of 41 mph.

L'Auto's front page screamed, "Two True Champions of France—Friol and Champion." On the front page the paper featured the Champion portrait by Elmer Chickering. Friol lacked such sophistication with the press. An artist sketched him in a rakish broad-brimmed hat like D'Artagnan.

"Champion rode with his usual courage and all the while he rode as a man of class, a man of quality, a man of great heart in the grand French tradition," Géorge Lefèvre wrote. "He is a man whose name preceded him well as a true champion of France."[141]

Le Vélo's Charles Ravaud added: "Champion, always marvelous to watch pacing behind the motors, will add his name to the glorious list of others he follows."[142]

Victor Breyer in *La Vie au Grand Air* declared, "Champion confirmed once again his excellent energy and endurance that we already knew he had."[143]

London's *Cycling Weekly* noted that Champion had raced at the Royal Aquarium. Champion told the correspondent: "This was the race of my life. I have been close on ten years and have at last gained my ambition, viz, to be champion of my own country. I can tell you I trained hard for one month, riding twice a day, and left the pleasures of life to others, Hence, my victory. Personally, I do not think I shall do much more bicycle racing. I have had such long innings, and my principal object to returning to Paris was to fix up with some big automobile firm to represent them in the United States of America where I have good connections."[144]

The correspondent brought up Champion's broken thigh bone. "This left him with one leg shorter than the other, while even at the present time he is suffering from a leg wound which would keep many plucky athletes in bed."

Champion pulled on his new national champion tricolor jersey for his lap of honor. The infield band once again played "La Marseillaise," this time the triumphant strains celebrating that Champion had accomplished his goal.

Afterward, there was champagne with Elise and friends.

"The next day he calmly took himself to Boucicaut [Hospital] as if he were going to mass," reported a journalist who had known him from their youth.[145]

The hospital, in the Fifteenth Arrondissement on the Left Bank, offered medicine's state-of-the-art natural ventilation with high vaulted ceilings, central steam heating, and modern plumbing with flush toilets. There a surgeon removed six bone chips from Champion's thigh, finally taking out the source of his painful abscess.[146] That night, however, Champion experienced yet another calamity. He woke in the middle of the night with his wound hemorrhaging.[147]

"But Champion did not panic," the account continued. "He calmly sprang from his bed and went to fetch the intern, who was able, in time, to beat back any serious repercussions. The next day, Champion recounted the episode laughing, while showing off the half-dozen bone chips that had been skillfully removed from his body."[148]

As he recovered, he received lucrative offers. Desgrange hired him to race on the Parc des Princes against Bruni, Walthour, and others through the end of October.

An offer—an appearance fee likely around $1,000—to race came from Dresden, one of Germany's most beautiful cities,[149] and Champion accepted. On a frosty and blustery October 9, Champion bundled up in wool tights, leather gloves, and his tricolor for 100 kilometers against German wunderkind Thaddeus Robl, Englishman Tommy Hall, and French compatriot César Simar. He lapped Robl seventeen times to even the score from their Berlin contest, and he buried the others even deeper. Champion crushed them.

Back in France on the last Sunday in October, Champion entered his final race at the Parc des Princes.[150] He paced behind Franz Hoffmann. Trained in Germany as a mechanical engineer, Hoffmann loved the motors and had gained a reputation in Germany, France, and America as a master in the art of pace driving. He had fine facial features and a small chin. In his cloth cap and leather jacket, he sat ensconced squarely upright over the rear wheel. He had led Robl to dozens of victories and Walthour to triumph at the London world championships. Hoffmann had paced Basil De Guichard to win thirty-nine races and Harry Elkes to win his last ten rides. In Elkes's fatal race, his last words to Hoffmann had been to speed up.

Champion won. Thousands of Parisians and a contingent of American expats surrounding the Parc des Princes oval gave him a rousing valedictory victory lap. He waved his clutch of flowers at everyone. "La Marseillaise" filled the air for his benefit for the umpteenth time.

Soon came an invitation to leave Paris for New York to ride an exhibition race against Tommy Hall at the next Madison Square Garden six-day.[151] However enticing, he had seen former idol Bouhours downgraded to a no-hoper. Champion's own receding hairline reminded him every day that his physical powers were on the wane. He opted to retire at the crest of la gloire!

It was time to disengage from his skein of a thousand races and exhibitions, to make a fresh career shift. The wised up were gravitating to autos. Desgrange's nemesis, *Le Vélo*, ten years old, surrendered in the circulation war and became *Le Journal de l'Automobile*.[152]

Champion stayed in Paris.[153] He apprenticed himself to auto companies to research how engines were built. His new endeavor was to become the sole US agent importing engine parts from French manufacturers.

10

DEBUT OF CHAMPION
SPARK PLUGS

THEY LOVE TO "SPARK" IN THE DARK OLD PARK,
AS THEY GO FLYING ALONG.
SHE SAID SHE KNOWS WHY THE MOTOR GOES.
THE "SPARKER" IS AWFULLY STRONG.
  —"IN MY MERRY OLDSMOBILE," GUS EDWARDS
      AND VINCENT P. BRYAN, 1905[1]

What fascinated Champion the most about autos were electrical components that powered gas-combustion engines—in particular spark plugs, magnetos, and the coil wires that connected them together.[2] While in Paris to prepare himself for importing French auto parts to America, two former motorpace rivals suffered excruciating deaths.

First, there was Jimmy Michael,[3] who had agreed to replace Champion for motorpace exhibitions in the Madison Square Garden six-day. However, he died while aboard the *La Savoie* en route to New York. The cause was a brain hemorrhage from his earlier accident racing on the Friedenau track in Berlin. Officers of the ship wanted to bury him at sea. A number of French, Belgian, Dutch, Italian, and Swiss cyclists accompanying Michael protested the tossing of his body into the cold Atlantic. They guaranteed the expenses of bringing him to New York. When *La Savoie* docked on October 26, Michael's comrades gave him a hasty burial in an unmarked grave in Brooklyn's Greenwood Cemetery.

Then there was Charles Brécy, pedaling snugly behind his driver, who was seated over the rear wheel of the motorcycle, around the Parc des Princes track on a world-record pace of 56 mph for 100 kilometers (62.5 miles).[4] Brécy had completed ninety-one kilometers as he flashed past a photographer with a camera mounted on a tripod at the end of the home straight. Brécy looked comfortable in the motorcycle's slipstream. A long-sleeved jersey and shorts was all he needed that mid-November day. A wool cap covered his receding hairline. Bare hands rested lightly on the handlebars. He sought to even the score after losing the national championship at this distance to Albert Champion. Seconds later on the back straight, without warning, the motorcycle engine quit. Brécy smashed into the roller bar hanging over the vehicle's rear wheel.[5] He was thrown to the cement and hurled with full force against the railing. An ambulance rushed him, bleeding from scrapes to his arms and legs, to Boucicaut Hospital. For twelve days, he shrieked in agony until he succumbed. He left a wife and three children.

French historian Pierre Chany summed up the arc of a baker's dozen such motorpace fatalities among Champion's cohorts: flying along, a false move, a fall, the hospital, and the cemetery. Chany called the years from 1900 to 1904, "The Game of the Massacre."[6]

Michael and Brécy were laid to rest while Champion, the rare motorpacer to retire at the top of his game, found employment in a succession of auto plants to build up his knowledge and create his own supply network. Paris, the birthplace of the modern automobile, was home to an array of marques. Among them were Panhard, Darracq, Renault, De Dion-Bouton, Mors, and Aster. It was natural that he would work for his former boss, Adolphe Clément-Bayard, at the factory in Levallois-Perret.

Clément-Bayard was purchasing from Edouard Nieuport the very electrical components that Champion planned to import to America, and, convenient for Clément-Bayard, Nieuport also had a plant in Levallois-Perret.[7] Nieuport was causing a sensation in the continent's auto world for producing spark plugs, magnetos, and coils for cars that were sweeping prestigious events in France and Belgium.[8] Nieuport was among Champion's oldest friends. He had won the race on the Vélodrome d'Hiver for the fastest lap in the program that culminated with Champion claiming the Paris city championship, Les Gosses Blanc.[9] Champion's employment included a stint at Nieuport's cramped factory at 13 rue des Frères Herbert.[10]

Edouard Nieuport had more coal-black hair on his head than he needed along with a thick mustache waxed with ends pointing up like a bull's horns. He was a proud Parisian, although he had been born in Blida, Algeria when his father, Colonel Edmund Deniéport, commanded the army garrison in the French colony.[11] He had attended an electrical engineering college in Paris and, though a top student, he'd abandoned classes at nineteen to race bicycles.[12] His parents were indignant that he chose what they regarded a foolhardy pastime. So the family name would not be tainted in the eyes of his parents, their shy, modest son competed under the assumed name of "Nieuport." He went by it for the rest of his life.

Short in stature, he had small hands and narrow shoulders. He also had a clever tactical mind and had racked up ten straight handicap victories one summer.[13] He and Champion would have seen each other in action at the Paris vélodromes. Nieuport had scored third in a national sprint championship. He was thrilled by speed and fearless; that is, until he competed in a paced race behind three men pedaling a triplet tandem on the Vélodrome de la Seine. He crossed the line first, only to black out and crash.[14] A doctor prescribed a different occupation.

Nieuport was eager to take what he had learned about aerodynamics from cycling and apply it to autos and new gliders that were gaining attention. In the summer of 1898, he had decided to invest prize money he had saved to go into business, although he had no plan. All he had was a fascination with autos and an irresistible curiosity about the mystery of the electrical ignition in gas-combustion engines, still scarcely explored as an area of expertise. Nieuport buried himself in the family library and read books and journals about the physical sciences, particularly the study of electricity.[15] His younger brother and sister had to tread quietly as he proceeded in his willful education about what makes electrons flow, the force of volts carrying electricity, and electricity's role in making autos go. Research led him to learn about the Belgian engineer Étienne Lenoir, who had lived in Paris and invented the first spark plug in 1860 for an engine to propel carriages. Lenoir's archetype was an integral unit containing the three elements used ever since—an insulator, two electrodes, and the spark gap. Back then, only a small number of engines were mounted on carriages. The engines were notoriously inefficient, loud, and prone to overheating. Nieuport overlooked their shortcomings and, indeed, considered their potential.

His mother grew concerned.[16] She prevailed on friends to find him an accounting job in a bank. Her son rejected the intrusion. He subsequently decided to manufacture spark plugs, spark coils, and magnetos. He rented a shop in Levallois-Perret. His funds, however, disappeared fast. Fortunately, despite the sting they had felt over his refusal to follow a military career like his father and both grandfathers, his parents did not hesitate to help.

Spark plugs are simple. They are narrow cylinders less than three inches long and weighing only ounces. In gas-combustion engines, however, they are indispensable in firing the pistons that propel vehicles weighing thousands of pounds.

The top of these modern spark plugs had a terminal connected by a wire to a magneto that created high-voltage electricity. An electrical insulator, printed with the name of the manufacturer, descended the length of the plug to provide electric insulation for the central electrode. A metal combustion seal prevented leakage from the combustion chamber. The bottom metal jacket removed heat from the insulator and acted as a ground for the spark passing through the central electrode to the side electrode. The outside of this metal jacket was threaded for fastening the spark plug to the engine. The magneto created an electric pulse strong enough to spark the gap between the center and side electrodes to ignite the fuel and air mixture in the chamber and drive the piston down.

Though more and more gas-powered autos chugged along roads in the 1890s, spark plugs were still a pesky work in progress. Motor enthusiasts inquired, "What is a spark plug?"[17] Ideal ones fired the spark that ignited gas fumes and air at the right time in the piston chamber to push the piston down for the power stroke, driving the vehicle ahead. Yet the vast majority of spark plugs for sale misfired. Nieuport examined how to improve spark plugs and produce efficient ones.

Nieuport figured that existing spark plugs performed poorly due to inferior materials. The best materials were as critical to spark plugs as the best ingredients are to a cook making a meal. For the central electrode point that fired in the engine, Nieuport settled on platinum,[18] or at least nickel as an alternative, because of the durability and tolerance of those metals for extremely high temperatures—hotter than one thousand degrees Fahrenheit. He devised spark plugs timed to hit the power stroke at the proper time. His products relied on porcelain as the electrical insulator to keep the plugs watertight. He ruled out the soapstone and lava insulators favored by other brands.

The craft of firing clay into porcelain for mass-producing dinner plates and vases had been around France for a couple centuries, thanks to King Louis XIV banning the import of foreign porcelain, chiefly from China, to protect French ceramists.[19] Nieuport's spark plugs with porcelain insulators were why cars that used his spark plugs won prizes.

Champion spent enough time with Nieuport to learn that his friend did a lot of thinking while driving a little blunt-nosed Darracq. While leaning over the steering wheel to scan the road ahead and avoid potholes, Nieuport formulated how to make a better, higher-voltage magneto—consisting of a coil of copper wire wound between the poles of a magnet to provide electrical current that ignited a spark plug.[20] After trial and error, he produced his Nieuport Magneto. He advertised it as simpler and stronger than other brands.[21] His magneto fitted in the palm of his hand, so light he could easily lift it with his fingertips. He also made Nieuport batteries.

Inferior electric components had caused the engine of the motorcycle pacing Brécy to cease working all of a sudden. If his pacing machine had kept going just minutes longer, he would have clinched the prized world record, assuring him higher appearance fees for the next season to support his family with more comfort. However, the motorcycle suffered a failure of its spark plugs, coils, or magneto—a frequent inconvenience, but fatal for Brécy. His driver had finished unharmed.[22] Nieuport and Champion, mindful of this tragic crash on a track they knew like the faces they shaved, were resolved to create better ignition accessories.

In the meantime, orders poured in for Nieuport's products. He was fascinated with autos and motorcycles, and even more passionate about combustion engines for what they would mean for flying airplanes.

Before Champion left Nieuport's factory to continue his study of autos, Nieuport agreed to sell him wholesale all the electric-ignition parts he wanted.

Frank Duane Stranahan grew impatient to embark on a new career before he turned thirty. For the last seven years, he had been managing the Savoy Hotel on Washington Street in downtown Boston's bustling shopping and theater district.[23] The hotel, celebrated for luxury and refinement, gave Stranahan a comfortable life and stature in the business community. Yet he had met all the challenges many times over. The hotelier's long hours, intermittent emergencies, and humdrum routines over time agitated him to do more with his talents. If he had been in the audience at Charles River Park witnessing Champion careen on his motorcycle around the track on his way to setting a new world record for the mile, Stranahan would have admired his freedom and his panache.

The automobiles rollicking and honking through city streets appealed to Stranahan as a way to change his life. He monitored their progress in the business community. In 1898 a half-dozen electric, steam, and gas-powered autos manufactured in Massachusetts had been accepted in a general exhibition that embraced all sorts of industrial machinery on display in the Mechanics Building.[24] Along Huntington Avenue on the Back Bay, the brick structure crouched with arches over windows like raised eyebrows. The Mechanics Building claimed the largest exhibition space in all six New England states.[25] As novelties, autos were exhibited in the basement; the street level was dedicated to displaying motor boats from the leading builders from around the country. At subsequent industrial exhibitions in the Mechanics Building, auto companies clamored for their own show. He heard the talk buzzing around town about meetings convened by the building's trustees to open additional street-floor space to auto exhibits.

When the Boston Automobile Dealers' Association took over the auto shows in 1903,[26] the building's Exhibition Hall and Grand Hall quickly sold out. Trustees had barred motor vehicles from Paul Revere Hall. Its polished wooden floor was rarely available except for dancing during major social occasions. Exhibition overflow was diverted up the avenue to the Horticultural Hall. To Bostonians accustomed to viewing rare commonwealth orchids and roses, huge motor trucks looked strange. By the next year, demand for more exhibition space forced trustees to surrender Paul Revere Hall to the invasion of motorcars.[27] Exhibits of motor boats were relegated to the basement. The Boston auto shows boasted that they ranked second only to those in New York's Madison Square Garden. Stranahan anticipated a new business ascending.

Savoy guests noticed Frank D. Stranahan, an earnest man with impeccable dress and good manners. His barbered dark hair and mustache could pass military inspection. He welcomed strangers and friends alike. His hospitality came from experience greeting customers, negotiating with shifty vendors, supervising disinclined staff, and managing income against expenses for his livelihood. As a result, he ensured return visits from tourists and business travelers. When traffic turned quiet, he headed to the billiard room to hone his shooting skills.

He had absorbed the hotel trade from his father, the wheeling and dealing if occasionally cavalier Robert Allen Stranahan, renowned as the ideal hotel man—open, generous, courteous, and solicitous of the welfare of his guests.[28] The *Boston Journal* called him one of Boston's most popular landlords. In 1896 when he bought the lease to the Savoy Hotel, he was only forty-six and suffering from tuberculosis. Frank ran the hotel's day-to-day affairs. In the summer of 1898 the elder Stranahan was thrown from a carriage and badly injured.[29] Soon afterward, he lost his battle against tuberculosis.[30]

As the eldest son of a Victorian-era household, Frank had stepped up to provide for his widowed mother Lizzie; sister Anna, sixteen; brother Spencer, fourteen; and twelve-year-old Robert Allen Jr. An older sister, Ada, lived with her husband in Brookline. Frank inherited his father's lease to the Savoy and inaugurated upgrades.[31] The restaurant enjoyed an excellent reputation. He brought in an orchestra to entertain evening diners. He opened a billiards parlor and furnished all rooms with every modern appliance and comfort. The *Boston Herald* predicted Frank could "become as popular in the hotel world as his late lamented father."[32]

In spite of the encouragement, he had an entrepreneurial streak and looked for a way to break from the hotel world—and his beloved father's shadow. Robert Allen Stranahan had been sued in 1889 for personal gain over a bond issue he was charged with floating under the guise of raising money for a gas company in Buffalo, where the family then lived.[33] The suit sullied his name and threw his financial stability into jeopardy. In the late nineteenth century, for almost all troubles short of murder you could give yourself a fresh start simply by leaving town. A third-generation Scotch-Irish, he had moved his family to Boston to blend among the large concentration of Irish and begin anew in the hotel business. Even after his father's death, however, Frank and his mother were left to clean up Robert Allen Stranahan's remaining debts from the Buffalo scandal. As a consequence, Lizzie, her curly dark hair graying, drilled Frank and his siblings well into their adulthood over the ethics of careful social and financial behavior.[34]

The Savoy located Frank Stranahan in the midst of Boston's theater district, which cultivated his taste for the stage and a passion for musicals. In May 1902 he had attended a road show of a Chinese musical comedy titled *San Toy* at the Boston Museum Theater on Tremont Street.[35] The cast included the chic, vivacious, and fetching Marie Celeste. She had been entertaining audiences and impressing theater critics with her singing and dancing for more than a decade.[36] Bewitched, Stranahan arranged to meet her after a show.

He had only two weeks to win her heart before she was to leave town with the troupe, and he had competition from a pack of stage-door Johnnies lavishing her with bouquets of roses and wedding proposals.[37] Caught in whirlwind courtship, he delegated duties at the Savoy so as to attend evening and matinee performances. Before the curtain went down after the final act, he elbowed through a bunch of male admirers and stole her away.

Beyond the footlights and without makeup, she was a demure, straightlaced New Yorker. She had studied music at a Gotham observatory as preparation to sing opera.[38] However, when she was sixteen, her father died, forcing her to earn a living. First, she had gone all the way to Halifax, Nova Scotia, to win an audition in a stock company. Later she moved to a company in Portland, Maine, to sing light opera. That led to performing as the leading woman on Broadway in *Mother Goose* and *Son Toy*. Her real name was Marie Celeste Martin. Stranahan campaigned to change her family name to his.

She assessed him as a capable businessman from a loving family—a loyal son and responsible older brother—and ardent about auditioning as her leading man. When *San Toy* concluded and the stagehands packed the sets to leave for their next engagement, the couple announced *their* engagement.[39] They married on the morning of June 2, 1902.[40] The ceremony in the nearly deserted Church of Our Savior lacked any of the usual wedding features. No marriage date was announced, a strategy he relied on to evade adversaries vying for her hand. Only twelve persons were present—Frank's mother and siblings and some of the bride's cast friends. Everyone had to pledge the utmost secrecy. The bride's mother was still in New York. After her vows,

Marie announced her retirement from the stage to live with her husband in Brookline.

By the time the trustees of the Mechanics Building acquiesced to make Paul Revere Hall available to the Boston Automobile Dealers for the auto show, Frank and Marie had a son, Duane. Frank decided to jump into the auto business in time for the third annual show in March 1905. Following his strategies from playing billiards, he planned at least three moves ahead.

In the spring of 1905 Champion and Elise returned to Boston. He brought trunks of Nieuport spark plugs, coils, magnetos, and storage batteries. Next he shopped for a location to rent and set up his import business. Most cars made in America relied on imported ignition parts and Champion sought to meet that demand.

Ample space beckoned in the South End. On Tremont Street loomed the landmark Cyclorama—a fortress-like round brick building festooned with towers and parapets. It had survived a fashionable form of entertainment popular in cities across North America that had rendered extravagant scenes from historic or biblical events. Boston's Cyclorama in the 1880s featured a huge painting of the Battle of Gettysburg, the Civil War's turning point. Paris artist Paul Dominique Philippoteaux had depicted a dramatic scene on canvas fifty feet tall and wrapping 400 four hundred feet around the building's inte-rior.[41] Ticket holders entered through a long, narrow hallway, trekked up a circular underground stairway, and discovered they were in the middle of the battlefield—looking at a panorama of rolling hills, valleys, open fields, ditches, stone walls, and soldiers in blue and gray uniforms firing rifles and cannons at each other. Life-size mannequins of troops standing on the floor with pitched tents and cannons augmented the scene to give viewers the frisson of witnessing the bloody battle.

The Cyclorama had boomed for several years before ticket sales waned. The painting went into storage and the artifacts were dispersed. Next, the building had hosted bare-fisted boxing matches, roller skating, and horseback riding. Then, finally, it was partitioned to attract commercial tenants.

One day Champion strolled in, looking to rent. The Cyclorama was mostly vacant. A mason occupied 517 Tremont Street.[42] A tenant at 525 Tremont Street built horse-drawn wagons. A pair of companies took up 541 Tremont Street—the Tremont Garage Company, incorporated in March 1905 to repair autos, and the Boston Buick dealership, one of the first on the East Coast.[43] Both of these enterprises were operated by Frank D. Stranahan.

Stranahan, seizing the opportunity to get into the auto business, had finally sold his lease on the Savoy Hotel. He had formed a partnership with W. E. Eldridge, importer of household goods.[44] The dealership took months to arrange with Buick headquarters in Flint, Michigan. At last, a two-cylinder Buick with four leather seats arrived by train. This model was called a tonneau, referring to its rear seats with a wooden body open to the sky like a rowboat. It came in time for Stranahan to enter it in the fourth annual Eagle Rock Hill Climb in West Orange, New Jersey, near Newark, on Thanksgiving Day, November 24, 1904.[45] When horses and buggies still ruled the roads, hill climbs demonstrated motor-vehicle reliability. The Automobile Club of New Jersey promoted its Eagle Rock Hill Climb as the first in America.[46]

Hundreds of spectators turned out to watch drivers race one by one for the fastest time over Eagle Rock Avenue's cobblestones. The avenue's steep grade proved too much for many vehicles. Successful ones powered all the way to sweep around the sharp left turn into Eagle Rock Reservation, a forest preserve and home to bald eagles. Frank in his Buick needed a little more than 2 minutes to win in record time in the division for autos costing between $850 and $1,250.[47] He had earned publicity and bragging rights.

It was in the Cyclorama that Champion and Stranahan met. The French national cycling champion and the former hotel manager realized that although they came from different backgrounds, they now shared the same vision for automobiles. Motor cars were so recent that the enterprise drew audacious men who on the whole came up from transportation or finance. Stranahan had run a bicycle shop before joining his father in the hotel trade and likely had followed the Frenchman's exploits in Boston papers or perhaps even watched him race around velodromes.

Stranahan valued celebrity star power as a commercial asset. Champion's world records, especially driving a motorcycle a mile under a minute, had promoted his name. In turn, Albert would have heard about the Savoy Hotel. Its classy reputation attested to Stranahan's bona fides in financial savvy and business management. The two men discussed how they could combine resources for their mutual benefit.

Stranahan doubled as president and treasurer of the Tremont Garage Company.[48] Younger sister Anna served as clerk.[49] Champion's inventory would complement the Tremont Garage Company's auto repairs. For discussions about joining the Frenchman's enterprise, Frank consulted younger brother Spencer. Spencer, with his thinner face and stronger jaw line, was a talented athlete,[50] and he had graduated from Prince High School at fifteen,[51] in the same class as Anna, who was three years older.[52] Their younger brother, Robert Allen Jr., was away at Harvard, the first in the family to attend college. Albert and Frank and Spencer agreed to run their businesses from the same address and share an economy of scale with billing and payments. They would all draw modest salaries while they built up the enterprise.

Frank D. Stranahan about the time he was treasurer of the Albert Champion Company. *Photo courtesy of Ann and Stephen Stranahan.*

The time was auspicious. Auto production and sales had rocketed ten-fold nationwide in five years, to 25,000 cars in 1905.[53] The Massachusetts Highway Commission announced that summer that it would start requiring licenses for drivers and autos; by the end of the year, the commission would claim it had registered 3,206 autos.[54]

Thus, on June 10, 1905, the two Stranahans and Champion combined their energy and vision for the future when they incorporated the Albert Champion Company at 541 Tremont Street in the Commonwealth of Massachusetts with capital of $5,000 as a wholesale business to import French auto parts.[55]

One hundred shares of $50 stock were issued.[56] Frank held majority ownership, fifty-one shares to Albert's forty-nine. Content with a big-name partner, Frank settled for the title of treasurer. Spencer was the clerk.

Albert Champion was president.

Precocious Spencer Stranahan was clerk in the Albert Champion Company. *Photo courtesy of Ann and Stephen Stranahan.*

The Albert Champion Company in Boston's South End was
incorporated in Massachusetts in June 1905 with $5,000 capital. *Photo
courtesy of Ann and Stephen Stranahan.*

Right away, Champion followed the example of his Paris boss, Clément-
Bayard, a devoted advocate of advertising, by launching the first in a stream
of ads in *Automobile* promoting the Albert Champion Company as the sole US
agent importing Nieuport's ignition products. Ads boasted: "Everything for
electrical ignition."[57]

The Albert Champion Company came to life with heavy wooden crates hitting
the Cyclorama's cement floor with a thud. The crates held spark plugs, spark
coils, magnetos, and batteries. Teamsters hauled them on handcarts from a
horse-drawn truck parked outside. Champion and the Stranahan brothers
unpacked inventory and sorted accessories into boxes on wooden shelves in
rows at the rear of 541 Tremont Street. Overstock went to off-site storage.

Consumed by his new career, Champion left his previous accomplishments—documented in his scrapbook—locked in a trunk to be discovered decades later.

Building the enterprise from scratch involved traveling by train to cities and towns around New England and down to New York. Champion had a network of contacts to exploit. He lugged a leather case packed with sample accessories to jobbers—wholesale merchants supplying retail auto and motorcycle companies. The former star athlete transformed himself into a sales rep. He joined the men's club of drummers in suits and shined shoes riding the rails to sell their wares. When he returned to the Cyclorama, he sat at his desk to fill out the paperwork that serves as the lifeblood of commerce. If he missed riding behind the heat of a fast motorcycle,[58] feeling the adrenaline rush of the chase, risking his life to make another conquest, he found what he desired on Long Island when he met the lovely French actress Olta de Kerman.

Olta de Kerman had accompanied her husband Jean Hallier to Mineola, NY, on a seasonably mild and cloudy Saturday, October 14, to watch the second-annual running of the Vanderbilt Cup Race. Sometime after the 6 a.m. start Champion met them among the five thousand chichi mingling on the grandstand,[59] which still smelled of the fresh-cut boards that had been used to erect the facility on the Jericho Turnpike.

The Vanderbilt Cup was America's premier international auto road race. The inaugural 283-mile event had been won by a low-slung, rakish Panhard.[60] The French car had averaged more than 50 mph. The Panhard's victory had attested that gas-powered autos had a technology advantage over steam and electric vehicles for driving long distances at high speed.

Behind the glorious cup race was railroad heir and pioneer racecar driver William K. Vanderbilt Jr. He had donated an ornate silver loving cup made by Tiffany and Company. The 10.5-gallon cup swelled to the breadth of a stout man's chest and weighed thirty pounds.[61] Called Willy K. by his friends,[62] Vanderbilt was a handsome, athletic aristocrat who had been cosseted in private schools in preparation for Harvard. He had married the daughter of a US senator who had amassed wealth from the Nevada Comstock silverlode. Vanderbilt and his wife, Virginia, had traveled in Europe, where he'd been awed by ultra-long car races on public roads and how much more advanced continental automakers were than their US counterparts. With the clout to challenge America's auto industry, complacent about holding short car races on horse tracks, and to propose the country's first long-distance road race, he had arranged for the American Automobile Association to sanction the event, and he'd invited foreign automakers to send cars and drivers. The competitive field was limited to five cars per country. Other than the challenge cup, his race offered no purse. Companies paid drivers substantial bonuses just for press coverage.

In the grandstand where Champion circulated, Vanderbilt held court with his wife, his sister Consuelo, the Duchess of Marlborough, and New York's fashionables. Another one hundred thousand folks watched along the 28.3-mile route on Nassau County dirt roads—one of the largest audiences ever to see a sporting event in America.[63]

Substantial crowds collected at all six turns. Men and women watched from the edge of the road, unprotected by a fence or any kind of barrier. When the nineteen muscular vehicles downshifted and braked to crawl around sharp corners, spectators were close enough to reach out and touch the cars, and when the autos charged through the turns, their unmuffled engines growling under the strain of making up lost time, tires would spray dirt at the feet of the gathered masses. The heavy chariots bounced over undulating roads past farm fields for ten laps, a grueling gauntlet of 283 miles. Posters nailed to trees and telegraph poles and pasted onto barns months before the event warned local residents, "Chain your dogs and lock up your fowls!"[64]

Five American cars and drivers lined up against fourteen renowned drivers and vehicles from France, Germany, and Italy. The stars and stripes snapped in the wind over the grandstands. Champion saw for the first time his future business partner, French-speaking Swiss native Louis Chevrolet, at the wheel of a Fiat in his first season racing in American. Like many drivers, Chevrolet peered through goggles and chomped on a cigar that served as a mouthpiece to keep him from breaking teeth while bumping over the roads. He held the bottom of the steering wheel with an underhand grip.

All but one car carried a large number on the front, big enough for anyone to spot from a distance. The exception was the car driven by American Albert Campbell. Issued "unlucky" number thirteen,[65] the superstitious Campbell had instead placed a large X across the nose of his Mercedes.

Louis Chevrolet, the Swiss-French racer, made the passenger car bearing his name and two Indy 500 winners. He and Champion were friends until Champion betrayed him. *Photo courtesy of General Motors Media Archive.*

After the first lap, accidents and equipment failures turned the contest into a race of attrition. Despite Albert Campbell's exorcising his Mercedes from the jinxing number thirteen, on the second lap his gas tank fell off.[66] During lap seven, Louis Chevrolet smashed at high speed into a telegraph pole on an S-curve.[67] The collision tore off a front wheel, bent the axle beyond repair, and crushed the front end into a tangled junk heap. Chevrolet barely escaped being killed. A photo of him sitting behind the steering wheel of the demolished Fiat contributed to his legend.

A two-sided scoreboard similar to those in ballparks stood above the stand reserved for press and officials, across the road from the grandstand, to provide updates on the standings and how many laps remained.[68]

The grandstand was filled with the privileged. They socialized while unpacking picnic baskets loaded with food and cases of drink to devour. Champion relaxed with Olta de Kerman and Jean Hallier and chatted in torrents of rapid French. Hallier preferred a tall, silk top hat to Champion's wool cap. Hallier's wife, one of the few women attending, looked stylish under a flowery hat secured with a wide ribbon tied under her delicate chin. White gloves protected her small hands. She was petite, like Elise, with elegant facial features. Olta's beauty bewitched Champion. For some five hours, as the fastest racecars on two continents thundered under the start-finish banner spanning the Jericho Turnpike and rumbled past the grandstand, setting off a tremendous ovation, Albert and Olta flirted with stolen glances and subtle winks.

The aptly named French driver, Victor Hemery, averaged a little over 60 mph to win in a Darracq that ran on Nieuport's electrical components.[69] Hemery claimed not only the Vanderbilt Cup to hold for a year but also $12,000 from the New York distributors of Darracqs and Michelin tires. Minutes later, a Panhard dashed over the finish line for second place. Once again, the Vanderbilt Cup turned into a French affair.

People swarmed from the grandstand onto the Jericho Turnpike to go home.[70] Vanderbilt, alarmed, fled the grandstand and yelled at officials to stop the race to prevent the injury of spectators and drivers. Officials waving checkered flags ran up the road to warn oncoming drivers that the race was over.

By the time Champion trundled down the grandstand, he and Olta de Kerman had arranged a liaison.

Champion had sold most of his inventory. A month after the Vanderbilt Cup event he shipped out to Paris on a mission to bring back more French ignition accessories. He left Elise behind. His month-long visit stretched through Christmas and New Year's Eve, ushering in 1906.

Gossip from friends in the City of Light reached Elise—Albert was escorting Olta de Kerman around. Elise, on her own, discovered that the actress and her husband lived at 260 West 25th Street in New York.[71] Elise communicated with Jean Hallier, at home. He confirmed his wife was overseas. By then he may have learned about his wife and Champion. Elise and Jean Hallier devised a plan.

On Tuesday, January 2, Albert and Olta returned to New York on the French steamship *La Loraine*. Huddled on the harbor pier in the freezing offshore wind were hundreds of friends and relatives of passengers as well as newspaper reporters. Elise, appearing greatly agitated, clutched tightly the arm of Jean Hallier, standing by her side.[72] Before the ship docked, Elise appealed to Officer Farley, a New York City policeman.[73] She explained that her husband was traveling with another woman and requested protection in case she was assaulted by her husband's companion.

Among the first to walk down the gangplank and come ashore were Albert and Olta.[74] Elise broke from Hallier and rushed to the gangway, followed closely by Hallier.

Elise wore a fur coat and dress that covered her feet. She moved as through on wheels as she rushed toward her husband. "You villain! How dare you deceive me in such a manner? Your little game is all known to me now. I shall immediately begin divorce proceedings."[75]

Before Albert had time to reply, she turned and walked away to the far end of the pier. Hallier joined her.[76] Albert hastened into the Customs Office.

"Mrs. Champion and Mrs. Hallier looked daggers at each other for a full half hour while Mrs. Hallier's baggage was being examined by the customs officers," reported the *New York World*. "The actress was approached by Hallier, who talked with her in French for several minutes."[77]

Their loud voices drew the attention of everybody on the pier. Hallier finally returned to Elise's side. They left together to intercept their spouses exiting the Customs Office.

Elise, with tears streaming from her eyes, told a reporter the story of her troubles with her husband. "A month ago Mr. Champion sailed for France. I learned that woman," she added, pointing at Mrs. Hallier and glaring at her like a tigress, "was to accompany him. He met her during the automobile races on Long Island. Ever since that time he has been infatuated with her."[78]

After clearing customs and claiming his luggage, Champion defended himself to journalists. "It is simply a case of a jealous woman," he said. "I have been guilty of no wrong-doing, and my wife has no cause to be jealous."[79]

Newspapers capitalized on the confrontation. The *World* broadcast, "Albert Champion, Bicycle Rider, and His Spouse Have Trouble."

Dispatches thrummed over national wire services. The *Boston Herald* repeated the New York accounts and published oval portraits of Elise and Olta adjacent to one another, like boxers promoting a bout. Line art represented the women quarreling as their men stamped away in opposite directions, Hallier in a top hat, coattail flying in the wake of his long strides, Champion in cloth cap. Shy Elise, a homemaker, had always avoided publicity. Now her picture, in fur coat and a fashionable hat, was printed for all of Boston to see and next to the very stranger who threatened her marriage, which must have intensified her humiliation. To her, the public spectacle could not be more louche. Or repulsive.

In due course Albert and Elise reconciled, though she had wised up to his cruelty.

For Champion, the affair was just one of those things. He shrugged off the Fourth Estate tattlers. Boston's papers were forever chasing sensational stories, concentrating on the bizarre and morbid.[80]

The brazenness of his affair cracked open a rift between Champion and the Stranahans, alert to a high standard of ethical behavior. The family matriarch Lizzie could hardly miss reading the *Herald*'s coverage and would have had a strong voice in family discussions about disassociating the Stranahan name from Albert Champion.[81] She recognized the damage his behavior could have to the family's name after their successful management of Boston's most important hotels. The Frenchman lived by his own rules, behaved like a pirate.

Ambitious to get back to work, Champion rationalized his conduct. He and his partners now had basic differences, like water and oil. Nothing they could do, however, would bother him. He did not need them, although they needed the prestige of his name.

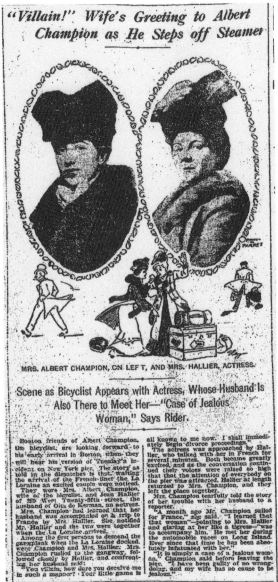

"Villain!" Wife's Greeting to Albert Champion as He Steps off Steamer

MRS. ALBERT CHAMPION, ON LEFT, AND MRS. HALLIER, ACTRESS.

Scene as Bicyclist Appears with Actress, Whose Husband Is Also There to Meet Her—"Case of Jealous Woman," Says Rider.

Boston friends of Albert Champion, the bicyclist, are looking forward to his early arrival in Boston, when they will hear his version of Tuesday's incident on New York pier. The story as told in the dispatches is that, waiting the arrival of the French liner the La Loraine an excited couple were noticed.

They were Mrs. Albert Champion, wife of the bicyclist, and Jean Hallier of 289 West Twenty-fifth street, the husband of Olta de Kerman, an actress.

Mrs. Champion had learned that her husband was accompanied on a trip to France by Mrs. Hallier. She notified Mr. Hallier and the two were together when the La Loraine arrived.

Among the first persons to descend the gangplank when the La Loraine docked were Champion and Mrs. Hallier. Mrs. Champion rushed to the gangway, followed closely by Hallier, and confronting her husband said:

"You villain, how dare you deceive me in such a manner? Your little game is all known to me now. I shall immediately begin divorce proceedings."

The actress was approached by Hallier, who talked with her in French for several minutes. Both became greatly excited, and as the conversation continued their voices were raised so high that that the attention of everybody on the pier was attracted. Hallier at length returned to Mrs. Champion, and they left the place together.

Mrs. Champion tearfully told the story of her trouble with her husband to a reporter.

"A month ago Mr. Champion sailed for France," she said. "I learned that that woman"—pointing to Mrs. Hallier and glaring at her like a tigress—"was to accompany him. He met her during the automobile races on Long Island. Ever since that time he has been absolutely infatuated with her."

"It is simply a case of a jealous woman," Champion said before leaving the pier. "I have been guilty of no wrongdoing, and my wife has no cause to be jealous."

Champion's affair with French actress Olta de Kerman, right, made for racy reading in newspapers, including this story in the *Boston Herald*. It marked a rare occasion when Champion's wife Elise, left, was in the news—for calling her husband a villain. The scandal caused tension between Champion and his business partners. *From the* Boston Herald, *January 4, 1906.*

More important to his way of thinking was the large consignment he had brought back of the latest ignition supplies from Edouard Nieuport.[82] While in Paris, Champion had visited Nieuport's large new factory on the rue de Seine in the western suburb of Surenes, offering a view of the Paris skyline. His friend inspired him to make his own products.

"One of the primary qualities of the spark plug should be its simplicity," Nieuport used to say. "Beware of spark plugs with odd shapes and complicated electrodes."[83] Champion heeded that advice—rather than worry about what his partners might think about him.

As part of the reconciliation between Albert and Elise, they left the clamor of the teeming city for the quiet seaside village of Magnolia on the North Shore, its rocky coastline interspersed with smooth sandy beaches.[84]

Albert had always provided for his mother and younger brothers, and they lived in the western suburb of Levallois-Perret.[85] He was protective of youngest brother Prosper, who had lost his right eye and wore a black eye patch.[86] Now eighteen, Prosper had limited job prospects. It is unknown when and how Prosper Champion suffered the disability, but Albert offered him passage to America and employment. He made the same offer to Louis and Henri, but they chose to remain in Paris. Elise wanted her younger sister, Gabrielle, twenty-two, to come and keep her company, as Albert worked long hours.

To finance the extra expenditure of buying a rustic cottage on the North Shore and picking up the tab for the ship's passage for Prosper and Gabrielle, Albert sold fifteen of his forty-nine shares of company stock to Frank Stranahan on June 20. The transaction bolstered Frank's majority holding to sixty-six shares while Albert held thirty-four shares. Albert's reduced stock holding diminished his personal attachment to the company, embarking on its second year.

When not traveling to drum up accounts, Champion commuted by trolley to the Cyclorama. He liked to be seated at his desk every morning by seven o'clock.[87] He plowed through paperwork, read trade journals, and organized himself to make the most of his time. He told an interviewer that one of his constant efforts was to manage his time "for more and better work."[88]

He explained that he always sought to improve everything he did. "I remember a salesman one time telling me that he knew the game from A to Z. He stated that nobody could tell him anything about selling. That was to me the best proof possible that he knew nothing about selling because those who really understand merchandising, manufacturing, or anything else that is important in life are those who realize how little they really know about it and how much there is to learn every day."[89]

Alfred P. Sloan, later credited with creating modern corporate management, said: "The keynote of his success was that he was never satisfied with the product of the job he was then doing. His mind was always open to the necessity for constant improvement."[90]

With a laugh, Champion once explained his passion for work during an interview. "You know the old line. Everybody who has a hobby, whether golf, fishing, baseball, tennis, or whatnot, always has some good arguments for indulging in it. They find those arguments because they like the game they play. Well, I like the game of work, and I can find good arguments for it, too."[91]

The Albert Champion Company had benefited from treasurer Stranahan's bookkeeping to keep pace in supplying customers in the escalating auto industry. Following the March 1906 Boston Automobile Dealers' Association Show, the company was ready to hire.

In August 1906 Prosper and Gabrielle arrived together in New York aboard the French liner *La Bretagne*.[92] An immigration officer at Ellis Island noted Prosper's disability.

Another Parisian joining Albert's payroll that summer was Basil De Guichard, retired from racing and ready to do whatever was needed at the Albert Champion Company. De Guichard arrived with his usual bonhomie and soon would become Albert's right-hand man and expert at quality control.

Albert deputized Prosper to travel and make business calls. As soon as Prosper could afford to, he replaced the eye patch with a glass eye.[93] His new look freed him from being stared at by strangers.

Off to a side in the Cyclorama building, Champion set up a workshop with hand tools. He made an engine battery and put his name on it—the Champion B.G.S. Battery. It caused a sensation when a Maxwell touring car drove a remarkable twenty-five hundred miles over rough New England dirt roads in 115 hours without having to recharge the Champion B.G.S. Battery. Maxwells were one of the country's premier brands.[94] The owner of the local dealership, the Maxwell-Briscoe Boston Company, wrote a letter with the company logo praising the battery for keeping the car going. Champion had been regularly buying small ads in *Automobile*—usually one of twenty-four on a page at the back of the book. For this testimonial, he sought to make the magazine readers take notice by reproducing the entire letter. He splurged for his first full-page advertisement.[95]

Youngest brother Prosper Champion followed Albert to America and worked as an engineer in Albert's companies. Prosper became a naturalized citizen and during World War II served as a volunteer in the US Army Air Corps. *Photo courtesy of Cherie Champion.*

One part integral to the ignition system that transformed the inert metal of an engine into a throbbing, noisy source of heat and horsepower was the spark coil. Champion calculated that spark coils, the component least understood by auto enthusiasts and consumers,[96] presented him with an opportunity. He designed original four-part spark coils: an iron core, primary and secondary windings, and a condenser. They created a high-voltage discharge that could jump the air gap between the spark plug electrodes to fire the fuel-air mixture in the combustion chamber.

Rolling up his shirtsleeves, he devised his spark coil prototype. After weeks of tests, he broke down the manufacturing process. Prosper, Spencer Stranahan, and some other new hires made the parts by hand and assembled them for finished products. De Guichard took over quality control.

By the spring of 1907, the Albert Champion Company was advertising Champion coils among its ignition products.[97] A new round of ads for Nieuport spark plugs relied on phonetic spelling, Nuport.[98] Champion's ads promoted a trademarked symbol—a Mercator projection drawing of the globe with *Champion* spelled out in a banner arranged diagonally across America.[99] He was making his bid to a national audience.

Next he added the Champion high-voltage terminals to Nuport spark plugs. His new Champion Nuport plugs were advertised with the trademarked logo in a full-page ad in *Automobile*.[100] The Albert Champion Company could now boast that it was both importer *and* manufacturer.

Champion was ambitious to build his own brand of spark plugs. However, they were far more difficult to make than spark coils. Even possessing the proper clay, the firing of clay to make porcelain, like treating steel, involves great care to get the proper temperature. If the clay is underheated, the resulting porcelain will not stand engine heat and cooling; overheating the clay causes the porcelain to blister. Champion required an artisan skilled in firing clay in a kiln to make porcelain. Through French connections, he learned about Henri Albert Schmidt, living in Brooklyn.

Schmidt, trained as an engineer in Paris, knew how to make porcelain and had immigrated in 1907. He was the older brother of Charles Schmidt,[101] who had recently been hired away, for twice the pay, from designing Packards in Detroit to instead work for the Peerless Motor Company in Cleveland, one of the Packard Motor Car Company's high-end rivals. Champion offered the older Schmidt a job.

Champion put his name on the globe promoting his Champion spark plug in *Automobile* magazine, May 16, 1907.

Albert Schmidt, as he preferred to be called, had a narrow face and a high, broad forehead. He was fluent in not only French and English but also German and Arabic, the last language a result of serving in France's African colonies during his compulsory military duty. Now forty, he held his head high as though still wearing a military collar.

Both Alberts hit it off—two excitable Gauls notorious for their short tempers. Champion purchased a kiln and accoutrements and installed them in the Cyclorama for his new employee. They imported from France and England the mixture of clays they needed to make porcelain, such as feldspar, flint, kaolin, and ball clay. Champion and Schmidt would argue in rapid-fire French over some detail at the top of their voices like enemies, then they would quickly make up and again be best friends—a pattern they would continue for years.[102]

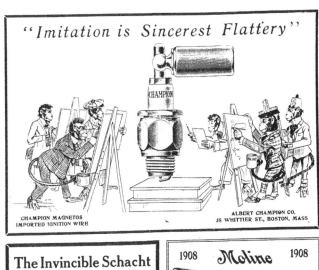

Soon after founding his Albert Champion Company in Boston's South End in June 1905, Champion introduced spark plugs bearing his name. In this ad, he poked fun at others who would copy his product—and his name. From Automobile magazine, February 6, 1908.

By early 1908, Schmidt had started to roll out spark plugs.[103] On the porcelain insulator, he stamped the name Champion.[104] Albert Champion bought half-page ads to promote his new Champion spark plugs. He was forming his traveling team of Frenchmen to split off from the Stranahans and set up another company in another city.

11

THE NAME GAME

I WAS THIRTY. BEFORE ME STRETCHED THE
PORTENTOUS, MENACING ROAD OF A NEW DECADE.
    —F. SCOTT FITZGERALD, THE GREAT GATSBY[1]

Unrest began to foment at the Albert Champion Company in 1907, possibly instigated by the youngest Stranahan. Twenty-one-year-old Robert Allen Stranahan Jr. boasted of a leave granted from Harvard after he had set a record for the college by completing all requirements of his four-year degree in two and a half years.[2] He had wasted a few months trying real estate and other vocations before giving his brothers' auto parts business a go,[3] breezing into the stock room.[4]

Robert, with the handsome features of his brothers, was the most assertive of the family—loquacious to the reserve of his brothers and sisters, a braggadocio to their modesty,[5] and boorish while his siblings considered how others felt. Over decades of family gatherings, Robert waxed eloquent about Spencer as the smartest and best of them while Frank, the steady eldest brother who had led them through the death of their father and paid for Robert's education so that he could become the first in the family to attend college, nodded politely. Frank was ten years Robert's senior, and he respected Champion as the company namesake. Robert saw only a bald guy with a tarnished reputation speaking awkward English and bumping along with a limp.

Lizzie Stranahan dreaded the effects of her sons' association with the Frenchman and his tawdry affair. It could wipe out all the goodwill from Frank's unimpeachable management of the Hotel Savoy. She was anxious to avoid blemishing the family name again as her late husband had in Buffalo. On occasions when her adult progeny and their spouses came together, she would have set her jaw in defiance and expressed her opinion of Champion.

Robert Allen Stranahan II completed his Harvard classes a year ahead
of schedule and in 1907 started working in the stock room of the
Albert Champion Company, where he learned to make spark plugs.
Photo courtesy of Ann and Stephen Stranahan.

Robert had come aboard as Frank engrossed himself in a new venture in
addition to operating the Buick dealership and running the Tremont Garage

Company. Frank had recently incorporated the dealership[6] with capital of $50,000 ($1.5 million in 2014)[7] and held majority ownership. His latest project was directing a Prest-O-Lite station.

Cars were then sold without headlights, although Buick offered a pair of brass kerosene lanterns as an option for $125.[8] Most drivers limited travel to daytime. The Prest-O-Lite Company of Indianapolis had introduced the first practical headlights for driving after dark.[9] Prest-O-Lite offered a cylindrical metal tank filled with compressed acetylene—the gas that lighthouses burned as beacons for ships—set along the running board with a rubber hose extending over the fender to the headlights. The driver ignited the gas by flipping a sparking switch. Twenty thousand customers in cities across North America counted on Prest-O-Lite. More than twelve hundred replacing stations[10] stored from six hundred to two thousand tanks for quick replacement.[11] When the containers emptied, customers would mail them to one of the stations; within a few days, the postal service would return a fully charged replacement. Frank oversaw the replacing station for the New England region. He also established a pumping plant in a brick building housing a big acetylene storage container for refills.[12] Pumping plants were prone to exploding. Frank directed one of only five in the United States and Canada.[13]

Robert had high expectations and had grown restless in the stock room. It is possible that he criticized Champion. Or perhaps the Cyclorama had become cramped from folks strolling into the Buick showroom. Or maybe processing Prest-O-Lite orders had interfered one way or another with Champion and his French cohorts producing spark plugs, coils, and magnetos. Whatever the cause, within weeks of Robert's joining the company, Champion cleared out. He and Prosper and compatriots packed the kiln and tools and relocated across town to a warehouse at 36 Whittier Street in the Roxbury neighborhood.[14] He broadcast the change of venue with a half-page advertisement in *Automobile*. Week after week, adverts listing the Whittier Street address hawked Albert Champion Company ignition supplies, as well as Champion spark plugs and Champion magnetos in all sizes to fit any car.

For Champion, 1908 ushered in every man's nemesis—his thirtieth birthday. Champion retrieved his bicycle from storage and pumped up the tires. Instead of relaxing on evenings and weekends over a glass of wine and conversation with his wife, brother, sister-in-law, and friends, he was pedaling fervently around the indoor Park Square board track. He mixed it up on the velodrome with younger pros to get back in shape for his battle against a stealthy adversary. On April 5, he would turn thirty—the gateway to middle age.

On the Park Square track a month before his milestone birthday, he entered his first race in years. Fans welcomed him with an ovation.[15] After the start gun fired, opponents he had beaten in his prime dashed away. He could only watch them go as though his legs were filled with water. A reporter wrote that he had overestimated his ability[16] and should have been "content to remain in his automobile supply store instead of returning to the track."

Albert, strong-willed, persisted, expecting to improve. A couple weeks later, he was trounced in two straight matches.

At home Elise would have narrowed her eyes at him and remarked that he had his share of La Gloire! His future lay ahead in business.

However reluctantly, he finally let go of his youth.[17]

Since he had immigrated, the early auto industry's Boston-Springfield-Hartford axis had vanished into the memories of pioneers. Michigan, a tranquil agricultural state, had transformed from its first new auto factory in 1900 to twenty-two in just five years.[18] It jumped over the previous leader, New York, which had twenty-one auto factories.[19] Ohio, Connecticut, and Massachusetts followed in motor production. Burton Becker of Elmore cars in Ohio declared motor vehicles were part of an unstoppable evolution: "You can no more get along without the automobile today than you could without the horse."[20]

The number of American car brands had ballooned to about three hundred.[21] Most were small-timers, including Elmore cars. The logo on the radiator featured the name *Elmore* written in cursive. Elmores came out of a bicycle company of the same name, after the Ohio village where the shop had begun.[22] Elmores and other garage outfits lacked resources to sell whatever they made, unlike concerns such as Buick, Maxwell, and Oldsmobile, with their factories, economies of scale, dealerships, and advertising budgets.

For the first time going back to the dawn of civilization, the hegemony of horses on urban roads was threatened. Horse-riding clubs in cities were losing members or closing their doors.[23] "Livery stables are losing money or being transformed into garages," noted *Automobile*.[24]

Michigan played a critical role in advancing America's standing abroad. The United States in 1906 had produced sixty thousand autos to overtake France— with fifty-five thousand motor vehicles—to lead the world.[25] America would sustain that eminence throughout the rest of the twentieth century.

By 1908, almost two hundred thousand cars were cruising US roads.[26] The city producing the greatest number was Detroit.[27] Car companies and allied trades employed more than eight thousand and maintained an annual payroll running into the millions. Detroit was on its way to becoming America's car capital, thanks to the unprecedented success of Ransom Olds and his Olds Motor Works plant,[28] constructed in 1900 as the country's first factory dedicated to manufacturing cars in quantity.[29] Sales of Oldsmobiles created modern fortunes. Three years after the factory began operations, Ransom Olds at age forty had earned "his million,"[30] as they used to say, in unparalleled speed from autos. He became embroiled in a management dispute and walked away to retire to a more leisurely life.[31] The city's business community invested in the capital-intense auto industry when Eastern bankers preferred to keep their money in traditional safe bets like steel, meat-packing, trolley trains, and utilities. Detroit car companies were paying laborers double the wages for comparable skills in the carriage trade—luring a talented labor force from around the country.[32] Detroit was to automobiles what Northern California's Silicon Valley later in the century became to computer technology.

Champion felt compelled to go back there, this time to get new orders. He had built a portable electrical ignition set that fit into a suitcase.[33] On a table he could quickly assemble the magneto, spark plug, and a wire connecting them. By turning a hand crank in the magneto, he built up volts, which created an electrical charge that flowed along the wire to the spark plug mounted on a metal stand to simulate being in the engine chamber. The plug fired its spark and demonstrated the superiority of his Champion porcelain spark plug, He packed his electrical ignition set and took a horse-drawn cab to Boston's South Station to board a train.

On his return to Detroit, like everybody obsessed with cars, Champion made a beeline for the Pontchartrain Hotel in central Detroit. He would have been familiar with the hotel's homage to French King Louis XIV's minister of state, the floridly named Louis Phélypeux, Comte de Pontchartrain,[34] who had never set foot in America. French explorer and fur trader Antoine de la Mothe Cadillac and his men had built a fort in 1702 and dubbed it Pontchartrain. The fort surrounded the fur-trading settlement called Ville d'Etroit, or "City of the Strait," which had been simplified to Detroit.

The Pontchartrain Hotel served as the unofficial auto-industry head-quarters. The saying went that you could meet anyone who was part of the automobile game in the club-like atmosphere of the lobby.[35] Inside the hotel, partnerships were formed and broken.[36] Outside, parked at the curb, new models made their debut.[37] People flocked to admire the latest whiz wagon. The Pontchartrain dining room, when emptied after lunchtime, revealed table-cloths that had been marked up with sketches of engine details, crankshafts, and all manner of mechanical devices.[38]

Champion booked a room but spent little time in it. The action unfolded at the rear of the hotel, in the barroom. There, every weekday morning when the black hands on the white marble wall clock struck 11:30, a spirited crowd of accessory manufacturers, journalists, dealers, racecar drivers, and other thirsty patrons converged under the ceiling of mahogany and gilded beams.[39] Everyone pressed against the polished brass rail and traded shoptalk while waiting for their drinks from a half-dozen bartenders frantically pouring drafts, uncorking wine bottles, and mixing cocktails. Industry gossip was heard first in the Pon-tchartrain.[40] A company buying a large vacant property signaled a new factory coming. If a senior executive had left for a better offer from a competitor, that could warn of a hard time ahead for his former employer. Drinking and dining at the Pontchartrain often broadcasted the future that loomed over the horizon.

Somewhere in the barroom, Champion had found an open table and set up his electrical ignition set.[41] The Pontchartrain's clientele was inclined to gather around and watch. Stories about his demonstrations circulated into Detroit's auto-community folklore.

Days later, he returned to Boston. He filed expenses in the Cyclorama building and regaled the Stranahans with stories. Not long afterward, he climbed aboard another train to Detroit. Commuting each way took thirty-some hours of nonstop swaying in the belly of train cars rumbling along at 35 to 40 mph, eating in the restaurant car, spending the night in a sleeper car over the rumble of rails. The time and expense of the journey were part of the price a company paid for being away from the throb of the Pontchartrain and the proliferating number of companies migrating to Michigan.

In the spring, Robert Allen Jr. was promoted from the stock room.[42] He received an executive title, although to his chagrin his salary remained meager.[43] Even so, he had become interested in how essential spark plugs, magnetos, and coils were to propelling autos.[44] He had found his career. He frequented the Whittier Street shop when Champion went out of town.

Robert was determined to work his way into the good graces of Albert Schmidt, the designer of Champion spark plugs. Artisans like Schmidt fiercely protected their craft secrets. The company had only one kiln, in a room of its own. Schmidt at first barred even Albert Champion from entering the kiln room, although Champion insisted that he be allowed to learn how spark plugs were made. A motivated Robert would have made himself useful in the tasks of machine-threading the steel shells and gland nuts, then assembling fired clay insulators between the two metal parts and carefully setting the spark plug gap.

Over time he won Schmidt's confidence. Schmidt needed more assistance and had showed Prosper Champion and Basil De Guichard the essential skills to operate a kiln and fire the clay into porcelain insulators. Schmidt also educated Robert in the art of the kiln.

Champion may have considered that moving his operation to Roxbury would sidestep the need to deal with Robert, whose ego rivaled his own, only to discover that the youngest Stranahan had inveigled his way into learning the craft of spark plug manufacture. Champion knew all too well that Yankee ingenuity led to rivals selling cheap knock-offs. He took out a half-page ad in *Automobile* lampooning monkeys copying his Champion spark plug.[45] The ad flaunted, "Imitation Is Sincerest Flattery." A half-dozen long-tailed monkeys stood with paint brushes before easels surrounding a human-sized Champion spark plug, posed like a nude model. Albert grew impatient with Robert butting into his shop, as Champion and the two elder Stranahan brothers had created the business before Robert joined their enterprise. Robert doubtless felt entitled to learn the business cofounded by his brothers.

A fistfight between Albert and Robert was inevitable. Legend handed down the corporate ranks from Robert to his son Robert III at Champion Spark Plug Company contends that after regular work hours Albert and Robert put up their fists and fought.[46] Albert fancied himself a good boxer. Robert, a couple inches taller, took pride in his wrestling. Neither had ever backed down from anybody.

The only way they could avoid each other was for Albert and Robert to alternate traveling back and forth between Boston and Detroit to sell orders. The strategy lasted until late into the summer.

The Stranahan-Eldridge Buick dealership had vacated the Cyclorama for a spacious facility on a side street near Commonwealth Avenue.[47] One early September day Champion heard, likely from Frank Stranahan, that the director of the Buick Motor Company, William C. Durant, was in town to survey the dealership. Durant had built up Buick in four years from almost nothing to the biggest selling car in the country.[48] Buick's sales of 8,820 cars that year surpassed the sales of Ford (6,181) and Cadillac (2,380).[49] His success was especially extraordinary when considering the fact that the production of Buicks tripled during the Panic of 1907, when the New York Stock Exchange had lost half its value and the country had cratered into recession.[50] Dozens of small auto companies that had been surviving on thin margins were forced to liquidate.[51] Durant had hired ambitious men in wholesale and retail branches, and he'd opened attractive dealerships in twenty-seven cities from coast to coast.[52] He had cruised through the national economic turmoil to a profit of about $1.1 million ($27.7 million in 2014) on sales of $4.2 million ($106 million).[53]

While in the Boston Buick dealership, Durant was arranging the sales room when Champion approached him with spark plugs samples.[54] Durant exuded calm and breathed success. Smartly trim all his life, he stood medium height, nearly as tall as Champion, and spoke in a soft voice.[55] He had a sharp and delicate nose that newspaper illustrators appreciated, a high forehead, and he never went in for facial hair. Now forty-six,[56] he was one of America's rare millionaires,[57] despite having dropped out of high school in Flint for a job paying seventy-five cents a day[58] in his grandfather's lumber business,[59] one of largest among the many Flint lumber mills. He had never heard of Champion and had missed the Albert Champion Company ads.

Champion, in his strong French accent, said, "I can make spark plugs out of porcelain."[60]

Durant paused. He realized at a glance that the samples were well made.[61] In a heartbeat he recognized that he and Champion were going to do business together.

Durant's deep-rooted love was selling—feeling a glow from the personal transaction in providing a good product to a customer.[62] He came from the school of salesmen who sold themselves first as trustworthy, credible citizens, and sold their product second. After a brief stint in lumber he had honed his skills as a vendor of cigars, groceries, patent medicines, and real estate.[63] By age twenty he'd grown impatient waiting around for customers to come into the store.[64] He wanted something he could go out and sell.[65] Young Durant had thrived on action.[66] He preferred to hustle,[67] take initiative, concentrate on the job at hand. Initially, he had become an insurance agent. The underlying current of dramatic tension in persuading people to buy a policy had intrigued him.

One of his guiding principles was to look for a something that practically sold itself, what he called a self-seller.[68] Another principle was if you couldn't find one, then make one.[69] In the 1890s he had come across an opportunity that changed his life. He paid $50 to purchase the patent for a light, two-wheeled horse cart that had a unique suspension system for a smooth ride despite steel-rimmed wooden wheels.[70] Durant formed a partnership with his friend Josiah Dallas Dort, a hardware clerk.[71] They hired a contractor to build ten thousand carts.[72] Durant scrambled day after day to sell them all in a short time, earning a reputation as a super salesman.[73] He and Dort put their profits into financing the Durant-Dort Carriage Company to turn out Blue Ribbon buggies and carriages. The company diversified with vehicles at different price points and models for a broad array of markets,[74] which they sold nationwide through farm-implement companies and mail-order houses.[75]

To guarantee a continuous supply chain to produce a steady quantity of finished products on time, Durant controlled ownership of sixteen local accessory plants that manufactured every part of the buggies, including a full line of wooden bodies, wheels, axles, forgings, stampings, leather, paint, even whip sockets.[76] His companies produced more than fifty thousand Blue Ribbon vehicles a year, which they sold nationwide.[77]

William Durant recruited Champion to make spark plugs in Flint before Durant founded General Motors. Durant took GM to the brink of bankruptcy twice in ten years. *Photo courtesy of General Motors Media Archive.*

His booming business had turned into a major employer. Durant acquired a legendary reputation for working longer hours than any of his employees,[78] needing only a few hours of sleep,[79] and greeting every morning with a smile.[80] The fawning Flint press referred to him as "the Little Giant."[81] Appreciative associates called him Billy.[82] Some dubbed him "The Man"[83] when passing on instructions.[84] By the turn of the twentieth century, the year before he turned forty, Blue Ribbon carriages had made Durant a millionaire.[85] The carriage market's vitality was on the wane.[86] Thus, he needed another endeavor to conquer, so he set off to New York to study Wall Street and the New York Stock Exchange.[87]

In August 1904 the owner of another carriage company invited the Little Giant back to Flint to turn around the floundering Buick Motor Company,[88] now the property of the Flint Wagon Works.[89] The wagon company's management looked to cars to take up the slack for a drop in carriage orders. Durant, however, regarded autos as noisemakers that shocked people and frightened horses.[90] A medical doctor friend invited him to take a ride on a September afternoon in the physician's Buick.[91] They motored over smooth roads, including one of Flint's few paved streets. Afterward, Durant borrowed the Buick and drove it alone. Over the following weeks, as his schedule allowed, he borrowed the doctor's Buick for off-road rambles. He steered into the countryside,[92] charging through swamps, bouncing over ruts, and grinding into stretches of soft sand. The engine powered up hills and persisted over rugged terrain that had stopped other makes.[93] He was impressed.

Flint civic leaders had proudly declared their town slogan, "The Vehicle City." Every Saturday farmers came to town in buggies and wagons to shop for supplies.[94] Their horses clip-clopped under the slogan printed on top of steel arches spanning Saginaw Street, the main downtown thoroughfare lined with storefronts and hitching posts and rails.

Another characteristic of Buicks caught Durant's attention.[95] Whenever he left the car parked unattended at the curb downtown on Saginaw Street, he noticed men and women hurrying over to look at his self-seller. He changed his mind about autos. He now believed that they *could* replace horses and buggies.

The car carried the name of David Dunbar Buick. Buick had deep-set, dark eyes, kept his pitch-black hair cut short and brushed up at the front, and wore a mustache. He'd been a child when his parents emigrated from Scotland to settle in Detroit.[96] Mechanically inclined, he developed a money-making plumbing-fixtures business. His patent for putting porcelain on cast iron,[97] essential for modern bathtubs and sinks, could have made him wealthy. Yet bathtubs and sinks failed to hold his attention. He rushed instead into reeking, noisy gas-combustion engines and built them for boats, farm vehicles, and then a car. In 1901 he produced his first auto, equipped with a tiller for steering and an uncomfortable bench seat wide enough for a passenger. He and two engineers designed a powerful and efficient two-cylinder engine with air-intake valves built directly over the pistons,[98] referred to as the "valve-in-head" engine (now called "overhead valve" engine).[99] It offered a more compact combustion chamber than the others engines in widespread use.

David Buick served a short term as president of the Buick Manufacturing Company,[100] but he was an impulsive, argumentative mechanic rather than a prudent entrepreneur.[101] The business blew through more money than it brought in. Rising debts pushed him out—he was among the first of the industry's many brilliant, progressive men who left their names behind while they faded into obscurity.[102]

Investors restructured the organization, moved it to Flint, and renamed it the Buick Motor Company. Despite the potential of its sturdy little engine, the enterprise floundered. Local leaders appealed to Durant. Out of loyalty to the town and his friends,[103] he agreed to do what he could. On November 1, 1904, he was elected to the Buick board of directors.[104] He declined the title of president or vice president,[105] but he took charge and was free to call the shots.

Every young industry needs a charismatic visionary like Durant to inject matchless energy and creativity. He had applied an efficient supply chain and a foundation of dealerships to make his carriage company a success. In the four years after he took control, Buicks came to rate first in speed, power, and durability.[106]

When Champion approached Durant in the Boston Buick dealership, the company in Flint employed twenty-five hundred people.[107] A new car rolled out of the factory every twelve minutes—a high standard for the era.[108] The Buick Motor Company was displacing the buggy trade. Buicks were destined to keep up Flint's slogan as the Vehicle City.

A few decades and twenty-five million General Motors cars later,[109] Durant in his last years finally sat down to compose his autobiography. In the third chapter he describes his momentous first meeting with Champion.[110] The Man noted that the spark plug that Champion had brought that day was unsuited for a Buick engine. Although he had no interest in buying what Champion showed him then, he was still impressed with the gadget. "I thought that anyone who could produce that kind of a device might do other worthwhile things as well."[111]

He recollected their discussion:

"Have you a factory?" I asked.
"No, just a shop."
"What are you making?"
"Magnetos and spark plugs."

"We do not use magnetos, but I am interested in spark plugs. Can you make a good one?"

Champion would have bragged that he made the best,[112] and he would not have failed to mention that he had been employed in Paris with automaker Adolphe Clément-Bayard and that he followed Clément-Bayard's production methods. Champion may also have brought up Edouard Nieuport's production of spark plugs, magnetos, and coils, which he had imported before manufacturing his own.

Durant's secret to selling was to engage the customer,[113] and though Champion wasn't a potential customer, Durant was certainly engaged. After a while he asked Champion to take him to his shop and give him a tour of the facility. Champion protested that it was quite some distance away, in Roxbury. Durant, a native of Boston and frequent visitor to the city, kept the conversation going.

"I later persuaded him to take me to his place of business," Durant wrote. "I landed in a part of Boston that was not familiar to me. On the third floor of a warehouse building, I found a very neatly arranged workshop with a small line of tools. It took him but a few moments to show me what he had."

Durant noticed the dozen or so men Champion employed, observed how they went about their jobs, eyed what their kiln produced, and gauged output capacity. At that point, he could have said in his polite soft voice that he had enjoyed their meeting and walked away. Instead, he chose to close the deal: "I began to quiz him about spark plugs."[114]

America's top-selling automaker sounded out Champion before nudging the focus toward recruiting him to Flint, a backwater town about sixty-five miles northwest of Detroit:

During our conversation I told him that we were having considerable difficulty in finding a spark plug suited to our needs, due to the fact that we had a very high-speed, high-compression, valve-in-head motor (twenty years ahead of the times) and had been able to find only one plug in the country that answered our purpose—the Rajah made in Bloomfield, New Jersey for which we were paying thirty-five cents each. If he were quite sure that he could make a plug that would answer our purpose, I suggested that we go to Flint, and if he liked the place and the layout, I would start an experimental plant, and if he could make good, I would give him an interest in the business. He had never been to Flint, knew nothing of the Buick, or the plans I had for the future.[115]

The two men had spent most of the day together, discussing autos, Durant talking in his rapid, easy way.[116] They were so nearly the same size—a tad under five feet eight inches and 140 pounds.[117] Anyone seeing them together might easily have mistaken them for brothers. They also shared the same dream in the future of autos.

Buick represented the biggest opportunity of Champion's career. Durant's serene confidence and proven success would have likely reminded Champion of his former Paris boss Adolphe Clément-Bayard—the locksmith who had started a small enterprise and developed it into one of the continent's great auto companies. Champion had no hesitation about leaving his partners for a fresh start in Michigan, the heartland of auto commerce. He could persuade Elise, Prosper, Schmidt, and fellow countrymen to follow him and leave the Stranahans behind.

Durant inquired about how much money Champion had in the business and if he had any partners. Champion replied that Frank Stranahan owned a majority of the company stock.[118] He said he would talk with Stranahan about buying him out.

To clinch the deal, Durant would have informed Champion that he intended to buy other car and accessory companies, although without disclosing details. He promised to put up the money to move Champion's outfit to Flint and to set him up in a factory where he could create the spark plugs for Buick's engine.[119]

The Man freighted the offer with three caveats.[120] First, Champion would have to make a spark plug that passed the strict test imposed by Buick engineers. Second, he had to produce the merchandise for less than the thirty-five-cent Rajahs. Third, he had one year to pay for Durant's cost of buying out his share and the moving expenses. Champion's revenue would come from savings generated by producing spark plugs at a lower cost than the price of Rajahs. Over the one-year trial, Champion and his cohorts would earn little more than basic living and operating expenses. If Champion fulfilled all conditions, Durant assured him a generous share of the business.[121]

They left the discussion there. Durant went back to his dealership.

Two mornings later, Champion found Durant at his office.[122] He reported that Stranahan had agreed to buy his share but would not sell Champion's name. Durant recounted: "I told him I was not interested in the name—I was interested in spark plugs. But he said, 'I am very much interested in the name. That is my name.' Strange as it may seem, I then asked the question, 'What is your full name?' Shrugging his shoulders—in real French style—he replied, 'Albert Cham-Pion.' I then said, 'We will have little use for a name unless you make good, but it would seem to me a company bearing your initials—"A.C."—would answer every purpose.' That suggestion pleased him, and the matter of the name was disposed of."[123]

Durant wrote a check to Stranahan for $2,000.[124] The next day, Champion returned with a bill of sale.[125] The Albert Champion Company, a little more than three years old, for all practical purposes had ceased.

"As soon as I could arrange it, I took Albert Champion to Flint, found a building near my office, and put him to work," Durant wrote.[126]

Albert, Elise, and their dozen compatriots climbed down from the train to stretch their legs and unload their possessions in Flint on September 10, 1908.[127] Flint was a runt of a burg, surrounded by rural farmland and forests. It could have fit in Boston or Paris as a small neighborhood. Flint was still a Saturday-night-horse-and-buggy town. Farmers came on wagons groaning under towering haystacks and tied their horses to the hitching posts and rails lining Saginaw Street. The wagons protruded deep into the street and created traffic hazards—streetcars sliding over rails barely squeezed past.[128]

It was a doughty town, the seat for the greater Genesee County, and expanding like an accordion—doubling in the last five years, from less than fourteen thousand inhabitants[129] to about twenty-five thousand.[130] Two railroads, the Grand Trunk and Pere Marquette, served Flint. The tracks crossed the flat plain along trails that had been cut by the French explorers and trappers who had made their way up the Flint River.

The Man set up Champion's operation in a corner of the Buick factory on the town's west side. Once again Champion was gambling but, as always, his confidence remained bulletproof as he entrusted his future to Durant and the Buick Motor Company.

Everything came down to creating a spark plug at least equal to the Rajah and cheaper. From early in the morning into the evening, Champion and his associates studied the Buick's valve-in-head engine. They examined the Rajah's construction compared with the spark plug Champion had been producing. He collaborated with Albert Schmidt to create a prototype. All of their careers depended on crafting an original device and producing it in mass quantities at less expense. After five weeks of dogged experiments and adjustments, he submitted his new device to Buick engineers. They subjected it to a strict test. Champion's spark plug performed without flaw. The engineers praised its genuine merit.[131] Champion directed his men to make a few hundred spark plugs a day.[132]

He was back on track with a whole new enterprise. For more than a year he had been emphasizing his company's Champion ignition products in ads. In Flint he decided to keep that name. On October 23, he incorporated the Champion Ignition Company of Flint in the state of Michigan with two business partners on capital of $60,000.[133]

Creating his new product had involved trying—and discarding—an array of materials, which led to an original discovery. Champion devised an invention to replace silver and copper conductors of electric currents with porcelain conductors to improve distribution of electricity flowing from the magneto to the spark plug.[134] His invention provided a compact, inexpensive, and effective holder for high-voltage currents. A patent lawyer conducted research to ensure that Champion had established a technical improvement before writing the patent application. A draftsman drew diagrams showing how the parts functioned. On November 3, 1908, Champion filed his invention for the insulator and conductor with the US Patent Office in Washington, DC.

Durant left Champion alone and rocketed all around the country on trains to bolster the Buick sales force and build up a supply chain to fulfill his greater idea. Part of the plan he had withheld from Champion was to make Buick the cornerstone of his grand new organization, which would compete with Henry Ford's low-cost car for the masses, the Model T, introduced that year.

Billy Durant lined up the purchase of Oldsmobile, the oldest brand on the market.[135] Before buying Oldsmobile, however, he founded a holding company that would allow him to create his new scheme. The articles of incorporation were filed on September 16 in Trenton, New Jersey, on capital stock of $2,000 ($52,200 in 2014) for the General Motors Company of New Jersey to build automobiles.[136] The officers in the company papers listed businessmen unknown to the Garden State press. As he had intended, the filing escaped public notice, even back in Flint, where the press tried to follow The Man's every movement.

Free from scrutiny, Durant operated boldly. Days after General Motors was formed he boosted its capitalization to $12.5 million ($322 million in 2014).[137] His control of both Buick and General Motors allowed him in six weeks to orchestrate General Motors' purchase of Buick for about $3.75 million[138] ($96.5 million) and Oldsmobile for a little more than $3 million[139] ($77.2 million).

The Common Council of Flint, the Vehicle City, finally decided to modernize the city's image by getting rid of the hitching posts and rails on Saginaw Street. "Roosting irons for loafers,"[140] complained an alderman in favor of traffic safety. Merchants protested that without a way to hitch horses, farmers would never again visit Flint and businesses would lose money. The council sided with traffic safety and issued an order to remove them one quiet weekday night in October.[141] Despite the cries of economic ruin, business went on as usual.

Buick paid Champion's company twenty-five cents for each spark plug, ten cents less than the Rajah.[142] Orders doubled.[143] Buick was now buying a thousand plugs a day,[144] saving Buick $100 a day.[145]

A year after Champion moved to Flint, The Man was back in his office to pore over the Champion Ignition Company balance sheet, which reported a net cash balance of $136,000.[146] His investment in Champion's company and operating expenses up to that time amounted to approximately $36,000.

"Champion had paid back the initial investment and had over $100,000 in the bank," Durant wrote. "I sent for Champion, told him I had seen his statement, was most pleased with the report. I congratulated him on his splendid success and reminded him that we had never discussed what his interest was to be if he made good, that up to that time he had only received living expenses."[147]

Durant organized Champion's company as a partially owned subsidiary of General Motors, with Champion as president.[148] In compensation for Champion's know-how, Durant awarded him with one-quarter of the Champion Ignition Company's stock, worth $25,000.[149]

"I asked him how he would like to have the stock issued," Durant remembered. "He said that a man by the name of Schmidt had come with him from Boston, had been very helpful and he would like him to have $7,500, the balance $17,500 issued to himself."[150]

Durant, who thrived on action, had also purchased Cadillac Motor Company.[151] The Champion Ignition Company was now making the spark plugs that powered Buicks, Oldsmobiles, and Cadillacs.

After Champion had decamped from Boston, Robert Stranahan took over as manager of the Albert Champion Company in partnership with Frank and Spencer.[152] Robert produced spark plugs in the Whittier Street warehouse and sold them under the Champion name.[153] He produced six Champion varieties, retailing from seventy-five cents to $1.50, for cars and motorcycles. Robert trekked at regular intervals to Detroit and Toledo to gain accounts for his Champion spark plugs.[154] The following summer the brothers renamed the business: The Champion Company.[155]

With Albert's Champion Ignition Company manufacturing an ever-greater number of spark plugs in Flint and Robert producing his line of Champion Company products, the two men and their companies were on course for another fight. Only one company would win the right to Champion's name.

12

CHAMPION AND
CHEVROLET SMASHUP

THE EARLY HISTORY OF AMERICAN CARS OVER HERE
MIGHT BE SAID TO BE THE EARLY HISTORY OF THE
CADILLAC CAR.
—LETTER FROM F. S. BENNETT OF
F. S. BENNETT LTD., OF LONDON,
THE PIONEER AGENT OF CADILLAC
IN THE BRITISH ISLES, 1924[1]

Buick racing cars, powered by Champion's spark plugs and magnetos,[2] kept roaring ahead of the competition in America's makeshift racing circuit over the 1908 and 1909 seasons. A select stable of Buick drivers were amassing more than five hundred trophies[3] along with a gush of publicity from winning half the races they entered.[4] Swiss-French driver Louis Chevrolet scored one of the most spectacular victories, capturing the ninety-one-mile Long Island Stock Chassis Derby in September 1909. He barreled around Suffolk County roads at an average speed close to 70 mph.[5] *Automobile* pronounced his deed "the greatest sustained flight ever accomplished in an American road race." Right behind followed teammate "Wild" Bob Burman for a one-two finish.[6]

Despite the spectacular show of cars thundering around the twenty-three-mile course on an ideal autumn Saturday, spectator turnout was sparse. The grandstand near the Riverhead start/finish failed to sell enough tickets. The event lost money.[7] All Chevrolet received for his skill and courage was a loving cup; Burman earned nothing. Nevertheless, they contributed to Buick's reputation for power and reliability, and they dodged the fate of one of the race's entrants, whose vehicle flipped over on a bend. The driver was seriously injured and his riding mechanic, in the shotgun seat, was killed.[8]

Durant encouraged racing. Before the phrase "research and development" gained currency, he supported a team dedicated to stressing cars and engines to their limits so engineers could devise improvements.[9] He ordered Buick's inventive engineer, Walter Marr, to develop racing engines and cars.[10] Marr's pointy Van Dyke beard gave him the look of a wizard, one with grease under his fingernails. He had helped David Buick build the original Buick engine. Marr was so compulsive about improving his motors that someone had to intervene and take the prototype away to put the latest version into production.[11]

A photo of the Buick racing team shows Chevrolet seated behind the steering wheel with Burman next to him, another A-list driver named Lewis Strang relaxing on the running board, and Marr leaning opposite Chevrolet, surrounded by twenty other mechanics, engineers, and drivers. At the end of the 1909 season, Durant awarded Chevrolet, Burman, and Strang a bonus of $10,000 ($260,000 in 2014) to share.[12]

Louis Chevrolet was a bear of a man, a hard-muscled six feet and 215 pounds.[13] He flexed every muscle steering the heavy, unforgiving vehicles of the day, hurling at high velocity around horse tracks and through S-turns and sharp corners on rough unpaved roads. He also had a rare mechanical flair. When he rolled up his shirtsleeves and shoved his arms into a car engine, always with a cigarette parked in a corner of his mouth and smoke curling up into his dark eyes, his hands performed magic on high-performance machinery.

His aptitude with engines was instilled in the French-speaking Swiss city of La Chaux-de-Fonds, where he had been born on Christmas Day 1878. Nestled in the Watch Valley at the base of the Jura Mountains, the city has been an international center of watch and clock making since the seventeenth century.[14] La Chaux-de-Fonds has been home to Heuer (predecessor to TAG Heuer), Omega, and Movado. Louis was the eldest son of a watch and clock maker.[15] The elder Joseph Félicien Chevrolet, the extended family, and neighbors earned their livelihoods doing fine workmanship by hand.[16] Social conversations branched into trade talk about turning out precise timepieces and novelty cuckoo clocks. Louis was ten and brother Arthur was two[17] when the family moved across the French border to Beaune, in the wine region of Burgundy.[18] There brother Gaston was born, eighteen years younger than Louis.[19]

Chevrolet's generation grew up hearing about France's legendary seventeenth-century governor of the French colonies in North America, the soldier-statesman Louis de Baude de Frontenac.[20] Frontenac ruled with Gaulic grandeur. He had extended France's North American empire from Montreal all the way to the Gulf of Mexico.[21] As a teenager Chevrolet had built a bicycle that he called *Frontenac*.[22] He had competed with some success, which encouraged him to market Frontenac bicycles—until automobiles completely usurped his attention.

When Louis left the provinces for Paris, he trained as a riding mechanic in the Darracq factory.[23] The French referred to him as a *mechanician*. His job was to sit next to the Darracq test driver, Victor Hemery, to serve as an extra set of eyes and ears and provide him with information while he concentrated on the road ahead. And when something broke down and the vehicle halted, it was the mechanician's job to hop out and make repairs. Chevrolet also held jobs in the factories of de Dion-Bouton, Panhard, and Mors.[24] In 1900 he shipped out, at twenty-one, to follow Frontenac's previous route to French-speaking Montreal.

In those days, anyone with his background could secure an assignment as a chauffeur.[25] Chauffeurs not only drove but also were responsible for all repairs from the wheels up. After six months he left Montreal to cross the US border on his way to Brooklyn and its French community, home to a de Dion-Bouton plant, his next employer. Among the French expats, Louis met the lovely, tall, dark-eyed Suzanne Treyvoux. To impress her he moved up to a better-paying job with more responsibility at Fiat in New York City.[26] Fiat management entrusted him to drive in races. On May 20, 1905, he had scored an impressive victory in the one-mile feature race around a horse track in Brooklyn against the formidable Barney Oldfield—Chevrolet clocked in at 52 seconds, for 69 mph.[27] Over the summer he beat Oldfield an impressive three times.[28] Louis Chevrolet acquired a national reputation. He was seen as one of the first Europeans in US auto races. His biggest prize, however, was winning Suzanne's heart.[29] At the end of the season, they married.

Unless a wheel fell off or some other disaster crippled his car, nothing kept Louis from finishing a race. Once while racing in Crown Point, Indiana, his car struck rocks in the road so hard that a cylinder was knocked out of commission, costing him one-quarter of his engine capacity, but he held on for victory. "I almost wanted to give up," he admitted, "but something told me to stay in.

It must have been the training I received while a mechanic for Hemery, the greatest motor-racing driver the world has ever known. He never has been known to give up. He taught me to drive that way in all my contests."[30]

Chevrolet brought his brothers to America. Arthur, eight years younger, followed him into racing. Louis and Arthur wanted to get hired to drive for the Buick team. In the spring of 1907 they took Gaston, age eleven, on the train to Flint. They heard that Durant was looking for a personal chauffeur, which paid well. The Man paired Louis and Arthur against each other in competition around a short dirt track outside the Buick factory dedicated to testing production models.[31] Louis dove aggressively into the turns, hugged the straights, and stirred up dirt clouds. Durant watched Louis give Arthur a thrashing defeat. Louis was chagrined when The Man picked Arthur for chauffeur.[32] Durant, looking out for his self-interests, appreciated that Arthur took no chances. Durant and Louis had only just met and already they had the first of several drastic misunderstandings. Both looked at the same thing with expectations poles apart, The Man every time holding the advantage.

Louis talked about how one day he would retire from racing to design his own car. He had in mind a light vehicle styled after French favorites he admired—one that caught the eye and was inexpensive. The Man expressed interest.

Buick racing cars had the same stock chassis and body as models for sale in showrooms. Model 10 with four cylinders served the Buick team well and led as the company's bestseller. Model 10 retailed for $900,[33] including Prest-O-Lite acetylene headlights and a bulb squeeze horn, which honked like a goose, but the sound penetrated through urban noise. Buick offered the option of a canvas top, priced at $50.[34] For the 1910 racing season, engineer Walter Marr oversaw the building of two identical Buick Bugs,[35] special stripped down race-cars. Instead of a flat front, they featured an aerodynamic nose and sat lower to the ground than most other racing models. On the hood was painted a big ram's head, as though the car's nose would butt through the wind.[36] The engine fired flames out the front-side exhaust ports and roared as loud as Niagara Falls.[37] The open-cockpit bucket seat was too small for a mechanician, which saved weight. Bugs were exclusively for Buick's headline drivers, Chevrolet and Burman.

While Chevrolet had more experience, Burman was six years younger and had taken a direct route to Buick. His start in the business had been painting wooden wheels of Durant's Blue Ribbon carriages.[38] Then, when Durant took over Buick, Burman tested some early models.[39] The Man encouraged him to tear around Flint's early morning, traffic-free streets to see how fast he could make the Buicks run and how they held up. Burman, slim and athletic, with big hands, entered a race around Detroit's Grosse Pointe horse track.[40] He was allowed to compete after several no-shows had reduced the field, and he drove against Barney Oldfield. Burman was out of his depth, yet he wasn't intimidated. His cheerful recklessness when driving had led to his nickname, Wild Bob.

Self-taught, Wild Bob lacked Chevrolet's sophistication. Wild Bob pressed his right foot on the gas pedal as though standing on one leg. His arms alternated turning the steering wheel left into the next turn then back to the right for the straight. He once explained that when the car held together, he won running wide open,[41] "or it breaks and I lose."[42]

At the Indianapolis Motor Speedway in May 1910, the year before the Indy 500 race made its debut, Burman snapped goggles over his eyes, stood on the gas pedal of his Bug, and recorded a thunderous 105.8 mph.[43] He won the prestigious Prest-O-Lite Trophy Race. That helped burnish the Bug's reputation as the fastest American-made car, conveniently overlooking the Frenchman whose company produced the ignition parts firing the engine.

Between publicity from the Buick racing team and increasing consumer demand for autos, Albert Champion managed to stay ahead of the propulsive growth in demand for Champion Ignition Company spark plugs, magnetos, and coils. His products were delivered on time to meet auto production schedules. Champion's goods were factory-installed in General Motors' Buicks, Cadillacs, and Oldsmobiles. Production in 1909 had more than doubled to twenty-four thousand,[44] led by Buick, which made up the lion's share. The next year production jumped 50 percent more,[45] in part from GM acquiring the Oakland Motor Company (predecessor to Pontiac Motor Company).

Phenomenal surging demand for Champion's products led to hiring new hands by the droves. The original operation on the third floor of the Buick Motor Company, where his outfit had started with fifteen men, grew cramped.

His company kept adding more workers and occupied a whole floor. Champion requested a building of his own.

Champion launched his twelve-hour workdays by seating himself at his desk by six o'clock.[46] He plowed through a mountain of paperwork and took care of a mass of details. Some days he left his desk only for lunch in the cafeteria. Now and then he strode around the shop floor, invariably accompanied by his right-hand man Basil De Guichard,[47] to monitor the production line. Over the decades, employees remembered the two Frenchmen as being as different from one another as chalk and cheese. Champion had a forceful personality, impatient and demanding, while De Guichard was even-tempered and tactful. Stories were passed down about Champion firing laborers on the spot if he felt they were slacking at their workstations, only to demand the next day to know why the workstation was vacant. Champion was strict about keeping production on schedule, and he expected his money's worth from wages he paid. De Guichard would track down the dismissed employee and offer his job back, presumably encouraging the worker to improve his output. Champion made a vivid impression on the shop floor, looking sharp in a pressed suit and shined shoes, sometimes giving laborers helpful pointers. They called him The Chief.[48]

Elise endowed their Flint home with a Parisian ambience. On weekends the Champions hosted De Guichard, the Chevrolet clan, including Louis and Suzanne's infant son, and extra compatriots. They chatted over meals in a nonstop gush of French while emptying cases of imported wine.

Albert and Louis had much in common—an intense passion for speed, the same birth year, and the rarely used middle name Joseph. They had set a fair number of world records although they were best remembered for one or two—Albert as the first to drive a motorcycle a mile under a minute and Louis steering an American car with a Darracq engine along the hard-packed shoreline of Daytona-Ormond Beach, Florida, in 1906 to the absolute world record of 119 mph.[49] They had survived high-speed crashes that put them in hospitals, sometimes convalescing for weeks. Louis would tally a good three years recovering from crash-related injuries.[50] Both men carried so many scars on their bodies they could regale an audience over drinks with a catalogue of outrageous stories about broken bones and mangled machines, enough yarns to consume an entire evening and stretch into the night. It was inevitable that they would go into business together.

The booming Flint economy strained Flint's infrastructure. Between 1908, the year of Champion's arrival, and 1910, the number of factory wage earners had tripled to fifteen thousand.[51] Auto production in 1910 in Flint reached thirty thousand—almost matching the output of Henry Ford's Model T.[52] Nearly all the finished cars were loaded onto trains bound for Kansas City, St. Louis, New York, San Francisco, and elsewhere. Few remained in town—only one hundred autos were licensed in Flint.[53] To accommodate the influx of laborers, farms left and right were subdivided to erect new houses. The town added seven square miles.[54]

In the summer of 1910, however, auto production halted. General Motors had run out of operating capital and fell into a financial crisis. Plans for Champion's new plant were put on hold. The Buick racing program was drastically scaled back. The unthinkable happened—pressure mounted for Durant's ouster.

During Durant's six years managing the Buick Motor Company, he enjoyed incomparable success. Unflagging energy and his love of making deals propelled him on round-the-clock workdays. In the period when he began negotiating to purchase the Olds Motor Works prior to filing the incorporation papers for General Motors, his schedule was so crowded that he only got around to touring the factory one weekday at 3 a.m.[55]

After Champion joined Durant in Flint, The Man acquired more than twenty car and accessory companies—a brisk rate of purchasing all or majority ownership of at least one manufacturer or supplier every month.[56] The parts businesses were in cities chiefly around Michigan but also in Ohio, Pennsylvania, and New York because Durant wanted to guarantee a continual flow of parts to support the GM network.

Part of Durant's charm was audacious faith in the future of automobiles. Over dinner one evening in 1906 with his carriage-making partner Josiah Dallas Dort and old friend Charlie Nash, Durant delivered a soliloquy about future growth of motorcars. He forecast the day was coming when one auto company alone might sell a hundred thousand cars or more in a year.[57] Nash and Dort looked at each other in silence.[58] Finally, Nash said, "Dallas, Billy's crazy."[59] Between friends, Nash and Dort didn't think Durant was moon-struck foolish but rather crazy like a prophet.

After General Motors was incorporated, he predicted that one year America would produce three hundred thousand autos.[60] The pronouncement shocked conservative bankers, especially in the East.[61] They were wary that most car companies were grossly undercapitalized, executives like Durant were dreamers, and autos were a passing fad like bicycles, which had caused many companies to lose money when consumer demand collapsed.

A journalist wrote in a profile of Durant that he impressed strangers as a man with intense but perfectly controlled energy.[62] One of The Man's hires was Alfred P. Sloan, destined to lead General Motors as its chief executive officer when it turned into the biggest auto company in the world, described Durant as sweet natured and well intended. "It was just Billy Durant's way. You accepted it, and perhaps liked it because you liked him."[63]

Durant's arrival to a factory he owned was compared to the visitation of a cyclone.[64] He strode through the door with staff trailing like pilot fish. As soon as he found a desk with a telephone, he took a seat, removed his suit jacket, and settled in. He held the phone with the mouthpiece in one hand, the other holding the receiver to his ear, and alternated politely issuing a flow of instructions to people around him and placing long-distance phone calls through the operator to dealerships and suppliers from New York to San Francisco, talking in his relaxed, confident manner. Long-distance phone calls were still considered unusual. The Man no sooner ended one phone conversation than he told the operator another number for his next call. It seemed natural that he had to speak to so many people so far apart. He alone kept the expanding GM system together. The numbers and names and details he kept in his head, conversing at a rate that would outpace his stenographer,[65] riveting everyone in his presence, making them feel as though they had a front-row seat to watch a compelling actor alone on stage. After some time, Durant would hang up the phone, set it back on the desk, and announce, "Well, we're off to Flint." He'd stand up, don his jacket, and lead his entourage out the door.

Some of Durant's acquisitions rated solid gold, including the Champion

Ignition Company,[66] Buick, and Cadillac. Others had patents that might prove useful, such as the Elmore Manufacturing Company, which produced Elmore cars. Too many, however, had either cost far more than they were worth, failed to meet expectations, or were liabilities. To complicate matters, management and accounting methods from company to company were uneven.[67]

The holding company, General Motors, was responsible for the bills rather than the twenty-plus individual businesses. Durant had been gliding along on his salesman's steadfast confidence, persuasive optimism, and access to local funding. General Motors had expanded so far that during the summer of 1910 it no longer had the money to finance expansions and buy supplies. Buick employees were laid off by the thousands.[68] Factories were down to skeleton crews. The Cadillac Motor Company was doing well enough on its own that two Detroit banks agreed to loan $500,000 to meet payroll.[69] Shares of GM stock plummeted from around $100 to $25,[70] and GM was removed from the New York Stock Exchange.

General Motors was engulfed in panic. The only way out for Durant was to accept a bailout for GM from a banking syndicate in Boston and New York. Eastern bankers acknowledged for the first time that the auto industry had potential. The Man had to accept harsh terms in order to save the company he had founded. After weeks of negotiations, the bankers agreed to supply a $15 million loan to GM at 6 percent interest over five years—$12.75 million for GM to pay its bills and stay in business and $2.25 million paid to the bankers.[71] The syndicate required full control of GM and insisted that Durant be expelled.

The announcement of the terms soon restored investor and consumer confidence in GM.[72] The value of GM stock shares rose in private trading.[73] The Buick plant returned to full production. Buick finished 1910 with another jump from the year before—producing nearly twenty-one thousand vehicles,[74] more than half of the more than thirty-six thousand total with Cadillac, Oakland, and Oldsmobile.[75]

Louis Chevrolet retired from racing in October.[76] He reminded Durant of his intention to build a new car.

Days before Thanksgiving of 1910, however, Durant was dismissed from directing GM. He was about to turn forty-nine and the big, complicated enterprise he had created was going on without him. The bankers holding the mortgage knew nothing about automobiles, yet they would retrench GM. The bankers closed down the Elmore Manufacturing Company along with a slew of other unprofitable ventures. Durant had no say about what the bankers did.

Rather than feel defeated, The Man saw a new opportunity open up. He held a substantial amount of GM stock. Under the bankers' settlement, he remained a GM vice president and served on GM's board as a member of the finance committee. He also had many allies in the Flint business community willing to join his next venture.

The Man intended to regain General Motors after the bankers let go of their hold in five years. He needed a new automobile. Louis Chevrolet was ready to build him such a new car.

In 1905 the Society of Automotive Engineers had been founded by like-minded auto manufacturers seeking to protect their patents,[77] solve common technical design problems, and develop engineering standards. SAE's first vice president was Henry Ford.[78] By 1910 SAE was headquartered in New York City. Its leaders invited Albert Champion to personally guide them on their first international trip to meet auto executives in France, England, Belgium, and Germany.[79]

Champion's summons may have been recommended by Charles Stewart Mott, manager of the Weston-Mott Company in Flint, which manufactured wheels and axles for General Motors. Charlie Mott, then in his mid-thirties, would serve sixty years on the GM board until his death at ninety-seven in 1973.[80] For decades he was the corporation's largest stockholder and one of America's wealthiest men.[81] In 1910 his factory was near Champion's operation. He valued the Frenchman's electrical ignition products and knew he could count on his cooperation for the notable trip to the continent.

Mott and Champion had widely different backgrounds but they played critical manufacturing roles in the buildup of Buick and General Motors, as a result William Durant had covered all expenses to move their businesses to Flint. Mott had grown up in Utica, New York, where his family owned a plant that produced bicycle wheels. Young Charlie would have gone cycling with

Charles Herman Metz, founder of the company that paid Champion's expenses to immigrate. Mott had studied engineering at the Stevens Institute in Brooklyn (predecessor to the Stevens Institute of Technology).[82] In 1900 he expanded the family business to produce car wheels and axles that gained a national reputation for quality.

Durant had lured Mott's business to Flint in 1906,[83] with expenses,[84] and had offered to construct a building for the Weston-Mott Company alongside a new huge Buick Motor Company factory. The two facilities on the north side of town shared offices and a powerhouse containing a 450-horsepower generator and a pair of engines with 300-horsepower each to provide electricity to operate the most modern machinery. Durant paid $45,000 to build the Weston-Mott plant and $75,000 for the Buick factory. Mott brought about one hundred employees with him.[85] The Buick Company drew several hundred mechanics and their families. Durant's factories introduced vertical integration in the auto industry,[86] a just-in-time delivery system for parts (a concept upon which Japanese industry would later increase.)

Mott had a reputation for methodical thinking.[87] He approached problems by gathering the facts. Mott saw an advantage in SAE membership. He was then influenced by SAE member Henry M. Leland's international coup. Its magnitude encouraged Mott and fellow masterminds to recruit Albert Champion as their guide for a trans-Atlantic expedition.

Henry Leland embodied New England machine-shop craftsmanship and Midwest pluckiness. Born in a Vermont village, he had come of age during the Civil War when firearm factories in Massachusetts and Connecticut had refined the practice of machining tools and parts to within one-thousandth of an inch.[88] Precision tooling opened the way for interchangeability of parts, essential for mass manufacturing of guns. Leland had trained as a skilled mechanic at the Federal Arsenal in Springfield, Massachusetts, and the Colt revolver factory in Hartford, Connecticut, and he'd worked twenty years at the famous Brown and Sharpe Manufacturing Company in Providence, Rhode Island.[89] In 1890 he moved to Detroit.

Leland stood out as a displaced flinty New Englander. He had not an extra ounce of fat and his shirts hung loose on narrow shoulders. His full head of hair had turned white as a birch tree. A broom-like beard and droopy mustache against shaved cheeks gave him the look of a sorcerer. Leland had made an engine for Ransom Olds, but Olds had used his own motor. A group of Detroit investors cherished Leland's superior engine and underwrote his founding the Cadillac Automobile Company. The name honored the French expedition leader who had founded the settlement of Detroit, Antoine Sieur de la Mothe de Cadillac. The company adopted the Frenchman's family coat of arms for its emblem.[90] Cadillac's company slogan decreed: "Craftsmanship a Creed, Accuracy a Law."[91]

That claim had been tested in 1908 in England. The London agency that imported Cadillacs for sale in the United Kingdom had submitted three from its stock to compete for the esteemed Dewar Trophy, an annual loving cup made of silver, awarded by the Royal Automobile Club of England for the car that had most advanced the industry.[92] The Dewar Trophy had been donated by the Scotch whiskey family and was the auto industry's equivalent to the Nobel Prize.

The three Cadillacs were driven twenty-five miles by RAC members to the Brooklands track where RAC mechanics completely dismantled the cars and scrambled everything into a single pile. A different RAC team, using only hand tools—wrench, hammer, pliers, and screwdriver—put the vehicles back together. Three other RAC members drove the reconstituted Cadillacs 500 miles around the Brooklands track. All three autos ran impeccably. Against considerable competition, Cadillac won the Dewar Trophy for flawless parts interchangeability.

Capturing the Dewar Trophy, a loving cup large enough to hold an infant, had given US autos in England tremendous credibility. The attendant acclaim in the press did much to overcome the prejudice against the poorly made American cars that had been dumped on an unsuspecting English market.[93] Leland's Cadillacs had opened the potential for greater US exports.

In October 1911 Albert and Elise sailed together, accompanied by two dozen SAE members,[94] including Mott and automakers Frederick S. Duesenberg and Harry Stutz,[95] from New York to Liverpool. They sailed across what Champion and his compatriots lightheartedly called *La Mare aux Harengs*, the Sea of Herrings.

On the eight-week trip, SAE members spent the most time in London, establishing a close liaison with the British Institution of Automotive Engineers.

Then to Paris, Berlin, and Antwerp. At the time it was unusual for a wife to accompany her husband on a business trip. Elise was the exception because she helped with translating to enhance business rapport wherever the group went. She and Albert educated the Americans about the use of different foreign currencies from country to country and assisted them to get what they needed in restaurants and hotels.

The SAE contingent met automakers and reached agreements. The Americans and Europeans had a mutual interest in the automobile industry. A critical global trade agreement Champion pushed for with success was to keep metric threads on spark plugs fastening into cylinder combustion chambers. He had always produced spark plugs with metric threads, standard on the continent—and in Cadillacs and the rest of GM's cars. Of the more than two thousand nuts and bolts holding American cars together, only spark plugs had metric threads—a standard that continues today, although with globalization American threading has been accepted.

The excursion broadened Champion's exposure as an auto industry ambassador on both sides of the Atlantic. He and Elise met automaker Frederick Duesenberg of Indianapolis. Albert's friendship with Frederick would later take them back to France together, with Frederick's brother Augie, and advance their careers as well as the reputation of American cars. Albert joined the SAE and remained a member for the rest of his life. He would regularly attend annual meetings and fill support roles in the society.

In December 1911 the SAE's mission concluded and it was time to go back home. The group sailed from Southampton to New York on the English White Star ocean liner *Olympic*, sister ship to the *Titanic*. The *Olympic* represented the ultimate in comfort and luxury, with a lavish grand staircase identical to the one on the *Titanic*. In 1980, when the organization celebrated its seventy-fifth anniversary, leaders looked back on its first international meeting from the perspective of the precarious circumstances behind the return.[96] If the trip had taken place early the next year, then Champion, Mott, Duesenberg, Stutz, and colleagues could have boarded the *Titanic* on its tragic voyage to New York. "Had the brains and ability of the SAE delegation to Europe been swallowed by the Icy Atlantic, the SAE could conceivably have suffered a premature death at the age of six!"[97]

Louis Chevrolet set up shop in the first weeks of 1911 on the second floor of a building in Detroit on Grand River Avenue.[98] He had funding from Durant. Louis's shop had ample space. He had the tools and time available to do the job right. Everything was going his way. However, he had no idea how perplexing life would be with The Man.

What appealed most to Durant about Chevrolet was his name, as much for the fame that Louis's motorsport career had achieved as for its phonetic spelling. Durant had an affinity for finding something that could sell itself. To him the right name was as essential to sales as perfect pitch is to a musician. Chevrolet, with its phonetic spelling, in French or English, had the edge over David Buick's name. Durant had worried that Buick could be mispronounced as *Boo-ick*,[99] a potential sticking point. Buick cars sold well anyway. The road was wide open as far as the eye could see for a car named Chevrolet.

Louis Chevrolet hired designer and compatriot Etienne Planche, one of the forgotten pioneers of auto design. They had probably met in a Brooklyn motor shop when they were young and New York held a brief reign as America's car capital.[100] Planche went on to design a motorcycle engine and a racing car that carried his name, the Roebling-Planche. He left the East Coast to join Louis in Detroit.[101]

While the two Frenchman experimented to produce the light French car they agreed upon, The Man played his own game. He repeated his past. Durant bought the Flint Wagon Works, which years earlier had originally backed the Buick Motor Company. By now carriage companies were on their way out, but he needed a factory. This one on the west side of town fit his plan. He brought in men from the Buick Motor Company willing to follow him again to build a new car company, even if they had to step around wooden wagon wheels and whip sockets. Such bygone paraphernalia could be sold to bring in cash to build new auto trial products. The Man incorporated a new car company in July, followed by a second, called the Little Motor Company, after William Little, Durant's general manager at Buick.

Louis Chevrolet and Etienne Planche built a full-sized four-door touring car. It had a blue body, electric headlights, three speeds, and low running boards resembling French cars. Louis deemed it worthy of his name and called it the Chevrolet Classic Six.

A story made the circuit around Detroit that Louis Chevrolet had tested one of his six-cylinder models by driving at four o'clock in the morning on a road on the outskirts of the city at 110 mph.[102] Such speed may be an exaggeration, but the car went fast enough to please Louis, a connoisseur of speed. A vehicle that swift without a muffler at full throttle and that time of the morning was bound to attract attention. On the return to Detroit, he was stopped at a roadblock and arrested for speeding.[103] A justice of the peace fined him $30—$5 for speeding and $25 for impersonating the famous race driver.[104]

Louis found the anecdote worth a laugh and told Durant. Any intended humor was lost on The Man. Durant's concern was that the Chevrolet Classic Six would retail for $2,150—the price of a luxury car in an exclusive and small market already competitive with Cadillac, Packard, and other established marques. The smaller and less powered Little cost only $1,285—a price closer to what Durant needed if he was to succeed in getting back into the car game.

On November 3, 1911, Durant incorporated the Chevrolet Motor Company of Michigan, his third new auto company that year. The eponymous Louis Chevrolet was listed as an incorporator with two others on capital of $100,000. The following month, The Man boosted the Chevrolet Motor Company capitalization to $2.5 million through stock sales. Louis was not listed as an officer. Louis Chevrolet was dealt out of the car company bearing his name. Durant compensated Louis with one hundred shares of the stock issue.[105]

Louis Chevrolet was satisfied with building the car he wanted, one worthy of the name Chevrolet. There were photo ops. Louis standing on the sidewalk next to a polished Chevrolet parked at the curb, the Chevrolet name spelled in cursive along the hood, the top folded down, The Man's grown son, Cliff Durant, ensconced behind the steering wheel next to Suzanne Chevrolet. She looked chic in a driving hat that covered her hair so it wouldn't get mussed in the wind.

The photo marked the high point for Louis. He had served his purpose to Durant, and he was on his way out. Louis Chevrolet and Billy Durant had different tastes. Louis wanted a stylish luxury car capable of going fast enough to get the driver arrested. The Man was trying to figure out how to produce a cheap car to challenge Henry Ford's industry-leading Model T.

The Chevrolet Classic Six auto went into production. Over the year 1912, Chevrolet cars sold modestly.[106] The next year Louis and Suzanne shipped out with their two sons for an extended trip to France.[107] They were gone long enough for The Man to incorporate more companies and merge some in pursuit of creating a mid-size car that cost less than the Chevrolet Six and could sell in big numbers. When Louis returned to Detroit, he discovered that his beloved Chevrolet Six had been discontinued. The Man had modified the Little Motor Car Company's auto, which was being sold as a low-cost Chevrolet.[108]

Louis was devastated. As if he had not endured enough humiliation with his dream car taken away from him, each time he talked with Durant, tension smoldered between them over Louis's cigarettes. The Man insisted that a gentleman carmaker should smoke cigars. Louis, like Albert Champion, came from the French working class. They had mustaches and wore flat wool caps. Durant was clean-shaven and wore felt hats. Louis smoked cigarettes and was not about to change his habit. But The Man would not let up on Louis; he persisted in attempting to persuade Louis to smoke cigars.

Louis was a tender and loving family man.[109] Nevertheless, Durant's action caused him to erupt in anger. "I sold you my car and I sold you my name, but I'm not going to sell myself to you," he bellowed. "I'm going to smoke my cigarettes as much as I want. And I'm getting out."[110]

By the end of 1913, the two men parted company. Embittered, Louis sold all his shares of Chevrolet Motor Company stock—to Durant.[111] He severed their relationship. (If he had held on to his shares, the stock would have made him a millionaire many times over. But no amount of money would change the way Louis felt about what Durant had done to him.)

The Man's Chevrolet Motor Company introduced two new models built in Flint—the Royal Mail roadster, evoking a romantic English association, and the Baby Grand touring car.[112] Both models were selling—for cash in the era before monthly payments were introduced—as fast as they were made. Durant now had a car company with a distinctive name and two models in the price range he wanted. All he needed was a catchy logo. He added the bow-tie badge to the Royal Mail and the Baby Grand, the first models to carry the Chevrolet bow tie. Now he was on track to regain control of General Motors.

Louis Chevrolet went back to what he knew best—racing. He planned to build a racecar. A successful one would prove reliability and Louis could adapt it as a passenger car.[113] This time he would name his esteemed auto after the great French patriot and former Governor General of New France, Louis de Baude Frontenac. To Louis Chevrolet, Frontenac was exceptional. A portion of the land Frontenac had claimed for France in North America was sold in 1803 as the Louisiana Purchase to the United States for $15 million (worth $314 million in 2014). The territory contained all or portions of what became fifteen US states. Frontenac's importance dwarfed that of his younger contemporary, Antoine Cadillac. Cadillac fell out of favor in the court of Louis XIV, was recalled back to Paris, and imprisoned briefly in the Bastille. Louis bet his future on an automobile named for Frontenac.

Louis had many friends and associates willing to back him. The first one to step up and offer to supply the capital he needed was Albert Champion.

Champion now had a plant of his own and employed hundreds. His Champion Ignition Company had moved into a two-story brick factory of more than thirty-three thousand feet of floor space at the corner of Harriet and Industrial Avenue, near the huge Buick complex.[114] His enterprise had matured from a startup to a going concern. Moving into the building had merited a ribbon-cutting ceremony in front of the new entrance. Elise would have attended the gala.

He also had deep pockets. Beyond his salary as chief executive of the Champion Ignition Company, Champion received $500,000 ($12.5 million in 2014) a year on dividends from his interest in the company.[115] Moreover, the US Patent Office in 1910 had issued him a patent for his insulator and conductor for electric currents, which were used in GM autos, resulting in a substantial annual royalty.[116]

In early 1914 Albert began sponsoring Louis's new Frontenac Motor Car of Michigan at Louis's shop on Grand River Avenue. They operated with the same arrangement Louis had in his early stages with Durant—underwriting without a corporate stake. Louis was conducting business as an individual. For the next year Albert paid the rent, utilities, material costs, and other expenses, and he also provided a basic salary for Louis, Etienne Planche as designer,[117] and Arthur Chev-rolet.[118] Louis expected to introduce his Frontenac racecar in the 1915 season.

The Chevrolet family and the Champions dined together often at one another's house, sometimes accompanied by De Guichard and Planche and their amours, making for raucous evenings. Albert noticed Suzanne Chevrolet, her long, dark hair, Gaulic poise.

Albert was experimenting with a new spark plug design, called the AC Titan Spark Plug. The latest high-speed racing engines increased cylinder pressure, which caused spark plugs to heat to a higher temperature and leak electricity, diminishing the plug's explosion in the combustion chamber and reducing engine power. Albert devised a new process for manufacturing the spark plugs to allow for metal expansion in a hot plug, which kept the electricity intact and the plug operating at high efficiency.

The Champion Ignition Company in the spring of 1914, leading up to the Memorial Day Indy 500, made AC Titan plugs plentifully available for the cars and teams on the race circuit so that they could test how they would perform in high-powered racing engines. That Albert Champion was funding Louis Chevrolet, a respected racer, lent credibility to his AC Titan plugs.

Chevrolet made progress on his Frontenacs. He had designs for two different ultramodern engines and a Frontenac finished in time for the 1915 season.[119] Arthur had two machines under construction.[120] Louis finally appeared ready to introduce his racecar. Yet he would lose another year before he introduced his adored Frontenacs.

The delay, the abrupt breakup between Louis and Albert, and Louis's sudden departure from Detroit was first accounted for by the late Griffith Borgeson,[121] acclaimed by the Society of Automotive Engineers as one of the world's preeminent automotive historians. Borgeson had interviewed more than one hundred people involved in the critical first third of the twentieth century, when the American auto industry was formed. He wrote his classic book *The Golden Age of the American Racing Car*, first published in 1966, with material based on the memories of the people who had made the history. Their recollections were checked and cross-checked. Borgeson noted that one day in early 1915 Louis was at work in Detroit when Albert visited Suzanne at home.

Albert must have become infatuated with her as he had been with French actress Olta de Kerman. He went to Suzanne with the intention of having an affair—and betraying Louis. Despite his considerable financial support and friendship with Louis, Albert risked everything. Suzanne spurned him. When Louis came home from work, she told her husband.

Louis exploded in rage. The following morning, Louis had fire in his eyes as he barged with bear-like strength through the door of his now ex-friend's private office, fuming that he had been mortally wronged.[122]

Albert stood up from behind his desk and yelled back in French.

The confrontation escalated like wildfire. Louis, a head taller and fifty pounds heavier, attacked Champion with his fists. Office staff members were shocked at the sight of men in The Chief's office throwing punches. Telephones crashed to the floor. Wooden trays holding reams of paper flew into the air and scattered documents all over the place. If the fight were a boxing match, ringside reporters would have scored it in favor of Louis, who beat Champion almost to death.[123] He warned Champion never to cross his path again or he would finish him off.

Louis was so enraged that as fast as he could he relocated his family to Indianapolis. The city, now famous for its motor speedway and the Indy 500, had a lot to offer. He never returned to Michigan in Champion's lifetime.

Elise always cared for Albert without hesitation. Yet there was a limit to what she would tolerate. His cruelty was threatening their marriage.

13

FIGHTING CHANCES

PROBABLY NO ONE BUSINESS OFFERS MORE
OPPORTUNITY FOR THE YOUNG MAN TO RISE THAN
THE AUTOMOBILE INDUSTRY, YET MOST OF THE
LARGE AUTOMOBILE FIRMS HAVE BEEN BUILT UP
FROM A SMALL BEGINNING.

—AUTOMOBILE, 1909[1]

Robert Stranahan had borrowed thousands of dollars from his brother Frank to jostle around on trains and sleep in hotels far away from his young wife as a traveling salesman from Boston calling on carmakers cropping up in the Midwest. It was all he could do to keep his Champion Spark Plug Company from going under. A trip to Toledo in the spring of 1910 changed all that.

There in the city abutting southern Michigan on the shore of Lake Erie, he offered his Champion spark plug samples to John Willys, a fast-rising captain of industry.[2] Willys owned the Overland Automobile Company, headquartered in Indianapolis.[3] He recently had moved his operation into a mammoth modern manufacturing campus of twenty-four buildings covering twelve acres in Toledo, ranking as one of America's largest auto-producing plants.[4] Robert had suggested to Willys that Champion spark plugs would improve the performance of Overlands.[5] Willys agreed to buy the spark plugs, but on the condition that Robert relocate his business to Toledo to ensure uninterrupted delivery.[6]

While Robert had been busy with the Willys proposition, his brother Spencer, the former precocious schoolboy and all-round athlete, had surprised the family. Walking into their mother's home in Brookline with blonde Marion Davenport at his side, he had announced, "I've been married, and this is my wife."[7] His bride was a pretty nineteen-year-old Boston nursing student from Portland, Maine. Afterward, the couple lived in Brookline. Spencer worked with Robert producing spark plugs in the Whittier Street shop in Roxbury.

Then, as unexpectedly as he had married, Spencer died in January 1909 at twenty-four from meningitis.[8] The close family was traumatized. So it was good news when Robert closed the deal with Willys. He was ready to leave Boston with his wife for a fresh start. Frank still had business pending in Boston, but he accompanied Robert to Toledo for a brief visit.

"We came to Toledo with spark plug manufacturing equipment loaded in two boxcars and saddled with a $22,000 debt ($548,000 in 2014)," Robert often recalled, to emphasize how he had worked his way up and overcome hard times.[9] Two weeks passed before the machinery arrived by rail. He set up shop in downtown Toledo, on the second floor of a brick commercial structure over the Holmes Snow Flake Laundry.[10] Doing business with Willys helped the Stranahans attract investors. The next month, the brothers reorganized the Champion Spark Plug Company as a Delaware corporation on $30,000 capital ($748,000 in 2014),[11] with Robert as president and Frank as treasurer.[12]

Willys had captured widespread attention for his swift ascent,[13] from practically nothing in two years to president of one America's largest car companies—one that in 1910 appeared capable of challenging Ford and Buick, especially with Buick faltering that summer.[14] John North Willys, called J. N. by his friends,[15] was thirty-seven. He had pleasant features, appeared urbane in business suits, and radiated a salesman's natural confident smile.

At the beginning of the decade Willys had been selling bicycles in Elmira, New York.[16] After three years one of the bicycle companies in Indianapolis shifted to turning out cars—called Overland. Right away he realized how autos would overtake bicycles,[17] the sales of which were already slumping. He put his considerable energy into selling Overlands as well as autos made by two other Indianapolis manufacturers. By 1909 he had moved to Indianapolis, had taken possession of the Overland plant, and had restructured the company. The cars were durable, eye-catching, and retailed for $1,200.[18] They were so popular that Willys was deluged with more signed contracts and deposits for orders than he could fill.[19] He needed a much larger factory—and right away, if his operation were to survive. The story of his rise read as though it were lifted from a fairy tale.[20]

Colonel Albert Pope,[21] America's first bicycle manufacturer and one of the original pioneer automakers, had put his Pope-Toledo factory up for sale. Pope had introduced the public to self-propelled personal transportation—first in the late 1870s selling Columbia bicycles, a brand still selling today, followed in 1898 by electric Columbia cars.[22] His Pope-Toledo model never caught on as he had envisioned, and in his sixties the Civil War veteran's health had deteriorated. Willys purchased his facility in April 1909 for $285,000 ($7.4 million in 2014). Five months later, Pope died of pneumonia.[23] Young Willys moved his company into the factory and continued Pope's legacy.

Frank Stranahan had lost the Boston Buick dealership when General Motors funding dried up and production shut down. After the bankers' trust took over GM and operations resumed, Frank became vice president of the Massachusetts Motor Company, incorporated in November 1910 in the Bay State to sell Oakland cars (predecessor to Pontiac) made by General Motors in Pontiac, Michigan.[24] He had four partners in the dealership, which opened sales rooms at 591 Boylston Street. Oaklands were powered by Champion Ignition Company spark plugs and magnetos, a rival of the Champion Spark Plug Company where Frank was also vice president. If he had overlooked such a conflict of interest, Robert would have scolded him to divest himself.

Robert took the helm of the Champion Spark Plug Company in Toledo and settled there with his wife, Agnes. Above the laundry shop, he acted as shop foreman, managed all company correspondence, kept the financial books, and served as chief salesman. He developed the reputation of a perfectionist.[25] His philosophy was to handle all details as if they mattered equally on the assumption that when a major problem arose he could treat it like another detail.

Revenue from supplying Willys's Overlands turned the Champion Spark Plug Company around into a moneymaker. The year 1910 concluded with the Overland Automobile Company producing a total of twenty thousand cars—twelve thousand in Toledo and eight thousand in Indianapolis.[26] Buick had about the same sum—its official tally exceeded Overland's by only one hundred.[27] Both Overlands and Buicks were running on spark plugs bearing Champion's name.

The supreme leader in auto sales was Henry Ford's Model T, his low-cost car for the multitudes,[28] with some twenty-six thousand sold. Robert determined he had to win the Ford account.[29]

Detroit and Henry Ford were a short train ride north from Toledo. When Robert had been an itinerant drummer from Boston, he had struck out trying to gain access to Ford. Now living in Toledo, he had a better chance. He joined several Masonic affiliations.[30] An ardent golfer, he became a member of area country clubs and the Detroit Athletic Club. He participated in local Republican politics. Over the next year he ingratiated himself with the right people and at last made a pitch to Henry Ford.

Robert promised he could provide better spark plugs than the existing supplier and, crucial to Henry, at a cheaper price. Henry agreed to try Robert's Champion spark plugs. The trial worked. The Champion Spark Plug Company became the sole supplier to the Ford Motor Company—an exclusive relationship that continued for half a century.[31]

The Ford and Overland accounts put the Stranahans in a position to take advantage of swelling auto sales. Robert was relieved from the need to travel constantly. He could now spend more evenings and weekends with Agnes and their children.

In 1912, President William Howard Taft signed the law admitting the territories of New Mexico and Arizona into the union,[32] finally giving America forty-eight contiguous states. The auto industry reached a sign of maturity, reflected in aftermarket sales for accessory manufacturing. Spark plugs had a short life and required frequent replacement. They became a popular consumer product.

A common problem plaguing spark plugs was porous or cracked porcelain, which caused electricity to leak. Electricity's natural propensity of taking the path of least resistance tended to ground the charge before reaching its designation. And the higher the engine temperature, the greater the electricity leakage. Reduced electric current weakened the spark's power. That led to the fuel mixture failing to fully ignite, which caused the cylinder to misfire and propel the vehicle as roughly as if its wheels were square. Most cars, like Buick and Ford Model Ts, had four cylinders, but autos with spark plugs that were leaking electricity drove as though they had three cylinders, and they sucked up more gasoline.

Albert Champion and Robert Stranahan, independently, experimented with how to make better spark plugs. They looked for ways to reduce the faults and increase the virtues—improvements that took them an inch, perhaps a foot, closer to the ideal, still decades away.

"I spent a fortune on spark plug experiments at the start," Champion later said. "My friends thought I was crazy. I said *no*. I *knew* I was right."[33] He put prototypes through long and rigorous tests before submitting patent applications.

Robert figured out one way to reduce electric current loss. It involved inserting gaskets between the metal and porcelain parts, which provided a more secure seal and improved insulation. As a result, the modified plug fired sparks more efficiently in the piston chamber—and made starting the engine easier in cold weather or when engine parts had chilled.[34] He submitted a patent application on February 1, 1912; in October, he was awarded the patent.[35] He marketed his design as the *Champion X*. It gave him an edge in the growing spark-plug competition.

After two years over the Snow Flake Laundry, the Champion Spark Plug Company relocated across town, into a four-story brick building on Upton Avenue. There was plenty of space for future expansion, which appeared inevitable, as accelerating demand for cars seemed boundless.

Profits allowed the Stranahans to buy out their early partners and split the shares. To retain the stock for safekeeping, the brothers created a holding company, Madison Securities.[36] Frank removed himself from his conflict of interest by selling his part of the Oakland dealership. Before he took his wife and son to live in Toledo, he dissolved the Albert Champion Company of Boston.[37] Frank, once a partner with Albert, had become his adversary.

Around that time, Robert and Frank brought their mother, Lizzie, as an equal partner in the Champion Spark Plug Company.[38] This was possibly a Solomon solution to help insulate her sons from difficulties sharing power and responsibilities.[39]

Brothers Frank D. Stranahan, left, and Robert, right, broke from the Albert Champion Company in Boston to found their Champion Spark Plug Company in Toledo. *Photo courtesy of Ann and Stephen Stranahan.*

The Stranahans in 1912 adapted the Champion name on the globe for the Champion Spark Plug Company. A lawsuit over the name *Champion* was inevitable. *From* Motor World, *March 7, 1912.*

A Solomon solution between the Stranahans and Albert Champion was out of the question. Their rivalry was turning more complicated. Magazine ads from the two companies sharing the Champion name started to look alike, and competing ads were sometimes published on facing pages.[40] Albert by 1912 distinguished his products by stamping the top of the porcelain of every spark plug with his initials, AC.[41] A full-page ad in *Motor World* to promote Robert's Champion X featured the globe with a Mercator projection and the *Champion* banner diagonally across North America—art lifted from Albert Champion Company ads five years earlier, complete with the same "trade-mark" symbol.[42]

Since the turn of the century, when most spark plugs had been imported from France or Germany, about two hundred domestic plug makers and assemblers had entered the fray to compete for annual sales of about 56 million spark plugs.[43] The two major brands accounting for half the market carried Champion's name.[44]

The Champion Spark Plug Company held a numerical advantage in sales over the Champion Ignition Company. Albert gained extra attention due to his products being used in cars that were regularly winning races. He generously contributed spark plugs to racing teams in exchange for their testing his products under motorsport's racking abuse. The Indianapolis Motor Speedway had introduced its five-hundred-mile endurance grind around the 2.5-mile oval on Memorial Day 1911. The famous winning car was Marmon, made in Indianapolis, among the growing number of independent passenger car companies running on Albert Champion's accessories. He supplied the expanding line of General Motors cars and trucks along with more than sixty independent motor companies, among them Duesenberg, Stutz, and Pierce-Arrow—all prominent marques.

Spark-plug manufacturers crowded into the market like prospectors flocking to the California gold rush. Many brands had reassuring names—Never-Miss, Constant, Sta-Rite,[45] Shur-Fire,[46] Reliance, and the American Indestructible. Others had whimsical appellations, like Rajah and Comet. Some sounded ambiguous, such as Duplex, or enigmatic, like Bougie B and S-M. The name Champion came across as simple and clean. It stood out as much for designating a winner as for the hard-earned reputation of Albert Champion, the Frenchman whose name was his destiny. In hostile business battles, however, names are a legal right rather than a birthright—as had been demonstrated by the sagas surrounding the Ransom Olds, David Buick, and Louis Chevrolet names.

The Stranahans were earning a fortune trading on Champion's name. In five years, the Champion Spark Plug Company had grown by 2,000 percent.[47] The prospects for future growth shined brilliantly. The Stranahans wanted their company to have exclusive rights to the name Champion. In the summer of 1916, they filed suit in US District Court in Cleveland against the Champion Ignition Company and Albert Champion for infringement of the Champion trademark and for unfair competition.[48] The Champion Spark Plug Company sought an injunction to restrain the Champion Ignition Company and Albert Champion from manufacturing, selling, or advertising spark plugs as "Champion."

The federal case became *Champion Spark Plug Co. v. Champion Ignition Co., et al.*[49]

Albert Champion filed a countersuit to dismiss the case.

Both companies had deep pockets to buy the best legal advice. Only one would win the Champion name.

In the meantime the eponymous Champion devoted his vigor to keeping up with the swelling auto industry. Manufacturing more than doubled every year, from about 210,000 vehicles produced in 1911 to some 1.6 million in 1916.[50] Improvements to cars included the introduction of electric starters, which eliminated laborious and hazardous hand-crank starters, and installation of electric lights for better nighttime driving. Americans now drove the roads in 3.5 million cars. Ford's Model Ts led the growth surge. Ford had been the innovative game changer,[51] introducing the moving assembly line and then boosting wages for laborers to $5 a day ($118 in 2014).[52] Ford Motor Company's profit of $37 million in 1913 ($885 million) showed that manufacturing cars created a new source of wealth. The auto industry further boosted the related industries of steel, rubber, and gasoline.

Flint puffed up from a rustic small town to a lively city topping fifty thousand folks. Some wanted the same urban amenities found in Detroit and Chicago. Albert Champion, Billy Durant, and Charles Stewart Mott joined a few dozen citizens to donate $500 each to found the Flint Country Club.[53] The group bought a farm out of town in Atlas Valley. An architect remodeled the colonial farmhouse into a clubhouse with a broad veranda and converted farmland into a respectable eighteen-hole golf course. The clubhouse was decorated throughout with a profusion of flowers arranged in gold baskets and white French wicker furniture. Men—and women—in leisure attire stretched their legs along carefully tended fairways and manicured putting greens to play. Nothing announced the city had come up in the world more convincingly than the Flint Country Club.

Swinging a wooden-shafted club to knock a ball down the fairway and tap it with a putter into a cup on the green scarcely appealed to Champion. His scores hovered around the rim of one hundred, in the duffer zone.[54] He only just tolerated the game, an excuse for a stroll in the sun—before the advent of golf carts. The game's salvation was an excuse to mingle outside with cohorts and engage in trade talk, which sometimes rewarded dishy gossip. Champion enjoyed playing in the company of the strong-willed Walter Chrysler. They shared a passion for cars and engines. Chrysler was a force in organizing production at Buick, GM's biggest-selling auto.

Champion and his wife joined the Flint Country Club for social cachet. She introduced herself by her first name, Julie, and reserved Elise, her middle name, for family and French-speaking friends. She and Albert hosted a dinner dance for 150 guests at the country club. The soirée offered a French-style seven-course menu.[55] Drinks were cooled by ice molded in the form of small pink-and-white automobiles.[56] Guests danced to the orchestra, which featured a xylophone player infusing the evening with the latest Chicago jazz riffs.

Everyone knew that Julie Champion played better golf than Albert. She took home silver loving cups and displayed them in the living room for winning the coveted Dort Cup Tournament and the Flint Country Club putting championship.[57]

More to Albert's style was rigorous exercise. "To work, you must keep fit," the former world-record-holding athlete liked to say.[58] Every morning at 5:40 he rose and trundled from the bedroom down the hall to a spare room designated as a gym.[59] He did sit-ups before he mounted a bicycle fixed to a steel frame, the rear wheel on a roller, for fifteen minutes of sweaty pumping.[60] Then he showered, donned a suit, and ate a sensible breakfast.[61] He would then commute to work in time to sit behind his desk before seven o'clock.

Driving to or from golfing could prove hazardous. One sunny afternoon at the end of May 1916 he had a narrow escape from a head-on collision while driving home from the Flint Country Club with Elise in the passenger seat of their Cadillac.[62] He came up behind a horse-drawn buggy in the road ahead and steered into the oncoming lane to pass as a roadster carrying three men approached from the opposite direction. Champion veered off the road into a ditch, which caused the car to flip over. The roadster had nowhere to go and crashed into the ditch. Elise suffered cuts to her head and face. Albert's right arm and right leg (his good one) were bruised. Both cars needed repairs for shattered windshields and bashed in radiators. The roadster's driver and passengers were unharmed. Elise was taken to the hospital for treatment and released. Champion had barely avoided another disaster.

The next day he was on the job when the astonishing news flashed around the auto world that Billy Durant had taken over General Motors as president. Champion's company was poised to grow with GM more than he could have ever dreamed.

After Durant had been forced out as the chief executive of GM, he had founded the Chevrolet Motor Company and developed a mid-priced passenger car retailing for up to $1,500. In a demonstration of creativity and tenacity, he had put together a nationwide organization. He had set up Chevrolet assembly plants in Michigan, New York City, St. Louis, Toledo, and Canada, along with wholesale offices around the United States and in Canada.[63] In 1915 about sixteen thousand Chevrolet cars—running on Champion Ignition Company accessories—were sold.[64] Chevrolet sales generated revenue of $11.7 million ($276 million in 2014) and a net profit of $1.3 million ($30.6 million). GM stock had returned to the New York Stock Exchange in the summer of 1911.[65] Durant had increased the value of Chevrolet Motor Company shares on the stock exchange and offered to trade five shares of Chevrolet stock for one GM share.[66] His strategy was for the Chevrolet Motor Company to amass enough GM shares to take over. Durant's tactic looked reckless, Sisyphean. Then he formed a strategic alliance with Pierre S. du Pont that changed the math.

Pierre S. du Pont, president of the DuPont Corporation of Wilmington, Delaware, directed the family business of making gunpowder and explosives.[67] The DuPont Corporation was exploiting the Great War, which had erupted in August 1914 on the continent. German troops had stormed through Belgium into northern France and destroyed everything in their path, forcing tens of thousands of civilians to flee to southern England and Holland. England declared war against Germany and allied with France and Belgium. DuPont was selling TNT and gunpowder to the governments and armies of both sides, which were slaughtering masses of troops with modern machine guns and cannons.

On the recommendation of his treasurer, John Jakob Raskob, Pierre du Pont had purchased a two thousand shares of General Motors stock.[68] Raskob, a streetwise bookkeeper from New York's Hell's Kitchen and a shrewd student of Wall Street,[69] looked ahead to when the war would someday end and the DuPont Corporation would have tens of millions of ready cash to invest (billions in 2014).[70] Raskob considered GM a good investment, despite Wall Street's worry that autos were risky business.[71] Over the next year, Pierre du Pont bolstered his shares of GM and Chevrolet until they made up more than half of his personal investment portfolio.[72]

The tally of Durant's GM shares of stock and thousands more owned by Pierre du Pont were augmented by holdings of The Man's cronies. Members of the Flint business community put their faith in him and traded GM stock for Chevrolet stock. Company owners like Albert Champion and Charles Stewart Mott, whom Durant had brought to GM, bought GM and Chevrolet shares. Durant maneuvered in the background as the Chevrolet Motor Company accrued 450,000 of GM's 825,589 outstanding shares.[73] And Durant also controlled the Chevrolet Motor Company's shares.[74] Still a vice president of GM, he attended the board meeting at a hotel in New York City on September 16, 1915. The date coincided with GM's seventh anniversary. The date also was two weeks from when GM was scheduled to pay the final $2.5 million of the $15 million loan it had received from the bankers' trust.[75] The bankers were unaware of the shift in the balance of power until Durant announced to them, "I'm in control of General Motors today."[76]

The bankers were astounded. Over the following months, the trust was dissolved. On June 1, 1916, The Man took over as president of General Motors.[77] He signed Walter Chrysler to a three-year contract as general manager of Buick.[78] It was time for another big show.

Soon The Man reorganized the General Motors Company of New Jersey into the General Motors Corporation, a Delaware corporation.[79] He transformed

GM into an operating company instead of a holding company—auto manufacturers like Buick and Cadillac and accessory companies such as the Champion Ignition Company became operating divisions.[80] General Motors was coming into its modern image. Durant had bigger plans ahead, more companies to purchase and bring into the GM fold.

Champion, encouraged by Albert Schmidt, himself a devotee of aviation during the early days of the sport in France,[81] foresaw a future in flight. Aircraft engines derived straight from car motors. The US aviation industry was small, with annual output measured in the dozens—ironic considering that America had claimed the airplane as a technical breakthrough only to let aviation languish.[82]

Across the Atlantic, France made bold progress in flying. Champion's comrade in Paris Edouard Nieuport had built early bi-wing and mono-wing Nieuport Aéroplanes. He had set world air-speed records in 1911.[83] He was the first ever to fly faster than 80 mph. Nieuport campaigned to pilot his plane at 100 mph, but he died in a crash at the end of the summer.[84] The Nieuport Company continued to use his name. During the Great War, French pilots in Nieuports were shooting German aviators from the sky in modern aerial combat.

America's neutrality was threatened in May 1915 after a German submarine sank the English passenger ship *Lusitania* in the Atlantic.[85] Among the twelve hundred passengers killed were 128 US citizens. Tensions rose between the governments of the United States and Germany—and among Americans about whether to enter the war. President Woodrow Wilson won reelection for a second term by speaking out against German aggression and the need for a strong US defense—he called for doubling the size of the army and funding a naval building program.[86]

The US federal government, meanwhile, requested a complete inventory of Flint's industries.[87] Champion was appointed to a special board with Charles Stewart Mott, a director of General Motors and the mayor of Flint, and three additional business leaders to conduct a survey of the city's factories for the Department of War (predecessor to the Defense Department) and US Navy. The survey was submitted in a confidential report intended to aid the federal government's planning for conversion of civilian factories for production of war materials.

In 1916 Champion designed a new AC Titan aviation spark plug to correct mechanical mishaps that had beleaguered plane engines.[88] He and his chemists experimented in the lab with different clays and unique grinding and mixing to improve porcelain insulation. They tried assorted steel alloys and varied copper thicknesses in their efforts to produce spark plugs that were more robust. His company distributed prototypes to aircraft companies for field tests.

Car racing had charged ahead to ever-faster records thanks to a new era of speedways, one or two miles around. Board surfaces had less rolling friction than asphalt, brick, and dirt. More steeply banked board turns meant drivers could fly around the ovals and average more than 100 mph in races up to 250 miles. Sustained high speeds caused carbon deposits to build up on spark plugs from the fuel-air mixture burning at intense heat inside the piston chamber. Frequently oil leaked into the chamber and collected. Carbon buildup on the central porcelain, which held the electrode tip in place, prevented the spark from jumping across the electrode gap—a misfiring known today as "fouling."

Champion created a new AC Cico spark plug and distributed prototypes for racecar teams to try out on the national circuit. More durable spark plugs would benefit passenger cars. "Keep ahead of the race," he said. "That is what brings success. It makes the great racer. It makes the successful businessman. No champion ever arrived resting on the oars."[89]

It was natural that journalists were drawn to the Frenchman as a business leader, more so in Flint. He was a player in the city's surging economic engine. Reporters saw Champion as a debonair continental, natty in a tailored suit, pushing forty but as energetic as men half his age. The *Flint Journal* described his hands-on approach to running all the departments. "If a universal eight-hour working day were compulsory, Albert Champion, president of the Champion Ignition Company and maker of A.C., AC Cico, and AC Titan spark plugs, would be an outlaw, as he is one of the busiest men in the automobile industry and thrives on work. Intensely enthusiastic and tirelessly energetic, he would resent any limitation being put on his hours of planning and execution."[90]

He climbed aboard trains taking him around the country to personally solicit business from blunt-talking, hard-working, ingenious, and singular carmakers shaping the industry—Fred and Augie Duesenberg, Harry Stutz, George Pierce producing Pierce-Arrows, and more.[91] Champion served as the purchasing agent, capable of talking with experts about the finest of raw materials found in America and imported from France and England.[92] He had a craftsman's knowledge of firing clay into porcelain.[93] He bought the materials and conducted exhaustive experiments, assisting his chief mechanical engineer Albert Schmidt and the chemists in his company laboratory. Adapting to manufacturing without precedent, he designed original machinery to save time and labor while raising the quality of his products.[94] He preferred to say that the three hundred people on his payroll did not so much work *for* Albert Champion as work *with* him.[95]

"I have always felt that the education and training I received as a bicycle racer was a great help in business because it is a game in which you train to fight and win," Champion told a *Detroit Daily News* scribe. He emphasized that experimenting and learning leads to progress. "I always remember what a friend of mine once told me. He was a well-known chemist, an authority in the automobile world. He said that four times during his life he has had to scrap his knowledge of chemistry and begin again at the start. He was not only happy about it. He is ready to do the same thing over and over when he finds it necessary."[96]

Even so, Champion was not without his quirks. Speaking to a *Flint Journal* reporter he brought up the Rudyard Kipling poem "The Vampire," to describe the construction of a spark plug. His taste for the Victorian English poet and other Victorian authors had been acquired from his former trainer-manager Choppy Warburton. Kipling's poem summarizes a woman as "a rag and a bone and a hank of hair." In that reductionist way, Champion suggested that a spark plug can be defined as a lump of clay, a cylinder of steel, and a copper disk. "But it is just as difficult a task to refine, shape, and assemble these raw materials into a spark plug as it would be to fashion a woman out of the ingredients of the Kipling formula."[97]

In his obsessive thoroughness, he devised quality-control inspections. The plugs went through two simple but effective tests prior to shipments. First, plugs were hooked up to a special machine connected to a thirty-thousand-volt transformer to measure electrical leakage.[98] The second tested compression leakage in the combustion chamber under very high air pressure.[99]

Germany's invasion of France had roused Albert Schmidt to return to his home-land. He was forty-eight, had gray in his mustache and the hair at his temples, but he wanted to offer his knowledge of engineering and aviation to help defend France. He made travel arrangements through the French consul in Detroit and shipped out. In Paris Schmidt bought a Blériot airplane and donated it to the government.[100] He flew a reconnaissance mission near Antwerp, a seaport in northern Belgium, and spotted thousands of German troops advancing. He flew back to his camp to report an impending attack. In an artillery barrage, he was knocked unconscious. He was captured but escaped to Antwerp. He fled in the dark to Holland and was smuggled out in a pile of coal on a boat to southern England. In Calais he was discharged from the French army for hearing loss from the explosion. His German-sounding name made English military officials suspicious that he was a spy until he produced a cablegram with Champion's name and the Champion Ignition Company address in Flint with instructions to take the French liner *Rochambeau* to New York.[101]

By 1917, production had spiked to nearly 1.9 million new cars.[102] Albert Champion had three new buildings erected in Flint, and he equipped them with energy-saving industrial machinery.[103] He had once regarded the manufacture of five thousand plugs as a good day, but his production now soared to sixty thousand plugs daily,[104] an annual rate of 12 million,[105] all stamped with his AC trademark on the porcelain. His labor force had expanded in nine years from fifteen to three hundred.[106] "In fact, the growth of the Champion Ignition Company is one of the many inspiring romances of the automobile world," burbled the *Boston Herald*.[107]

In April 1917 the United States declared war against Germany, joining France and England in the fight. Congress approved the Selective Service Act, which required that men aged eighteen to thirty register for the draft. The Buick factory geared up to make Liberty airplane motors, tanks, artillery shells, and parts for ambulances bound for France.[108]

Champion's efforts to develop AC Titan spark plugs for aircraft engines and test them for a year assured that his company was well prepared. The Champion

Ignition Company stepped up to furnish AC Titans for Liberty, Wright, and Hispano-Suiza aircraft engines in US Army planes that would be shipped across the ocean as soon as they were built.[109]

The next month the case of *The Champion Spark Plug Company v. Champion Ignition Co. et al.* was transferred from the US District Court in Cleveland to the US District Court in Detroit.[110]

The Stranahans filed a motion to dismiss Champion's counterclaim on the grounds that the District Court in Detroit lacked jurisdiction to entertain a counterclaim.[111]

Champion fought to distinguish his products from those of his adversaries. On June 4, 1917, he filed an application with the US Patent Office for a spark plug that reduced electricity leakage with an improved electrode and insulation of the inner, exposed end of the electrode.[112] The new design also cut the cost of manufacturing the spark plugs.

More than two hundred thousand American troops landed in France in the summer of 1917 as part of the American Expeditionary Force under US Army commander John J. "Black Jack" Pershing. The AEF consisted of five divisions of Army and Marine Corps. They were the vanguard of what would reach a million US troops over the next year. The American soldiers and marines were deployed to the front lines. The Great War had expanded into World War I.

Champion was saddened by the news of the losses of Marius Thé,[113] driver of the motorcycle he had paced behind to win the French national motorpace title, killed at the Battle of the Somme along with Emile Friol, the national sprint champion.[114] German audiences had cheered Champion, but German soldiers had destroyed the landmark Roubaix Velodrome,[115] where he had scored one of his greatest victories. Germans blew up the auto factory that his boss Adolphe Clément-Bayard had operated in Mézières.[116] In 1915 a German submarine had sunk the *Majestic*, the ship Champion had first sailed on to America.[117] Jean Hallier,[118] husband of Champion's amour Olta de Kerman, was killed flying in a dogfight. The Battle of the Somme in the summer of 1916 had killed or wounded more than one million French, English, and German troops.[119]

Champion was still fighting the Stranahans in federal court. France and America, allied with England and Belgium, were battling Germany. His only way to fight was to endure and win, so Champion threw himself into his work.

On November 22, 1917, US District Court judge Arthur J. Tuttle denied the Stranahans' motion to dismiss Champion's counterclaim.[120]

Judge Tuttle noted in writing his opinion that the Stranahans and the Champion Spark Plug Company had been for the last ten years engaged in continuous manufacture and sale of spark plugs under the trade name and trademark of "Champion." That left open the issue of whether Albert Champion had interrupted the use of his name after he had moved.

The case remained in the US District Court of Detroit.

By the end of that month, Champion had filed his third patent with the US Patent Office, for a spark plug that reduced carbon deposits on the porcelain insulator to ensure continuous firing.[121]

The court case contesting his name was hanging over him like the sword of Damocles. Yet it would take a different lawsuit, involving another woman, to resolve who would win his name.

14

STARS AND STRIPES
CAPTURE THE
GRAND PRIX DE FRANCE

FOR ONE THING IT IS QUITE LETHALLY
DANGEROUS. FOR ANOTHER, HARDLY ANYONE MAKES
A PENNY OUT OF IT, AND MOST PARTICIPANTS
LIVE LIVES OF REAL SACRIFICE IN ORDER TO BE
PART OF IT.

—GRIFFITH BORGESON,
THE GOLDEN AGE OF THE
AMERICAN RACING CAR[1]

Forty-year-old Albert Champion, formerly a draft dodger in his native country, registered under the US Selective Service Act in the final weeks of America's combat involvement in helping its allies France, England, and Belgium at last to win.[2] Following the armistice of November 11, 1918, after four years of artillery bombardments and trench warfare had devastated major sections of France and Belgium, the Allies looked ahead to massive reconstruction.

As America's participation in the Great War escalated to a deployment of one million soldiers and marines fighting in France by 1918,[3] General Motors president Billy Durant was wheeling and dealing in high gear. Pierre du Pont had come aboard GM as chairman, giving the corporation credibility on Wall Street.[4] Durant added several companies to GM, and GM bought all the shares of the Chevrolet Motor Company, completing the company's modern lineup. The Man arranged for GM to acquire the company that had supplied its bearings, and he brought in its president, Alfred P. Sloan, as the new GM director and president in charge of accessory operations.[5] General Motors purchased the Dayton Engineering Laboratories (Delco) and hired its founder, Charles

Kettering,[6] inventor of the automobile electric starter, which replaced manual hand cranking and aided the auto industry's growth. Kettering joined GM as a vice president and director of research. Sloan and Kettering were rare college graduates with degrees in electrical engineering—Sloan from MIT and Kettering from Ohio State University.

In the spring of 1919, diplomats from around the globe converged in Paris to sign the Versailles Treaty, which officially ended the Great War. The treaty created new countries and changed national boundaries on three continents. Durant organized a group of GM executives to go there in the late summer to look for overseas investment opportunities.

Champion was a likely pick. Following the war's end, declassified documents disclosed that every day the Champion Ignition Company in Flint had been manufacturing forty thousand spark plugs capable of fifty-hour runs in Liberty and Hispano-Suiza high-compression aircraft engines.[7] Within only a few months after the entry of the United States into the war, Champion had ramped up his company as the sole provider of aviation spark plugs to US military planes.[8] The Champion Ignition Company had produced more aviation plugs daily than any factory in Europe. In addition, AC Titan plugs powered 90 percent of US military tanks and trucks.[9]

Champion intended to establish branch plants in France and England for manufacturing AC spark plugs and, his new pursuit, speedometers, to supply foreign automakers.[10] He and Elise and her sister Gabrielle joined GM brass, including Alfred Sloan, Charles Kettering, Charles Stewart Mott, and Walter Chrysler—all traveling with their wives.[11] They shipped out in late August on the S.S. *France*,[12] a lavish French liner graced with portraits of Louis XIV and his Bourbon family adorning the first-class cabins. In Paris, they checked into the luxurious Ritz.

"Champion is a famous guide," Mott wrote in a letter to the *Flint Journal*.[13] The group toured several auto companies to see about acquiring a share. Among the factories they visited were Clément-Bayard, De Dion-Bouton, Panhard, Hispano-Suiza, Ballot, and Citroën. "It seems that all of the auto manufacturers here were in the bicycle game—riding, pacing, or training him, and they all know him and like him."[14]

The weather cooperated. So did the rate of exchange—from the prewar rate of five francs to a dollar to a postwar rate of eight francs to a dollar. The group traveled to Lyon to tour the Peugeot factory and to Turin, Italy, to survey the Fiat operation.[15]

Champion was forced to face the immense suffering France had endured. Industry and trade remained unorganized, and there was a shortage of every sort of material.[16] He offered brothers Louis and Henri employment in America. Louis accepted his help and moved to New York,[17] where he founded a company that imported essential oils for food processing.[18] Henri opted to stay in Paris, near their mother.

Four years of bloody trench warfare in northern France had destroyed roads that Champion had ridden to win Paris-Roubaix. The event had resumed in April 1919. A Paris journalist, appalled by bomb craters that devastated the countryside, had declared that Paris-Roubaix was crossing "the Hell of the North."[19] Long after the roads were repaired, the description stuck as a metaphor for the arduous Queen of the Classics.

Champion renewed acquaintances with Constant Huret and former pace manager Pierre Tournier. Champion located a spark plug company in Levallois-Perret,[20] and he designated Tournier to inquire how much it would cost to purchase and replace old machinery with the latest technology. He also visited England and decided on a plant he could purchase in Birmingham.[21]

Of all the potential purchase targets in France and Italy, only André Citroën was willing to sell to General Motors.[22] Weeks of negotiations followed, with Champion translating back and forth. Barriers arose. The French government sneered at the prospect of an American auto company acquiring a French one, especially Citroën, which had made important contributions during the war.[23] The Citroën production facilities required a greater investment than the initial cost.[24] Worse, its management was deemed inadequate.

One possibility emerged in which either Sloan, six feet tall and 130 pounds, or Chrysler, robust and hardy, would move to Paris and run the company. Sloan and his wife did not have children, giving them more flexibility than Chrysler and his wife, parents of four. Yet Chrysler was a stronger candidate, since he and Durant often clashed on business matters, and Chrysler's contract as president of Buick, the cornerstone of General Motors, was soon to expire. Moving him to Paris would keep him at GM. After eight weeks of lengthy discussions, on the group's final day in Paris, they decided to pass on buying Citroën.[25]

Since Durant had taken over General Motors the second time, the company prospered as it grew. Production of vehicles had jumped by nearly 60 percent over the previous year, from 251,000 vehicles in 1918 to 378,000 in 1919. Net profits had quadrupled, from $15 million in 1918 to $60 million in 1919. General Motors in 1919 had turned into a vast network of divisions and subsidiaries, which employed a workforce of 86,000.

A $20 million ($269 million in 2014) building corporation was formed to construct a new headquarters in Detroit, where GM would relocate.[26] Plans called for the world's largest office building—a limestone structure fifteen stories high with thirty acres of floor space to accommodate seventeen hundred offices.[27]

However tempted Champion might have been to follow GM to Detroit, he kept his operation in Flint and concentrated on improving spark plugs. He submitted papers to the US Patent Office for three new patents. One of the new inventions, on which he'd collaborated with Albert Schmidt, was designed to improve how the insulator is seated in the shell during assembly without the liability of fracture.[28] Another was intended to more effectively insulate the spark plug.[29] Yet another enabled production of a better outer electrode.[30] Together, the new patents raised his total to six.

His AC Titan spark plugs were setting world records in three spheres of travel—flying to the roof of the world and speeding on water and land. Roland Rohlfs, chief test pilot for the Curtiss Aeroplane Company in Garden City, Long Island,[31] bundled up in heavy leather coveralls, goggles, and a mask over his head, and breathed oxygen from a metal bottle to fly a triple-wing Curtiss Wasp six miles up, to 34,610 feet.[32]

Gar Wood, the ace of speedboat pilots,[33] set the world power boat record of 77 mph on the Detroit River. Racecar stalwart Tommy Milton drove a sixteen-cylinder Duesenberg over the hard-packed Florida sands at 156 mph.[34] Milton's Duesenberg zoomed through the mile in 23.07 seconds powered by sixteen AC Titan spark plugs firing 9,870 sparks. Every second, 428 jets of flame converted the gas-oil mixture into record-smashing power.[35] Duesenberg drove faster than the American airplane record, set by army lieutenant C. C. Mosley on his way to winning the Pulitzer Cup and the American national flying championship piloting a Verville-Packard plane equipped with AC Titans to a speed of 136 mph.[36]

Champion, the former bicycle courier who had earned six francs a week, a little over a dollar, had become a multimillionaire and now served as a director of the First National Bank of Flint.[37] The bank paid 4 percent on savings deposits,[38] and it had capital of $200,000 ($2,320,000 in 2014) and resources of $4,400,000 ($51,100,000 in 2014).[39]

Instead of moving to Detroit, however, GM faced a crisis brought on by a national depression. The armistice had set off a brief spending spree, but in the summer of 1920 the US economy tanked. More than a hundred thousand banks failed.[40] Sales of GM cars and trucks virtually vanished. General Motors share prices on the New York Stock exchange plunged from a high of $420 a share to $12 by November.[41] Durant's finances were spread thinly among a vast number of stock shares he owned on price margins, and in their freefall he had only hours to make up the difference. His personal wealth had disintegrated from more than $90 million in paper value to a debt load of $30 million to his bankers and brokers.[42] His only alternative was to turn to GM director Pierre du Pont and plead for help. Du Pont realized that if Durant failed to pay his debts, GM's outstanding 4.3 million shares of stock would decline so fast that the corporation would likely suffer a fatal blow. Du Pont formed a syndicate and joined the J. P. Morgan partners to bail out Durant.[43] Once again it was time for Durant to leave GM, this time for the long goodbye.

At the end of November 1920, The Man resigned.[44] He was succeeded by du Pont as president and chairman. Du Pont appointed Sloan as vice president of operations.

Sloan concluded that GM had grown too large and too complex for the one-man show Durant had favored. Sloan overhauled the corporation, dividing it into five automobile divisions and a central administration with a strong office that had financial and advisory staffs to coordinate corporate policies—thus eliminating the prevailing culture of management by crony and implementing an organizational management that prevailed for most of the rest of the century.[45]

Alfred P. Sloan, one of the great captains of industry of his age, observed that the keynote of Albert Champion's success was that he always kept his mind open to constant improvement. *Photo courtesy of General Motors Media Archive.*

For several years auto company executives, journalists, salesmen, distributors, and advertisers had reminisced at trade shows about the "good old days" through dinners fueled with drinks and cigars, in the process discussing ways to honor pioneers for their roles in building the industry.[46] All the discussions culminated at the banquet of the January 1921 Chicago Automobile Show. In the Gold Room of the Congress Hotel, they established the Old Timers Club.[47] The agreement was to levy annual dues of five dollars. Dues payers would receive a lapel button inscribed with the year the possessor broke into the industry. Members guffawed that the money collected would go to help the down-and-outs who had missed their chance early on and needed assistance, like the fund for indigent actors.

"We gave Elwood Hanes No. 1 membership card in recognition of his claim to having built America's first gasoline car," Chris Sinsabaugh recalled when he was editor of *Automotive News*. "We elected Albert Champion, founder of the AC Spark Plug Company, our first president."[48]

Sinsabaugh was renowned in Detroit restaurants favored by auto execs as the creator of the celebrated Chris Sinsabaugh Martini,[49] served up in a glass suitable for holding three times the ordinary quantity and without the olive, which he banished for wasting space. He probably knew about Champion for the longest time among the Fourth Estate, going back to his rookie reporter days in Chicago at *Bearings*, which first introduced the Frenchman to American readers. From there he moved on to the *Chicago Daily News* and bestowed the new Chicago National League baseball team with the name "Cubs."[50] He mostly covered the fledgling auto industry, which took him to New York for a job as editor of the American Automobile Association flagship magazine. He later became editor of *Automotive News* in Detroit. Over the years, he studied racing lore.

Upon being elected president of the Old Timers Club, Champion asked around for recommendations for how to promote the club. "I came into the picture with a suggestion that clicked with the president," Sinsabaugh recalled. "I knew that American cars and drivers in the past had made miserable showings in the European road races."[51] Sinsabaugh noted that over the past fifteen years, the records showed that only one American had finished any of the contests, and that was a sorry seventeenth place. He brought up the Grand Prix de France in July and pointed out that the deadline for entry was soon to close. "I suggested that he personally send an American entry to the French Grand Prix," Sinsabaugh said. "That way, he would be helping his homeland and also his adopted country."[52]

Sinsabaugh had proposed a major mission. The Grand Prix de France was tempting because it ranked as Europe's—and the world's—most prestigious road race. The cost of shipping vehicles and crews out and back across the Atlantic plus other travel expenses was prohibitive. None of the large American auto manufacturers building racecars was willing to pay that kind of money.

Champion had the resources and the will to succeed for his native France, for his adopted America, and for la gloire! He knew from everyone he came into contact with on a daily basis that in recent years US racing cars and drivers had moved up in class. They were at long last ready to challenge the French, English, and Italian racing creations in the strenuous 321-mile Grand Prix over public roads. The best way to prove it, and to promote his spark plugs, was to send an American team for the first time in the history of the famous speed classic. He agreed to underwrite the show.

Another collaborator joined him in the cause—Barney Oldfield, employed by Firestone, which marketed a tire in the old star's name and was willing to supply new Oldfield gum tires.[53] General Motors directors agreed GM would cover half the entry fee.

The matter of which American car to send was obvious to Champion—Duesenbergs, made by his fellow Society of Automotive Engineers member Fred Duesenberg and younger brother Augie. The Duesenberg brothers had become a name to reckon with in racing. Their Duesenbergs won national-level events of grand-prix distances. Among them were the previous season's 250-milers on California board speedways in Beverly Hills and Fresno.[54] Both victories were scored by the talented Duesenberg team driver from San Francisco, Jimmy Murphy.

The Automobile Club of France organized the grand prix, which dated back to 1906. The 1921 edition would be the first postwar contest, ending a six-year hiatus. Automobile Club of France officials reacted to the news that an American team was coming by selecting Le Mans, some 130 miles southwest of Paris, where the population appreciated what US troops had done to save France during the war.[55] That *beau geste* was the most the ACF could come up with—the organization offered no prize money.

The Duesenberg brothers had been building a new passenger car intended for the commercial market. Rather than entering a one-off auto produced exclusively for the grand prix, Fred Duesenberg decided to enter three of the production models. He sent a cable to the English journalist, W. F. Bradley, who was in Paris serving as the go-between for the American contingent. Fred told Bradley to enter three Duesenbergs. Fred had neglected to send money for the entries so the American team had missed the February 1 deadline.[56] The ACF, however, allowed a grace period ending March 1, at the cost of the fee doubling to a hefty 83,000 francs ($10,375 then and $135,000 in 2014).[57]

In the intervening thirty days, Fiat bowed out,[58] and a composite French-English team of Sunbeam-Talbot-Darracq also withdrew.[59] The director of the Automobile Club of France prepared to cancel the race if the Duesenberg entry fee failed to materialize by the end of the grace period, March 1.[60]

After Champion's intervention, half the entry fee was paid by General Motors,[61] half by the team of Frenchman Albert Guyot, a veteran driver of the Indy 500, and his compatriot Louis Inghibert.[62] Guyot and Inghibert made up a fourth Duesenberg team. W. F. Bradley received the Duesenberg entry money for four teams a week before the due date. However, Bradley held on to the check to make the ACF director worry that the grand prix could turn into a complete fiasco.[63] Not until the church bells across Paris were tolling 6 p.m. on March 1 did Bradley enter the ACF headquarters on the Place de la Concord.[64] As the final bell rang, he threw open the door of the ACF director's office, strode up to the man's desk, and laid down a packet of cash. "This is for four Duesenbergs," Bradley said. "Now perhaps you'll have a race."[65]

The first postwar Grand Prix de France was saved. Then the Sunbeam-Talbot-Darracq organization announced it would enter four teams,[66] raising the total to thirteen contestants representing three nations on the July 25 race day.[67]

America's first-ever contingent to the Grand Prix de France shipped out with Augie Duesenberg, son Dennis, and a team of four drivers, riding mechanicians, and some support folks. Fred and Augie Duesenberg supplied the cars. Firestone donated Barney Oldfield tires. The $60,000 tab ($781,000 in 2014) for transportation and housing was picked up by the American Automobile Association and Albert Champion.[68]

The Duesenberg brothers were notorious for being chronically late and short on money, but the crew arrived in Le Mans in time for some days of practice runs. The cars were state of the art and streamlined, with a narrow nose, open cockpit for the driver and mechanician, and a stubby tail. They were painted white, and the stars and stripes were displayed discretely on both sides behind the driver and mechanician. Drivers wore a shirt and tie under their Duesenberg jumpsuits. Their only protection from flying stones and debris were goggles and thin leather headgear with a chinstrap, only good for protecting them from airborne dirt and oil.

On test laps around the 10.7-mile course laid out on public roads, drivers found the surface slippery. The roads consisted of stone beds beneath a sand composition that had been spread and rolled. One of the French cars, a Ballot, crashed, totaling the vehicle and killing the driver.[69] Jimmy Murphy was driving a Duesenberg into a bend in the road when a horse ran in front of him. His foot hit on the brakes, which locked up and sent the car skidding sideways before rolling over. Riding with him was Frenchman Louis Inghibert, who suffered a broken rib and contusions. Inghibert had paid his portion of half the Duesenberg race entry fee, but all he got was a trip to the hospital and confinement to a bed while he recovered.[70] The Duesenberg he was intended to drive was given to André Dubonnet, a French wine magnate and avid motorist.[71]

Murphy had an easy-going personality, charming and radiant with a thousand-watt smile, but behind the wheel he was serious and aggressive. Orphaned at age eleven when his parents were killed in the 1906 San Francisco earthquake and fire, he was brought up in a modest household by relatives in Los Angeles.[72] Fascinated with autos, by eighteen Murphy worked as a mechanic for the Duesenberg brothers. They treated him like a son.

On July 25, Murphy, despite his accident, was on the start line, taped from hips to armpits.[73] Next to him was mechanician Ernie Olsen, serving as extra eyes to warn him if someone was coming up from the outside. Murphy was twenty-six, at the height of his powers.

The thirteen starters lined up in pairs in front of the grandstand, which was packed with spectators strung out about a mile down the home straight. Each pair of starters was flagged off at thirty-second intervals. Murphy was in the second row. On the second lap, he moved up to the lead, followed by another Duesenberg car.

At the end of the first hour, the autos pounding over the road had torn the course apart. The sand blew away, exposing bare rock, which broke up into chunks the size of a man's fist and flew like shrapnel at velocities approaching 100 mph.[74] Tires of the heavy and powerful Sunbeam-Talbot-Darracq vehicles shredded so badly that the teams kept pulling into the pits for wheel changes until they ran out of tires.[75]

On lap seven, Murphy pulled into the pits to check on his tires, gum-dipped Oldfields. His crew gave them the thumbs up. Seconds later, he dashed back onto the road. He zoomed into the lead on lap seventeen, 181 miles, marking the halfway point of the grand prix.[76] Teammate Albert Guyot moved into second place, which he could have held till the end—except that a hurling rock struck his mechanician with great force on the skull.[77] Guyot pulled into the pit. The wounded man was pulled from the vehicle and whisked right away for medical treatment. Another man replaced him and Guyot roared back onto the road, now in sixth place.

A constant barrage of rocks punctured radiators, fuel tanks, and oil tanks, knocking out contenders.[78] On lap twenty-nine, Murphy's race lead was suddenly in at risk as the result of a rock bashing through his car's radiator core.[79] A heartbeat later, a tire blew. He had twelve miles to go, only three tires, and water gushing from the radiator. Murphy did not let up, rationalizing that his momentum would keep him going long enough to reach his pit. The closer the car came to the pit, the more it seemed that every bolt and rivet would bust. Once in the pit, mechanician Ernie Olsen leaped out to change the wheel. Murphy kept the engine revving as the support crew ladled water into the red-hot engine block. Olsen swung his hammer but missed the wheel wing nut. The hammer slipped from his grip and flew twenty feet.[80] He had to run over and pick up the hammer before he could change the wheel. Finally, Murphy steered back onto the course. Water they had just taken on poured out.

Eight miles remained when another tire exploded.[81] Luckily, Murphy had just enough lead to bump over the finish line in first place. Fourteen minutes passed before the runner-up crossed the finish in a French car called Ballot.[82] André Dubonnet drove his Duesenberg to fourth place; Albert Guyot's Duesenberg came in sixth.

News flashed around the world that the white Duesie with the American flag on the side had won. Duesies had scored three of the top six spots.

Champion, second from the right, crossed his right leg over the knee of his left to stand upright and compensate for one leg being shorter than the other. Here he joined famous names in international motorsport. From the left are E. C. Chenry who would succeed Champion as company president, André Boillot, English journalist W. F. Bradley, J. Origet, automaker E. U. Ballot, C. E. Sorenson, Champion, and French racecar driver Albert Guyot. *From the collections of The Henry Ford.*

Murphy's beaming smile, his fair skin burned by the sun and covered with dirt and oil outlining where his goggles had been, was published in newspapers and magazines worldwide.

His victory drew an enormous cheer from the audience. However, his triumph in an American Duesenberg upset some French stalwarts. Officials neglected to have the band perform "The Star-Spangled Banner."[83]

The 1921 Grand Prix de France amounted to what the French call a *succès d'estime*—a critical success, but no money. For all his effort, at the victory banquet Murphy received from the Automobile Club of France a small medal that fit in the palm of his hand. The rest of the Duesenberg crew headed home with little more than stories to tell of their experiences in France.

The journalist W. F. Bradley wrote in *Automobile* that Murphy's win, averaging 78.1 mph, had bettered the average speed of the winner of the last grand prix, held in 1914, which had been 65.5 mph. Advancements had been made over the past seven years, and American cars and drivers were at the forefront of international motorsport.[84] Forty-one years would pass before another American, Dan Gurney, would win the Grand Prix de France.

Legend has it that Albert Champion was back in Paris taking care of last-minute business before returning to America when two gendarmes knocked on his hotel room door.[85] They came to arrest him for deserting the French army. Although the matter of his military duty had been resolved years earlier, the United States Embassy, so it is said, intervened to spring the spark-plug tycoon from the rap, and he never returned to the land of his birth.

There is no record that he left Flint for the grand prix. Nevertheless, if he had gone and the incident with the gendarmes had persuaded him to remain permanently in America, it might have saved his life.

15

A STORM THAT
BREAKS LOOSE

*MY MILLIONAIRES WERE AS BEAUTIFUL AND DAMNED
AS THOMAS HARDY'S PEASANTS.*
—F. SCOTT FITZGERALD, THE CRACK-UP[1]

As Jimmy Murphy made motorsport history at the Grand Prix de France, a private detective hired by Elise reported that Albert was carrying on an affair in New York with Edna Crawford, a seamstress.[2] Elise had been suspicious about her husband since the New York Auto Show in January.[3] Champion had met Edna, single and twenty-four, at a party in the gilded Waldorf-Astoria Hotel one evening during the auto show.[4] Elise turned the detective's mounting evidence over to her attorney and grew troubled.[5] In early August she totaled the Cadillac coupé she was driving in a head-on collision in Flint with a heavy truck.[6] Her sister Gabrielle suffered a cut to an eyelid that required stitches.[7] Soon after, the detective phoned to say Albert was driving with Edna from Niagara Falls to a lakeside hotel in the southwest corner of New York State.[8] Elise said she would meet the detective there the next day so she could have her husband arrested.[9]

Elise boarded a train bound for New York. The detective waited for her at the Beamus Point station, on Chautauqua Lake outside Jamestown.[10] On their drive to the Beamus Point Hotel, where her husband and Edna had a room, the detective's car passed their vehicle traveling in the opposite direction.[11] The detective continued to the hotel, where he and Elise ascertained that Albert and Edna had registered as Mr. and Mrs. A. Chapman.[12] Then the detective drove Elise to the sheriff's office in nearby Mayville.[13] She filed a complaint with a justice of the peace,[14] charging her husband and Edna Crawford with disorderly conduct.[15]

While Elise waited in the sheriff's office late on the afternoon of Wednesday, August 24, her husband parked his car across the street. The sheriff walked over with the warrant,[16] arrested him, and escorted him to his office. Elise sat in an adjoining room.[17]

Albert realized what was taking place when his wife stepped out and confronted him.[18] He blushed in surprise, but said nothing.[19] He was arraigned before a justice of the peace.[20] He pleaded guilty and paid a fine of $50.[21]

Later, when Albert returned to their house in Flint to pick up his things, he said he had found a woman who understood him.[22]

"Understands you!" Elise retorted. "Why, I understand you, Albert, after all these years."[23]

Champion protested that he wanted to live large and take advantage of his growing wealth like other motor magnates in Flint and Detroit.[24]

Elise was cautious about money and uninterested in the role of grand social hostess. She and Albert had recently bought their house from Walter Chrysler after his General Motors contract expired and he moved to Toledo with an unprecedented $2 million contract ($23.2 million in 2014) to rescue the Overland Automobile Company following John Willy's disastrous reversal of fortune,[25] which had left him indebted to 127 bankers for $46 million ($599 million in 2014) due to Billy Durant–like mismanagement. Companies were rising and falling with the regularity of the change of seasons. Twice in ten years Elise had seen General Motors narrowly miss bankruptcy.

She must have been brokenhearted. Nevertheless, after enduring Champion's liaisons and his recent affair, she filed suit in the Genesee County circuit court to divorce her husband of eighteen years on grounds of extreme cruelty.[26]

The case of *Julie Elise Champion vs. Albert Champion* added to Albert's pending case with the Stranahan brothers.

On November 1, the court granted Elise's divorce decree. She and Albert had settled out of court, granting her the house, which they had purchased for $40,000 ($521,000 in 2014) along with $250,000 cash (worth $3.25 million in 2014).[27] She and Gabrielle shipped out to Paris to spend time with their family.

Walter Chrysler and Champion occasionally played golf together at the Flint Country Club, and when Chrysler left Flint to work in Toledo, he sold Albert and Elise Champion his house. *Courtesy of General Motors Media Archive.*

Edna Josephine Crawford had wide-set brown eyes, a broad forehead, and a straight nose. Similar to other young women, she had her brown hair cut short and wavy. Whenever possible, she wore high heels, their tapping sound following her around.[28] In stocking feet, she measured five feet six; in heels next to Champion, she stood a little taller than him.[29]

They had met by chance. Edna had delivered a dress she had sewn to a society woman who told her there was a gasoline-society swanky event at the Waldorf-Astoria, the grand hotel at Fifth Avenue and 34th Street (present site of the Empire State Building).[30] Edna brought along her sister, Emily, one of the eye-candy Ziegfeld Girls from the Ziegfeld Follies vaudeville productions.[31] Emily acted under the stage name of Emlee Haddone in theater and one-reeler movies,[32] including *Hitchie Koo*, and *Broadway Brevities*.[33]

She gave her age as twenty-four to Albert's forty-four,[34] although she was actually thirty-two.[35] Somewhere in the chitchat between Edna and Champion she mentioned that they shared the name Champion.[36] Her mother, born Elizabeth Jane Champion, of Welsh descent,[37] had married Wylie Crawford. Like Albert, Edna was the eldest of her siblings; she had two brothers and two sisters.

She likely told him about growing up in Kansas City, Missouri, which would have registered with Champion. His sister-in-law, Prosper's wife Flora, was from Kansas City, Kansas.[38] Edna attended Northeast High School.[39] By age thirteen she was working full-time as a cashier in a dry goods store.[40] Her early marriage at seventeen to Arba K. Mills was best forgotten.[41] She had divorced him by her twentieth birthday and moved to New York, where her mother took the family following the desertion of Wiley Crawford.[42] Elizabeth Crawford had decided that the prospects for marrying her lovely daughters off to wealthy men were superior in America's city of cities, already nicknamed the Big Apple for its bounteous prizes. Edna helped support the family by running a power machine in a shirtwaist factory.[43] Long arduous hours motivated her to take advantage of her talent for needlework,[44] necessary to make clothes for herself and her siblings, and to improve upon it for employment as a seamstress.[45] She sewed costumes for Emily to wear on stage.[46]

What Champion cared the most about was Edna's rapt attention. She was a pretty, younger woman, and this fit the new decade's accent on youth. And she cherished his wealth and the casual way he could buy her clothes, an emerald ring, and a pearl necklace.

Following the collapse of his marriage, Champion stayed in New York to be near Edna. He took advantage of the office building that General Motors owned at 224 West 57th Street.[47] It became his base while trusted Basil De Guichard ran the factory in Flint. Champion kept up a brisk work schedule during the day and courted Edna in the evenings. New York was the gaudiest, greatest city, and it continues to be the nation's center of theater, the arts, and jazz. Congress had passed the Eighteenth Amendment outlawing the sale of alcohol,[48] but, for a price, New York restaurants dodged Prohibition and kept liquor, beer, wine, and champagne flowing—thus fulfilling the fundamental economic chase of supply meeting demand.

Champion submitted another application with the US Patent Office, this one for producing spark-plug shells from cast metal, which reduced material, eliminated waste, and lowered costs.[49] Over the past year, he had filed five other patents for spark plugs, including terminator connectors. One patent application introduced rotary grinders that fashioned spark-plug exteriors, which saved time and money over the previous system of rotating knives that had needed constant replacement. His surge in applications would raise the count of his total US patents to eleven.[50]

In early February 1922, Champion announced his engagement to Edna Crawford,[51] described as the daughter of a Kansas City wholesale grocer and a student in the National Academy School of Fine Arts.[52] Tuition for the academy, dedicated to aspiring professional artists, was nominal, but the academy has no record of her attending.[53] Nonetheless, the cover story played well. A photo-studio portrait of Edna, glamorous in a fur coat, made its way across the wires, enriched by the stirring caption, "Art Student to Wed Millionaire."[54]

Champion had always examined how best to organize himself for more and better work. He would have assessed his stressful divorce and his planned marriage to Edna. The economy had recovered. Car sales had jumped, proving not only that autos were here to stay but also that the market was far from approaching saturation. His factory output was thriving. General Motors had finally moved out of Flint to the large new limestone office building, officially designated as the General Motors Building.[55] Champion looked to the future with optimism.

Edna Champion in a glamour photo, from seamstress to millionaire's wife in the Jazz Age. *Photo courtesy of Kerry Champion Williams.*

On February 15, 1922, he ended his legal hassles with the Stranahans by signing papers in Lansing, the state capital, which officially changed the name of the Champion Ignition Company of Michigan to the AC Spark Plug Company of Michigan.[56] Like Ransom Olds, David Buick, and Louis Chevrolet, his name continued in business without him.

A week later, he and Edna were married by a justice of the peace in New York City.[57] His wedding present to her was $40,000 worth of General Motors stock.[58] They sailed to France to begin their honeymoon aboard the recently completed French liner S.S. *Paris*, which, at 764 feet in length, was the largest liner under the French flag.[59]

Their time overseas stretched to five months, and it included business trips to shop for factories in England and France.[60] In his absence, Basil De Guichard ran the day-to-day operations. De Guichard had married Mae Nash, daughter of esteemed automaker Charlie Nash, who produced Rambler motor cars.[61] De Guichard ranked among the auto industry's nobility.

Edna Crawford Champion, Albert's second wife, strikes a flapper pose, 1922. *Photo courtesy of Kerry Champion Williams.*

Once Albert and Edna returned to America, they moved into a custom estate called Colberry on Woodward Avenue in Flint's tony neighborhood of Bloomfield Hills.[62]

Champion lived large at his Colberry Estate in Flint. Looking dapper and casual in his customary pose to conceal his left leg being two inches shorter as a result of injuries from his near-fatal car crash. *Photo courtesy of Kerry Champion Williams.*

Champion came back full of ambitions and was encouraged by the changed attitude he'd seen in Europe. "The fine service of American automotive equipment during the war undoubtedly helped to awaken this appreciation," he told the *Flint Journal*. "The victory of the American car in the Grand Prix last year also had its effect."[63]

Champion acquired a spark plug company called Oleo, which was located on the Seine in Levallois-Perret outside Paris, and renamed it Société des Bougies A.C.-Titan.[64] He arranged for shipping American machinery and clay from Flint to the Paris operation.[65] In six months, A.C.-Titan was making AC-Titan spark plugs using the same shell and electrode operations, assembly, and inspection processes that were used in the home Flint plant.[66] AC-Titan spark plugs were installed in more than two dozen French auto brands, including Peugeot, Renault, Bugatti, De Dion, and Ballot, and they were also distributed to French-controlled countries in Africa and Asia.

Champion also took over the Sphinx Manufacturing Company in Birmingham, England.[67] He purchased the business, reorganized it, and rebuilt the plant with the latest American machinery. It was renamed A.C. Sphinx Sparking Plug Ltd. Its A.C. Sphinx sparking plugs were produced from American clay.[68] The plugs were used in cars made in England, including Talbot, Vauxhall, and Morris-Cowley. The Birmingham factory supplied A.C. products to wholesalers and dealers in the British Isles, the Scandinavian countries, Egypt, Iraq, Turkey, Iran, Australia, and New Zealand.[69]

Champion and his three younger brothers united for the last time in March 1924 at the funeral of their mother, who'd passed away at the age of seventy-one and was buried in the north Paris section of St. Cloud.[70]

Brother Prosper, a machinist at AC Spark Plug, became a naturalized US citizen in January 1924.[71] Prosper and his French-speaking wife had three sons, all brought up to speak French at home.[72] The eldest was Albert Prosper Champion, who was then nine years old and talking to his uncle Albert about working in the factory when he grew older. Albert's other nephews were Louis and Paul.

Albert talked to his brother Prosper about setting up a trust for his three nephews.[73] It was something he meant to get around to when nephew Albert Prosper Champion turned thirteen.

During the first four years of his second marriage, Champion filed thirteen more patents for improved spark plugs and dashboard speedometers, including lighting the speedometer after dark—a breakthrough in 1926.[74] His company's products were factory installed in more than two hundred brands of autos made in America, France, and Great Britain, and across Europe, the Middle East, Australia, and Japan.[75]

By 1926 he had twenty-five US patents, and more testing was under way for further improvements, and he was broadening his products into air filters and oil filters. General Motors that year would manufacture more than 1.2 million autos.[76] Leading the way were sales of nearly seven hundred thousand Chevrolets.[77] Champion's payroll expanded to thirty-five hundred employees.[78]

General Motors had started the same year that Henry Ford introduced his Model T, the nation's biggest-selling car, with more than 2 million Model T sales between 1923 and 1925. Yet Ford's advantage of selling Model Ts for prices as low as $500 was a competitive liability in the used-car market, and consumers preferred more modern autos such as GM's Chevies, Buicks, Cadillacs, and Oldsmobiles. General Motors was one year away from surpassing Ford.

Champion's career was soaring. His domestic life, however, had turned fractious. Even though Edna was a Midwesterner, she chaffed at living in Flint. She preferred the bright lights and hustle of New York. The wives of Champion's colleagues gave her the cold shoulder as the "other woman."[79] Elise still lived in the house on Kearsley Street.

Edna discovered that her multimillionaire husband thought nothing of buying a new car with cash, but he refused to give her money of her own.[80] He allowed her to purchase clothing and merchandise from stores around Flint and charge it to his account.[81] Edna wanted to give money to her widowed mother, Elizabeth. Albert provided Edna with $50,000 to buy a big house in Flint and allowed his mother-in-law to live in one half and rent the other half for income.[82]

At the end of the summer in 1926 Champion prepared to attend the annual Paris Auto Salon in October as well as its counterpart in London. For the 1926 edition, Edna elected to stay in Flint with her siblings for a few weeks before joining her husband in Paris. Albert agreed. He would ship overseas with GM big shots after the first of October to attend the trade show, and she would follow.[83] He had to inspect his factories in Levallois-Perret as well as those across the channel in Birmingham.

Champion always had a lot of friends to visit in Paris. He was surprised to discover Barney Oldfield, honeymooning with his third wife, Hulda Rae Braden, a San Diego woman a decade younger than Oldfield.[84] Champion took a break from the grind of morning-to-midnight meetings and conferences and dinners to go with Oldfield on an outing at the Atlantic coastal resort of Deauville. They were photographed together on the shore—America's famous racecar driver and the inventor-manufacturer enjoying cigars.[85]

On the day Edna's ship arrived in Le Havre, some 130 miles from Paris, Albert was too busy to meet her train from Le Havre to the Gare du Nord.[86] He wanted Oldfield to meet her. He knew where to find Oldfield—at the bar of the famed Hôtel Crillon in the Tuileries. It was late in the afternoon and Oldfield, good friend that he was, had settled in to enjoy drinks with an American expat he had recently met, a war veteran from San Francisco named Charles Brazelle. Oldfield hated the idea of being a messenger, even for Champion. Albert pleaded with Barney to collect Edna until Barney relented, as long as he could be accompanied by Brazelle.

Oldfield and Brazelle made it to the train station on time. There, on the crowded train platform, the handsome Charlie Brazelle and Edna met. "I loved her the moment I set eyes on her," he admitted afterward. "Later, she told me it was the same with her."[87]

Brazelle minded his manners in front of Oldfield as they escorted Edna by taxi to the Hôtel Meurice, in the Tuileries, where Champion had a suite. He joined them for a drink.

Charlie Brazelle was living in Paris, trying to sell stock shares in a company to launch a new casino near France's Atlantic resort of Biarritz.[88] He was estranged from his second wife, St. Louis socialite Roberta Acuff, owner of a mansion in Biarritz. He'd had no employment since mustering out of the army after the 1918 armistice.

To bask in Oldfield's celebrity, he ingratiated himself by throwing a dinner party at the fashionable Henry's restaurant.[89] Brazelle even invited reporters willing to accept a free meal and the chance to report gossip. The November 21, 1926, *Seattle Daily Times* ran news from Europe about the dinner for Oldfield.

"It was Charles Brazelle's farewell to Barney Oldfield, and among the guests was Albert Champion, whose name is inseparably connected with the spark plug industry."[90] Line art depicted men laughing, but the fun would soon turn tragic.

16

PERMANENT PARISIAN

*IT WAS A WORLD OF A VERY DIFFERENT TIME
SECTOR, AND IT IS HARDLY COMPREHENSIBLE TO
US NOW.*

—GRIFFITH BORGESON,
*THE GOLDEN AGE OF THE
AMERICAN RACING CAR*[1]

For years telegrams had been inundating the AC Spark Plug Company headquarters testifying to races won and records set by cars powered by the company's spark plugs. Peter DePaolo won the 1925 Indy 500 driving a Duesenberg that Champion had bought for him to test spark plugs and air and oil filters. He made Indy history as the first winner to average 100 mph.[2] DePaolo, one of the monarchs of motorsport, was so grateful that he visited Albert and Edna Champion at their Colberry estate.[3] One morning the Indy 500 winner took over the Cadillac from Champion's chauffeur,[4] Conrad A. Ramberg, and drove The Chief to work. Flashing his gap-toothed grin as he shifted gears with consummate precision into turns, DePaolo had no problem driving the distance in record time. "We had some ride," Ramberg recalled of how fast DePaolo went.[5]

On May 9, 1926, US Navy pilot Richard E. Byrd and pilot-mechanic Floyd Bennett flew circles around the North Pole in brilliant sunlight as part of their sixteen-hour roundtrip from Spitsbergen, Norway, with AC Spark Plugs firing the triple engines of their heavy German Fokker.[6] Byrd, a lieutenant commander, was hailed in the press as an American hero. He received a ticker-tape parade up Broadway in New York City. President Calvin Coolidge decorated him in the White House with the Congressional Medal of Honor, the nation's highest US military honor.

Byrd was widely seen as the most likely aviator to fly nonstop across the

Atlantic, between New York and Paris, to at last claim the prestigious $25,000 Orteig Prize ($329,000 in 2014), which had been up for grabs since 1919.[7] The prize had been offered by the New York hotelier Raymond Orteig to commemorate the friendships between pilots from the United States and France during the war.[8] Orteig was impressed with Eddie Rickenbacker, America's most illustrious ace pilot. Rickenbacker had flown Nieuports in the famous Lafayette Esquadrille (small squadron) because the US Army lacked combat aircraft. Rickenbacker had said in a speech that he looked forward to the day when the two countries would be linked by air routes. Orteig, a native of southern France, had immigrated to New York at age twelve and had made his fortune as owner of the Hotel Lafayette and Hotel Brevoort. In the spirit of Franco-American cooperation, he had donated the cash prize, which was available to flyers from any nation and administered under the auspices of the not-for-profit National Aeronautic Association.[9]

Champion regarded aviation as the ultimate test for technology. He was liberal about distributing aviation spark plugs to Byrd and other pilots, who would in turn provide their thoughts on ways to improve reliability. The prospect of flying nonstop across the Atlantic had powerful skeptics. The eminent insurance company Lloyds of London announced odds of ten to one against anyone making the flight successfully to claim the Orteig Prize.[10]

April 1927 proved cruel to attempts to beat those odds. Navy Commander Byrd's Fokker crash-landed on a training flight.[11] New Yorker Clarence Chamberlain survived his plane's landing gear tearing loose on takeoff.[12] Crewmen of Noel Davis and Stanton Wooster were killed in a test flight.[13] In early May French aviators Charles Nungesser and François Coli, both decorated war veterans, took off from Le Bourget Aérodrome outside Paris, bound for New York—only to disappear.[14]

None of the disastrous news discouraged twenty-five-year-old US Air Mail pilot Charles Lindbergh. He took off alone on May 20 in the sleek, single-wing *Spirit of St. Louis* from Roosevelt Field on Long Island and flew thirty-six hundred miles in thirty-three hours to land safely at Le Bourget Aérodrome.[15] The plane's Wright "Whirlwind" nine-cylinder air-cooled engine ran perfectly on AC Spark Plugs.[16]

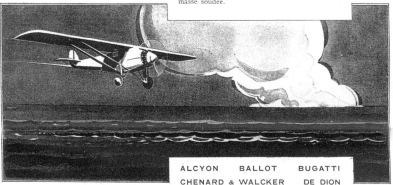

AC Champion Spark Plugs fired 28,944,000 sparks to keep the engine of Lindbergh's *Spirit of St. Louis* flying over the Atlantic into history. This ad from 1927 lists some of the two hundred automobiles that also used AC equipment.

Commenting on the record flight, Champion told reporters: "There is no question but what speedway records of distance from short spurts of a mile or two, upwards to a total of 500, are a severe test for spark plugs, but they cannot compare with the terrific strain endured in flights of this kind.[17] The slightest defect in any one would spell the difference between success and disaster. One will realize the severe service the spark plugs are required to render when it is figured that at the average estimated speed of Captain Lindbergh's plane, about 115 miles per hour, the spark plugs were called upon to deliver without failure a total of 28,944,000 sparks."

Lindbergh had made aviation history. Overnight he became an international folk hero. Paris cafés overflowed with celebrators. New Yorkers lauded him in a rousing parade up Broadway. President Calvin Coolidge invited him to meet in Washington, DC. And, of course, Lindbergh laid claim to the Orteig Prize—the hotelier presented him with a medal and the $25,000 check in a ceremony at his Hotel Brevoort.[18]

In early June Clarence Chamberlain took off from Roosevelt Field and flew to Eisleben, Germany,[19] a distance of nearly four thousand miles. Later that month, Byrd followed as the third pilot to fly across the Atlantic—cloud cover prevented him from landing at Le Bourget Aérodrome, so he circled back and made an emergency landing, without injury, on the coast of Normandy.[20]

Champion said that of his achievements, he was most proud that aviators had staked their lives on his products.[21] Some of their success shined on him as a Franco-American success.

He took out ads in magazines promoting Lindbergh's iconic plane flying low over the Atlantic, and in newspapers promoting both Lindbergh and Chamberlain.

That spring Champion oversaw the introduction of innovative fuel pumps for feeding gasoline to auto engines that have been standard ever since.[22] He employed thirty-five hundred workers in factories occupying sixteen acres on a twenty-acre site in Flint.[23] Plants in England and France employed another five hundred. His AC Spark Plug Company made the world's greatest number of dashboards, air and oil filters, and spark plugs.[24] He submitted more patents applications, including for air and oil filters,[25] from the US Patent Office, for what came to be a total of thirty US patents. His advancements and products contributed to GM car and truck sales topping 1.5 million in 1927,[26] with nearly 1 million Chevies sold.[27] Henry Ford, admitting that his beloved Model T had been left behind by the competition, shut down "Tin Lizzies" to introduce the new Model A. General Motors leaped over Ford to dominate the auto industry worldwide—a status GM held for most of the century.

Despite all Champion's success, he and Edna bickered more and more often about money. She came to realize that work was more important to him than marriage. It didn't help that her younger sister, Emily, the actress, had taken Champion's prized Marmon Speedster for an eventful joy ride. When a Model T cost $500, Cadillacs ranged up to $3,000; Marmon Speedsters went for $5,300.[28] Marmons were the fastest production car in American and were bought for their speed. A Stutz Bearcat could do 80 mph. Marmon Speedsters were capable of cruising 85-plus mph. Emily, his sister-in-law, lost control of his Marmon and drove it into a lake.[29] He never forgave her.[30]

When Champion left the factory around five o'clock, he carried with him a leather briefcase, which he dubbed his "traveling desk."[31] He filled it with letters and memoranda that crossed his desk during the day so he could read as chauffeur Conrad Ramberg drove him some forty minutes home to Colberry. Once there, he walked the two family dogs around the grounds. He dined with Edna at the usual time. Then he extracted more papers from his traveling desk to prepare for the next day's agenda.

At forty-nine, he had no intention of slowing down his schedule. A concession to age was depending on eyeglasses. During the traditional slow news month of August, the *Detroit News* ran a feature titled "Work Is Albert Champion's Main Pastime—Says He Can't Quit Now."

"People say to me, 'Albert, you have all the money you'll ever want, why in the world don't you stop and have a good time?' I always laugh. If they only realized it. I am having the time of my life right now."[32]

When Champion returned home after his work days, he relaxed with a cigar and took his dogs for a walk. He taught the puppies commands in French, which his wife, Edna, did not speak. As a result, she was unable to control them. *Photo courtesy of Kerry Champion Williams.*

Champion monitored the progress of employee Albert Guyot Jr., the son of the French racecar driver who had finished sixth driving a Duesenberg at the 1921 Grand Prix de France. The junior Guyot was being groomed for management at Champion's Levallois-Perret factory.[33] Another in management was the famous French aviator, war hero, and ace Captain Alfred Heurtaux. "He has eight sons, and they will come to me when they are old enough," Champion said. "We both want to make men of them."[34]

Champion also provided a summer job for his nephew Albert Prosper Champion, age twelve, the eldest son of Prosper Champion. The youngster punched the time clock, in and out four times a day as employee number 51-121.[35] He sorted mail and distributed it through the sprawling factory. "I know every department in the plant and who's responsible for it," nephew Champion said. "Have to know that to take the mail and carry messages. I know everything we make and whom we make it for."[36]

Albert took a keen interest in his nephew and Prosper's two other sons. He promised to fund scholarships for his nephews to attend college.[37] He told Prosper he would rewrite his will, which left everything to Edna, and make sure that half his estate would go to his nephews. But first he had to attend the annual Paris Auto Salon. For the first time since the Paris Auto Salon resumed after the war it was admitting German automakers and journalists, a sign that things were returning to the prewar normal.

Edna Champion on a trip to Miami Beach in early 1927, one of the last trips she and Albert took together. *Photo courtesy of Kerry Champion Williams.*

On October 1, Champion and Edna sailed from New York on the luxury French liner *Île de France*, celebrated for its modernistic Art Deco designs,[38] with Walter Chrysler and GM leaders Alfred Sloan, Charles Kettering, Charles Stewart Mott, and Laurence Fisher of the Fisher autobody division. Other passengers included author Anita Loos, on a business trip to promote foreign editions of her new novel *Gentlemen Prefer Blondes*, and French tennis star and sportswear manufacturer René Lacoste.

Once again in Paris, Champion shuttled between a series of meetings. Edna, left alone, renewed her friendship with Charles Brazelle, still estranged from his wife in Biarritz and residing in the Hôtel Crillon, one of the City of Light's most prestigious accommodations. He turned on the charm and listened to her marriage woes.

On Wednesday evening, October 26, Albert and Edna dined with his longtime friend Henri Desgrange, publisher of the sports newspaper *L'Auto* and director of the Tour de France. The newspaper's editor and dinner host Charles Faroux wrote: "All this time Albert Champion is happy, enthusiastic as usual, bubbly about grandiose projects, once more communicating to us his ardor for life, his combative alacrity, his love of action, which constituted a personality so moving."[39]

After dinner, they all met Alfred P. Sloan and spent the rest of the night hobnobbing.[40] For Edna, it must have been a relief to talk in English with Sloan, as she was isolated from the others carrying on in streams of French.

The next morning, Albert and Edna quarreled in their Hôtel Meurice suite. Edna declared that she wanted to leave Albert for Charlie Brazelle.[41] Albert argued that she needed him because she had no money. She reminded him that he had given her $40,000 of GM stock.[42] He threatened that he had an enormous number of shares and could manipulate them to drive down their value.[43] She retorted that she had $50,000 worth of jewelry that she could sell.[44] Champion seized her jewelry box and had it locked up in the hotel safe.[45] Then he left. He had a busy day, starting with an appointment with Pierre Tournier for a tour of the renovated AC Titan factory in Levallois-Perret. Later he planned to have dinner with his friend Constant Huret.

Early that afternoon he returned with Tournier to the suite at the Hôtel Meurice, where Champion expected to find Edna waiting. The suite was empty. Champion and Tournier walked across the Tuileries Quarter to the Hôtel Crillon.

Champion spotted Edna in a gilded-oak gallery lounge. Chic, with bobbed hair cut at her jaw line straight as a ruler below a cloche hat, she leaned across a marble table. She gestured with a cigarette in her fingers, talking to Charlie Brazelle. Albert approached the table, close enough now to smell the scent of perfume he had watched Edna apply that morning. The well-mannered hush of the lounge was suddenly broken when he demanded that his wife accompany him immediately back to their hotel.[46]

Brazelle stood, shrugging his shoulders and murmuring in French.[47] A former US Army officer, he'd been stationed in France during the war and had polished his command of the language. He was stout, taller than Champion, and closer to Edna's age. A confrontation seemed imminent. Champion erupted with jealousy.

The *New York Daily News* would report that he and Brazelle argued over Edna, their words escalating louder and harsher: "Finally blows were struck by Charlie and Albert, both sputtering in French, which Edna did not understand. Then Champion staggered off."[48]

As Champion and Tournier shuffled back through the Tuileries Quarter to the Hôtel Meurice, by chance they were but a short kilometer from where Champion had grown up as the son of a widowed washerwoman who struggled to feed him and three younger brothers. At one point, he slowed down and halted.[49] Perhaps Tournier thought about the punch Champion had taken, but he had seen him endure disastrous crashes. Champion intended to relax in his suite in the Hôtel Meurice and wait for Edna to join him at 5:30 for cocktails and dinner with life-long friend Constant Huret.

In the Tuileries Quarter, however, Champion complained of a stomach-ache.[50] He and Tournier detoured to a pharmacy.[51] Champion described his symptoms to a pharmacist who dispensed aspirin and advised him to consult a doctor right away.

Tournier accompanied him to his suite. When Champion reclined on his bed, his forehead broke into beads of sweat.[52] Tournier called for the house doctor, but Albert died at 4:30 in Tournier's arms.[53]

An hour later, Constant Huret arrived at the hotel to meet his buddy for dinner. Instead, he learned the sad news that Champion was dead.[54]

News of Champion's unexpected death, attributed to a heart attack, set the massive iron printing presses thundering at newspapers in Paris, around

Europe, and in the United States. Paris's *Figaro* called Champion "the astonishing Frenchman among Americans."[55] The *Boston Globe* headlined his life: "Brilliant Career."[56] The Associated Press wire-service coverage in US newspapers stated: "His death closed a career as brilliant as that of any Horatio Alger hero, from errand boy in Paris, France, to millionaire automobile accessories manufacturer in America."[57]

Gendarmes arrested Edna and Brazelle and held them in jail during an investigation.[58] Witnesses from the Hôtel Crillon were interviewed. Brazelle claimed Champion always had a weak heart and got mad once too often, which caused a heart attack. The US Army veteran, who had done his duty aiding the French to win the war, held an advantage over Champion the draft dodger lying dead in the morgue. Edna, in mourning, pleaded that she had to make arrangements either to bring her late husband's body back to Flint or to have him buried in Paris at Père Lachaise.

Finally Brazelle and Edna were released without charge, in time to attend Champion's memorial service on the afternoon of November 3, seven days after his death, at the Church of the American on Avenue Georges V.[59] Prosper Champion and his wife and their three sons came from Flint for the funeral,[60] and brother Louis arrived from New York.[61] Hundreds filled the church and hundreds more collected outside.

Edna was robed in widow's black and behaved with grace in the pew. Brazelle, in mourning clothes, sat next to her. She had been living without her multimillionaire husband allowing her to have her own money. Now he was gone and she inherited his millions. She would no longer have to live in Flint; she could now afford a luxurious life in New York. Later it was said that she giggled and laughed into her handkerchief through the ceremony.[62] Her in-laws, however, thought they had heard the muffled sounds of grief.

Edna followed her husband's wishes and ordered a mausoleum built of marble for him in Paris's revered Père Lachaise cemetery, celebrated today as the final resting place of Honoré de Balzac, Sarah Bernhardt, Georges Bizet, Frédéric Chopin, Edith Piaf, and, the rare American Jim Morrison. Edna also commissioned a sculptor to make a bust of him.[63] Almost a year later, on July 24, 1928, she returned to Paris to have her late husband entombed in his mausoleum. It had an opening on one side a few feet from the ground to display the bust, since hidden behind a frosted-glass window. Edna arranged to have the remains of his mother, Marie Blanche Champion, moved from the cemetery in St. Cloud to rest with him as permanent Parisians.[64]

Albert Champion rests with his mother, Marie Blanche Carpentier Champion, in the famous Paris cemetery Père Lachaise. Neighbors include rocker Jim Morrison and singer Edith Piaf. *Photo courtesy of Bernadette Murphy.*

17

THE LOWDOWN

"I'm no gigolo!" Charles Brazelle Tells Why.
—New York Daily Mirror, April 26, 1935[1]

Edna and Charlie lived together in a New York hotel and Brazelle's wife stayed in France while Champion's estate was settled over the next year.[2] General Motors bought the stock that Champion had amassed and took over the company as a division, surviving today as ACDelco. Basil De Guichard served as executor of his estate,[3] and he succeeded Champion as president of AC Spark Plug Company.[4]

In 1928 Edna inherited about $12 million ($163 million in 2014), making her one of the richest women in America in charge of her own fortune.[5]

Charlie said he wanted a penthouse apartment.[6] It took a while to find something that suited his taste. Edna came upon a two-story penthouse containing ten rooms atop the twenty-story Medical Arts Building, a hospital for the affluent at 57 West 57th Street. To please him, she bought the entire building.[7] As coolly as if she were a tourist jotting a note on a postcard, she wrote a check for $1.3 million ($17.7 million in 2014).[8]

A burst of Puritan conscience about living openly with her lover prompted her to order him out of her bedroom.[9] They converted the dining room into his bedroom. She purchased a Louis XVI canopy bed for her bedroom and two Watteau paintings.[10] Then she had a third floor built on top just for her and Charlie. They held open house on the first floor of their penthouse for parties, drinking, and dancing the Charleston and the Lindy Hop to music blaring from the phonograph around the clock. Edna stocked a room with cases of champagne and drank the bubbly from an extra tall iced-tea glass.[11]

Charlie took over the second floor of the Medical Arts Building as a gentleman stockbroker.[12] He created a dummy corporation in Panama and sold her General Motors stock for $5 million.[13] When the stock market crashed in 1929, he lost $3.5 million of Edna's money.[14]

His wife Roberta Acuff Brazelle died at age thirty-five in a Paris hotel of pneumonia in April 1930.[15] He proposed marriage to Edna, but she was wary of becoming his third wife. He plied her with champagne and narcotic drugs from the hospital until her sisters and brothers-in-law packed his bags and banished him from her life.[16] He moved into the New York Athletic Club. Desperate to reconcile, he kept coming back, again and again.

Edna's liver failed and the hospital she lived above could not help. She hired guards to protect her from Brazelle.[17] On March 18, 1935, she was lying on her Louis XVI bed when he smashed through a glass-panel bedroom door, waving a pistol and shouting her name.[18] Guards beat him up, blackened both eyes, and threw him bleeding into the street.[19] He went by ambulance for treatment at the Flower-Fifth Avenue Hospital.[20]

Hours later, Edna died. Her estate, valued at $8 million, went to her surviving mother and siblings.[21]

Brazelle sued her estate in Manhattan Surrogate's Court for $650,000 as her common-law husband.[22] Edna's family ratted out Brazelle in court, claiming that he had slugged Champion fatally in the bar of the Hôtel Crillon during an argument over Edna.[23] The circumstances behind Champion's death had not hit the streets in the New York-Detroit-Flint axis until the *New York American* headline of June 15, 1935, screamed: "Millionaire's Death Laid to Boxer's Punch in Suit over Champion Estate."[24]

A hard fist to the chest from husky six-foot Brazelle could set off atrial fibrillation, causing a heart attack.[25] Relatives fed details to reporters and, surprisingly, he verified their version to bolster his claim as common-law husband. Newspapers treated the trinity of money, sex, and betrayal as a bonanza.

The salacious stories fizzled in December when Brazelle was taken by ambulance for treatment of gastric ulcers to Flower-Fifth Avenue Hospital—where Champion had recovered from his 1903 compound leg fracture. There on December 20 at age forty-four Charlie Brazelle died.[26]

The spark-plug designs, dashboard speedometers, and companies Champion started have stood the test of time. Today the Champion Spark Plug and ACDelco brand names are recognized around the world. More than two hundred thousand people a year attend performances at the Boston Center for the Arts in the landmark Cyclorama Building in Boston's South End, all passing the brass plate celebrating his Albert Champion Company, where he had made his first Champion spark plugs. Approximately 50 million vehicles operating in the United States are currently on the road with ACDelco spark plugs, filters, brakes, and other components.[27] And every April at the Paris-Roubaix Queen of the Classics bicycle race, another winner's name is added to Albert Champion's on the roster of legends.

ACKNOWLEDGMENTS

Albert Champion's story has been lying around for nearly a century, the accounts of his life widely scattered on both sides of the Atlantic. To collect source material, I have benefited from the generous help and cooperation of many people in five countries. To everyone, I express my heartfelt appreciation.

Thanks to Lorne Shields in Toronto for bringing to my attention the big concept of the bicycle industry in the late nineteenth century creating the foundation of our modern transportation system. Roger White, museum specialist in the Transportation Division of the Smithsonian Institution's National Museum of American History, generously and patiently granted me regular access over several years to read old leather-bound volumes of *Bearings*, *Automobile*, and many other periodicals.

Cheri Champion, granddaughter of Prosper Champion, Albert Champion's youngest brother, provided family stories and the scrapbook that Albert kept of his professional cycling career and the scrapbook Prosper collected containing French and English obituaries.

Kerry Champion Williams, great-niece of Albert's second wife, Edna Crawford, shared family stories as well as a scrapbook collected by her grandmother, Emily.

Stephen and Ann Stranahan shared personal recollections and family reminiscences about their grandfather, Frank D. Stranahan, and Frank's younger brother, Robert Allen Stranahan II. Stephen and Ann provided records of the Albert Champion Company of Boston, the genesis of both the Champion Spark Plug Company and the General Motors division ACDelco.

Virginia L. Smeyers, curatorial associate at Harvard University Archives in Pusey Library, supplied copies of entries from Robert Allen Stranahan II, class of 1908, *Anniversary Reports*.

Anne McMahon, university archivist at Santa Clara University, supplied documents on Charles Brazelle, class of 1908. Jessica Miller, archivist at the

Archives of Michigan, guided me on the dates of the founding of the Champion Ignition Company of Flint and its later name change to the AC Spark Plug Company, since merged with another division and continuing as ACDelco. Melissa Phillips, manager of the Research Library at the American Automobile Association, generously provided helpful historical information.

Dennis Renault kindly tutored me and gave a broadsheet he had written and illustrated on the intricate nineteenth-century letter-copying book process. Vincent Bakich provided helpful background into the Marmon Speedster. Gary McCoy shared some of his vast knowledge of motorcycles, especially the Clément Gladiator. Stewart Harris provided a copy of his erudite and puckish college thesis on Boston's Newspaper Row and its eight dailies around the turn of the twentieth century. Waltham Museum volunteers Albert Arena, Louise Butler, and Jack Vallely were always helpful in supplying information on Charles Herman Metz and Champion's early days in America working for Metz.

For medical consulting, thanks to W. Scott Schroth, MD, MPH; Bill Mallon, MD; Andrew Lovy, OD; and Lainie Holman, MD.

For translations thanks to Steve Moyer, who also suggested books on Paris and France, and to Jean-Claude Laboudigue, my friend in Pau, France.

As always, I am fortunate to have inspiration and support from Louise Blum, Don McDermott, and Dan (Hoss) Lee.

Frank K. Gallant and Hank Banta patiently listened as I shared some early findings. Thanks to Buck Peacock, Jere Cunningham, Andrew Homan, Ken Moffett, Steve Lassahn, Alan Côté, John Howard, Jack Nadolski, Janet Brown and Roy Drinkwater, Ben Valley, Bill Driscoll, Pete and Sally Swan, Clint Page and Dar Webb Page, Russell Howe, Bill and Carol McGann, Ken and Pam Williams, Bob Keough, Gerry Ives, Jacques Seray, Gérard Salmon, Butch Baker, Andrew Ritchie, Rich Street, Dylan Klemper, Ed Ruesing, Owen Mulholland, the late Rich Carlson. And thanks to Marine Corps sharpshooter Lawrence Herman for his calls with news reports and to inquire about my progress.

For guidance on General Motors, I thank Daniel L. Dolan in media relations at the AC Rochester Division of General Motors, since renamed ACDelco; also, Kathleen Adelson, researcher at the General Motors Heritage Center.

Thanks to Jim Orr at the Benson Ford Research Center at the Henry Ford Museum in Dearborn, Michigan, and Dave Larzelere, librarian at the *Flint*

Journal. Dave White at the Kettering University Archives and the William C. Durant Collection in Flint was always attentive and helpful in providing material about The Man and his creation known around the world as General Motors.

Mentors from the Goucher College MFA in Creative Writing gave me much kind support and editorial direction. A special thanks to Suzanna Lessard, Tom French, Jacob Levenson, Dick Todd, and Patsy Sims.

I am indebted to volunteer researchers who constantly impressed me with their diligence and brilliance. Bernadette Murphy in Paris tracked down records and background information in and about Paris that inspired me to continue digging into Champion's story. Alain Pernot, also in Paris, provided helpful material and insights on the 1921 Grand Prix de France. Renate Franz in Cologne, Germany, found material on Champion in Berlin. Dick Croft in Manchester, England, diligently researched nineteenth-century files in the public library of Haslingden for information on Haslingden's very own James "Choppy" Warburton. David Herlihy, a Boston-based world traveler, and Stuart Stanton, a Welshman living in Leeds, England, and Janis Keough in Oak Harbor, Washington, were indefatigable in discovering information that solidified the biography's narrative.

My gallant and persevering agent John Rudolph at Dystel and Goderich Literary Management pushed hard to get this story in print. Thanks to John and to Steven L. Mitchell, editor-in-chief at Prometheus Books, who saw the value of Champion's biography as a crossover history of the automobile industry. The crew at Prometheus Books applied their considerable talents to produce the book, led by the sharp-eyed and rigorous editor Brian McMahon, proofreader Mariel Bard, designer Jacqueline Nasso Cooke, and production manager Cate Roberts-Abel.

My special appreciation goes to Trever Igor Nye for sharing his deep knowledge of engines and passion for spicy Indian food.

Most of all, I thank my wife Valerie with deep appreciation and love for her patience over the years I was researching and pulling the story together and, especially, for reading drafts and offering invaluable editorial expertise. She influences me in many ways every day. I could not have written this book without her.

NOTES

A note on sources. In my research about Albert Champion and his circle, his great niece, Cherie Champion, the granddaughter of his youngest brother, Prosper Champion, generously provided the scrapbook that Albert had kept of his cycling career 1896 and 1904 and another scrapbook that Prosper Champion had collected of his brother. These scrapbooks yielded a treasury of newspaper and magazine clippings and photographs. Some included information is incomplete as clips were cut out and pasted onto pages in a casual way. A scrapbook about Champion and his second wife, Edna Crawford Champion, was collected by her younger sister, Emily Crawford, including material about Edna's lover, Charles Brazelle. A copy was made courtesy of Emily's granddaughter, Kerry Champion Williams. For converting money amounts to their purchasing power in 2014, I relied on MeasuringWorth, http://www .measuringworth.com/ppowerus.

PROLOGUE

1. Chris Sinsabaugh, *Who Me? Forty Years of Automobile History* (Detroit: Arnold-Powers, 1940), p. 224.

2. "Motor Racing in America—at the Empire City Track," *New York Sun*, June 6, 1903.

3. Ibid.

4. John J. Donovan, "Champion Rides a Mile in 58-4/5S," *Boston Globe*, July 12, 1903, describes his four-cylinder, 10-hp engine on his Clément Gladiator motorcycle imported from Paris when US motorcycles had one or two cylinders. Champion bored the cylinder holes wider to boost his engine capacity to 22 hp, noted *Motorcycle Illustrated*, September 1, 1908, p. 30.

5. "World's Record Broken—Champion Does Mile on Motor Cycle in 1m. 4 1-5s," *Boston Herald*, May 31, 1903.

6. "1900: 8,000 Automobiles, 4 billion Cigarettes," in *Chronicle of America: From Prehistory to Today* (New York: Dorling Kindersley, 1995), p. 529.

7. "Motor Racing in America" *New York Sun*; "World's Record Broken," *Boston Herald*.

8. Henry Ford Museum display, from author visit October 24, 2013, at the 1902 Ford "999" Race Car, Dearborn, MI. More information available at American Heritage, http://

www.americanheritage.com/content/1902-Ford-999-race-car-built-henry-ford (accessed June 11, 2014).

9. John B. Rae, *The American Automobile: A Brief History* (Chicago: University of Chicago Press, 1965), p. 17.

10. William F. Nolan, *Barney Oldfield: The Life and Times of America's Legendary Speed King* (New York: G. P. Putnam's Sons, 1961), p. 38.

11. "American Leads in Numerical Value," *Automobile*, February 21, 1907, p. 352.

12. Henry Ford Museum display.

13. "Motor Racing in America," *New York Sun*.

CHAPTER 1. BALANCING ON ONE WHEEL

1. Chris Sinsabaugh, *Who Me? Forty Years of Automobile History* (Detroit: Arnold-Powers, 1940), p. 15.

2. "Albert Champion, Head of AC, Dies in Paris Hotel," *Flint Journal*, October 28, 1927.

3. Ibid.

4. Archives de Paris, 18 Boulevard Sérurier, 75019 Paris, on microfilm #869 (accessed September 10, 2004). Also available at http://canadp-archivesenligne.paris.fr.

5. John Colletta, lecturer in a French Genealogical Workshop, US National Archives, Washington, D.C., August 27, 1996.

6. Patrice Higonnet, *Paris: Capital of the World*, trans. Arthur Goldhammer (Cambridge, MA: Harvard University Press, 2002), p. 69.

7. Michael Poisson, *Paris: Buildings and Monuments: An Illustrated Guide with over 850 Drawings and Neighborhood Maps* (New York: Harry N. Abrams, 1999), p. 287.

8. Edouard de Perrodil, *Albert Champion: His Triumphs, His Adventures, His Voyage to the United States*, brochure published in Paris, 1904, by *L'Auto*, pp. 6–7, translated by David Herlihy.

9. Ibid.

10. US Draft Registration Card, Division No. 1, Flint, MI, September 12, 1918.

11. Perrodil, *Albert Champion*, p. 7.

12. Ibid.

13. Ibid.

14. Ibid.

15. Paul-Henri Lecuyer, archivist at Noisy-le-Sec, in e-mail to author, March 3, 2014.

16. Perrodil, *Albert Champion*, p. 7.

17. Ibid.

18. Charles Ravaud, "The Death of Albert Champion: His Career—From Cycling Champion to Industrialist," *L'Auto*, October 28, 1927.

19. Perrodil, *Albert Champion*, p. 7.

20. "Champion's Death a Shock to Friends: Industry Loses Most Colorful Figure," *Automobile Topics Illustrated*, November 5, 1927.

21. Archives de Paris, canadap-archivesenligne.paris.fr/archives_etat_civil/avant_1860 -fichiers_etat_civil_reconstitute/fecr_visu_img.php?registre=V3E_N_0430&type=ECRF&&bdd-en -cours=etat_civil_rec-fichiers (accessed January 17, 2014).

22. Michael Kimmelman, "Glimpsing a Lost Paris, Before Gentrification: Charles Marville's Pictures Show What Was Destroyed," *New York Times*, March 9, 2014.

23. Poisson, *Paris*, p. 11.

24. Robert A. Caro, *The Years of Lyndon Johnson: The Path to Power* (New York: Alfred A. Knopf, 1982), chapter 27, "The Sad Irons," pp. 508–509, describes the universal labor involved in manual clothes washing.

25. Record for Alexandre Champion, Ancestry.com, http://search.ancestry.com/cqi -bin/sse.dll?h=282016&db=ARFIDOmarriages&indiv=try (accessed June 5, 2012).

26. Archives de Paris, Marriages, 1873–1882, 17e arr. D1M9 481, p. 6, record for Alexandre Champion, http://canadparchivesenligne.paris.fr/archives_etat_civil/1860_1902_tables _decennales/td_visu_img.php?registre=D1M9_481&type=TD&vue_tranche_debut=AD075TD _D1M9_481_0045&vue_tranche_fin=AD075TD_D1M9_481_0065&ref_histo=14404&cote =D1M9%20481 (accessed January 17, 2014).

27. Ibid.

28. Alastair Horne, *Seven Ages of Paris* (New York: Alfred A. Knopf, 2002), p. 262; Rupert Christiansen, *Paris Babylon: The Story of the Paris Commune* (New York: Viking, 1994), p. 244.

29. Ibid.

30. David McCullough, *The Greater Journey: Americans in Paris* (New York: Simon and Schuster, 2011), p. 286. McCullough notes that the taste of brewery rats surpassed that of sewer rats.

31. Horne, *Seven Ages of Paris*, p. 270; Higonnet, *Paris*, p. 109; Christianson, *Paris Babylon*, p. 366.

32. Poisson, *Paris*, p. 263.

33. US National Parks Service, http://www.nps.org/wamo/index.htm (accessed June 11, 2014).

34. Archives de Paris, Décès, 1883–1892, 17e arr. D1MP890, Parish Register, p. 16, http:// canadparchivesenligne.paris.fr/archives_etat_civil/1860_1902_tables_decennales/td_visu_img .php?registre=D1M9_890&type=TD&vue_tranche_debut=AD075TD_D1M9_890_0062&vue _tranche_fin=AD075TD_D1M9_890_0082&ref_histo=13330&cote=D1M9%20890 (accessed January 17, 2014).

35. Researcher Bernadette Murphy consulted the Paris Archives on March 24, 2014, checking the conscription and tax records of each of Paris's twenty arrondissements from 1849 to 1939, but found no mention of Alexandre Champion anywhere.

36. "Work Is Albert Champion's Main Pastime—Says He Can't Quit Now," *Detroit News*, August 21, 1927.

37. Perrodil, *Albert Champion*.

CHAPTER 2. THE FEARLESS KNIGHT

1. Légion d'Honneur file, archived at the Centre Historique Archives de Paris, ref. L0549039, http://www.culture.gouv.fr/documentation/leonore/pres.htm (accessed March 3, 2006). Clément was awarded Chevalier de la Légion d'Honneur on April 2, 1894.

2. Henri Desgrange, "Mort de Clément-Bayard," *L'Auto*, May 11, 1928, p. 1.

3. Ibid.

4. Légion d'Honneur file. After Chevalier de la Légion d'Honneur followed Officier de la Légion d'Honneur, on December 6, 1904, then Commandeur Légion d'Honneur, November 20, 1912.

5. "The French Dunlop Tires," *To-Day* (London), July 18, 1896, p. 331.

6. Desgrange, "Mort de Clément-Bayard."

7. "The Romance of Business: A Word on the Birth and Growth of a New Industry," *Westminster Budget* (London), May 1, 1896, p. 26.

8. Ibid.

9. Sir Arthur du Cros, *Wheels of Fortune: A Salute to Pioneers* (London: Chapman and Hall, 1938), p. 90.

10. Ibid., p. 92.

11. Gérard Hartmann, *Clément-Bayard: Sans Peur et Sans Reproche*, 2006, p. 4, http://www.hydroretro.net.etudegh/clement-bayard.pdf (accessed August 29, 2013).

12. "Pierrefonds, Un Lieu, Une Histoire. . . ." http://www.members.lycos.fr/decouvrir/Pierrefonds.html (accessed January 27, 2003).

13. Ibid.

14. Hartmann, *Clément-Bayard*, p. 4.

15. Pierre Terrail Bayard, *Dictionnaire de Bibliographie Français* (Paris: Librairie Letouzey et Ané, 1959), pp. 995–96; *The New Encyclopedia Britannica* (London: 2005).

16. Ibid., p. 996.

17. Desgrange, "Mort de Clément-Bayard."

18. Graham Robb, *The Discovery of France: A Historical Geography from the Revolution to the First World War* (New York: W. W. Norton, 2007), p. 158.

19. Ibid.

20. Ibid., p. 243.

21. Desgrange, "Mort de Clément-Bayard."

22. Joan DeJean: *The Essence of Style: How the French Invented High Fashion, Fine Food, Chic Cafés, Style, Sophistication, and Glamour* (New York: Free Press, 2005), p. 136.

23. Ibid., p. 212.

24. Ibid.

25. Desgrange, "Mort de Clément-Bayard"; Jack Rennert, *Poster Ecstasy*, vol. 28 (New York: Poster Auctions International, 1998), Clément & Cie., poster of 1886, plate no. 1, p. 3.

26. Desgrange, "Mort de Clément-Bayard."

27. Ebria Feinblatt and Bruce Davis, eds., *Toulouse-Lautrec and His Contemporaries: Posters of*

the Belle Epoque, from the Wagner Collection (New York: Los Angeles County Museum of Art, in association with Harry N. Abrams, 1985), p. 15; Jules Chéret's address on posters through 1890 at 18 rue Brunel, including 1879 poster, *Les Girard: L'Horloge, Champs-Elysées*, 1879, and *Théâtrophone*, 1890, place no. 33.

28. Desgrange, "Mort de Clément-Bayard."

29. *Dictionnaire de Biographie Français*, vol. 8 (Paris: Librairie Letouzey et Ané, 1959), pp. 1432–33.

30. "Uniting the Houses of Charron-Clément," *Automobile*, March 21, 1907, p. 500.

31. Listed among the medals he won at trade shows in Le Mans, Tours, Nice, Epernay, and Alençon, cited in February 8, 1904, for his Officier de la Légion d'Honneur, ref. L0549039.

32. Desgrange, "Mort de Clément-Bayard."

33. "Uniting the Houses of Charron-Clément."

34. Légion d'Honneur file.

35. S. S. Wilson, "Bicycle Technology: This Humane and Efficient Machine Played a Central Role in the Evolution of the Ball Bearing, the Pneumatic Tire, Tubular Construction, and the Automobile and the Airplane," *Scientific American*, March 1973, pp. 81–91. J. K. Starley of Coventry, England, is widely recognized for introducing the Rover safety bicycle, with the first chain drive and same-size wheels on the diamond frame, in 1885 at the Stanley Show in London, the bicycle industry's annual trade show. Geoffrey Williamson, *Wheels within Wheels: The Story of the Starleys of Coventry* (London: Geoffrey Bles, 1966), pp. 103–105. Prior Dodge, *The Bicycle* (Paris: Flammarion, 1996), pp. 94–102.

36. Desgrange, "Mort de Clément-Bayard."

37. Patrice Higonnet, *Paris: Capital of the World*, trans. Arthur Goldhammer (Cambridge, MA: Harvard University Press), p. 357.

38. Desgrange, "Mort de Clément-Bayard."

39. du Cros, *Wheels of Fortune*, p. 63.

40. Ibid., p. 70.

41. Ibid.

42. "Romance of Business."

43. du Cros, *Wheels of Fortune*, p. 31.

44. Ibid.

45. Ibid.

46. Ibid.

47. Ibid., p. 33.

48. Ibid., p. 41.

49. Ibid., illustration, p. 103.

50. Ibid., pp. 102–103.

51. Ibid., p. 99.

52. Ibid., p. 124.

53. "The French Dunlop Tyre," p. 331.

54. Jack Rennert, *100 Years of Bicycle Posters* (New York: Darien House, 1973), p. 3; Ebria

Feinblatt and Bruce Davis, "The Posters of Toulouse-Lautrec: Art for the Pavement Public," pp. 10–35, and "The Art of Persuasion: Sources of Style and Content in Belle Epoque Posters," pp. 38–47, in Feinblatt and Davis, eds., *Toulouse-Lautrec and His Contemporaries: Posters of the Belle Epoque, from the Wagner Collection* (New York: Los Angeles County Museum of Art, in association with Harry N. Abrams, 1985).

CHAPTER 3. A BEAUTIFUL DEVIL

1. "The French Dunlop Tyre," *To-Day* (London), July 18, 1896, p. 331.

2. Edouard de Perrodil, *Albert Champion: His Triumphs, His Adventures, His Voyage to the United States*, brochure published in Paris, 1904, by *L'Auto*, p. 8, translated by David Herlihy.

3. Pierre Chany, *La Fabuleuse Histoire du Cyclisme: Des Origines à 1955* (Paris: Nathan, 1988), p. 94.

4. Graham Robb, *The Discovery of France* (New York: W. W. Norton, 2004), p. 226.

5. Chany, *La Fabuleuse Histoire du Cyclisme*.

6. Ibid.

7. Ibid.

8. Ibid., p. 97.

9. Sir Arthur du Cros, *Wheels of Fortune: A Salute to Pioneers* (London: Chapman and Hall, 1938), p. 41.

10. Ibid.

11. Ibid.

12. Ibid.

13. Ibid.

14. Ibid.

15. "The Brothers Who Seized an Opportunity," European Automotive Hall of Fame, http://www.autonews.com/files/euroauto/inductees/michelin2002.htm (accessed February 27, 2003).

16. Ibid.

17. Ibid. Edouard Michelin studied under Adolphe William Bouguereau (1825–1905), famous for his iconic cherubic angels reproduced on note cards, key chains, and umbrellas. He was an influential member of the French Royal Academy of Painting and Sculpture, and he prevented avant-garde works from showing at the academy's official exhibitions.

18. Chany, *La Fabuleuse Histoire du Cyclisme*, p. 47.

19. Sylvane de Saint-Seine, "Angellis, Fords, Toyodas . . . Armand Peugeot Beat Them All," European Automotive Hall of Fame, 2003 induction, http://www.autonews.com/files/euroauto/inductees/apeugeot2003.htm (accessed February 3, 2003).

20. Chany, *La Fabuleuse Histoire du Cyclisme*, p. 99.

21. Ibid.

22. Ibid., p. 95.

23. Ibid., p. 98.

24. Ibid.

25. Ibid.

26. Ibid., p. 100.

27. Perrodil, *Albert Champion*, p. 11.

28. The Clément catalogue of 1888, p. 20, lists the basic price as 450 francs, plus assorted equipment upgrades that raise the price to a total of 725 francs.

29. Perrodil, *Albert Champion*, p. 11.

30. Ibid.

31. The Man in the Street (likely Charles Ravaud of *L'Auto*, a journalist who had covered Champion's progress while writing for other publications, including *Vélo*), "Cycling Gossip," *La Pédale* (Paris), October 8, 1924, p. 12, translated by David Herlihy.

32. Edouard Moussett, "Les Miettes du Cyclisme: Brique Pilée" (The Crumbs of Cycling, Wiping the Floor), *Le Véloce-Sport* (Bordeaux), November 11, 1897, p. 18.

33. Perrodil, *Albert Champion*, p. 11.

34. Ibid.

35. Moussett, "Miettes du Cyclisme."

36. Perrodil, *Albert Champion*, p. 11.

37. Ibid.

38. Advice offered unsolicited in the early 1960s from James Armando, member of the US Olympic Cycling team that competed in the 1924 Paris Olympics, and subsequent interviews in the 1980s with other veterans for Peter Nye's *Hearts of Lions: The History of American Bicycle Racing* (New York: W. W. Norton, 1988).

39. "French Dunlop Tire," p. 331.

40. Ibid.

41. Citation in Chevalier de la Légion d'Honneur, file archived at the Centre Historique Archives de Paris, ref. L0549039.

42. Ibid.

43. Ibid.

44. Perrodil, *Albert Champion*, p. 11.

CHAPTER 4. THE "HUMAN CATAPULT"

1. "Cycling in France," *Westminster Budget* (London), October 9, 1896, p. 28.

2. Robert Kanigel, *The One Best Way: Frederick Winslow Taylor and the Enigma of Efficiency* (Cambridge, MA: MIT Press, 2005), pp. 132–33.

3. Edouard de Perrodil, *Albert Champion: His Triumphs, His Adventures, His Voyage to the United States,"* brochure published in Paris, 1904, by *L'Auto*, p. 12, translated by David Herlihy.

4. Ibid.

5. "Albert Champion, Head of AC, Dies in Paris Hotel," *Flint Journal*; 6 francs also cited

in an Associated Press wire story carried in more than a hundred US dailies, including the *Boston Globe*, "Champion, Who Rose to Wealth, Dead: From Six Francs a Week, He Became a Millionaire," October 28, 1927.

6. "This and That," *Le Rappel* (The Reminder), May 21, 1921, cites Tournier's managing world-class riders, including Floyd McFarland of San Jose, CA, when he raced in Paris in 1900. Tournier became a father figure for Champion as well as a trusted colleague and director of Champion's AC Titan factory in suburban Levallois-Perret.

7. Ibid.

8. Perrodil, *Albert Champion*, p. 12.

9. Ibid.; The Man in the Street (likely Charles Ravaud of *L'Auto*), "Cycling Gossip," *La Pédale* (Paris), October 8, 1924, p. 12.

10. The Man in the Street's 1924 "Cycling Gossip."

11. Ibid.

12. Ibid.

13. Norman Beasley, "Albert Champion: The Office Boy Who Was Taught That a Race Is Won before the Race and There Is No Such Thing as 'Good Enough,'" *MoTor*, September 1926, reprinted as *Biography of Albert Champion, President, AC Spark Plug Company, Flint, Michigan*.

14. "Story of Champion's Life: Narrative of French Errand Boy Who Became a $20,000-a-Year Cycle Race Winner, and Later a Leading Figure in Automotive Industry," *Motor West*, November 15, 1927, pp. 32–34. This article by an anonymous writer describes Champion's early days under Adolphe Clément with details (including sweeping and dusting, attending the hearth fires, and washing windows) also appeared in other publications over the years. *Motor West* had offices in Los Angeles, San Francisco, New York, and Chicago.

15. Ibid.

16. Ibid.

17. Henri Desgrange, "Mort de Clément-Bayard," *L'Auto*, May 11, 1928, p. 1.

18. "Story of Champion's Life."

19. Dennis Renault, "Book Press Ink and Paper: The History of the Nineteenth Century Letter-Copying Book Process," excerpted from W. B. Proudfoot, *The Origin of Stencil Duplicating* (London: Hutchinson and Company, 1972), reprinted with permission and illustrated as a folio keepsake for the Sacramento Book Collectors Club (Sacramento, CA: Mockingbird Press, 1996).

20. Ibid.

21. Author interview with Dennis Renault in Carmel, CA, May 15, 1998.

22. Ibid.

23. Pierre Terrail de Bayard, *Dictionnaire de Bibliographie Français* (Paris: 1959), Librairie Letouzey et Ané, pp. 994–96; *The New Encyclopedia Britannica* (London: 2005).

24. Ibid.

25. Légion d'Honneur file, archived at the Centre Historique Archives de Paris, ref. L0549039, http://www.culture.gouv.fr/documentation/leonore/pres.htm (accessed March 3, 2006).

26. Desgrange, "Mort de Clément-Bayard."

27. "Réne Panhard," *The New Encyclopedia Britannica* (London: 2005).

28. "Émile Levassor," *The New Encyclopedia Britannica* (London: 2005).

29. John B. Rae, *The American Automobile: A Brief History* (Chicago: University of Chicago Press, 1965), p. 7.

30. Ibid.

31. Ibid.

32. Ibid.; Arthur Pound, *The Turning Wheel: The Story of General Motors through Twenty-Five Years, 1908–1933* (Garden City, NY: Doubleday, Doran and Company, 1934), p. 36.

33. Ibid.

34. David V. Herlihy, *The Bicycle: The History* (New Haven, CT: Yale University Press, 2004), pp. 86–87. Herlihy discusses Lallement's US patent, in 1866, and the patent's sale and resale, pp. 208–209.

35. Kanigel, *One Best Way*, p. 156.

36. Geoffrey Williamson, *Wheels within Wheels: The Story of the Starleys of Coventry* (London: Geoffrey Bles Publishers, 1966), pp. 48–49.

37. Desgrange, "Mort de Clément-Bayard."

38. Ibid.

39. Roger Bastide, Robert Chapatte, and Dominique Grimault, *Les Légendaires: Des Temps Héroïques* (Paris: La Maison du Sport, 1988), sidebar bylined Roger Bastide, "L'Empereur du Tour, Henri Desgrange Avait le Culte de Napoléon," p. 79.

40. Ibid., p. 246.

41. Birth certificate of Julie Elisa Delpuech, December 4, 1876, Archives de Paris, 18 Boulevard Sérurier, 75019 Paris, on microfilm #950 (accessed September 10, 2004). Also available from http://canadp-archivesenligne.paris.fr.

42. Ibid.

43. Bastide et. al., *Les Légendaires*, discuss Desgrange organizing weekend races in the 1890s, serving him well when he would introduce the Tour de France in 1903, p. 246.

44. Spectator of the Third Arrondissement (pen name for Desgrange), *Le Cycle* (Paris), April 12, 1896, page unnumbered.

45. Ibid.

46. The Man in the Street (possibly Charles Ravaud), *La Pédale*, October 8, 1924, p. 12; Perrodil, *Albert Champion*, p. 14. Champion's performance generated more than a dozen recollections over the years. All accounts are consistent and indicate that the event marked his career debut.

47. The Man in the Street's 1924 recollection.

48. Ibid.

49. Perrodil, *Albert Champion*, p. 12.

50. Ibid.

51. Spectator of the Third Arrondissement, *Le Cycle*.

52. Perrodil, *Albert Champion*.

53. Les Woodland, *Paris-Roubaix: All the Bumps of Cycling's Cobbled Classic* (Cherokee Village, AR: McGann Publishing, 2013), p. 14.

54. Charles Ravaud, "The Death of Albert Champion: His Career—From Cycling Champion to Industrialist," *L'Auto*, October 28, 1927, p. 2.

55. Ibid.

56. Ibid.

57. The Man in the Street's 1924 recollection.

58. Ibid.

59. Légion d'Honneur file.

60. Pierre Terrail de Bayard, *Dictionnaire de Biographie Français* (Paris: Librairie Letouzey et Ané), p. 996.

61. Desgrange, "Mort de Clément-Bayard."

62. "The French Dunlop Tyre," *To-Day* (London), July 18, 1896, p. 331.

63. Jack Rennert, *Prima Posters* (New York: Poster Auctions International, 1994), vol. 14, no. 45, by artist Paul Dupont, advertising Clément Cycles, including the company's capital of 4 million francs.

64. Desgrange, "Mort de Clément-Bayard."

65. Ibid.

66. Ibid.

67. David Herlihy, "Bicycle Story," *Invention and Technology* (New York) (Spring 1992): 59; Herlihy, *Bicycle*, p. 278.

68. Ibid.

69. "Men of Mark in the Cycling World: M. Albert Champion," *Hub* (London), February 20, 1897, p. 101.

70. Ibid.

71. Ibid.

72. "Work Is Albert Champion's Main Pastime," *Detroit News*, August 21, 1927.

73. W. A. Pritchard, "Albert Champion a Cycle Marvel: Wonderful Records Made by Manufacturer in his Younger Days Are Recalled," *New York Sun*, January 7, 1917.

74. "Men of Mark in the Cycling World."

75. Pierre Chany, *La Fabuleuse Histoire du Cyclisme: Des Origines à 1955* (Paris: Nathan, 1988), pp. 186–88. Warburton has long been the subject of articles, many repeating earlier accounts accusing him of drugging his stars. One notorious account goes back to Welshman Arthur Linton winning the 1896 endurance grind of some 370 miles from Bordeaux to Paris, earning a prize three thousand francs, sufficient to live on comfortably for a year. Weeks later, however, Linton died in a hospital of cholera. Warburton was blamed for giving him a fatal drug, possibly cocaine, although nothing was proved and drug testing was decades in the future.

76. "Men of Mark in the Cycling World."

77. Ibid.

78. Ibid.

79. Ibid.

80. Ibid.

81. Major Halstead, "'Choppy' Warburton and the Old Athletic Club," *Haslingden Observer* (Haslingden, England), January 22, 1898.

82. Ibid.

83. Ibid.

84. Ibid.

85. Ibid.

86. Ibid.

87. Ibid.

88. Ibid.

89. Major Halstead, "Choppy 'Beats Hazael,'" *Haslingden Observer*, January 29, 1898.

90. Halstead, "'Choppy' Warburton."

91. Ibid.

92. David Wallechinsky, *Complete Book of the Olympics* (New York: Little, Brown, 1991), p. 51.

93. Ibid., p. 54.

94. Halstead, "'Choppy' Warburton."

95. *Manchester Athletic Club Magazine* (England), January 1894, p. 2.

96. H. O. Duncan, *Vingt Ans de Cyclisme Pratique: Étude Complète du Cyclist de 1876 a Ce Jour* (Paris: F. Juven, 1896), pp. 64–66. Duncan, an Englishman and one of cycling's first generation of professionals, describes Warburton's regimen for Champion, which had earlier worked wonders for world champion Jimmy Michael of Wales.

97. Ibid.

98. "Men of Mark in the Cycling World."

99. Beasley, "Albert Champion."

100. Ibid.

101. Graham Robb, *The Discovery of France: A Historical Geography from the Revolution to the First World War* (New York: W. W. Norton, 2007), p. 162.

102. Ibid., p. 161.

103. Ibid., p. 162.

104. "Work Is Albert Champion's Main Pastime."

105. Ibid.

106. Beasley, "Albert Champion."

107. "Work Is Albert Champion's Main Pastime."

108. Ibid.

109. Clément, Légion d'Honneur file, archived at the Centre Historique Archives de Paris, ref. L0549039, http://www.culture.gouv.fr/documentation/leonore/pres.htm (accessed March 3, 2006).

110. "Men of Mark in the Cycling World."

111. Ibid.

112. Herlihy, *Bicycle*, p. 278; author interview with Colonel Pope's great-grandson, Albert Pope of Millbrook, New York, on March 1, 2002.

113. Stephen B. Goddard, *Colonel Albert Pope and His American Dream Machines: The Life and Times of a Bicycle Tycoon Turned Automotive Pioneer* (Jefferson, NC: McFarland and Company, 2000), pp. 17, 145, 157.

114. Ibid., p. 10.

115. Jack Rennert, *100 Years of Bicycle Posters* (New York: Darien House, 1973), p. 4.

116. Goddard, *Colonel Albert Pope*, p. 163.

117. David A. Hounshell, *From the American System to Mass Production, 1800–1932: The Development of Manufacturing Technology in the United States* (Baltimore: Johns Hopkins University Press, 1985), p. 189.

118. Ibid.

119. Herlihy, *Bicycle*, p. 278.

120. "Champion, 'Choppy' Warburton's Latest Find," *Bearings*, February 11, 1997, p. 105.

121. "Men of Mark in the Cycling World." Champion graces the cover, photo credited to Thiele and Company, Chancery Lane.

122. Duncan, *Vingt Ans de Cyclisme Pratique*, p. 185.

123. *Velocipede Illustré* (Paris), May 3, 1896, cover.

124. "Men of Mark in the Cycling World."

125. "Au Royal Aquarium: Lisette-Champion," January 16, 1897 (Champion scrapbook, unnamed newspaper).

126. "Champion, the Boy Champion," *Bearings*, February 11, 1897, p. 105.

127. Ibid.

128. Ibid.

129. Ibid.

130. Ibid.

131. Ibid.

132. Ibid.

133. Ibid.

134. Ibid.

135. Ibid.

136. Ibid.

137. Victor Breyer, "Great Star of Sport, Then of Industry, Albert Champion Is Dead!" *Echo des Sports*, October 28, 1927, p. 1, publishes the photo.

CHAPTER 5. A NEW CENTURY, ANOTHER COUNTRY, A FRESH START

1. "An Elaborate Programme Has Been Arranged—The Meet Will Be One To Be Remembered," *Montreal Daily Star*, August 5, 1899.

2. "Aluminum," *The New Encyclopedia Britannica* (London: 2005).

3. Ibid.

4. Georges-Thadée Bouton, *Dictionnaire de Biographie Français*, vol. 7 (Paris: Librairie Letouzey et Ané, 1956), p. 63.

5. Ibid. "A Versatile, Trendsetting, Automotive Pioneer," inducted 2004 into the European Automotive Hall of Fame, Automotive News, http://www.autonews.com/fileseuroauto/inductees/dedion2004.htm (accessed February 2, 2004).

6. Ibid.

7. Ibid.

8. Bob Rimel, "Reed Martin's 1899 DeDion Bouton," *Classic Cycle Review* (Harrisburg, PA) 2, no. 4 (April 1995): 37. More information on how the De Dion-Bouton motorcycle works came from an author interview with Reed Martin on May 9, 1995, at his home in Cabin John, MD.

9. Victor Breyer, "Paris-Roubaix: Victoire de Champion," *Vélo*, April 3, 1899.

10. "Champion Rides Like a Demon," *Bearings*, February 25, 1897, p. 326.

11. Sir Arthur du Cros, *Wheels of Fortune: A Salute to Pioneers* (London: Chapman and Hall, 1938), p. 59.

12. Ibid.

13. Ibid.

14. Author e-mail correspondence with cycling historian Les Woodland of Silfield, England, May 5, 2005.

15. Victor Breyer and Robert Coquelle, *Les Rois du Cycle: Comment Sont Devenus Champions* (Paris: Le Vélo, 1898), p. 153.

16. Ibid.

17. Ibid.

18. "Ce qu'en Pense Champion (The Thoughts of Champion)," *Vélo* (Paris), from Champion's scrapbook, likely written by Victor Breyer.

19. Victor Breyer, "Grande Vedette du Sport, Puis de L'Industrie, Albert Champion Est Mort!" *Echo des Sports*, October 28, 1927, p. 1.

20. Victor Breyer, "International Memories of Half a Century: Men and Events I," *Cycling* (London), February 12, 1947, p. 142; *Who's Who in France*, 1959–1960, 4th ed. (Paris: 1959), p. 146.

21. René Bibere, "La Bonté de Champion (The Kindness of Champion)," *Intransigeant* (Paris), October 31, 1927, describes Champion giving 700 francs to Marie of Porte Maillot so she could purchase firewood through the winter as an example of Champion's generosity to people in his old neighborhood.

22. Breyer and Coquelle, *Les Rois du Cycle*, p. 153.

23. Ibid.

24. Ibid., p. 145.

25. H. O. Duncan, *Vingt Ans de Cyclisme Pratique: Étude Complète du Cyclist de 1876 a Ce Jour* (Paris: F. Juven, 1896).

26. "Tidbit," *Véloce Sport*, June 10, 1897.

27. "'Choppy' Warburton Dead: Famous English Trainer Dies Suddenly at Wood Green Track," *Cycle Age and Trade Review* (Chicago), December 23, 1897, p. 238.

28. "Cause of 'Choppy's' Death," *Cycle Age and Trade Review*, January 13, 1898, p. 378.

29. Ibid.

30. Inscription from photo of tombstone supplied by historian Stuart Stanton of Leeds, England, e-mailed to author November 1, 2009.

31. Birth certificate of Julie Elisa Delpuech, December 4, 1876, Archives de Paris, 18 Boulevard Sérurier, 75019 Paris, on microfilm #950 (accessed September 10, 2004). Also available at http://canadp-archivesenligne.paris.fr.

32. Ernest Hemingway, *A Moveable Feast* (New York: Scribner's Sons, 1964) p. 65.

33. Roger De Maertelaere, *100 Jaar Zesdaagsen de Mannen van de Nacht* (Eeklo, Belgium: De Eecloonaar, 2000), p. 11.

34. "American 6-Day Races in the Nineteenth Century," Sixday.org, http://www.sixday .org/html/usa_19th_century.htm (accessed June 19, 2014).

35. "Bouhours Contre Champion," undated clip from Champion's scrapbook.

36. "Champion à Agen: Champion Tout Seul," undated clip from Champion's scrapbook.

37. *Cycle Age and Trade Review*, December 1, 1898, p. 146.

38. Les Woodland, *Paris-Roubaix: All the Bumps of Cycling's Cobbled Classic* (Cherokee Village, AR: McGann Publishing, 2013), p. 56.

39. Ibid., p. 49; Pascal Sergent, *A Century of Paris-Roubaix* (London: Bromley Books, 1998), p. 19.

40. Victor Breyer, "Paris-Roubaix: La Grande Épreuve de Demain," *Le Vélo*, April 1, 1899.

41. Sergent, *Century of Paris-Roubaix*, p. 8.

42. Ibid.

43. Ibid., p. 18.

44. "La Course Paris-Roubaix, 4e Année," *Journal de Roubaix*, April 4, 1899. p. 1.

45. Chany, *La Fabuleuse Histoire du Cyclisme*, p. 159.

46. "La Course Paris-Roubaix, 4e Année."

47. Breyer, "Paris-Roubaix," April 1, 1899.

48. Woodland, *Paris-Roubaix*, pp. 35–37. Woodland researched the claim that Garin's father had given him away and found it was based on an underlying truth. France had laws prohibiting French children from working inside chimneys, but youngsters from across the border were exploited. Maurice Garin was indeed a chimney sweep, as was a younger brother, Joseph-Isidore Garin.

49. Sergent, *Century of Paris-Roubaix*, p. 12.

50. Ibid.

51. Ibid., p. 14.

52. Victor Breyer, "Paris-Roubaix: Derniers Détails," *Le Vélo*, April 2, 1899.

53. Ibid.

54. Ibid.

55. Sergent, *Century of Paris-Roubaix*, p. 19.

56. "La Course Paris-Roubaix, 4e Année."

57. Sergent, *Century of Paris-Roubaix*, p. 18.

58. "La Course Paris-Roubaix, 4e Année."

59. Breyer, "Paris-Roubaix," April 3, 1899.

60. Ibid.

61. Ibid.; Sergent, *Century of Paris-Roubaix*, p. 19.

62. "La Course Paris-Roubaix, 4e Année."

63. Breyer, "Paris-Roubaix," April 3, 1899.

64. Ibid.

65. Ibid.; Sergent, *Century of Paris-Roubaix.*

66. "La Course Paris-Roubaix, 4e Année."

67. Breyer, "Paris-Roubaix," April 3, 1899.

68. "La Course Paris-Roubaix, 4e Année."

69. Ibid.

70. Breyer, "Paris-Roubaix," April 3, 1899.

71. "La Course Paris-Roubaix, 4e Année."

72. Ibid.

73. Ibid.

74. "Paris-Roubaix Road Race," *Cycle Age and Trade Review*, April 20, 1899, p. 775.

75. Victor Breyer, "Vitesses Comparées," *Le Vélo*, April 3, 1899.

76. John J. Donovan, "Albert Champion Dies, Millionaire at 47: Brilliant Career of Ex-Bicycle Racer, Who Got His Manufacturing Start in Boston," *Boston Globe*, October 28, 1927.

77. John J. Donovan, "Memorial Day Races Promise to Play Havoc with Records," *Boston Globe*, May 27, 1900.

78. Breyer, "International Memories," pp. 142–43.

79. "Foreign Invasion Begins: Champion, the Frenchman, Arrives Wednesday," *Cycle Age and Trade Review*, November 16, 1899, p. 616.

80. "A Versatile, Trendsetting, Automotive Pioneer," inducted 2004 into the European Automotive Hall of Fame, Automotive News, http://www.autonews.com/fileseuroauto/inductees/dedion2004.htm (accessed February 2, 2004).

81. "Foreign Invasion Begins."

82. Thomas S. LaMarre, "One Piece at a Time: The Cars of C. H. Metz," *Automobile Quarterly* (Kutztown, PA) 32, no. 3 (January 1994): 6.

83. Franklin B. Tucker, "C. H. Metz: Automotive Pioneer," *Antique Automobile* (Hershey, PA) (March-April 1967): 8.

84. Jack Rennert, *Prima Posters* (New York: Poster Auctions International, 1994), vol. 14, no. 47.

85. Tucker, "C. H. Mentz," p. 6.

86. Ibid., pp. 9–10.

87. Ibid.

88. Ibid.

89. LaMarre, "One Piece at a Time," p. 6; Tucker, "C. H. Metz," p. 11.

90. LaMarre, "One Piece at a Time," p. 6; Tucker, "C. H. Metz," p. 11.

91. Donovan, "Memorial Day Races Promise to Play Havoc with Records."

92. David V. Herlihy, *The Bicycle: The History* (New Haven, CT: Yale University Press, 2004), pp. 293–94.

93. "May Prove Means of Saving Millions in Transportation," *Cycle Age and Trade Review*, July 11, 1899, p. 454.

94. "An Elaborate Programme Has Been Arranged."

95. Ibid.

96. US Census Bureau figures, http://www.census.gov/population/estimates (accessed April 12, 2014).

97. "1900: 8,000 Automobiles, 4 billion Cigarettes," in *Chronicle of America: From Prehistory to Today* (New York: Dorling Kindersley, 1995), p. 529.

98. Stephen B. Goddard, *Colonel Albert Pope and His American Dream Machines: The Life and Times of a Bicycle Tycoon Turned Automotive Pioneer* (Jefferson, NC: McFarland and Company, 2000), pp. 157, 183.

99. A museum dedicated to the twins, Francis Edgar and F. O. Stanley, is maintained in their native Kingfield, Maine. See Stanley Museum, http://www.stanleymuseum.org (accessed June 20, 2014).

100. "No Use for Horses: Springfield Mechanics Devise a New Mode of Travel," *Springfield Evening Union* (Massachusetts), September 12, 1896.

101. Goddard, *Colonel Albert Pope and His American Dream Machines*, p. 188.

102. Laurence Gustin. "Sights and Sounds of Automotive History," *Automotive History Review* (New London, CT), no. 52 (Summer 2010): 5; Arthur Pound, *The Turning Wheel: The Story of General Motors through Twenty-Five Years, 1908–1933* (Garden City, NY: Doubleday, Doran and Company, 1934), illustration, p. 39.

103. LaMarre, "One Piece at a Time," p. 6; Tucker, "C. H. Metz," p. 7.

104. LaMarre, "One Piece at a Time," p. 6; Tucker, "C. H. Metz," p. 8.

105. LaMarre, "One Piece at a Time," p. 6.

106. US Census Bureau figures, http://www.census.gov/population/estimates (accessed April 12, 2014).

107. LaMarre, "One Piece at a Time," p. 6.

108. Ibid.

109. Ibid.

110. Ibid.; Tucker, "C. H. Metz," p. 5.

111. LaMarre, "One Piece at a Time," p. 6; Tucker, "C. H. Metz," p. 5.

112. Tucker, "C. H. Metz," p. 5.

113. Ibid.

114. Ibid.

115. Ibid.; LaMarre, "One Piece at a Time," p. 6.

116. Tucker, "C. H. Metz," p. 5; LaMarre, "One Piece at a Time," p. 6.

117. Tucker, "C. H. Metz," p. 5; LaMarre, "One Piece at a Time," p. 6.

118. City of Waltham website: http//:www.waltham-community.org/Waltham4History.html, see Key dates in the history of Waltham (accessed June 20, 2014).

119. Ibid.

120. Ibid.

121. Ibid.

122. "Economic Fluctuations: Stability and Instability: Business Cycles. Historical Studies of Cycles," *The New Encyclopedia Britannica* (London: 2005).

123. LaMarre, "One Piece at a Time," p. 6; Tucker, "C. H. Metz," p. 7.

124. "What the Boys Are Doing Now," *Bicycling World* (New York), November 17, 1906, p. 217, estimated his worth upon retirement at more than $100,000, and his investments included a telephone company in Detroit.

125. "Baseball's Milestone Contracts," *Sports Illustrated*, http://www.sportsillustrated.cnn.comsi.com/mlb/photos/2014/02/24/baseball-milestone-contracts#1 (accessed May 15, 2014) cites Wagner's salary as having doubled in 1908 to $10,000, considered a milestone contract for major league baseball.

126. Tucker, "C. H. Metz," p. 8.

CHAPTER 6. "PACEMAKERS KILLED"

1. John J. Donovan, "Pacemakers Killed: Miles and Stafford on Motor Tandem Hurley to Death," *Boston Globe*, May 31, 1900, p. 1.

2. "Fire Destroys Boston Saucer," *Bicycling World and Motorcycle Review*, January 23, 1909, p. 670.

3. "Worse than 'Bicycle Face': Harry Elks and John Nelson May Die Any Minute," *Omaha World Herald*, July 31, 1901, p. 8.

4. "Elkes Still the Champion: Wins Fifty-Mile Race in World's Record Time," *Cycle Age and Trade Review*, September 21, 1899, p. 564.

5. Ibid.

6. "New French Cycle Board," *Cycle Age and Trade Review*, March 1, 1900, p. 606; Clément, Légion d'Honneur file, archived at the Centre Historique Archives de Paris, ref. L0549039, http://www.culture.gouv.fr/documentation/leonore/pres.htm (accessed March 3, 2006).

7. "Harry Elkes Killed in Bicycle Race: Traveling at Nearly a Mile a Minute When a Tire Burst," *New York Times*, May 31, 1903, p. 1. The article notes that Elkes had been studying medicine with Dr. Chase of Chelsea, Massachusetts, and had intended to retire from racing at the end of the summer to enter the University of Pennsylvania.

8. Stewart Harris, "Have You Seen the *Globe* Today? A History of the Boston Newspaper," class paper, Boston University, 1981, p. 18.

9. John J. Donovan, "Albert Champion Dies," *Boston Globe*, October 28, 1927.

10. Joseph Durso, *Madison Square Garden: 100 Years of History* (New York: Simon and Schuster, 1979), p. 73.

11. "Interest in Racing Not Dead," *Cycle Age and Trade Review*, December 7, 1899, p. 214.

12. William A. Brady, *Showman: My Life Story* (New York: E. P. Dutton and Co., 1937), p. 77.

13. Ibid., p. 209.

14. Roger De Maertelaere, *100 Jaar Zesdaagsen de Mannen van de Nacht* (Eeklo, Belgium: De Eecloonaar, 2000), p. 11; Six Day Racing, http://www.6dayracing.ca (accessed March 1, 2014).

15. Brady, *Showman*, p. 228.

16. Ibid., p. 229. The law passed by the New York legislature was signed into effect by New York governor Teddy Roosevelt.

17. Ibid.

18. "Bicycle Cracks Compete: Elkes and French Racer in 25-Mile Paced Match," *New York Times*, December 3, 1899.

19. Ibid.

20. Ibid.

21. Ibid.

22. Ibid.

23. "Gossip of the Wheelmen: Racing Season Will Open at Waltham, May 30," *Boston Globe*, May 13, 1900.

24. Donovan, "Albert Champion Dies."

25. US Federal Census of Cambridge, Massachusetts, June 8, 1900, lists them both as servants living at 19 Cottage Street, where Champion and Dudley Marks lived as boarders.

26. "Passing of Michael: Most Famous of Little Men Dies in Mid-Ocean—His Remarkable Career," *Bicycling World*, November 20, 1904, p. 201, discusses Michael deserting cycling to race horses in New Orleans and Paris.

27. "To Give Up Horses," *Cycle Age and Trade Review*, December 29, 1898, p. 266.

28. Ibid.; "Passing of Michael."

29. John J. Donovan, "Crowd Watches the Racers," *Boston Globe*, May 14, 1900.

30. "Trouble with Spark Plugs," *Bicycling World*, May 8, 1902, p. 171, discussed problems of De Dion spark plugs.

31. Ibid.

32. Donovan, "Crowd Watches the Racers."

33. Ibid.

34. "Gen Wheeler's Speech: Hero of Two Conflicts Tells of the Glories and Benefits of Just and Successful War," *Boston Globe*, May 31, 1899.

35. The US Department of Veterans Affairs web site notes that Decoration Day was organized on May 5, 1868, by Union veterans of the Civil War to honor the graves of fallen warriors with flowers. "Memorial Day History," US Department of Veterans Affairs, http://www.va.gov.opa/speceven.memday.history.asp (accessed July 15, 2014).

36. "Massachusetts Men at Gettysburg: Record They Made during Those Three Days of Fearful Struggle When They Met and Measured Steel and Courage with the Flower and Chivalry of the Southland," *Boston Globe*, May 29, 1900.

37. Ibid.

38. "Big Bicycle Day: Waltham's Plans Going on an Elaborate Scale," *Boston Globe*, May 20, 1900, published block print art of Champion on his bicycle.

39. "Memorial Day Races Promise to Play Havoc with Records," *Boston Globe*, May 27, 1900, with art showing the motor-tandem called "Typhoon," carrying the driver, Charles Henshaw, and stoker, Oscar Hedstrom.

40. Ibid.

41. "MacEachern at Waltham," *Boston Globe*, May 29, 1900.

42. "McEachern Falls to His Death," *Bicycling World*, May 15, 1902.

43. Donovan, "Pacemakers Killed."

44. Ibid.

45. Ibid.

46. Ibid.

47. "Two Killed at Waltham: W. F. Stafford and H. E. Miles Run off the Track on Motor Tandem, Colliding with Pole," *Cycle Age and Trade Review*, May 31, 1900, p. 124.

48. Donovan, "Pacemakers Killed."

49. *Boston Directory: City Record, Directory of the Citizens, Business Directory* (Boston: Sampson, Murdock, 1901), cites US Census of Massachusetts, 1900, and lists Waltham's population at 23,431, p. 15.

50. Donovan, "Pacemakers Killed."

51. Ibid.

52. Ibid.

53. Ibid.

54. Ibid.

55. Ibid.

56. Ibid.

57. Ibid.

58. Ibid.

59. Ibid.

60. Ibid.

61. Ibid.

62. Ibid.

63. Ibid.

64. Ibid.

65. Ibid.

66. Ibid.

67. Ibid.

68. Ibid.

69. Ibid.

70. Ibid.

71. Ibid.

72. "The Last Star Event of the Racing Season," *Automobile*, November 7, 1903, p. 474.

73. Donovan, "Pacemakers Killed."

74. Ibid.

75. Ibid.

76. Ibid.

77. Ibid.

78. Ibid.

79. Ibid.

80. Ibid.

81. Ibid.

82. "'Fixed' the Motor: Tampering, Marks Thinks, Caused Waltham Tragedy: Tandem Out of Order," *Boston Post*, June 2, 1900.

83. "Two Killed at Waltham."

84. Donovan, "Pacemakers Killed."

85. "Death Race," *Boston Herald*, May 31, 1900.

86. John J. Donovan, "Nelson Shows the Way," *Boston Globe*, July 10, 1900.

87. "Pacemaker Tournier," *Boston Globe*, undated clip pasted into Champion's scrapbook.

88. Franklin B. Tucker, "C. H. Metz: Automotive Pioneer," *Antique Automobile* (Hershey, PA) (March-April 1967): 11.

89. Chris Sinsabaugh, *Who, Me? Forty Years of Automobile History* (Detroit: Arnold-Powers, 1945), p. 24.

90. Tucker, "C. H. Metz," p. 7.

91. O. L. Stevens, "Stabling Automobiles around Harvard," *Automobile Magazine* (New York), January 1901, p. 52.

92. Ibid.

93. Ibid.

94. Ibid.

95. Ibid.

96. Ibid.

97. Ibid.

98. Ibid., p. 53.

99. Ibid.

100. Ibid.

101. "Boston Saw the Start of Champion's Fortune," *Boston Globe*, October 28, 1927. The unsigned article remarked, "He was one of the first men in Massachusetts consistently arrested for speeding his motorcycle."

102. "Motor Notes," unidentified newspaper clip from Champion's scrapbook.

103. "John J. Donovan," *Boston Globe* obituary, May 28, 1950.

104. Ibid.

105. *Boston Directory*, p. 471.

106. "John J. Donovan."

107. Donovan, "Albert Champion Dies."

108. Ibid.

109. Ibid.

110. Ibid.

111. Ibid.

112. John J. Donovan, "Hurled to Earth: Albert Champion Badly Hurt at Readville," *Boston Globe*, unidentified date, from Champion's scrapbook.

113. Ibid.

114. Ibid.

115. Ibid.

116. John J. Donovan, "M. Champion Hurt in Road Accident: Tricycle Breaks While Traveling Speed in Road Accident and He Narrowly Escapes Death," *Boston Globe*, July 16, 1900.

117. Ibid.

118. Ibid.

119. "Albert Champion on His New Motor Cycle," caption to photo in the *Boston Post*, August 5, 1900, p. 7.

120. Ibid.

121. Ibid.

122. Ibid.

123. Ibid.

124. Jerry Hatfield, *American Racing Motorcycles* (Osceola, WI: Motorbooks International, 1989), p. 213.

CHAPTER 7. AMERICA'S FASTEST MAN ON WHEELS

1. John Maynard Keynes, *The General Theory of Employment, Interest, and Money* (New York: Harcourt, Brace and World, 1936), preface, p. viii.

2. "Results of the Events on the Track," *Motor Vehicle Review* (Chicago), September 27, 1900, p. 37; "News for Wheelmen," *Boston Globe*, September 19, 1900.

3. "Results of the Events on the Track"; "News for Wheelmen."

4. "Results of the Events on the Track."

5. "To Continue Auto Meet," *Chicago Daily News*, September 19, 1900.

6. John B. Rae, *The American Automobile, A Brief History* (Chicago: University of Chicago Press, 1965), p. 5.

7. "Michigan Street, Near Rush, Where Trucks Sink to Hubs in Mud," *Chicago Tribune*, September 1, 1900, p. 1.

8. Ibid.

9. Ibid.

10. Ibid.

11. Ibid.

12. "Lowers Ten-Mile Record: Fast Time at Opening Day of Automobile Races," *Chicago Tribune*, September 19, 1900.

13. Ibid.

14. "Mini-Historical Statistics," US Census Bureau, http://www.census.gov/statab/hist/HS-07.pdf (accessed April 12, 2014).

15. "Results of the Events on the Track."

16. Ibid., p. 38; "Best Racing Card of the Week," *Chicago Tribune*, September 22, 1900.

17. "Results of the Events on the Track."

18. Alexander Winton, Automotive Hall of Fame, Dearborn, Michigan, http://www

.automotivehalloffame.org/inductee/alexander-winton/704/ (accessed December 15, 2013). Winton was inducted in 2005.

19. Ibid.

20. Ibid.

21. Ibid.

22. The Cleveland Historical Team, "Winton Motor Carriage Co.," Cleveland Historical, http://clevelandhistorical.org/items/show/267 (accessed December 15, 2013).

23. Ibid.

24. Rae, *American Automobile, A Brief History*, p. 22; Sinsabaugh, *Who, Me?* pp. 54–55.

25. Rae, *American Automobile, A Brief History*, p. 22; Sinsabaugh, *Who, Me?* pp. 54–55.

26. John J. Donovan, "Albert Champion at Chicago Makes Fast Time: Frenchman Rides the Three-Wheeler One-Mile in 1m 19 1-5s: Also Breaks World's Records up to 50-Miles—Nervy Chauffeur On Horse Track Goes the Long-Hoped For 40 Miles in One Hour," *Boston Globe*, September 23, 1900.

27. Ibid.

28. Ibid.; "Lowers Ten-Mile Record: Fast Times at Opening Day of Automobile Races."

29. "Lowers Ten-Mile Record."

30. Ibid.

31. "Best Day of Auto Meet: Washington Park Track Now Dry Enough for Speed Trials," *Chicago Daily News*, September 20, 1900.

32. "Too Soft for Automobiles: Condition of Washington Park Track Postpones the Racing Card," *Chicago Tribune*, September 20, 1900.

33. Laura Hillenbrand, *Seabiscuit: An American Legend* (New York: Ballantine Books, 2002), p. 63, referring to analysis by George Pratt of the Massachusetts Institute of Technology to gauge the top speed of quarter horses.

34. "Best Day of Auto Meet."

35. Donovan, "Albert Champion at Chicago Makes Fast Time."

36. "Champion Beats Skinner," *Chicago Tribune*, September 21, 1900.

37. "Results of the Events on the Track."

38. Ibid.

39. Donovan, "Albert Champion at Chicago Makes Fast Time." The subhead included: "Also Breaks World's Records up to 50 miles—Nervy Chauffeur on Horse Track Goes the Long-Hoped-For 40 miles in One Hour."

40. Ibid.

41. Ibid.

42. Ibid.; "Automobile Record Broken," *Chicago Daily News*, September 22, 1900.

43. Donovan, "Albert Champion at Chicago Makes Fast Time." Donovan also reported that Champion won another $500 in a side bet with Kenneth A. Skinner.

44. "The Great St. Louis Fair: Fair Grounds To-Day," *St. Louis Globe-Democrat*, October 3, 1900.

45. "Big Thursday at the Fair: Close on to 100,000 People Entered the Gates Yesterday," *St. Louis Globe-Democrat*, October 5, 1900.

46. Ibid.

47. US Census Bureau, http://www.census.gov/population/estimates (accessed April 12, 2014).

48. "Big Thursday at the Fair."

49. Ibid.

50. Ibid.

51. "Fair Attendance Grows," *St. Louis Globe-Democrat*, October 4, 1900.

52. Sinsabaugh, *Who, Me?* p. 54.

53. US Census Bureau.

54. Sinsabaugh, *Who, Me?* p. 55.

55. Stacy Perman, *A Grand Complication: The Race to Build the World's Most Legendary Watch* (New York: Atria Books, 2013), p. 22.

56. Ibid., p. 38.

57. Sinsabaugh, *Who, Me?* p. 55.

58. Stephen B. Goddard, *Colonel Albert Pope and His American Dream Machines: The Life and Times of a Bicycle Tycoon* (Jefferson, NC: McCarland and Company, 2000), p. 179.

59. Ibid., p. 163.

60. Sinsabaugh, *Who, Me?* p. 56.

61. Rae, *American Automobile, A Brief History*, p. 13.

62. Goddard, *Colonel Albert Pope and His American Dream Machines*, p. 151.

63. Ted Case, *Power Plays: The U.S. Presidency, Electric Cooperatives, and the Transformation of Rural America* (Wilsonville, OR: Ted Case, 2013), p. ix, discusses President Franklin Delano Roosevelt on May 11, 1935, signing the executive order establishing the Rural Electrification Administration under the US Department of Labor that would bring electricity for the first time to 90 percent of US farms.

64. "Battery Facts," http://www.batteryfacts.co/uk/BatteryHistory/Edison.html (accessed February 15, 2014).

65. Rae, *American Automobile, A Brief History*, pp. 13–15.

66. "The Stanley Steamer, Why the Fascination?" http://www.stanleymotorcarriage.com/GeneralTechnical/Generalinfo.htm (accessed June 23, 2014).

67. Rae, *American Automobile, A Brief History*, p. 49.

68. Ibid. Between 1907 and 1910 the price of a gallon of gas jumped from around 9 cents a gallon to 17 cents.

69. Sinsabaugh, *Who Me?* p. 56; Alfred P. Sloan with Boyden Sparkes, *Adventures of a White-Collar Man* (New York: Doubleday, Doran, and Company, 1941), p. 42; photo of the track can be found at http://wcbsfm.cbslocal.com/photo-galleries/2013/07/31/10-famous-new-york-buildings-that-no-longer-exist/ (accessed January 5, 2014).

70. Sloan, *Adventures of a White-Collar Man*, p. 14.

71. Ibid., p. 41.

72. Ibid., p. 42.

73. Sinsabaugh, *Who Me?* p. 56.

74. Ibid., pp. 56–57.

75. Ibid.

76. Ibid.

77. Julie Husband and Jim O'Loughlin, *Daily Life in the United States, 1870–1900* (Westport, CN: Greenwood Press, 2004), p. 36.

78. "List of Defunct Automobile Manufacturers in the United States, *Wikipedia*, http://www.en.wikipedia.org/wiki/List_of_defunct_automobile_manufacturers_of_the_United_States (accessed April 12, 2014).

79. Charles Leerhsen, *Blood and Smoke: A True Tale of Mystery, Mayhem, and the Birth of the Indy 500* (New York: Simon and Schuster, 2011), p. 110.

80. L. Spencer Riggs, "Carl G. Fisher, Indiana's Best Kept Secret," *Automobile Quarterly*, May 1996, p. 68.

81. Rae, *American Automobile, A Brief History*, p. 17.

82. Sinsabaugh, *Who Me?* p. 39.

83. "1900: 8,000 Automobiles, 4 Billion Cigarettes," in *Chronicle of America: From Prehistory to Today* (New York: Dorling Kindersley, 1995), p. 529.

84. Ibid.

85. Birth certificate of Julie Elisa Delpuech, December 4, 1876, Archives de Paris, 18 Boulevard Sérurier, 75019 Paris, on microfilm #950 (accessed September 10, 2004). Also available at http://canadp-archivesenligne.paris.fr.

86. "Where Is Fournier Chauffeur?" clip in French from unidentified newspaper in Champion's scrapbook.

87. "An Expert on Falls: Albert Champion Tells of Many Falls, On Crutches Still from His Latest Experience," unidentified clip, possibly *New York Sun*, from Champion's scrapbook.

88. Ibid.

89. Ibid.

90. Ibid.

91. "Champion Makes New Mile Motor Record," unidentified clip from Champion's scrapbook.

92. Grantland Rice, "Cycle Kings to Settle Title," *Atlanta Journal*, September 16, 1903.

93. Personal interviews 1985–1987 with Alf Goullet and Freddie Spencer, who had competed on the professional US cycling circuit. Goullet participated between 1910 and 1925, and Spencer between 1920 and1936.

94. Rice, "Cycling Kings to Settle Title."

95. Reed Browning, *Cy Young: A Baseball Life* (Amherst: University of Massachusetts Press, 2003), p. 219.

96. Andrew Ritchie, *Major Taylor: The Extraordinary Career of a Champion* (Baltimore: Johns Hopkins University Press, 1996), pp. 159–160.

97. "A New Cycling Record: Albert Champion Rides a Mile in 1:29 4-5 and Defeated Taylor," *New York Times*, August 8, 1901.

98. "Racing Cyclist Injured: John Nelson's Leg Mangled in Race against 'Jimmy' Michael," *New York Times*, September 5, 1901.

99. Ibid.

100. "Cyclist Nelson's Racing Days Over," *New York Times*, September 8, 1901.

101. "Cyclist Nelson's Funeral To-Day," *New York Times*, September 11, 1901.

102. Pierre Chany, *La Fabuleuse Histoire du Cyclisme: Des Origines à 1955* (Paris: Nathan, 1988), p. 141.

103. "Dies Making Records: Harry Elkes Killed While Riding His Fastest Race on New Charles River Track," *Bicycling World*, June 6, 1903, p. 321.

104. "Harry Elkes Killed in Bicycle Race," *New York Times*, May 31, 1903.

105. Ibid.

106. 1920 US Census, City of Flint, MI, January 12, 1920. Elise reported that she immigrated in 1901.

107. Address listed on Marriage Registration, Cambridge City Hall, Cambridge, MA, October 31, 1902.

108. Thomas S. LaMarre, "One Piece at a Time: The Cars of C. H. Metz," *Automobile Quarterly*, January 1994, p. 6; Franklin B. Tucker, "C. H. Metz: Automotive Pioneer," *Antique Automobile* (March-April 1967): 13.

109. "Patrick T. Powers," *Wikipedia*, http://en.wikipedia.org/wiki/Patrick_T._Powers (accessed September 21, 2013).

110. Ibid.

111. "Joseph Pulitzer," *The New Encyclopedia Britannica* (London: 2005).

112. Ibid.

113. Ibid.

114. Ibid.

115. "Michael and His Mascot 'Trixy,'" *New York World*, December 7, 1901.

116. "Walthour Wins Six-Day Race by Scant Yard," *New York World*, December 15, 1901.

117. Ibid.

118. Ibid.

119. Ibid.

120. Ibid.

121. Ibid.

122. Ibid.

123. Ibid.

124. Ibid.

125. LaMarre, "One Piece at a Time," p. 6; Tucker, "C. H. Metz," p. 13.

126. LaMarre, "One Piece at a Time," p. 6; Tucker, "C. H. Metz," p. 13.

127. LaMarre, "One Piece at a Time," p. 6; Tucker, "C. H. Metz," p. 13.

128. "He Trained Here," *Washington Star*, June 9, 1902.

129. Ibid.

130. Ibid.

131. Ibid.

132. "Elkes' Return," *Boston Herald*, May 25, 1902.

133. "To Ride a Clément Is to Be Happy," Clément catalogue, 1904.

134. US Passport application of Basil De Guichard, May 16, 1924.

135. "Basil W. de Guichard, Former AC Head, Dies," *Flint Journal*, May 30, 1958.

136. Ibid.

137. US Passport application.

138. *Cycle Age and Trade Review*, advertisement, August 7, 1902.

139. "He Trained Here."

140. "Tonight's Big Race: Champion and Freeman Meet at Coliseum in Ten-Mile Event," *Washington Star*, June 11, 1902.

141. "He Trained Here."

142. Ibid.

143. Ibid.

144. Ibid.

145. "Racing," *Bicycling World*, July 24, 1902, p. 467.

146. "Racing," *Bicycling World*, August 28, 1902, p. 572.

147. "Racing," *Bicycling World*, September 11, 1902, p. 511.

148. Ibid.

149. Rice, "Cycle Kings to Settle Title"; W. A. Pritchard, "Albert Champion a Cycle Marvel: Wonderful Records Made by Manufacturer in His Younger Days Are Recalled," *New York Sun*, January 7, 1917.

150. Marriage Registration in Cambridge, MA, City Hall, October 31, 1902.

151. Ibid.

152. Ibid.

153. LaMarre, "One Piece at a Time," p. 6.

154. Tucker, "C. H. Metz," p. 14.

155. "The History of the AMA," website of the American Motorcyclist Association, http://www.americanmotorcyclist.com/about/history (accessed June 23, 2014).

156. "Automobile Topics of Interest," *New York Times*, May 24, 1903.

157. John J. Donovan, "Champion Rides a Mile in 58 4-5s: Wonderful Performance of the Frenchman at Charles River Track," *Boston Globe*, July 12, 1903, p. 1.

158. Ibid.

159. "Within the Fold: The Motor Was Brought to This Country from Paris by Albert Champion and Originally Cost $1,500," *Motorcycle Illustrated* (New York), September 1, 1908, p. 30.

160. Andrew M. Homan, *Life in the Slipstream: The Legend of Bobby Walthour Sr.* (Washington, DC: Potomac Books, 2011), p. 108.

161. Ibid.

162. Ibid.

163. "Automobile Topics of Interest."

164. Ibid.

165. Ibid.

166. Ibid.

167. Henry Ford Museum display, text from author visit, October 24, 2013, at the 1902 Ford "999" Race Car, Dearborn, MI. More information available at American Heritage, http://www.americanheritage.com/content/1902-Ford-999-race-car-built-henry-ford (accessed June 11, 2014)

168. William F. Nolan, *Barney Oldfield: The Life and Times of America's Legendary Speed King* (New York: G. P. Putnam's Sons, 1961), p. 51.

169. "Automobile Topics of Interest."

170. Amos G. Batchelder, "Motor Racing in America—At the Empire City Track," *New York Sun*, June 6, 1903; Nolan, *Barney Oldfield*, p. 51.

171. Rae, *American Automobile, A Brief History*, p. 46. By 1910 all US automakers had abandoned mounting the steering wheel on the left side to meet conditions of American driving.

172. Batchelder, "Motor Racing in America"; "World's Record Broken: Champion Does Mile on Motor Cycle in 1m. 4 1-5 s," *Boston Herald*, May 31, 1903.

173. Batchelder, "Motor Racing in America."

174. Ibid.

175. Ibid.; "World's Record Broken: Barney Oldfield of Toledo Makes a Mile in 1m 1 3-5s. at Yonkers, *Boston Herald*, May 31, 1903.

176. Batchelder, "Motor Racing in America."

177. Nolan, *Barney Oldfield*.

178. Ibid.

179. Ibid.

180. Ibid.

181. Ibid.

182. "World's Record Broken."

183. "The Auto Race Meet Proves a Big Success," *Boston Herald*, May 31, 1903.

184. "Harry Elkes Killed in Bicycle Race," p. 1.

185. John J. Donovan, "Harry Elkes Killed in Fearful Bicycle Mix-up," *Boston Globe*, May 31, 1903, p. 1.

186. Ibid.

187. Ibid.

188. Ibid.

189. Ibid.

190. Ibid.

191. Ibid.

192. Ibid.

193. Ibid.

194. Ibid.

195. Ibid.

196. Ibid.

197. Ibid.

198. Ibid.

199. Ibid.

200. "The Track Mile under a Minute: Barney Oldfield in Match Race at Indianapolis Meet Breaks 1 and 5-Mile Records, Making Mile in 59 3-5 Seconds," *Motor Age*, June 25, 1903, p. 6; "Marvelous Driving in Oldfield-Cooper Match Race in Indianapolis," *Automobile*, June 27, 1903, p. 663; Nolan, *Barney Oldfield*, p. 53.

201. Nolan, *Barney Oldfield*, p. 21.

202. Ibid.

203. Ibid., p. 24.

204. Ibid.

205. Ibid., p. 25.

206. Ibid.

207. Ibid.

208. Ibid.

209. Ibid.

210. Ibid., p. 30.

211. Ibid., p. 37.

212. "Death Comes to Tom Cooper in Auto Accident, *Detroit News*, November 20, 1906.

213. "Cooper Is the Phenomenon of '95," *Bicycling World* advertisement by Monarch Cycling Manufacturing Company, December 18, 1895, p. 899.

214. *Chicago Tribune* quote in a full-page Monarch ad, *Bicycling World*, October 30, 1896, p. 22.

215. William A. Brady, *Showman: My Life Story* (New York: E. P. Dutton and Company, 1937), p. 224.

216. "Death Comes to Tom Cooper in Auto Accident."

217. Ibid.

218. "Cycle Cracks Sail for Europe," *Brooklyn Eagle* (New York), July 25, 1900.

219. Nolan, *Barney Oldfield*, p. 37.

220. Ibid., p. 38.

221. Ibid.

222. Ibid.

223. Ibid., p. 39.

224. Ibid.

225. Ibid., p. 40.

226. Ibid.

227. "What the Boys are Doing Now," *Bicycling World*, November 17, 1906, p. 217.

228. Nolan, *Barney Oldfield*, p. 40.

229. Ibid.

230. Ibid., p. 41.

231. Ibid., p. 43.

232. Ibid.

233. Ibid.

234. Ibid., p. 44.

235. Ibid.

236. Ibid.

237. Ibid.

238. Ibid., p. 45.

239. Ibid., p. 46.

240. Ibid.

241. Ibid.

242. Ibid.

243. Ibid., p. 48.

244. Ibid.

245. Ibid.

246. Ibid.

247. Ibid., p. 49.

248. Ibid.

249. Ibid.

250. "Oldfield Won from Winton," *Cleveland Plain Dealer*, October 26, 1904, p. 4.

251. Ibid.

252. Nolan, *Barney Oldfield*, p. 49.

253. Ibid.

254. Ibid., p. 50.

255. Jerry M. Fisher, *The Pacesetter: The Untold Story of Carl G. Fisher, Creator of the Indy 500, Miami Beach, and the Lincoln Highway* (Fort Bragg, CA: Lost Coast Press, 1998), p. 18.

256. "Marvelous Driving in Oldfield-Cooper Match Race at Indianapolis," p. 663; "New Automobile Records: Barney Oldfield Figures from One to Five Miles on a Round Track," *New York Times*, June 21, 1903, p. 9.

257. "Marvelous Driving in Oldfield-Cooper Match Race at Indianapolis," p. 663; "New Automobile Records," p. 9.

258. Nolan, *Barney Oldfield*, p. 52.

259. Fisher, *Pacesetter*, p. 4; L. Spencer Riggs, "Carl G. Fisher, Indiana's Best Kept Secret," *Automobile Quarterly* (Kutztown, PA) (May 1996): 68.

260. Fisher, *Pacesetter*, p. 4.

261. Ibid., p. 8.

262. Ibid.

263. "Great Card for Auto Meet," *Indianapolis Star*, June 20, 1903.

264. "Track Mile under a Minute," p. 6.

265. Ibid.

266. "Marvelous Driving in Oldfield-Cooper Race at Indianapolis."

267. Ibid.; "Track Mile under a Minute"; "New Automobile Records"; "World's Records Cut," *Motor World*, June 25, 1903.

268. "Marvelous Driving in Oldfield-Cooper Race at Indianapolis."

269. Ibid.

270. Donovan, "Champion Rides a Mile in 58 4-5s."

271. "Piloting Motor Driven Races," *Motor*, December 1903, p. 18.

272. "Many Died in Fearful Heat," *Boston Globe*, July 12, 1903, p. 1.

273. Donovan, "Champion Rides a Mile in 58 4-5s."

274. Ibid.

275. Ibid.

276. "Walthour's Close Shave: Tried Champion's French Motor and Did Not Know How to Stop It," *Bicycling World*, July 18, 1903, p. 498.

277. Ibid.

278. Ibid.

279. Ibid.

280. Ibid.

281. Ibid.

282. Ibid.

283. Ibid.

284. Ibid.

285. Ibid.

286. John J. Donovan, "By 1-1/3 Laps: Champion Wins again from Walthour," *Boston Globe*, August 16, 1903; Grantland Rice, "Coliseum Is Fixed for Races Tonight," *Atlanta Journal*, September 15, 1903.

287. Donovan, "By 1-1/3 Laps."

288. "News for Wheelmen: Albert Champion Promises to Give Bobbie Walthour a Beating in Their Next Race," *Boston Globe*, May 5, 1902.

289. "New Automobile Records: Oldfield Makes World's Figures of 0:55 4-5 for mile," *New York Times*, July 26, 1903.

290. Ibid.

291. Ibid.

292. John J. Donovan, "Goes a Mile in 56s: Albert Champion Cuts His Record on a Motor Cycle," *Boston Globe*, September 4, 1903.

293. Ibid.

294. Ibid.

295. Ibid.

296. Ibid.

297. Ibid.

298. "Elkes Monument Erected: Now in Place at the Grave and Will be Dedicated June 19," *Bicycling World*, June 11, 1904, p. 347.

299. Ibid.

300. John J. Donovan, "Champion and Hurley: Stars at the Afternoon Meet," *Boston Globe*, September 7, 1903; "Cyclist Champion Won Long Race," *New York Times*, September 7, 1903.

301. John J. Donovan, "Champion Goes a Mile in 552/5S: Clips Three-Fifths of a Second off His Own Motorcycle Record at Charles River Park," *Boston Globe*, September 8, 1903.

302. Ibid.

303. Ibid.

304. Ibid.

305. "The 'Gray Wolf' Racer," *Automobile*, September 19, 1903, p. 293.

306. "How the Gray Wolf Came to Grief," *Automobile Topics Illustrated* (New York), November 7, 1903, p. 239.

307. Ibid.

CHAPTER 8. "NEARLY KILLED AT BRIGHTON!"

1. Griffith Borgeson, *The Golden Age of the American Racing Car*, 2nd ed. (Warrendale, PA, Society of Automotive Engineers, 1998), p. 3.

2. Andrew Homan, *Life in the Slipstream: The Legend of Bobby Walthour Sr.* (Washington, DC: Potomac Books, 2011), p. 115; "Crack Riders Race Tonight: Walthour and Champion to Decide Championship of World," *Atlanta Constitution*, September 17, 1903, notes that Walthour had won thirty-eight races.

3. Grantland Rice, "Walthour Is Back From Northern Tracks," *Atlanta Journal*, September 10, 1903.

4. "Bobby Won Best Race Seen Here: Walthour Had to Break Track Record to Beat Champion," *Atlanta Constitution*, September 18, 1903.

5. Russ Gatlin, "The Wooden Wonders," *Automobile Quarterly* (Kutztown, PA) (Spring 1971): 258.

6. Ibid.; Larry L. Ball Jr., "John Shillington 'Jack' Prince," National Sprint Car Hall of Fame and Museum induction, 2003, see http://www.sprintcarhof.com (accessed July 16, 2014). Prince (1859–1927) became legendary in the 1910s and 1920s when he multiplied his formula for constructing board tracks for bicycle races by a factor of ten to construct larger board auto-racing tracks, called "toothpick saucers."

7. "Prince's Coliseum Plans," *Cycle Age and Trade Review*, May 24, 1900, p. 100.

8. Ibid.

9. Gatlin, "Wooden Wonders"; Ball, "John Shillington 'Jack' Prince."

10. "Prince's Coliseum Plans."

11. Homan, *Life in the Slipstream*, p. 1.

12. "One by One, States Join Confederacy," *Chronicle of America: From Prehistory to Today* (New York: Dorling Kindersley, 1995), p. 364.

13. Homan, *Life in the Slipstream*.

14. Ibid., p. 2.

15. Ibid., p. 11.

16. Ibid., p. 13.

17. New Georgia Encyclopedia, http://www.georgiaencyclopedia.org (accessed October 14, 2013).

18. Grantland Rice, "Coliseum Is Fixed for Races Tonight," *Atlanta Journal*, September 15, 1903.

19. Grantland Rice, "Monroe Here Ready for Race," *Atlanta Journal*, September 11, 1903.

20. William A. Harper, *How You Played the Game: The Life of Grantland Rice* (Columbia: University of Missouri Press, 1999), p. 6.

21. Ibid., p. 122.

22. Ibid.

23. Homan, *Life in the Slipstream*, p. 87.

24. Ibid., p. 131.

25. Grantland Rice, "Riders Are Ready for Big Race Tonight," *Atlanta Journal*, September 14, 1903.

26. Grantland Rice, "Cycle Kings to Settle Title: Both Walthour and Champion Claim to Be Holders of Championship and Test Begins Tomorrow Night," *Atlanta Journal*, September 16, 1903.

27. Ibid.

28. Grantland Rice, "Champion Says He Did His Best," *Atlanta Journal*, September 18, 1903.

29. Ibid.

30. Ibid.

31. Ibid.

32. Ibid.

33. Ibid.

34. Ibid.

35. "Frenchman Beaten Two Straight Heats," *Atlanta Constitution*, September 18, 1903.

36. Beverly Rae Kimes, "Packard Gray Wolf," *Automobile Quarterly* (Kutztown, PA) (Third Quarter, 1981): 296.

37. William F. Nolan, *Barney Oldfield: The Life and Times of America's Legendary Speed King* (New York: G. P. Putnam's Sons, 1961), p. 56.

38. Kimes, "Packard Gray Wolf," *Automobile Quarterly*, p. 296.

39. Ibid.

40. Ibid.

41. Ibid.

42. Ibid.

43. Ibid.

44. Ibid., p. 303.

45. Ibid.

46. Evan P. Ide, *Packard Motor Car Company* (Charlestown, SC: Arcadia Publishing, 2003), p. 34.

47. Kimes, "Packard Gray Wolf," p. 299.

48. "How the Gray Wolf Came to Grief," *Automobile Topics Illustrated* (New York), November 7, 1903, p. 239.

49. "Surprises Develop at Detroit Races: Oldfield and 'Baby Bullet' Meet Their Equals in Cunningham" *Automobile*, September 12, 1903, p. 263.

50. "How the Gray Wolf Came to Grief."

51. Kimes, "Packard Gray Wolf," p. 300.

52. "How the Gray Wolf Came to Grief."

53. Ibid.

54. "Notes of Brighton Beach Race Meet," *Automobile*, November 7, 1903, p. 489.

55. "How the Gray Wolf Came to Grief."

56. Ibid.

57. Ibid.; "Serious Accident Mars Motor Races: Albert Champion Hurled from His Machine at Brighton Beach," *New York Times*, November 1, 1903.

58. "How the Gray Wolf Came to Grief."

59. "Notes of Brighton Beach Race Meet," p. 475.

60. Ibid., p. 474.

61. Ibid.

62. Ibid., p. 475.

63. "Serious Accident Mars Motor Races."

64. Ibid.

65. Ibid.

66. Ibid.

67. "Hurt in 'Auto' Race: Albert Champion Breaks Hip," *New York Tribune*, November 1, 1903.

68. Ibid.

69. "How the Gray Wolf Came to Grief."

70. "Serious Accident Mars Motor Races."

71. "Last Star Event of the Racing Season," *Automobile*, November 17, 1903, p. 474.

72. Ibid.; "Serious Accident Mars Motor Races"; "Hurt in 'Auto' Race."

73. "How the Gray Wolf Came to Grief."

74. "Serious Accident Mars Motor Races."

75. "Notes of Brighton Beach Race Meet," p. 489.

76. "Notes on the Sport," *Automobile*, November 7, 1903, p. 492.

77. "Track Racing Is Safe," *Automobile Topics Illustrated*, November 7, 1903, p. 255.

78. "Racing Autoist Nearly Killed at Brighton!" *New York World*, November 1, 1903, p. 1.

79. "Serious Accident Mars Motor Races."

80. "Champion Hurt," *Boston Globe*, November 1, 1903.

81. "Champion in Smash," *Boston Herald*, November 1, 1903.

82. Kimes, "Packard Gray Wolf," p. 302.

83. Interviews with Dr. W. Scott Schroth at the George Washington University Hospital, November 19, 2001, and Dr. Andrew Lovy, at A. T. Still University, April 4, 2013; e-mails in October 11, 2010 and August 28, 2012 with Dr. Bill Mallon, of Duke University Medical Center.

84. John J. Donovan, "Albert Champion Still Undaunted," *Boston Globe*, November 10, 1903.

85. "Notes," *Automobile*, December 14, 1903, p. 526.

86. "Albert Champion Still Undaunted."

87. Ibid.

88. "Notes."

89. Ibid.

90. Albert Champion, "Piloting Motor Driven Racers," *Motor* (New York), December 1903, p. 19.

91. Ibid.

92. "Albert Champion Still Undaunted."

93. Ibid.

94. Albert Champion, "All Kinds of Machines at the Automobile Show," *Boston Traveler*, January 19, 1904.

95. "Chauffeurs Tell of Thrilling Accidents and Narrow Escapes," *New York Sun*, undated in Champion's scrapbook, but likely from around January 19, 1904. Champion's reference to the "Great Reaper" rather than the traditional "grim reaper" reflects his grappling with English. The unsigned article could have been written by Amos Grant Batchelder, on the staff of the *New York Sun* as well as chairman and president of the US National Cycling Association, the governing body for American cycling, which issued his professional license. Batchelder went on to serve as editor of the American Automobile Association's flagship magazine and as a member of the AAA's executive committee. After his death in a plane crash, he was eulogized in the July 1921 *American Motorist* for his role among the foremost advocates working to bring the federal government into a national highway system. When President Woodrow Wilson signed the Federal Aid Road Act of 1916, establishing a national highway system, he presented his gold pen to Batchelder.

96. Ibid.

97. Ide, *Packard Motor Car Company*, pp. 47–49.

98. "Champion Will Be Racing Again," *Boston Globe*, undated, about February 1904, from Champion's scrapbook.

99. Ibid.

100. Pierre Chany, *La Fabuleuse Histoire du Cyclisme: Des Origines à 1955* (Paris: Nathan, 1988), p. 160; the Paris journalist signing his name as The Man in the Street, likely *L'Auto* journalist Charles Ravaud, in "Cycling Gossip," *La Pédale* (Paris), October 8, 1924, pp. 12–13, described Champion as "being handicapped by an extraordinarily short leg."

101. The Man in the Street, "Cycling Gossip."

102. Beverly Rae Kimes, "The Dawn of Speed," *American Heritage* (New York), November 1987, online at Vanderbilt Cup Races, http://www.vanderbiltcupraces.com (accessed September 27, 2012).

103. Ibid.

104. "Champion Will Race Again."

105. Chris Sinsabaugh, *Who, Me? Forty Years of Automobile History* (Detroit: Arnold-Powers, 1940), p. 55.

CHAPTER 9. NATIONAL CHAMPION OF FRANCE

1. Pierre Chany, *La Fabuleuse Histoire du Cyclisme: Des Origines à 1955* (Paris: Nathan, 1988), p. 160.

2. "Champion Is Back in Town," *Boston Globe*, May 5, 1904.

3. "In Collision Huret Is Hurt by Michael," *Atlanta Journal*, September 6, 1902.

4. Stephen B. Goddard, *Colonel Albert Pope and His American Dream Machines: The Life and Times of a Bicycle Tycoon Turned Automotive Pioneer* (Jefferson, NC: McFarland and Company, 2000), p. 51.

5. Ibid., p. 45.

6. John B. Rae, *The American Automobile: A Brief History* (Chicago: University of Chicago Press, 1965), p. 20; Roger J. Sherman, "The Decline of Pierce-Arrow in the 1920s," Table 1, Timeline of the Pierce-Arrow Company, in *Automotive History Review* (Maple Grove, MN: Society of Automotive Historians, 2004), p. 21.

7. "Champion May Retire," *Boston Globe*, June 2, 1904.

8. "American Auto Owners Will Enter Oldfield, Champion, and Others," Champion's scrapbook, unidentified newspaper.

9. Ibid.

10. Andrew M. Homan, *Life in the Slipstream: The Legend of Bobby Walthour Sr.* (Washington, DC: Potomac Books, 2011), p. 139.

11. "The French Championships," *Cycling Weekly* (London), September 28, 1904, p. 272.

12. "Champion May Retire."

13. Ibid.

14. "Automobile Races at Readville," *Boston Herald*, June 5, 1904.

15. Adolphe Clément's Légion d'Honneur file, archived at the Centre Historique Archives de Paris, Ref: L0549039, http://www.culture.gouv.fr/documentation/leonore/pres.htm (accessed March 3, 2006).

16. Frank A. Munsey, "The Automobile in America," *Automobile*, February 1, 1906, p. 313, from an article appearing in *Munsey*, January 1906.

17. Ibid.

18. Rae, *American Automobile*, p. 23.

19. Ibid.

20. Ibid.

21. Ibid.

22. US Census, http://www.census.gov (accessed April 12, 2014).

23. "Bob Dunbar's Sporting Chat," *Boston Journal*, May 4, 1904.

24. "Henry Contenet," Gazzetta, http://www.cycling4fans.de/index.php?id=2298&no_cache=1&sword_list[]=contenet (accessed February 6, 2006).

25. Harry Van Den Brent and Rene Jacobs, *Velo Plus, Het Nieublad Sportwereld* (Gent, Belgium, 1987), p. 189-E, lists Marius Thé as winner of the 1897 national classic race from Marseille to Nice, 125 miles.

26. F. Mercier, "The Return of Champion," *L'Auto*, July 1, 1904; "Champion again in France," *Bicycling World*, July 23, 1904.

27. Mercier, "The Return of Champion."

28. John J. Donovan, "Victory of Albert Champion," *Boston Globe*, June 6, 1904.

29. Ibid.

30. A. G. Batchelder, "Victory of Champion," *New York Sun*, June 9, 1904.

31. "Moran's Winning Streak," *Bicycling World*, June 11, 1904, p. 353.

32. "Champion Will Return to France," *Washington Post*, June 19, 1904; "Albert Champion Going Home," *Bicycling World*, May 28, 1904, p. 298.

33. "Leander Killed on Track: Six Day Winner Meets His Fate While Following Pace in Paris," *Bicycling World*, August 22, 1904.

34. John J. Donovan, quoted in Andrew Homan, "The Windy City Fat Boy," *Road Bike Action* (Valencia, CA) (January 2010): 102–106.

35. "Six-Day Bicycle Race Ended in a Riot," *Boston Evening Transcript*, January 6, 1902.

36. Victor Breyer, "Return from America," *La Vie au Grand Air* (Paris), July 14, 1904, p. 544.

37. Homan, *Life in the Slipstream*, p. 135.

38. Ibid., p. 129.

39. Ibid., p. 135.

40. Ibid.

41. "Champion Hurt in Fast Race: Injury Was Received While Slowing up after Race," *Atlanta Constitution*, June 16, 1904.

42. "Cycling Notes of Interest," *New York Times*, June 30, 1904.

43. Mercier, "Return of Champion."

44. Serge Laget, "How the Tour Was Born," foreword to *The Official Tour de France Centennial 1903–2003* (London: Weidenfeld and Nicolson, 2004); Chany, *La Fabuleuse Histoire du Cycling*, pp. 167–75.

45. Laget, "How the Tour Was Born"; Chany, *La Fabuleuse Histoire du Cycling.*

46. Laget, "How the Tour Was Born"; Chany, *La Fabuleuse Histoire du Cycling.*

47. Henri Desgrange, "Death of Clément-Bayard," *L'Auto*, May 11, 1928, p. 1.

48. Laget, "How the Tour was Born"; Chany, *La Fabuleuse Histoire du Cycling.*

49. Laget, "How the Tour was Born"; Chany, *La Fabuleuse Histoire du Cycling.*

50. Mercier, "Return of Champion."

51. Chany, La Fabuleuse Histoire du Cycling, p. 170.

52. Géorge Lefèvre, "Champion against Contenet," *L'Auto*, July 10, 1904.

53. Victor Breyer, "Retour d'Amérique: Un Revenant," *La Vie Au Grand Air*, July 14, 1904, p. 544.

54. Desgrange, "Death of Clément-Bayard."

55. Légion d'Honneur file.

56. Ibid.

57. Ibid.

58. Mercier, "Return of Champion."

59. Chany, *La Fabuleuse Histoire du Cycling*, p. 160.

60. Photo, Champion's scrapbook.

61. Lefèvre, "Champion against Contenet."

62. Chany, *La Fabuleuse Histoire du Cycling.*

63. Laget, "How the Tour was Born."

64. "Henry Contenet."

65. Homan, *Life in the Slipstream*, p. 130; "Une Belle Reunion," *Le Vélo*, March 21, 1904.

66. Lefèvre, "Champion against Contenet."

67. Charles Ravaud, "The Return of Champion," *Le Vélo*, July 10, 1904; Géorge Lefèvre, "Beautiful Return of Champion," *L'Auto*, July 11, 1904.

68. Franz Hoffmann, "The Art of Pacemaking," *Cycling Weekly* (London), November 16, 1904, p. 408. Hoffmann explained: "On the Continent pacemakers generally start about 200 meters behind the riders, and at the first explosion of the motors the pistol is fired for the start of the riders."

69. Lefèvre, "Champion against Contenet."

70. Ibid.

71. Ibid.

72. Charles Ravaud, "Triumphal Return of Champion," *Le Vélo*, July 11, 1904.

73. Ibid.

74. Lefèvre, "Champion against Contenet."

75. *Bicycling World*, August 22, 1904, p. 632.

76. Photo on the cover of *La Vie Au Grand Air*, "Au Vélodrome Buffalo—La Rentrée de Champion," July 14, 1904.

77. "Legs of Champions," *La Vie Au Grand Air*, July 28, 1904, pp. 840–41.

78. Victor Lefèvre, "Michael-Simar against Leander," *L'Auto*, July 17, 1904.

79. Victor Lefèvre, "Poor Champion!" *L'Auto*, July 17, 1904.

80. Ibid.

81. Ibid.

82. "Champion Is Better," unsigned two-paragraph article, *L'Auto*, July 21, 1904.

83. Ibid.

84. "The French Championships: Chat with Champion," *Cycling Weekly* (London), September 28, 1904, p. 272.

85. Edouard de Perrodil, *Albert Champion: His Triumphs, His Adventures, His Voyage to the United States* (Paris: *L'Auto*) sold for thirty centiemes, July 29, 1904.

86. "Paris-Milan (1489 kilomètres): Par M. de Perrodil, Sur Une Bicyclette Acatène-Métropole," *Vélocipede Illustraté*, April 25, 1895.

87. Géorge Lefèvre, "This evening at the Buffalo: The Series of the Grand Prix of Summer—Guignard and Simar against Champion for 50 kilometers," *L'Auto*, July 28, 1904.

88. Géorge Lefèvre, "Champion All Alone," *L'Auto*, July 29, 1904.

89. Ravaud, "Return of Champion."

90. Charles Ravaud, "Course of 90 Kilometers," *Le Vélo*, August 8, 1904.

91. Géorge Lefèvre, "The Championships of France: 100 Kilometers and Pure Sprinters," *L'Auto*, September 18, 1904.

92. "The Defeat of Champion by Leander," *L'Auto*, August 1, 1904.

93. Ibid.

94. Ravaud, "Course of 90 Kilometers."

95. "Motorcycle Racing in the Early Days," *Baltimore Sun*, January 16, 1916.

96. Géorge Lefèvre, "An Emotional Course: Victory by Leander, Superb Effort by Bruni and Champion," *L'Auto*, August 8, 1904.

97. Franz Reichel, "The Moral Winner Is Champion," *La Vie Illustrée*, August 12, 1904, p. 319.

98. Lefèvre, "An Emotional Course."

99. Homan, *Life in the Slipstream*, p. 142.

100. "Leander Killed on Track."

101. Walter Rutt, unpublished memoir in a collection by Sammlung Wolfgang Gronen, *Zentralbibliothek der Sportwissenschaften der Deutschen Sporthochschule Köln*, no. 15, Cologne, Germany, translated by Renate Franz.

102. Ibid.

103. Ibid.

104. "Cyclisme: Victoire de Lawson a Berlin," unattributed article in French newspaper, possibly *Le Vélo*, from the scrapbook of Iver Lawson, winner of the Berlin Grand Prix sprint event on August 21, 1904, when Champion rode in the motorpace event. Lawson, a Swede, had immigrated to the United States in the mid-1890s and lived in Chicago. Lawson's scrapbook is in a collection at the US Bicycling Hall of Fame, 303 3rd St., Davis, CA 95616.

105. Franz Hoffmann, "Hoffman Discusses Tragic End of Harry Elkes and Jimmie Michael," *Atlanta Journal*, April 10, 1904. Hoffman relates that he was Michael's driver for two years in France and Germany, and the last time he paced Michael was at the Friedenau Sportpark in Berlin when Michael's front tire blew out and Michael fell. One of the other motors struck Michael in the face, tearing flesh open from his mouth to ear and giving him a concussion. He was not expected to live, but after six months in the hospital he walked out. However, Hoffmann said Michael was never the same and suffered memory loss and headaches. Six months after Hoffmann's visit to Atlanta and his article in the *Journal*, Michael died.

106. "Cyclisme: Victoire de Lawson a Berlin."

107. Homan, *Life in the Slipstream*, p. 142; "Leander Killed on Track."

108. Homan, *Life in the Slipstream*, p. 143.

109. Homan, "Windy City Fat Boy,"

110. Géorge Lefèvre, "Two True Champions of France," *L'Auto*, September 19, 1904, shows line art of Champion wearing a helmet on the start line of the national middle-distance championship; Victor Breyer, "The Champions of France 1904," *La Vie Au Grand Air*, September 23, 1904, p. 772, shows close-up photo of Champion on his aero bike at the national championship start line, wearing a leather helmet.

111. "The Union Vélocipedique de France in Selecting Their Representatives for the London World's Championships Rejected the Demands of Albert Champion," *Bicycling World*, August 22, 1904, p. 632.

112. Charles Ravaud, "The Grand Course of 50 Kilometers Is a Brilliant Win by Champion," *Le Vélo*, Champion's scrapbook.

113. "Lawson off for Paris," *Bicycling World*, June 11, 1904, p. 352.

114. Ravaud, "Grand Course of 50 Kilometers Is a Brilliant Win by Champion."

115. Lefèvre, "Championships of France: 100 Kilometers and Pure Sprinters," includes a list of winners from 1885 along with their times in a sidebar titled "The Preceding Champions of the Distance."

116. Ibid.

117. Ibid.

118. Ibid.

119. Jack Rennert, *Prima Posters* (New York: Poster Auctions International, 1994), vol. 14, text for a Georges A. Bottini poster of Cycles Médinger, 1897, poster no. 18.

120. Joan DeJean, *The Essence of Style: How the French Invented High Fashion, Fine Food, Chic Cafés, Style, Sophistication, and Glamour* (New York: Free Press, 2005), p. 7.

121. Ibid., p. 91.

122. Lefèvre, "Two True Champions of France."

123. Ernest Mousset, "Cyclisme: World Championships and the Championship of France," *Paris-Sportif Illustré*, undated, p. 281.

124. Ibid.

125. Breyer, "Champions of France 1904," p. 772.

126. Ibid.

127. F. Mercier, "Each Has His Chance," *L'Auto*, September 1, 1904.

128. Lefèvre, "Championships of France." Bouhours had won the middle-distance championship in 1897 and 1898 with human tandem pacing and in 1900 pacing behind a motor-tandem. In 1900, he was the first to win the title over one hundred kilometers in under two hours, finishing in 1 hour 38 minutes 20 seconds. See http://www.cycling4fans.de/index.php?id=2303 (accessed January 29, 2004). Pascal Sergent, "Bouhours Demonstration," *A Century of Paris-Roubaix, 1896–1996* (Eeklo, Belgium: De Eecloonaar, 1997).

129. "Paul Guignard," Gazzetta, http://www.gazzetta.cycling4fans.com/index.php?id=2434 (accessed February 6, 2006).

130. In Lefèvre, "Championships of France," a paragraph on Bruni described him as often racing with irregular results.

131. Ibid.; "Louis Darragon," Gazzetta, http://www.gazzetta.cycling4fans.com/index.php?id=2442 (accessed August 15, 2013).

132. "Charles Albert Brécy," Gazzetta, http://www.gazzetta.cycling4fans.com/index.php?id=2116 (accessed August 15, 2013).

133. Lefèvre, "Two True Champions of France."

134. Ibid.

135. Ibid.

136. Harry Van Den Bremt and Rene Jacobs, *Velo Plus, Het Nieuwsblad* (Gent, Belgium, 1987), list of world championship motorpace results, p. M-260.

137. Lefèvre, "Two True Champions of France"; Mousset, "Cyclisme: World Champions and Champions of France," p. 281; Charles Ravaud, "The Champions of France: Friol and Champion Succeed de Thau and de Contenet," *Le Vélo*, September 19, 1904, p. 1.

138. Lefèvre, "Two True Champions of France"; Mousset, "Cyclisme: World Champions

and Champions of France," p. 281; Charles Ravaud, "The Champions of France: Friol and Champion Succeed de Thau and de Contenet," *Le Vélo*, September 19, 1904, p. 1.

139. Lefèvre, "Two True Champions of France."

140. Ibid.

141. Ibid.

142. Ravaud, "Champions of France."

143. Breyer, "Champions of France 1904."

144. "The French Championships Chat with Champion."

145. A Man in the Street, "Cycling Gossip," *La Pédale* (Paris), October 8, 1924, p. 13; Chany, *La Fabuleuse Histoire du Cyclisme*, p. 160.

146. A Man in the Street, "Cycling Gossip."

147. Ibid.

148. Ibid.

149. "Champion Triomphe à Dresde," *Cyclisme*, possibly from *Paris-Sportif Illustré*, in Champion's scrapbook.

150. Hoffmann, "Art of Pacemaking."

151. Ibid.

152. Laget, "How the Tour was Born."

153. Norman Beasley, "Albert Champion: The Office Boy Who Was Taught That a Race Is Won before the Race and There Is No Such Thing as 'Good Enough,'" *MoTor*, September 1926, and reprinted as "Biography of Albert Champion, President, AC Spark Plug Company, Flint, Michigan."

CHAPTER 10. DEBUT OF CHAMPION SPARK PLUGS

Three labors of love provided invaluable information. Background on the Stranahan family comes from a 2004 monograph, *An American Chronicle: The Stranahan Chronicles*, by Ann Stranahan of Perryville, Ohio, for family members to learn about their ancestry in America since 1818. Material was culled from boxes of letters and photos. A similar family effort on French pioneer aviator Edouard Nieuport is *Nieuport: A Biography of Edouard Nieuport* by grandsons Gérard and Bertrand Pommier (Atglen, PA: Shiffer Publishing, 2002). Howard Kroplick, a research volunteer at the Suffolk County Vanderbilt Museum on Long Island, published *Vanderbilt Cup Races of Long Island* (Charleston, SC: Arcadia Publishing, 2008), to preserve the memory of America's early automobile road races, from 1904 through 1910, on Long Island. Howard also maintains an informative website devoted to each of the seven Vanderbilt Cup races at http://www.vanderbiltcupraces.com (accessed February 15, 2014).

1. Gus Edwards and Vincent P. Bryan, "In My Merry Oldsmobile," 1905, *Wikipedia*, http://en.wikipedia.org/wiki/In_My_Merry_Oldsmobile (accessed November 3, 2013).

2. Norman Beasley, "Albert Champion: The Office Boy Who Was Taught That a Race Is Won before the Race and There Is No Such Thing As 'Good Enough,'" *MoTor*, September 1926, and reprinted as "Biography of Albert Champion, President, AC Spark Plug Company, Flint, Michigan";

Richard P. Scharchburg, "Albert Champion," *Encyclopedia of American Business History and Biography: The Automobile Industry, 1896–1920* (New York: Broccoli Clark Layman, 1990), p. 79.

3.   "Passing of Michael: Most Famous of Little Men Dies in Mid-Ocean," *Bicycling World*, November 20, 1904, p. 201. Michael's grave in Green Wood Cemetery in Brooklyn remained neglected and unmarked for decades. In the late 1940s, Charles (Mile a Minute) Murphy, who had raced Michael, found the grave overgrown with weeds. Murphy had retired from a career as a New York cop and had made his way around in a wheelchair after amputation of a leg from a motorcycle accident in the line of duty. He and some twenty surviving pros from the 1890s had formed the Bicycle Racing Stars of the Nineteenth Century. With financial support from Chicago bicycle manufacturer Frank Schwinn, they purchased a gravestone of polished granite and perpetual care. On June 13, 1949, a memorial service with Murphy and some twenty surviving pros dedicated the headstone and bronze tablet to Michael's memory.

4.   Pierre Chany, *La Fabuleuse Histoire du Cyclisme: Des Origines à 1955* (Paris: Nathan, 1988), pp. 142–43.

5.   Ibid., p. 141.

6.   Ibid.

7.   Gérard and Bertrand Pommier, *Nieuport: A Biography of Edouard Nieuport* (Atglen, PA: Shifter Publishing, 2002), p. 31.

8.   Ibid., p. 31.

9.   "Champion, the Boy Champion," *Bearings*, February 11, 1897, p. 106.

10.   Champion advertised Nieuport's accessories every week in *Automobile*, beginning July 6, 1905, p. 41, and continuing in a steady stream for the next four years.

11.   Gérard and Bertrand Pommier, *Nieuport* , p. 18.

12.   Ibid.

13.   Ibid.

14.   Ibid.

15.   Ibid., p. 30.

16.   Ibid.

17.   Arthur Pound, *The Turning Wheel: The Story of General Motors through Twenty-Five Years, 1908–1933* (Garden City, NY: Doubleday, Doran and Company, 1934), p. 456, reprinted in 2012 by Forgotten Books.

18.   Gérard and Bertrand Pommier, *Nieuport*, p. 31.

19.   Joan DeJean, *The Essence of Style: How the French Invented High Fashion, Fine Food, Chic Cafés, Style, Sophistication, and Glamour* (New York: Free Press, 2005), p. 113.

20.   Gérard and Bertrand Pommier, *Nieuport*, pp. 21–22.

21.   Ibid.

22.   Chany, *La Fabuleuse Histoire du Cyclisme*, p. 142.

23.   "Improvements at the Savoy," *Boston Herald*, October 9, 1898; Stranahan, *American Chronicle*, p. 14.

24.   "Boston's Show History: Automobiles Were Exhibited in Mechanics Building in 1898: Automobiles Were Exhibited in 1898," *Automobile*, March 8, 1906, p. 475.

25. "Boston Will Have a Great Show," *Automobile*, March 8, 1906, cover story.

26. Ibid., p. 476.

27. Ibid.

28. "Robt. A. Stranahan Dead: Last Summons for Popular Hotel Proprietor," *Boston Globe*, August 10, 1898; "Obituary: Robert A. Stranahan," *Boston Journal*, August 11, 1898; "Obituary: Robert A. Stranahan," *Boston Daily Advertiser*, August 11, 1898.

29. "Robt. A. Stranahan Dead: Last Summons for Popular Hotel Proprietor," *Boston Globe*, August 10, 1898; "Obituary: Robert A. Stranahan," *Boston Journal*, August 11, 1898; "Obituary: Robert A. Stranahan," *Boston Daily Advertiser*, August 11, 1898.

30. "Robt. A. Stranahan Dead: Last Summons for Popular Hotel Proprietor," *Boston Globe*, August 10, 1898; "Obituary: Robert A. Stranahan," *Boston Journal*, August 11, 1898; "Obituary: Robert A. Stranahan," *Boston Daily Advertiser*, August 11, 1898.

31. "Improvements at the Savoy."

32. Ibid.

33. Stranahan, *American Chronicle*, p. 5.

34. Stephen Stranahan, grandson of Frank D. Stranahan, e-mail August 6, 2004.

35. "Boston Museum: Two Weeks Only, The Augustin Daily Musical Co.," advertisement, *Boston Globe*, May 5, 1902.

36. "At the Plays," *Philadelphia Inquirer*, interview with Marie Celeste by a reporter using the name, The Call Boy, April 6, 1902. The Call Boy noted her struggles to get on stage "will prove interesting to my readers, especially that small army of girls and youths," since the interview was about what it took to get a chance to shine behind the footlights.

37. Stephen Stranahan, e-mail, November 13, 2013.

38. Call Boy, "At the Plays."

39. "An Engagement Announced," *Boston Globe*, June 1, 1902.

40. "Stranahan-Martin: Well-Known Hotel Proprietor Weds Actress at Church of Our Savior in Brookline," *Boston Globe*, June 3, 1902; "Miss Celeste Married: Prominent Light Opera Soubrette Now the Wife of Frank D. Stranahan, and Will Live in Brookline," *Boston Journal*, June 3, 1902.

41. *Boston Center for the Arts: An Architectural History* (Boston: Boston Center for the Arts, 1995). The Boston Center for the Arts has its headquarters today in the building at 539 Tremont Street, Boston, MA 02116. Other sources for details about the Cyclorama Building are Robert Campbell and Peter Vanderwarker, *Cityscapes of Boston: An American City through Time* (Boston: Houghton-Mifflin, 1992), p. 191; Jane Holtz Kay, *Lost Boston* (Boston: Houghton-Mifflin, 1980), pp. 204–205. Philip Kennicott, "Coming Full Circle: Gettysburg Cyclorama Is Painstakingly Restored to Its Original Pageantry," *Washington Post*, September 20, 2008, describes the $15 million restoration effort to restore Philippoteaux's original painting. It is on permanent display at the Gettysburg, Pennsylvania, cyclorama, maintained by the National Parks Service. A video tour and panoramic views of the Gettysburg Cyclorama are available on the *Washington Post* website at http://www.washingtonpost.com/museums (accessed September 20, 2008).

42. City of Boston Tax Receipts, Assessors' Plan No. 6, Block No. 4, Back Bay District, Section No. 4, 1906, p. 1.

43. Ibid.

44. "Automobile Legislation: Various Bills Are Certain to Be Presented at Five New England Capitols This Year," *Boston Globe*, January 1, 1905. The article includes a photo of Stranahan at the wheel of the Buick tonneau and three companions. "Buick Car," *Boston Globe*, March 12, 1905, describes Stranahan's demonstration model.

45. "Automobile Legislation."

46. Ibid.; "Eagle Rock Hill Climb: Overall History," provided by the West Orange History website, http://www.westorangehistory.com/eagle_rock_hill_climb.htm (accessed November 12, 2013).

47. "Automobile Legislation."

48. City of Boston Tax Receipts, 1906.

49. Ibid.

50. "Introduced Wife, Surprised Mother: Spencer U. Stranahan, Brookline, and His Bride Marry without Publicity," *Boston Herald*, May 31, 1907.

51. Prince High School 1898 Yearbook, Diplomas of Graduation, p. 259.

52. Ibid.

53. Frank A. Munsey, "The Automobile in America," *Automobile*, February 1, 1906, p. 313; "American Leads in Numerical Value," *Automobile*, February 14, 1907, p. 352.

54. "More than 3,200 Autos Registered in Massachusetts," *Automobile*, December 19, 1905, p. 642.

55. Massachusetts incorporation record, on the state's secretary general's website, at http://www.sec.state.ma.us/corpWeb/CardSearch.aspx (accessed September 15, 2013); "Recent Incorporations," *Automobile*, June 29, 1905, p. 796.

56. Stephen Stranahan supplied copies of stock certificates, including one with Frank D. Stranahan as owner of fifty-one shares.

57. *Automobile*, July 6, 1905, p. 41, classified ads, twenty-four to a page, including the Albert Champion Company.

58. Howard Kroplick, *Vanderbilt Cup Races of Long Island* (Charleston, SC: Arcadia Publishing, 2008), p. 45.

59. Ibid.

60. Ibid., p. 8. The Vanderbilt Cup is at the Smithsonian Institution's American History Museum in Washington, DC.

61. Ibid.

62. Ibid., p. 9.

63. Ibid., p. 55.

64. Ibid., p. 22. Nassau County supervisors approved the use of public roads for the auto race as an opportunity for businesses to take advantage of free-spending visitors, although many farmers relied on horses for transportation and regarded motorcars as playthings for the rich.

65. Ibid., p. 47. Albert Campbell's Mercedes became the only Vanderbilt Cup racecar without a number.

66. "Mercedes X (1905)," Vanderbilt Cup Races, http://www.vanderbiltcupraces.com/cars/car/Mercedes_x_1905 (accessed February 15, 2014).

67. Kroplick, *Vanderbilt Cup Races of Long Island*, p. 50.

68. Ibid., p. 46.

69. Ibid., p. 56.

70. Ibid., p. 55.

71. "Albert Champion, Bicycle Rider, and His Spouse Have Trouble," *New York World*, January 2, 1906; the same article and headline ran January 14, 1905, in the *Salt Lake Herald* (Utah). Olta de Kernan's address was listed at 260 West 25th Street in New York.

72. "Albert Champion, Bicycle Rider, and His Spouse Have Trouble."

73. "La Touraine Met Gales: Stormy Time also Awaited Albert Champion, Bicycle Rider, When He Landed on the Deck," *Brooklyn Eagle*, January 2, 1906. The newspaper had misspelled *La Loraine*.

74. Ibid.; "'Villain!' Wife's Greeting to Albert Champion as He Steps off Steamer," *Boston Herald*, January 4, 1906.

75. "Albert Champion, Bicycle Rider, and His Spouse Have Trouble"; "'Villain!' Wife's Greeting to Albert Champion as He Steps off Steamer."

76. "Albert Champion, Bicycle Rider, and His Spouse Have Trouble"; "'Villain!' Wife's Greeting to Albert Champion as He Steps off Steamer."

77. "Albert Champion, Bicycle Rider, and His Spouse Have Trouble."

78. "'Villain!' Wife's Greeting to Albert Champion as he Steps off Steamer."

79. "Albert Champion, Bicycle Rider, and His Spouse Have Trouble."

80. Stewart Harris, "Have You Seen the *Globe* Today? A History of the Boston Newspaper," class paper at Boston University, 1981, p. 18.

81. Stephen Stranahan, e-mails January 8, 2014, and January 10, 2014.

82. Champion launched a steady stream of weekly ads in the *Automobile*, listing the Albert Champion Company, Importers. They touted Nieuport's patented spark plugs, spark coils, ignition wires, and magnetos. The ads continued for the next few years. In 1905 and 1906 most Albert Champion Company ads were among the twenty-four to a page alongside the ads of other competitors, including Constant Spark Plugs, Alpha Spark Plug, and S-M Spark Plug.

83. Gérard and Bertrand Pommier, *Nieuport*, p. 31.

84. Ship passenger list of Prosper Champion and Gabriel Delpuech's arrival on *La Bretagne*, sailing from Le Havre, France, to New York, August 4, 1906, destined to join Albert and Elise Champion, living in Magnolia, MA. Prosper lists his previous address as Levallois-Perret.

85. Ibid.

86. Ibid.

87. "Albert Champion, Head of AC, Dies in Paris Hotel," *Flint Journal*, October 28, 1927.

88. Beasley, "Albert Champion."

89. Ibid.

90. "Champion's Death Blow to Associates: Alfred P. Sloan's Tribute," *Motor Age*, November 10, 1927.

91. Beasley, "Albert Champion."

92. Ship passenger list.

93. Ibid.

94. *Automobile*, November 8, 1906, p. 66.

95. Ibid.

96. "Concerning Spark Coils: Just How They Are Made and How They Perform Their Functions," *Bicycling World*, May 28, 1904, p. 299.

97. *Automobile*, May 2, 1907.

98. Ibid.

99. *Automobile*, May 9, 1907, p. 62.

100. *Automobile*, May 16, 1907, p. 84.

101. "AC Pioneer Is Dead: H. Albert Schmidt Was a Founder," *Flint Journal*, November 13, 1942.

102. Ibid.

103. Half-page ad in *Automobile*, February 6, 1908, p. 96.

104. *Automobile*, November 7, 1907, p. 69.

CHAPTER 11. THE NAME GAME

1. F. Scott Fitzgerald, *The Great Gatsby* (New York: Scribner, 2004), p. 135.

2. Robert Allen Stranahan II, *Harvard Class of 1908, Quidecennial Report*, 1923, p. 514.

3. Ibid.

4. Robert Allen Stranahan, *Harvard Class of 1908, Anniversary Reports, Second Class Report*, 1914, p. 297.

5. Ann Stranahan, e-mail recollection of her in-law Robert and his older brother, Frank, July 13, 2004; great-nephew Stephen Stranahan, e-mail, February 9, 2005.

6. Beverly Rae Kimes, *Standard Catalogue of American Cars, 1805–1942* (Detroit: 1979), p. 1359. On October 5, 1906, five hundred shares of $100 each were issued for the Tremont Garage Company. Frank D. Stranahan received Stock Certificate No. 1 for 54 shares and Certificate No. 3 for 220 shares, totaling 274 shares at $100 each, valued at $27,400. Copies of the stock certificates supplied November 19, 2001, by Stephen Stranahan, grandson of Frank D. Stranahan. Thus Frank D. Stranahan held majority ownership.

7. Measuring Worth, http://www.measuringworth.com/ppowerus (accessed December 15, 2013).

8. Arthur Pound, *The Turning Wheel: The Story of General Motors through Twenty-Five Years, 1908–1933* (New York: Doubleday, Doran and Company, 1934), p. 88.

9. Mark Dill, "Prest-O-Lite History," The First Super Speedway, http://www.first superspeedway.com/articles/prest-o-lite (accessed December 5, 2013).

10. Prest-O-Lite full-page ad in *Automobile*, August 1, 1907, p. 104.

11. Ibid.

12. "News and Trade Miscellany," *Automobile*, October 18, 1906, p. 524.

13. "News and Trade Miscellany," *Automobile*, December 27, 1906, p. 937.

14. *Automobile*, half-page ad, November 7, 1907, p. 69. The ad includes art of a Champion spark plug and a magneto sold through the Albert Champion Company at 36 Whittier Street, Boston. The Whittier Street address continues in all the company's ads through 1908, when Champion left the company and moved to Flint, MI.

15. "Champion Overestimates Self: Defeat by MacLean Marks His Return to the Track," *Bicycling World and Motorcycle Review*, March 14, 1908, p. 849.

16. Ibid.

17. "Second Defeat for Champion," *Bicycling World and Motorcycle Review*, March 28, 1908, p. 17.

18. "Official Figures on American Auto Production," *Automobile*, June 13, 1907, p. 963.

19. Ibid.

20. "The Automobile Is in the Nature of an Evolution," *Automobile*, January 9, 1908, p. 61.

21. Richard P. Scharchburg, ed., *The GM Story: Corporation Created by Dynamic Flint, Bold Men* (Flint, MI: General Motors Institute, 1958), p. 1.

22. Alfred P. Sloan Jr. with John McDonald, *My Years with General Motors* (New York: Doubleday, 1963), p. 6.

23. Victor Lougheed, "The Horse and the Automobile," *Automobile*, February 14, 1907, p. 315.

24. Ibid.

25. "America Leads in Numerical Value," *Automobile*, February 21, 1907, p. 352.

26. Scharchburg, *GM Story*.

27. "Detroit's Auto Interests," *Automobile*, October 18, 1906, p. 512.

28. Pound, *Turning Wheel*, p. 46.

29. Ibid., p. 52.

30. Ibid., p. 62.

31. Lawrence R. Gustin, *Billy Durant: Creator of General Motors* (Flushing, MI: Craneshaw Publishers, 1984), p. 98.

32. Ibid., p. 92. A carriage trimmer could earn two dollars daily while car manufacturers paid four dollars for about the same labor.

33. Bernard A. Weisberger, *The Dream Maker: William C. Durant, Founder of General Motors* (Boston: Little, Brown and Company, 1979), p. 140.

34. "Pontchartrain (Louis Phélypeux, compte de)," *Grand Dictionnaire Encyclopédique Larousse* (Paris, 1984).

35. Alfred P. Sloan, *Adventures of a White-Collar Man*, written in collaboration with Boyden Sparkes (New York: Doubleday, Doran and Company, 1941), p. 79.

36. Ibid., p. 80.

37. Ibid.

38. Ibid.

39. Ibid., p. 79.

40. Ibid.

41. Weisberger, *Dream Maker*.

42. Stranahan, *Harvard Class of 1908, Anniversary Reports*, p. 297.

43. Ibid.

44. Ibid.

45. *Automobile*, March 12, 1908, p. 96.

46. Don Ramsdell, telephone interview, April 9, 2009. Ramsdell of Holland, Ohio, was an executive at the Champion Spark Plug Company from 1953 to 1988. He said the story of Robert Stranahan II and Albert Champion fist fighting was passed from Stranahan to his son, Robert Allen Stranahan III. The prospect of the fisticuffs jibes with the personalities of the two men.

47. Stephen Stranahan, e-mail, February 9, 2005.

48. Scharchburg, *GM Story*, p. 2.

49. Gustin, *Billy Durant*, p. 87; Sloan, *My Years with General Motors*, p. 5.

50. Ron Chernow, *The House of Morgan: An American Banking Dynasty and the Rise of Modern Finance* (New York: Grove Press, 1990), p. 121.

51. Gustin, *Billy Durant*, p. 85.

52. Ibid., p. 20; Pound, *Turning Wheel*, p. 27.

53. Sloan, *My Years with General Motors*, p. 5.

54. William C. Durant, *William C. Durant: In His Own Words, The Unedited Memoirs of William C. Durant* (Flint, MI: Scharchburg Archives at Kettering University, 2008), p. 20.

55. Gustin, *Billy Durant*, p. 15.

56. Durant, *William C. Durant*, p. 20. Durant says he was born December 8, 1861, in Boston.

57. Gustin, *Billy Durant*, p. 49.

58. Ibid., p. 33. Durant dropped out of Flint High School a half year short of graduation to work in the family lumber company.

59. Pound, *Turning Wheel*, p. 78.

60. Sloan, *Adventures of a White-Collar Man*, p. 108.

61. Durant, *William C. Durant*, p. 20.

62. Ibid. Durant discusses how selling was born to him: "It thrills me as it does every other real salesman to close a clean sale."

63. Gustin, *Billy Durant*, p. 18.

64. Pound, *Turning Wheel*, p. 78.

65. Ibid.

66. Ibid.

67. Ibid.

68. Durant, *William C. Durant*, p. 17.

69. Ibid.

70. Pound, *Turning Wheel*.

71. Ibid.

72. Ibid.

73. Gustin, *Billy Durant*, p. 65.

74. Ibid., p. 48.

75. Ibid.

76. Durant, *William C. Durant*, p. 19.

77. Pound, *Turning Wheel*, p. 79.

78. Ibid., p. 84.

79. Ibid.

80. Ibid.

81. Ibid.

82. Ibid.

83. Ibid.

84. Ibid.

85. Ibid.; Gustin, *Billy Durant*, p. 49.

86. Pound, *Turning Wheel*, p. 79.

87. Ibid.

88. Ibid.

89. Ibid.

90. Gustin, *Billy Durant*, p. 67.

91. Ibid.

92. Ibid., p. 69; Weisberger, *Dream Maker*, p. 92.

93. Gustin, *Billy Durant*.

94. Scharchburg, *GM Story*, p. 3.

95. Ibid.

96. Ibid., p. 56.

97. Scharchburg, *GM Story*; Pound, *Turning Wheel*, p. 69.

98. Scharchburg, *GM Story*; Pound, *Turning Wheel*.

99. Scharchburg, *GM Story*; Pound, *Turning Wheel*.

100. Gustin, *Billy Durant*, p. 57; Pound, *Turning Wheel*, p. 69.

101. Gustin, *Billy Durant*, p. 57; Pound, *Turning Wheel*, p. 69.

102. Gustin, *Billy Durant*, p. 57; Pound, *Turning Wheel*, p. 69.

103. Gustin, *Billy Durant*, p. 57.

104. Ibid., p. 69.

105. Ibid.

106. Scharchburg, *GM Story*, p. 3.

107. Ibid.

108. Ibid.

109. Durant, *William C. Durant*, p. 82; Sloan, *Adventures of a White-Collar Man*, pp. 145–46. On January 12, 1940, GM celebrated the 25 millionth GM car rolling off the assembly line at the Chevrolet division plant in Flint. The next day in New York before an audience of five thousand celebrating at a dinner pageant, Sloan paid tribute to Durant on the stage as founder of GM.

110. Durant, *William C. Durant*, p. 20. Durant titled the third chapter "The A.C. Spark Plug."

111. Ibid.

112. Ibid. Durant notes that Champion said he had "worked for a number of years with Mr. Renault of Paris," but Durant may have been confused. Durant had started composing his memoir at age eighty in 1942. By then he had suffered three major reversals of fortune, lost the last of his money

in the 1929 stock market crash, and was managing a bowling alley in Flint and working as a short-order cook in a corner food counter. Durant may have been unfamiliar with Champion's influence under Adolphe Clément-Bayard and Clément-Bayard's role in the French auto industry, which had been wiped out. During World War I, most of Clément-Bayard's auto plants had been destroyed. What was left was his Levallois-Perret auto plant in suburban Paris, which he had sold in 1918 to carmaker André Citröen. Clément died in 1928.

113. Ibid. What is revealing so early in Durant's autobiography is his discussion of how he likes to sell a good product. In the next paragraph, he recalls meeting Champion in the Boston Buick dealership. The account of their meeting continues for four pages, including dialogue, as Durant recalled it. This scene Durant recalled had taken place about two weeks before September 16 when he filed incorporation papers for General Motors.

114. Ibid.

115. Ibid.

116. Pound, *Turning Wheel*, p. 95. Recollection about Durant from Lee Dunlap, general manager of the Oakland Motor Car Company in Pontiac, MI, one of the companies purchased by Durant and subsequently the basis for the Pontiac brand.

117. Gustin, *Billy Durant*, p. 124, notes that Durant was just under five feet eight inches tall; Champion's trainer, Choppy Warburton, had measured Champion at five feet seven and a half inches. "Men of Mark in the Cycling World," *Hub* (London), February 20, 1897, p. 101.

118. Durant, *William C. Durant*, p. 21. Durant wrote that Champion's company was "not making any money, and the future did not look very bright." This may not be accurate, as Albert Champion bought weekly ads and the company was adding staff. Champion may have colored the situation over his personal conflicts with Robert Allen Stranahan II.

119. Sloan, *My Years with General Motors*, p. 7.

120. Durant, *William C. Durant*, p. 23.

121. Ibid.

122. Ibid., p. 22.

123. Ibid. Durant recalls meeting Stranahan to discuss opening a Buick dealership and contends that "the firm of Stranahan & Eldridge was organized," when it already had been a going concern for three years.

124. Ibid.

125. Ibid.

126. Ibid.

127. Scharchburg, *GM Story*, p. 3.

128. Ibid.

129. Pound, *Turning Wheel*, p. 72.

130. Scharchburg, *GM Story*.

131. Durant, *William C. Durant*.

132. Pound, *Turning Wheel*, p. 456.

133. Articles of Association of Champion Ignition Company, State of Michigan Department of Licensing and Regulatory Affairs, Corporations, Securities and Commercial Licensing Bureau,

Corporation Division. The $60,000 capital was divided into six hundred shares of $100 each. Champion owned one share, F. A. Allen owned one share, and Arnold M. Goss owned 598.

134. US Patent Office, Patent 959,052, application filed November 3, 1908, granted May 24, 1910.

135. Gustin, *Billy Durant*, p. 111.

136. Ibid.

137. Ibid.

138. Ibid., p. 112.

139. Ibid.

140. Scharchburg, *GM Story*.

141. Ibid.

142. Durant, *William C. Durant*, p. 23.

143. "Calendar Production Figures for GM," *The First 75 Years of Transportation Products* (Princeton, NJ: Automobile Quarterly Productions; Detroit: General Motors, 1983), p. 216. From 8,220 Buicks in 1908 to 14,606 in 1909.

144. Durant, *William C. Durant*.

145. Ibid.

146. Ibid.

147. Ibid.

148. Ibid.

149. Ibid.

150. Ibid.

151. Pound, *Turning Wheel*, p. 109.

152. Stranahan, *Harvard Class of 1908, Anniversary Reports*, p. 297.

153. *Automobile*, December 31, 1908, half-page ad, p. F-15.

154. Stranahan, *American Chronicle*, p. 48.

155. The Champion Company: http://www.sec.state.ma.us/CorpWebCardsearch.aspx, card file, p. 3 (accessed September 15, 2013). The date of the company's name change was July 1, 1909.

CHAPTER 12. CHAMPION AND CHEVROLET SMASHUP

1. Arthur Pound, *The Turning Wheel: The Story of General Motors through Twenty-Five Years, 1908–1933* (New York: Doubleday, Doran and Company, 1934), p. 107, quoting a letter from F. S. Bennett of London, the pioneer agent of Cadillac in the British Isles, published in *Automobile Trade Journal*, December 1924.

2. "Champion Will Make Magnetos," *Automobile*, November 10, 1908, p. 729.

3. Lawrence R. Gustin, *Billy Durant: Creator of General Motors* (Flushing, MI: Craneshaw Publishers, 1984), p. 91.

4. Ibid.

5. "Chevrolet 70 M.P.H. in Long Island Derby," *Automobile*, September 30, 1909.

6. Ibid.

7. Ibid.

8. Ibid.

9. Gustin, *Billy Durant*, p. 89.

10. Ibid.

11. Ibid.

12. Ibid., p. 93.

13. Griffith Borgeson, *The Golden Age of the American Racing Car* (New York: Bonanza Books, by agreement with W. W. Norton, 1966), p. 54.

14. La Chaux-de-Fonds, http://www.chaux-de-fonds.ch (accessed December 16, 2013).

15. Borgeson, *Golden Age of American Car Racing*, p. 53.

16. Ibid.

17. Ibid.

18. Ibid.

19. Ibid.

20. "Frontenac, Louis de Baude, comte de Pallau et de," *The New Encyclopedia Britannica* (London, 2005). See also Historical Narrative of Early Canada, http://www.uppercanadahistory.ca (accessed June 29, 2014).

21. "Frontenac, Louis de Baude, comte de Pallau et de"; Historical Narrative of Early Canada.

22. Borgeson, *Golden Age of American Car Racing*, p. 62.

23. "Chevrolet's Opinion of the Big Race," *Automobile*, June 24, 1909, p. 1014.

24. Borgeson, *Golden Age of American Car Racing*, p. 54.

25. Ibid.

26. Ibid.

27. Ibid.; citation of Louis Chevrolet's 1992 induction into the International Motorsports Hall of Fame in Talladega, Alabama, Talladega Superspeedway, http://www.talladegasuperspeedway.com/Hall-of-Fame-and-Museum.aspx (accessed May 3, 2000); "Louis Chevrolet, Auto Pioneer, Dies: Builder of First Car to Bear His Name, Once World's Leading Racing Driver, Set Mile Speed Record," *New York Times*, June 7, 1941.

28. Borgeson, *Golden Age of American Car Racing*, p. 54.

29. Ibid., p. 60.

30. "Chevrolet's Opinion of the Big Race," p. 1014.

31. Pound, *Turning Wheel*, p. 143.

32. Pound, *Turning Wheel*, p. 143; Gustin, *Billy Durant*, p. 91.

33. Gustin, *Billy Durant*, pp. 92–93.

34. Ibid.

35. Ibid., p. 137; Bernard A. Weisberger, *The Dream Maker: William C. Durant, Founder of General Motors* (Boston: Little, Brown and Company, 1979), p. 140.

36. Weisberger, *Dream Maker*, p. 140.

37. Ibid.

38. Gustin, *Billy Durant*, p. 88.

39. Ibid.

40. Ibid., p. 89.

41. Charles Leerhsen, *Blood and Smoke: A True Tale of Mystery, Mayhem, and the Birth of the Indy 500* (New York: Simon and Schuster, 2011), p. 49.

42. Ibid.

43. Gustin, *Billy Durant*, p. 137.

44. "Calendar Production Figures for GM," *GM: The First 75 Years of Transportation Products* (Princeton, NJ: Automobile Quarterly Productions; Detroit: General Motors, 1983), p. 216.

45. Ibid.

46. "Albert Champion, Head of AC, Dies in Paris Hotel," *Flint Journal*, October 28, 1927.

47. Phone interview with Daniel L. Dolan, Media Relations, AC Rochester (predecessor to today's ACDelco division), January 31, 1994. Dolan discussed stories passed down from retired AC Spark Plug workers.

48. "Albert Champion, Head of AC, Dies in Paris Hotel."

49. Citation of Louis Chevrolet's 1992 induction into the International Motorsports Hall of Fame; Borgeson, *Golden Age of American Car Racing*, p. 55.

50. Borgeson, *Golden Age of American Car Racing*, p. 106.

51. Gustin, *Billy Durant*, p. 94.

52. Ibid.

53. Ibid.

54. Ibid.

55. Beverly Rae Kimes, "The Early Years of the Marque: Launching the Chevrolet," *Automobile Quarterly* (Kutztown, PA) (Third Quarter 1980): 228.

56. Pound, *Turning Wheel*, p. 120; Gustin, *Billy Durant*, p. 123.

57. Weisberger, *Dream Maker*, p. 112.

58. Ibid.

59. Ibid.

60. Pound, *Turning Wheel*, p. 125.

61. Ibid., p. 126.

62. Gustin, *Billy Durant*, p. 125, citing a 1909 profile by Louis E. Rowley in *Detroit Saturday Night*.

63. Alfred P. Sloan Jr. with Boyden Sparkes, *Adventures of a White-Collar Man* (New York: Doubleday, Doran and Company, 1941). p. 113.

64. Pound, *Turning Wheel*, p. 95.

65. Ibid.

66. Gustin, *Billy Durant*, p. 124.

67. Ibid., p. 134.

68. Ibid., p. 136; Richard P. Scharchburg, ed., *The GM Story: Corporation Created by Dynamic Flint, Bold Men* (Flint: MI: General Motors Institute, 1958), p. 5.

69. Gustin, *Billy Durant*, p. 139.

70. Ibid.

71. Ibid., p. 141; Pound, *Turning Wheel*, p. 128.

72. Gustin, *Billy Durant*, p. 142.

73. Ibid.

74. "Calendar Production Figures for GM," p. 216.

75. Ibid.

76. Richard P. Scharchburg, *W. C. Durant: "The Boss"* (Flint, MI: General Motors Institute, 1973), p. 31.

77. "An Abridged History of SAE," Society of Automotive Engineers International, http:// www.sae.org/about/general/history (accessed June 22, 2014).

78. Ibid.

79. "Albert Champion," *Journal of the Society of Automotive Engineers* (November 1927): 617.

80. Al Rothenberg, "The Mystifying Millionaire: The Best Known and Least Known of GM's Leaders," *Automotive News*, September 16, 1983; "Mott, Charles Stewart," *The New Encyclopedia Britannica* (London: 2005).

81. Rothenberg, "Mystifying Millionaire"; "Mott, Charles Stewart."

82. Rothenberg, "Mystifying Millionaire."

83. "Buick and Weston-Mott Plants," *Automobile*, February 1, 1906, p. 324.

84. Sloan, *Adventures of a White-Collar Man*, p. 48, mentions that Durant provided $100,000 cash for expenses and construction of the plant.

85. Ibid.

86. William Pelfrey, *Billy, Alfred, and General Motors: The Story of Two Unique Men, a Legendary Company, and a Remarkable Time in American History* (New York: American Management Association, 2006), p. 100.

87. Sloan, *Adventures of a White-Collar Man*, p. 49. Sloan wrote that he liked to work with Mott: "Neither of us took pride in hunches. We left all the glory of that kind of thinking to such men as liked to be labeled 'genius,'" a swipe at Durant, who was content to let the press credit him as a genius.

88. Pelfrey, *Billy, Alfred, and General Motors*, p. 61.

89. Ibid., p. 61; Pound, *Turning Wheel*, p. 101.

90. Pound, *Turning Wheel*, p. 104.

91. Ibid.

92. Ibid., p. 106; Pelfrey, *Billy, Alfred, and General Motors*, p. 134.

93. Pound, *Turning Wheel*, p. 107.

94. "Albert Champion."

95. "Presentation to A. L. Clayden," *SAE. Bulletin*, 1912, p. 15.

96. *SAE 70th Anniversary Book* (Warrendale, PA: Society of Automotive Engineers International, 1980), p. 16.

97. Ibid.

98. Kimes, "Early Years of the Marque," p. 232; Gustin, *Billy Durant*, p. 145.

99. Kimes, "Early Years of the Marque," p. 232.

100. Borgeson, *Golden Age of the American Racing Car*, p. 99.

101. Ibid., p. 100.

102. Kimes, "Early Years of the Marque," p. 233.

103. Ibid.

104. Ibid.

105. Ibid., p. 239; Gustin, *Billy Durant*, p. 157; Borgeson, *Golden Age of the American Racing Car*, p. 55.

106. Borgeson, *Golden Age of the American Racing Car*.

107. Kimes, "Early Years of the Marque," p. 236.

108. Gustin, *Billy Durant*, p. 156.

109. Borgeson, *Golden Age of the American Racing Car*, p. 53.

110. Kimes, "Early Years of the Marque," p. 239; Gustin, *Billy Durant*, p. 157.

111. Borgeson, *Golden Age of the American Racing Car*, p. 56.

112. Ibid.; Pound, *Turning Wheel*, p. 146.

113. Borgeson, *Golden Age of the American Racing Car*, p. 100.

114. David J. Andrea, "AC Spark Plug," *Encyclopedia of American Business History and Biography, the Automobile Industry, 1896–1920* (New York: Bruccoli Clark Layman, 1990), p. 3; Richard P. Scharchburg, "Albert Champion," p. 80; "Albert Champion," *The AC Rochester 85th Anniversary* (Linden, MI: McVey Marketing and Advertising, 1993), p. 19.

115. William C. Durant, *William C. Durant: In His Own Words, The Unedited Memoirs of William C. Durant* (Flint, MI: Scharchburg Archives at Kettering University, 2008), p. 23.

116. US Patent No. 959,052, issued May 24, 1910.

117. Borgeson, *Golden Age of the American Racing Car*, p. 99.

118. Ibid.

119. Ibid.

120. Ibid., p. 100.

121. Ibid., p. 56. Borgeson, editor-in-chief of *Motor Trend* and writer for *Sports Car Illustrated*, predecessor of today's *Car and Driver*, conducted several interviews in the 1950s with Cornelius Willett van Ranst, who was in charge of engineering the engines of Frontenac racecars that won the Indy 500 in 1920 and 1921, a rare occasion when the same manufacturer won back-to-back titles. Borgeson's *The Golden Age of the American Racing Car* was acclaimed by the Society of Automotive Engineers International for rescuing the memory of the era of brilliant racecar work in America. In 1977 SAEI published a second edition of the book, which is still in print.

122. Ibid., p. 56; Kimes, "Early Years of the Marque," p. 239. Kimes (1939–2008) was a leading automotive writer renowned as a stickler for accuracy and detail in her plethora of articles and books. She cites Borgeson in describing the fight between Champion and Chevrolet.

123. Borgeson, *Golden Age of the American Racing Car*.

CHAPTER 13. FIGHTING CHANCES

1. "How Willys Entered Auto Industry," *Automobile*, October 28, 1909, p. 738.

2. Ibid.

3. Ibid.

4. "Overland Buys Pope-Toledo Factory," *Automobile*, April 8, 1909, p. 590.

5. "Stranahan Brought Firm, Heavy Debt to Toledo in 1910: Industrial Empire Built from Modest Start, Sold His Product to Willys, Ford," *Toledo Blade*, February 8, 1962.

6. "General Trade News," *Automobile*, June 2, 1910, p. 1031; Ann Stranahan, *An American Chronicle: The Stranahan Chronicles* (Perrysburg, OH: 2004), p. 16.

7. "Introduced Wife, Surprised Mother: Spencer U. Stranahan, Brookline, and His Bride Marry without Publicity," *Boston Herald*, May 31, 1907.

8. Copy of Record of Death, Town Clerk's Office, Brookline, MA.

9. "Stranahan Brought Firm, Heavy Debt to Toledo in 1910"; "Robert A. Stranahan Sr. Dead; Founded Champion Spark Plug," *New York Times*, February 10, 1962; "Company Profile, Champion Spark Plug Co., Toledo, Ohio," *Motor Age* (December 1976): 55.

10. "Stranahan Brought Firm, Heavy Debt to Toledo in 1910."

11. Stephen Stranahan, "The Entrepreneurial Years," in Ann Stranahan's family memoir *An American Chronicle*, unnumbered pages, June 6, 2006, based on corporate records in the family.

12. Ibid.

13. "How Willys Entered Auto Industry."

14. Ibid.

15. Ibid.

16. "John Willis," *Encyclopedia of World Biography* (New York: 2004), http://www.encyclopedia.com/doc/1G2-3404707705.html (accessed February 1, 2014).

17. Ibid.

18. Ibid.

19. "Overland Buys Pope-Toledo Factory."

20. Ibid.

21. Honored by the US Postal Service in the 1990s as the subject of a first-class thirty-two-cent stamp.

22. "Overland Buys Pope-Toledo Factory."

23. "Col. Pope Passes Away," *Bicycling World and Motorcycle Review*, August 14, 1909, pp. 779–81.

24. "News in Brief from the East, West, and South," *Automobile*, December 1, 1910, p. 940.

25. "Stranahan Brought Firm, Heavy Debt to Toledo in 1910."

26. "How Willys Entered Auto Industry."

27. "Calendar Year Production Figures for GM," *GM: The First 75 Years of Transportation Products* (Princeton, NJ: Automobile Quarterly Productions; Detroit: General Motors, 1983), p. 216.

28. Robert Lacey: *Ford: The Men and the Machine* (New York: Ballantine Books, 1987), p. 112. Lacey lists Ford Model Ts selling 18,664 cars in the fiscal year of October 1, 1909, to September 30, 1910, and 34,528 cars sold in the next fiscal year.

29. "Stranahan Brought Firm, Heavy Debt to Toledo in 1910."

30. Ibid.

31. "Champion Seeks to Sell Its Spark Plugs to Ford after Sale of Autolite," *Wall Street*

Journal, April 21, 1972. The Champion Spark Plug Company was Ford's exclusive supplier of spark plugs from 1911 through 1961, when Ford acquired Autolite.

32. "Union Adds Arizona and New Mexico," *Chronicle of America: From Prehistory to Today* (New York: Dorling Kindersley, 1995), p. 573.

33. "Work Is Albert Champion's Main Pastime—Says He Can't Quit Now," *Detroit News*, August 21, 1927.

34. Patent Number 1,042,619, granted October 29, 1912, from the US Patent Office.

35. Ibid.

36. Stranahan, *American Chronicle*.

37. Corporate card file, http://www.sec.state.ma.us./CorpWeb/CardSearch.aspx (accessed September 15, 2013).

38. Stranahan, *American Chronicle*.

39. Ibid.

40. *Motor World*, March 7, 1912, p. 1070, published a Champion Spark Plug Company advertisement facing a Champion Ignition Company ad, p. 1071.

41. Ibid.

42. *Motor World* full-page ad, March 7, 1912, p. 1082.

43. Albert Champion, "Spark-Plugs for High-Speed Engines," *1917 Transactions* (New York: Society of Automotive Engineers, 1918), p. 354.

44. Ibid.

45. *Automobile*, February 6, 1905, p. 41.

46. *Automobile*, January 24, 1907, p. 44.

47. "Keeping Pace with 2000% Growth: What Burroughs Direct-to-Ledger Posting Has Done for the Champion Spark Plug Company," Burroughs Adding Machine Company advertisement, *Daily Register Gazette* (Rockford, IL), April 19, 1917.

48. "In the Courts," *Bay City Times* (Bay City, MI), May 8, 1917.

49. Ibid.

50. Alfred P. Sloan with John McDonald, *My Years with General Motors* (New York: Currency and Doubleday, 1990), p. 8.

51. "Ford Assembly Line Open," in *Chronicle of America: From Prehistory to Today* (New York: Dorline Kindersley), p. 580.

52. "To Sell Cars to the Common Man, Ford Offers Workers $5 a Day," in ibid., p. 582.

53. "History of the Atlas Valley Country Club," http://www.atlasvalleycountryclub.com (accessed June 29, 2014).

54. "Country Club Celebration on Labor Day," *Flint Journal*, September 5, 1916. His score for eighteen holes was 101.

55. "Dinner Dance at Country Club," *Flint Journal*, September 21, 1916.

56. Ibid.

57. "Cups Offered in Golf Tournament," *Flint Journal*, September 18, 1916; "Mrs. Albert Champion Wins Women's Putting Contest," *Flint Journal*, September 4, 1917.

58. "Work Is Albert Champion's Main Pastime."

59. Ibid.

60. Ibid.

61. Ibid.

62. "Runs Automobile into Ditch to Avoid Collision: Albert Champion Has Narrow Escape from Serious Injury," *Flint Journal*, May 31, 1916.

63. Arthur Pound, *The Turning Wheel: The Story of General Motors through Twenty-Five Years, 1908–1933* (New York: Doubleday, Doran and Company, 1934), p. 150.

64. Lawrence R. Gustin, *Billy Durant: Creator of General Motors* (Flushing, MI: Craneshaw Publishers, 1984), p. 164.

65. Ibid., p. 165.

66. Gustin, *Billy Durant*, p. 165; Sloan, *My Years with General Motors*, pp. 9–10.

67. William Pelfrey, *Billy, Alfred, and General Motors: The Story of the Two Unique Men, a Legendary Company, and a Remarkable Time in American History* (New York: American Management Association, 2006), p. 183.

68. Ibid., p. 185; Gustin, *Billy Durant*, p. 165.

69. Pelfrey, *Billy, Alfred, and General Motors*, 194.

70. Ibid.

71. Sloan, *My Years with General Motors*, p. 12.

72. Ibid., p. 187.

73. Ibid., p. 193; Gustin, *Billy Durant*, p. 178.

74. Sloan, *My Years with General Motors*, p. 188; Gustin, *Billy Durant*, p. 168.

75. Gustin, *Billy Durant*, pp. 167–68.

76. Ibid., p. 170.

77. Ibid., p. 178; Sloan, *My Years with General Motors*, p.11; Pelfrey, *Billy, Alfred, and General Motors*, p. 194.

78. Gustin, *Billy Durant*, pp. 181–83.

79. Ibid., p. 173; Sloan, *My Years with General* Motors, p. 11; Pelfrey, *Billy, Alfred, and General Motors*, p. 190.

80. Sloan, *My Years with General Motors*.

81. "Under Fire of Aeroplane Guns of the Germans, Albert Schmidt Returns to Flint after Five months in French Army," *Flint Journal*, January 20, 1915, p. 1.

82. John B. Rae, *The American Automobile, A Brief History* (Chicago: University of Chicago Press, 1965), p. 72.

83. Gérard and Bertrand Pommier, *Nieuport: A Biography of Edouard Nieuport* (Atglen, PA: Shifter Publishing, 2002), pp. 65–73.

84. Ibid., p. 86.

85. "America Irate over Lusitania's Sinking," in *Chronicle of America*, p. 587.

86. "United States Enters the War 'To Save Democracy,'" in ibid., p. 599.

87. "Plan Flint Industrial Survey for Defense," *Daily Telegram* (Adrian, MI), May 20, 1916.

88. "Puts New Spark Plugs on Market: One of New Devices Is for Use in Aviation to Stop Mishaps," *Cleveland Plain Dealer*, December 31, 1916.

89. "Work Is Albert Champion's Main Pastime."

90. "Albert Champion Is One Busy Man: Head of Ignition Company Is Director of Many Departments," *Flint Journal*, February 20, 1917.

91. Ibid.

92. Ibid.

93. Ibid.

94. Ibid.

95. Ibid.

96. "Work Is Albert Champion's Main Pastime."

97. "Albert Champion Is One Busy Man."

98. "What Spark Plug Means to the Motor: Facts Concerning Making of Important Little Contrivance," *Flint Journal*, February 23, 1917.

99. Ibid.

100. "Under Fire of Aeroplane Guns."

101. Ibid.

102. Rae, *American Automobile*, p. 66.

103. "Once Champ Rider Now Spark Plug King: Albert Champion Has Increased the Output of His Factory to 12,000,000 a Year and Now Leads in This Field—A Pioneer in This Line," *Boston Herald*, March 4, 1917, p. 55.

104. Ibid.

105. Ibid.

106. Ibid.

107. Ibid.

108. "United States Enters the War 'To Save Democracy.'"

109. Richard P. Scharchburg, ed., *GM Story: Corporation Created by Dynamic Flint, Bold Men* (Flint, MI: General Motors Institute), p. 10.

110. "In the Courts."

111. "Cases Argued and Determined in the Circuit Courts of Appeals and the District Courts of the United States, March-April 1918," *Federal Reporter*, vol. 247 (St. Paul: West Publishing Company, 1918), *CHAMPION SPARK PLUG CO. v. CHAMPION IGNITION CO., et al.* (District Court, E.D. Michigan, N.D. November 22, 1917), pp. 200–207.

112. US Patent 1,263,038 granted April 16, 1918.

113. Pascal Sergent, "1919: Henri Pélissier, Winner of 'The Hell of the North,'" in *A Century of Paris-Roubaix* (Brussels, Belgium: De Eecloonaar, 1997), unnumbered page.

114. "Champion French Cyclist Killed," *New York Times*, December 25, 1916.

115. Pascal Sergent, "1914: Crupelandt before the Storm," in *A Century of Paris-Roubaix*, unnumbered page.

116. Henri Desgrange, "Mort de Clément-Bayard," *L'Auto*, May 11, 1928.

117. "HMS *Majestic* 1895," *Wikipedia*, http://en.wikipedia.org/wiki/HMS_Majestic_1895 (accessed August 26, 2004).

118. "Mort au combat au 1917," Topic Topos, http://fr.topic-topos.com/vitrail-edern (accessed February 2, 2014).

119. Jeff Shesol, "The Somme," review of *The Great War* by Joe Sacco, *New York Times Book Review*, December 8, 2013, p. 17.

120. "Cases Argued and Determined in the Circuit Courts of Appeals and the District Courts of the United States, March-April 1918," *Federal Reporter*, p. 210.

121. US Patent 1,338,674, granted May 4, 1920.

CHAPTER 14. STARS AND STRIPES CAPTURE THE GRAND PRIX DE FRANCE

1. Griffith Borgeson, *The Golden Age of the American Racing Car* (New York: Bonanza Books, by arrangement with W. W. Norton, 1966), p. 3.

2. Registration Card of September 12, 1918. He listed his birthday as April 2, compared with the April 5 date on his birth certificate, possibly facetiously, as he had won Paris-Roubaix on April 2, which led to his contract to race in America, which changed the course of his life.

3. "Million American Troops Stem the Tide," in *Chronicle of America: From Prehistory to Today* (New York: Dorling Kindersley, 1995), p. 606.

4. Lawrence R. Gustin, *Billy Durant: Creator of General Motors* (Flushing, MI: Craneshaw Publishers, 1984), p. 193.

5. Ibid., p. 193.

6. Ibid., p. 195.

7. "40,000 Spark Plugs Champion Co.'s Daily Average," *Flint Journal*, November 30, 1918, p. 9.

8. Ibid.

9. Ibid.

10. "Champion Co. Plans Branch Plants in France and England," *Flint Journal*, July 18, 1919, p. 1.

11. "Gen. Motors Party Now Seeing Paris: Albert Champion Is Famous Guide, Says C. S. Mott in Letter," *Flint Journal*, September 20, 1919, p. 8.

12. Ibid.

13. Ibid.

14. Ibid.

15. Ibid.

16. Ibid.

17. "Louis A. Champion," *New York Times* obituary, August 11, 1947.

18. Ibid.

19. Pascal Sergent, "1919: Henri Pélissier Winner of "The Hell of the North," in *A Century of Paris-Roubaix* (Brussels, Belgium: De Eecloonaar), 1977, pages unnumbered.

20. "Gen. Motors Party Now Seeing Paris."

21. Ibid.

22. Alfred P. Sloan with John McDonald, *My Years with General Motors* (New York: Currency and Doubleday, 1990), p. 317.

23. Ibid.

24. Ibid.

25. Ibid.

26. Gustin, *Billy Durant*, p. 199.

27. Ibid.

28. US Patent application filed September 25, 1918, for Patent 1,441,783, granted January 9, 1923.

29. US Patent application filed November 24, 1919, for Patent 1,501,021, granted July 8, 1924.

30. US Patent application filed March 8, 1920, for Patent 1,583,870, granted May 19, 1925.

31. "They Carried Roland Rohlfs to the Roof of the World," Champion Ignition Company advertisement, *Literary Digest*, January 10, 1920.

32. Ibid.

33. Albert Champion, "Uncle Same Now Supreme in Two Speed Classes," *Duluth News-Tribune* (Minnesota), February 21, 1921, p. 10.

34. Ibid.

35. Ibid.

36. Ibid.

37. "The First National Bank Extends to All a Happy and Prosperous New Year," advertisement, *Flint Journal*, January 1, 1920, p. 14.

38. Ibid.

39. Ibid.

40. "Depression Hurting; Hoover Has Job Plan," in *Chronicle of America*, p. 618.

41. Gustin, *Billy Durant*, p. 214.

42. Ibid.

43. Ibid., p. 218.

44. Ibid., p. 222.

45. Ibid.

46. Chris Sinsabaugh, *Who, Me? Forty Years of Automobile History* (Detroit: Arnold Powers, 1940), pp. 219–21.

47. Ibid., p. 223.

48. Ibid.; "Old-Timers Choose Albert Champion to Head New Auto Club," *Flint Journal*, January 22, 1921, p. 12.

49. George Slocum, foreword to Sinsabaugh's memoir, *Who, Me? Forty Years of Automobile History*. Slocum, publisher of *Automotive News*, regarded Sinsabaugh as the foremost authority on auto history and encouraged him to write articles about it for *Automotive News*. The articles were collected for his memoir.

50. Sinsabaugh, *Who, Me?* p. 44. He had coined "Cubs," one less letter than "Colts," to fit in the confines of a single column seventeen spaces wide in the *Chicago Daily News*.

51. Ibid., p. 223.

52. Ibid., p. 224.

53. "America Enters Grand Prix This Year," *Evening Tribune* (San Diego, CA), April 1, 1921, p. 18.

54. Borgeson, *Golden Age of the American Racing Car*, appendix 3, "Winners of Major American Races, 1915–1929," p. 328.

55. Ibid., p. 167.

56. Ibid., p. 168.

57. Ibid., p. 169.

58. Ibid.

59. Ibid.

60. Ibid.

61. Gary D. Doyle, *King of the Boards: The Life and Times of Jimmy Murphy* (Tempe, AZ: Ben Franklin Press, 2002), p. 208.

62. Ibid.

63. Borgeson, *Golden Age of the American Racing Car*, p. 169.

64. Ibid.

65. Ibid.

66. Ibid.

67. Ibid., p. 172.

68. Doyle, *King of the Boards*, p. 209.

69. Borgeson, *Golden Age of the American Racing Car*, p. 170.

70. Ibid.

71. Ibid.

72. Doyle, *King of the Boards*, p. 7.

73. Borgeson, *Golden Age of the American Racing Car*, p. 172.

74. Ibid.

75. Ibid., p. 173.

76. Ibid.

77. Ibid.

78. Ibid.

79. Ibid.

80. Ibid., p. 174.

81. Ibid.

82. Ibid.

83. Ibid.

84. Ibid., pp. 175–76.

85. Ibid., p. 176.

CHAPTER 15. A STORM THAT BREAKS LOOSE

1. F. Scott Fitzgerald, *The Crack-Up* (New York: New Directions, 1993), p. 87.

2. "Flint Manufacturer Arrested in Hotel on Wife's Complaint: Mrs. Albert Champion Finds Husband in Company with 'Other Woman,'" *Flint Journal*, August 25, 1921, p. 1.

3. Ibid.

4. Kerry Champion Williams, Edna's great-niece, e-mail, April 11, 2014.

5. "Flint Manufacturer Arrested in Hotel on Wife's Complaint."

6. "Two Women Hurt in Auto Accidents: Coupe Hits Truck—Car Crowded into Ditch," *Flint Journal*, August 2, 1921, p. 12.

7. Ibid.

8. "Flint Manufacturer Arrested in Hotel on Wife's Complaint."

9. Ibid.

10. Ibid.

11. Ibid.

12. Ibid.

13. Ibid.

14. Ibid.

15. Ibid.

16. Ibid.

17. Ibid.

18. Ibid.

19. Ibid.

20. Ibid.

21. Ibid.

22. Martha Martin, "Sparkplug Millions Explode in Tragedy: Death Wipes out Triangle of Champion, No. 2 and Gigolo," *New York Sunday News*, April 26, 1935.

23. Ibid.

24. Ibid.

25. Vincent Curcio, *Chrysler: The Life and Times of an Automotive Genius* (New York: Oxford University Press, 2000), pp. 265–66.

26. "Champion Divorce Decree Is Filed: Property Settlement Made out of Court—Wife Goes to France," *Flint Journal*, November 1, 1921, p. 15.

27. Ibid.

28. Kerry Champion Williams e-mail, September 30, 2003.

29. Ibid.

30. Kerry Champion Williams e-mail, April 11, 2014.

31. Ibid.

32. "Pride of Albert Champion and Her Sister Now in Motion Pictures—Both Former Kansas City Girls," *Kansas City Star*, February 22, 1922, p. 3.

33. Ibid.

34. "Crawford-Champion," *New York Times*, February 9, 1922.

35. Ancestry.com lists her birth date as February 17, 1889 in Raymore, MO, http://www.Ancestry.com (accessed May 17, 2012).

36. Kerry Champion Williams phone interview, September 10, 2003. Edna's mother was Elizabeth Jane Champion, born in February 1869 in Springfield, IL.

37. Ibid.

38. "Mrs. Prosper Champion Dies," *Flint Journal*, June 18, 1944.

39. "Pride of Albert Champion and Her Sister Now in Motion Pictures."

40. *Hoye's 1902 Directory*, Kansas City, MO, p. 271.

41. "Marriage Licenses," *Kansas City Star*, September 2, 1906.

42. Martin, "Sparkplug Millions Explode in Tragedy."

43. Kerry Champion Williams phone interview, September 10, 2003.

44. Ibid.

45. Kerry Champion Williams e-mail, April 11, 2014.

46. Ibid.

47. *GM: The First 75 Years of Transportation Products* (Princeton, NJ: Automobile Quarterly Productions; Detroit: General Motors, 1983), p. 216.

48. "Prohibition Begins: America Goes Dry," in *Chronicle of America: From Prehistory to Today* (New York: Dorling Kindersley, 1995), p. 613.

49. US Patent 1,511,199 for Spark Plug and Method of Making the Same, filed April 14, 1921, and granted October 7, 1924.

50. US Patent 1,491,079 for Device for and Method of Forming Ceramic Objects, filed January 20, 1921, and granted April 22, 1924; US Patent 1,672,201 for Terminal Connector for Electric Supply Cables, filed May 18, 1921, and granted June 5, 1928; US Patent 1,566,465 for Terminal Connector for Spark Plugs, filed May 18, 1921, and granted December 22, 1925; and US Patent 1,552,274 for Spark Plug, filed October 10, 1921, and granted September 1, 1925.

51. "Crawford-Champion"; "Champion Head to Wed an Arts Student."

52. Ibid.

53. Marshall Price, assistant curator at the National Academy Museum, e-mail June 20, 2005. "Tuition was basically free," Price said, "and it was a much more serious art school for aspiring professional artists, so if she were here then it would be in the records."

54. "Art Student to Wed Millionaire," *New Orleans Item*, February 13, 1922.

55. Lawrence R. Gustin, *Billy Durant: Creator of General Motors* (Flushing, MI: Craneshaw Publishers, 1984), p. 206.

56. Corporations Division of the Michigan Department of Licensing and Regulatory Affairs, Order Number 1212745.

57. "Flint Business Man Weds Art Student," *Saginaw News* (Michigan), February 23, 1922.

58. Martin, "Sparkplug Millions Explode in Tragedy."

59. "Ocean Travelers," *New York Times*, February 21, 1922.

60. "Europe Respects U.S. Auto Craft: Albert Champion Finds Changed Attitude during Trip Abroad," *Flint Journal*, October 12, 1922.

61. "Basil W. de Guichard, Former AC Head, Dies," *Flint Journal*, May 30, 1958.

62. Martin, "Sparkplug Millions Explode in Tragedy"; "Work Is Albert Champion's Main Pastime—Says He Can't Quit Now," *Detroit News*, August 21, 1927.

63. "Europe Respects U.S. Auto Craft."

64. Ibid.

65. "Work Is Albert Champion's Main Pastime."

66. Ibid.

67. Ibid.

68. Ibid.

69. Ibid.

70. Passenger List of French liner S. S. *Savoie* from Le Havre, France, arriving Port of New York, December 22, 1924, including entries for Prosper Champion, wife Flora, and their three sons.

71. Supreme Court of Brooklyn, New York, Record Number 442754, January 29, 1924, cited on above passenger list.

72. Cherie Champion, granddaughter of Prosper Champion, phone interview, July 15, 2002.

73. Ibid.

74. US Patent 1,631,191 for Terminal Connector for Spark Plugs, filed October 28, 1921, and granted June 7, 1927; US Patent 1,537,586 for Self-Cleaning Spark Plug, filed October 28, 1922, and granted May 12, 1925; US Patent 1,670,841 for Drive Unit (dashboard speedometer cable), filed May 31, 1924, and granted May 22, 1928; US Patent 1,713,860 for Indicating Instrument (dashboard speedometer), filed September 19, 1924, and granted May 21, 1929; US Patent 1,619,969 for Spark Plug filed March 30, 1925, and granted March 8, 1927; US Patent 1,705,045 for Terminal Clip (spark plug), filed May 4, 1925, and granted March 12, 1929; US Patent 1,651,374 for Terminal Connector for Spark Plugs, filed July 20, 1925, and granted December 6, 1927; US Patent 1,680,012 for Instrument Panel (speedometer), filed October 7, 1925, and granted August 7, 1928; US Patent 1,668,525 for Lighting Means for Instrument Boards (speedometer), filed January 7, 1926, and granted May 1, 1928; US Patent 1,688,522 for Instrument Assembly (speedometer), filed February 17, 1926, and granted October 23, 1928; US Patent 1,675,639 for Instrument Panel (speedometer), filed July 2, 1926, and granted July 3, 1928; US Patent 1,683,023 for Flexible Tube Support (speedometer cables), filed July 2, 1926, and granted September 4, 1928; and US Patent 1,658,552 for Speedometer Drive Shaft, filed August 11, 1926, and granted February 7, 1928.

75. "Work Is Albert Champion's Main Pastime."

76. "Calendar Production Figures for GM," *GM: The First 75 Years of Transportation Products*, p. 217, lists 1,237,600 autos produced in 1926.

77. Ibid. There were 693,386 Chevrolets manufactured in 1926.

78. "Work Is Albert Champion's Main Pastime."

79. Martin, "Spark Plug Millions Explode in Tragedy."

80. Ibid.

81. Ibid.

82. Ibid.

83. Ibid.

84. William F. Nolan, *Barney Oldfield: The Life and Times of America's Legendary Speed King* (New York: G. P. Putnam's Sons, 1961), p. 219.

85. "A Year Ago," *Los Angeles Examiner*, December 21, 1927, from scrapbook of Prosper Champion.

86. Tony Mayfair, "Fatal Romance behind a Suit by a 'Common Law Husband,'" *New York Daily Mirror*, July 7, 1935.

87. Ibid.

88. Basil Woon, "A Bit of Gossip," *Seattle Daily Times*, November 14, 1926.

89. Basil Woon, "Dinner for Oldfield," *Seattle Daily Times*, November 21, 1926.

90. Ibid.

CHAPTER 16. PERMANENT PARISIAN

1. Griffith Borgeson, *The Golden Age of the American Racing Car* (New York: Bonanza Books, by agreement with W. W. Norton, 1966), p.13.

2. Ibid., p. 330: "Winners of Major American Races, 1915–1929," De Paolo averaged 101.1 miles per hour; ibid., p. 343: "Performance Trends—Indianapolis Winners, 1911–1929."

3. "Champion was 'A Regular Fellow and Good Boss,' Chauffeur's Tribute," unidentified newspaper clip from Prosper Champion's scrapbook.

4. Ibid.

5. Ibid.

6. "Byrd and Bennett Fly over North Pole," in *Chronicle of America: From Prehistory to Today* (New York: Dorling Kindersley, 1995), p. 632.

7. A. Scott Berg, *Lindbergh* (New York: G. P. Putman's Sons, 1998), p. 91.

8. Ibid.

9. Ibid.

10. Ibid., p. 104.

11. Ibid.

12. Ibid.

13. Ibid.

14. Ibid., p. 105.

15. "Lucky Lindy Hops over the Atlantic," in *Chronicle of America*, p. 635.

16. "28,944,000 Sparks Required by Flight: Plugs Put to Terrific Test by Lindbergh's Hop from New York to Paris, Says Albert Champion," *Seattle Daily Times*, May 29, 1927.

17. Ibid.

18. Berg, *Lindbergh*, p. 159.

19. Ibid., p. 150.

20. Ibid., p. 155.

21. "Spark Plug King First Won Fame as Bicycle Racer," *New York Herald, Paris* (predecessor to the *International Herald-Tribune* and today's *International New York Times*), October 8, 1927.

22. Arthur Pound, *The Turning Wheel* (New York: Doubleday, Doran and Company, 1934), p. 337.

23. Ibid.

24. Ibid.

25. US Patent 1,753,773 for Chromium Plated Worm Shaft (speedometer), filed October 1, 1926, and granted April 8, 1930; US Patent 1,727,808 for By-Pass and Filter Connection, filed

May 6, 1927, and granted September 10, 1929; US Patent 1,731,209 for Mounting for Oil Filters, filed August 17, 1927, and granted October 8, 1929; US Patent 1,840,831 for Air Cleaner, filed August 5, 1927, and granted January 12, 1932; US Patent 1,757,411 for Speedometer Case (dashboard), filed September 1927 and granted May 6, 1930; and US Patent 1,840, 832 for Air Cleaner, filed September 2, 1927, and granted January 12, 1932.

26. "Calendar Production Figures for GM," *GM: The First 75 Years of Transportation Products* (Princeton, NJ: *Automobile Quarterly Magazine*; Detroit: General Motors, 1983), p. 217.

27. Ibid.

28. Vincent Bakich of Bakersfield, California, letter of October 13, 2005, to the author about a 1921 Marmon Speedster he had restored and the place Marmon Speedsters had among 1920s American autos.

29. E-mail from Kerry Champion Williams, April 14, 2014.

30. Ibid.

31. "Work Is Albert Champion's Main Pastime—Says He Can't Quit Now," *Detroit News*, August 21, 1927.

32. Ibid.

33. Ibid.

34. Ibid.

35. Ibid.

36. Ibid.

37. Telephone interview with Cherie Champion, August 21, 2005.

38. "Ile-De-France Docks Late," *New York Herald*, Paris, October 8, 1927.

39. Charles Faroux, "Albert Champion Est Mort!" *L'Auto* (Paris), October 28, 1927, p. 1.

40. Ibid.

41. Martha Martin, "Sparkplug Millions Explode in Tragedy: Death Wipes out Triangle of Champion, No. 2 and Gigolo," *New York Sunday News*, April 26, 1936.

42. Ibid.

43. Ibid.

44. Ibid.

45. Ibid.

46. Ibid.

47. Ibid.

48. Ibid.

49. Charles Ravaud, "The Last Moments of Albert Champion," *L'Auto*, October 28, 1927.

50. Ibid.

51. Ibid.

52. Ibid.

53. Ibid.

54. Ibid.

55. "The Death of Albert Champion," *Le Figaro*, October 29, 1927.

56. John J. Donovan, "Brilliant Career," *Boston Globe*, October 28, 1927.

57. "Life of Albert Champion Like That of Alger Hero: Errand Boy and Bicycle Racer, He Dies a Wealthy Man," *Boston Traveler*, October 28, 1927.

58. Martin, "Sparkplug Millions Explode in Tragedy." On April 12, 2006, Bernadette Murphy, my Paris researcher, visited the Paris police archives in search of the commissariat reports for the First and Eighth Arrondissements, where the Hôtel Crillon and Hôtel Meurice are located, and discovered that all files from 1920 into the early 1930s for both arrondissements have disappeared—either accidentally misplaced or deliberately destroyed.

59. Ibid.

60. Program of the memorial service at the Church of the American on Avenue Georges V, listing the Champion brothers along with Basil de Guichard, Pierre Tournier, and their families, nephews, nieces, and friends.

61. Ibid.

62. Martin, "Sparkplug Millions Explode in Tragedy."

63. Phone interview with Kerry Champion Williams, October 15, 2005. Family photos of the late 1920s show the bust of Champion, no longer in view.

64. Bernadette Murphy in an e-mail of October 13, 2004, reported that she had interviewed the St. Cloud cemetery caretaker, a character out of a Balzac novel. The caretaker in his small office pulled from the top of a wardrobe armoire a huge old leather-bound cemetery register. It indicated that Marie Blanche Champion's remains were exhumed on July 25, 1928, and "transferred across Paris." Records in Père Lachaise Cemetery indicate Albert and his mother were placed in metal coffins on July 25, 1928, one on either side of the cavity, which contains room for six more family members.

CHAPTER 17. THE LOWDOWN

1. "'I'm No Gigolo!' Charles Brazelle Tells Why," *New York Daily Mirror*, April 26, 1935, p. 1.

2. Martha Martin, "Sparkplug Millions Explode in Tragedy: Death Wipes out Triangle of Champion, No. 2 and Gigolo," *New York Sunday News*, April 26, 1936.

3. "Widow Given Champion Gold," *Detroit Times*, November 16, 1927.

4. "New Executive Name for AC Spark Plug Co.," *Detroit News*, November 25, 1927.

5. Martin, "Sparkplug Millions Explode in Tragedy."

6. Ibid.

7. Ibid.

8. Ibid.

9. Ibid.

10. Ibid.

11. Ibid.

12. Ibid.

13. Ibid.

14. Ibid.

15. "Mrs. Brazelle Dies in Paris of Pneumonia: She Spent Girlhood in St. Louis—Former Wife of David G. Joyce," *St. Louis Post-Dispatch*, April 11, 1930; "Mrs. Acuff Brazelle Succumbs in Paris: Former St. Louisan Stricken with Pneumonia after Italian Tour," *St. Louis Globe-Democrat*, April 11, 1930; "Mrs. C. L. Brazelle Dies in Paris," *New York Times*, April 12, 1930.

16. Martin, "Sparkplug Millions Explode in Tragedy."

17. Ibid.

18. Ibid.

19. Ibid.

20. Ibid.

21. "Champion's Widow Leaves $8,000,000: Three Michigan Relatives Are Included in Five Sharing in Estate," *Flint Journal*, March 26, 1935; "Champion Kin Get 8 Million: Estate Is Bequeathed to Family Here," *Detroit Free Press*, March 28, 1935.

22. L. L. Stevenson, "Charge 6 Million Will Plot: Friend Begins Court Battle—N.Y. Club Man Says He Lived with Mrs. Champion for 8 Years in Penthouse," *Detroit News*, April 23, 1935; Tony Mayfair, "Widow's Estate Sued in Common Law: Rich Mrs. Champion Lived with War Vet, He Says in Suit—Claims Family Fed Her Liquor to Keep Her Hidden Away," *New York Mirror*, April 22, 1935; "Hearing Set on Champion Will Battle: Brazelle Admits Living as 'Man and Wife' with Widow of Spark Plug King," *Flint News-Advertiser*, April 25, 1935; Joseph Cowan, "Dead Widow's Friend Sues for Estate: Brazelle Charges Conspiracy to Bar Him from Woman," *New York Evening Journal*, April 22, 1935; "Family Named in Suit on Will of Mrs. Champion: Turned Widow of Spark Plug Manufacturer against Him, Charles Brazelle Charges," *New York Herald-Tribune*, April 23, 1935; Hal Burton, "Lover Sues Spark Plug Widow's Kin," *New York News*, April 23, 1935; Tony Mayfair, "Brazelle Bares Story of Love: 'Common Law' Hubby Fights for Estate," *New York Daily Mirror*, April 26, 1935; "Seeks to Break Spark Plug Will: 'Protégé' of Champion's Widow Says He Shared Her Penthouse," *Cleveland Plain Dealer*, April 23, 1935.

23. "Boxer Fights A. C. Champion Widow's Will: Share in $6,000,000 Estate Demanded on Claim of 'Common-Law Husband,'" *Detroit Times*, June 16, 1935; "Charge Terrorism in Champion Suit: King of Spark Plug King's Widow Accuses Former Boxer," *Grand Rapids Press* (Michigan), June 15, 1935; "Violent Death of Plug King Bared in Suit," *New York Daily News*, June 15, 1935.

24. "Millionaire's Death Laid to Boxer's Punch in Suit over Champion Estate," *New York American*, June 15, 1935; "Ex-Pug, Who Made Widow of Late Lover, Seeking Part of Fortune," *State Times-Advocate* (Baton Rouge, LA), June 15, 1935.

25. Lainie K. Holman, staff physician of Physical Medicine and Rehabilitation at Cincinnati Children's Hospital Medical Center, Cincinnati, OH, interview October 18, 2010, with the author in New York; e-mails October 11, 2010, and August 28, 2012, with Bill Mallon, MD, of Duke University Medical Center.

26. "C. L. Brazelle Dead; Sanitarium Manager," *New York Times*, December 20, 1935.

27. Scott R. Lawson, General Director for Marketing Services at ACDelco in Grand Blanc, MI, letter of May 3, 2012, to author.

BIBLIOGRAPHY

Allen, Frederick Lewis. *Only Yesterday: An Informal History of the 1920s.* New York: Harper and Row, 1931.

Bastide, Roger, Robert Chapatte, and Dominique Grimault. *Les Légendaires: Des Temps Héroïques a l'Avenèment de Coppi, 1869–1942.* Paris: La Maison du Sport, 1988.

Berg, Frederick Lewis. *Lindbergh.* New York: G. P. Putnam's Sons, 1998.

Borgeson, Griffith. *The Golden Age of the American Racing Car,* 2nd ed. Warrendale, PA: Society of Automotive Engineers, 1998.

Brady, William A. *Showman: My Life Story.* New York: E. P. Dutton and Company, 1937.

Breyer, Victor, and Robert Coquelle. *Les Rois du Cycle: Comment Sont Devenus Champions.* Paris: Le Vélo, 1898.

Browning, Reed. *Cy Young: A Baseball Life.* Amherst: University of Massachusetts Press, 2003.

Brinkley, Douglas. *Wheels for the World: Henry Ford, His Company and a Century of Progress.* New York: Viking Press, 2003.

Case, Ted. *Power Plays: The U.S. Presidency, Electric Cooperatives, and the Transformation of Rural America.* Wilsonville, OR: Ted Case, 2013.

Chany, Pierre. *La Fabuleuse Histoire du Cyclisme: Des Origines à 1955.* Paris: Nathan, 1988.

Chernow, Ron. *The House of Morgan: An American Banking Dynasty and the Rise of Modern Finance.* New York: Grove Press, 1990.

Christiansen, Rupert. *Paris Babylon: The Story of the Paris Commune.* New York: Viking, 1995.

Chrysler, Walter P., with Boydon Sparkes. *Life of an American Workman.* New York: Curtis Publishing, 1938.

Curcio, Vincent. *Chrysler: The Life and Times of an Automotive Genius.* New York: Oxford University Press, 2000.

Dodge, Prior. *The Bicycle.* Paris: Flammarion, 1996.

Doyle, Gary D. *King of the Boards: The Life and Times of Jimmy Murphy.* Tempe, AZ: Ben Franklin Press, 2002.

du Cros, Arthur. *Wheels of Fortune: A Salute to Pioneers.* London: Chapman and Hall, 1938.

Duncan, H. O. *Vingt Ans de Cyclisme Pratique: Étude Complète du Cyclist de 1876 a Ce Jour.* Paris: F. Juven, 1897.

Durant, William C. *William C. Durant: In His Own Words, The Unedited Memoirs of William C. Durant.* Flint, MI: Scharchburg Archives at Kettering University, 2008.

Durso, Joseph. *Madison Square Garden: 100 Years of History.* New York: Simon and Schuster, 1979.

Erwin, John M., and A. A. Zimmerman. *Zimmerman Abroad and Points on Training.* Chicago: Blakely Printing Company, 1895.

Farber, David. *Sloan Rules: Alfred P. Sloan and the Triumph of General Motors.* Chicago: University of Chicago Press, 2002.

Feinblatt, Ebria, and Bruce Davis. *Toulouse-Lautrec and His Contemporaries: Posters of the Belle Époque, from the Wagner Collection*. New York: Los Angeles County Museum of Art in association with Harry N. Abrams, Inc., Publishers, 1985.

Fisher, Jerry M. *The Pacesetter: The Untold Story of Carl G. Fisher, Creator of the Indy 500, Miami Beach, and the Lincoln Highway*. Fort Bragg, CA: Lost Coast Press, 1998.

Fitzgerald, F. Scott. *The Crack-Up*. New York: Scribner, 1931.

————. *The Great Gatsby*. New York: Scribner, 1925.

Frey, Julia. *Toulouse-Lautrec: A Life*. New York: Viking, 1994.

Galbraith, John Kenneth. *The Great Crash*. Boston: Houghton Mifflin, 1954.

Gladwell, Malcolm. *Outliers: The Story of Success*. Boston: Little, Brown and Company, 2008.

————. *The Tipping Point: How Little Things Can Make a Big Difference*. New York: Back Bay Books/ Little, Brown, and Company, 2000.

Glasscock, Carl Burgess. *The Gasoline Age: The Story of the Men Who Made It*. New York: Bobbs-Merrill Company, 1937.

Goddard, Stephen B. *Colonel Albert Pope and His American Dream Machines: The Life and Times of a Bicycle Tycoon Turned Automotive Pioneer*. Jefferson, NC: McFarland and Company, 2000.

————. *Getting There: The Epic Struggle Between Road and Rail in the American Century*. New York: Basic Books, 1994.

Gustin, Lawrence R. *Billy Durant: Creator of General Motors*. Flushing, MI: Craneshaw Publishers, 1984.

Harper, William A. *How You Played the Game: The Life of Grantland Rice*. Columbia: University of Missouri Press, 1999.

Hatfield, Jerry H. *American Racing Motorcycles*. Osceola, WI: Motorbooks International, 1989.

Hemingway, Ernest. *A Moveable Feast*. New York: Charles Scribner's Sons, 1964.

Herlihy, David. *Bicycle: The History*. New Haven, CT: Yale University Press, 2004.

————. *The Lost Cyclist: The Epic Tale of an American Adventurer and His Mysterious Disappearance*. New York: Houghton Mifflin Harcourt, 2010.

Higonnet, Patrice. *Paris: Capital of the World*. Cambridge, MA: Harvard University Press, 2002.

Hillenbrand, Laura. *Seabiscuit: An American Legend*. New York: Ballantine Books, 2002.

Hofstadter, Richard. *The Age of Reform: From Bryan to F.D.R.* New York: Vintage Books, 1955.

Homan, Andrew M. *Life in the Slipstream: The Legend of Bobby Walthour Sr.* Washington, DC: Potomac Books, 2011.

Horne, Alistair. *The Seven Ages of Paris*. New York: Alfred A. Knopf, 2002.

Hounshell, David A. *From the American System to Mass Production, 1800–1932: The Development of Manufacturing Technology in the United States*. Baltimore: Johns Hopkins University Press, 1985.

Husband, Julie, and Jim O'Loughlin. *Daily Life in the United States, 1870–1900*. Westport, CT: Greenwood Press, 2004.

Ide, Evan P. *Packard Motor Car Company*. Charlestown, SC: Arcadia Publishing, 2003.

Kanigel, Robert. *The One Best Way: Frederick Winslow Taylor and the Enigma of Efficiency*. Cambridge, MA: MIT Press, 2005.

Kaplan, Rachel. *Little-Known Museums in and around Paris*. New York: Harry N. Abrams, 1996.

Keynes, John Maynard. *The General Theory of Employment, Interest, and Money*. New York: Harcourt, Brace and World, 1936.

Kluger, Richard. *The Paper: The Life and Death of the New York Herald Tribune*. New York: Vintage Books, 1989.

Kroplick, Howard. *Vanderbilt Cup Races of Long Island*. Charleston, SC: Arcadia Publishing, 2008.

Lacey, Robert. *Ford: The Men and the Machine*. New York: Ballantine Books, 1986.

LaMarre, Thomas S. *One Piece at a Time: The Cars of C. H. Metz*. Kutztown, PA: *Automobile Quarterly* 32, no. 3 (January 1994).

Larson, Erik. *The Devil in the White City: Murder, Magic, and Madness at the Fair That Changed America*. New York: Vintage Books, 2009.

Leblanc, Jean-Marie. *The Official Tour de France Centennial: 1903–2003*. London: Weidenfeld and Nicolson, 2004.

MacMillan, Margaret. *Paris 1919: Six Months That Changed the World*. New York: Random House, 2002.

Madsen, Axel. *The Deal Maker: How William C. Durant Made General Motors*. New York: John Wiley and Sons, 1999.

Maertelaere, Roger de. *De Mannen van de Nacht, 100 Jaer Zesdaagsen*. Eeklo, Belgium: De Eecloonaar, 2000.

McCullough, David. *The Greater Journey: Americans in Paris*. New York: Simon and Schuster, 2011.

McDonald, John. *A Ghost's Memoir: The Making of Alfred P. Sloan's General Motors*. Cambridge, MA: MIT Press, 2002.

Mead, Marion. *Bobbed Hair and Bathtub Gin: Writers Running Wild in the Twenties—Edna St. Vincent Millay, Dorothy Parker, Zelda Fitzgerald, and Edna Ferber*. New York: Harcourt, 2004.

Nolan, William F. *Barney Oldfield: The Life and Times of America's Legendary Speed King*. New York: G. P. Putnam's Sons, 1961.

Orlean, Susan. *Rin Tin Tin: The Life and the Legend*. New York: Simon and Schuster, 2011.

Pelfrey, William. *Billy, Alfred, and General Motors: The Story of the Two Unique Men, a Legendary Company, and a Remarkable Time in American History*. New York: American Management Association, 2006.

Perman, Stacy. *A Grand Complication: The Race to Build the World's Most Legendary Watch*. New York: Atria Books, 2013.

Poisson, Michael. *Paris: Buildings and Monuments*. New York: Harry N. Abrams, 1999.

Pommier, Gérard and Bertrand. *Nieuport: A Biography of Edouard Nieuport*. Atglen, PA: Shifter Publishing, 2002.

Pound, Arthur. *The Turning Wheel: The Story of General Motors through Twenty-Five Years, 1908–1933*. New York: Doubleday, Doran and Company, 1934.

Rae, John B. *The American Automobile, A Brief History*. Chicago: University of Chicago Press, 1965.

———. *American Automobile Manufacturers: The First Forty Years*. Philadelphia: Chilton, 1959.

Rennert, Jack. *100 Years of Bicycle Posters*. New York: Darien House, 1973.

———. *Poster Ecstasy*, vol. 28. New York: Poster Auctions International, Inc., 1998.

———. *Prima Posters*, vol. 14. New York: Poster Auctions International, 1994.

Ritchie, Andrew. *Flying Yankee: The International Cycling Career of Arthur Augustus Zimmerman*. Cheltenham, UK: John Pinkerton Memorial Publishing Fund, 2009.

———. *Major Taylor: The Extraordinary Career of a Champion*. Baltimore: Johns Hopkins University Press, 1996.

Robb, Graham. *The Discovery of France: Historical Geography from the Revolution to the First World War.* New York: W. W. Norton, 2006.

Scharchburg, Richard P. *W. C. Durant: "The Boss."* Flint, MI: General Motors Institute, 1973.

Sergent, Pascal. *A Century of Paris-Roubaix.* Brussels, Belgium: De Eecloonaar, 1997.

Sinsabaugh, Chris. *Who Me? Forty Years of Automobile History.* Detroit: Arnold-Powers, 1940.

Sloan, Alfred P. Jr., with Boyden Sparkes. *Adventures of a White Collar Man.* New York: Doubleday, Doran and Company, 1941.

Sloan, Alfred P. Jr., with John McDonald. *My Years with General Motors.* New York: Currency and Doubleday, 1990.

Thurow, Lester. *Fortune Favors the Bold.* New York: HarperBusiness, 2003.

Weisberger, Bernard A. *The Dream Maker: William C. Durant, Founder of General Motors.* Boston: Little, Brown and Company, 1979.

Williamson, Geoffrey. *Wheels within Wheels: The Story of the Starleys of Coventry.* London: Geoffrey Bles, 1966.

Woodland, Les. *Paris-Roubaix: The Inside Story, All the Bumps of Cycling's Cobbled Classic.* Cherokee Village, AR: McGann Publishing, 2013.

OTHER DOCUMENTS

Beasley, Norman. "Albert Champion: The Office Boy Who Was Taught That a Race Is Won before the Race and There Is No Such Thing as 'Good Enough.'" *MoTor* (New York), September 1926. Reprinted by AC Spark Plug Company.

Champion, Albert. "Piloting Motor Driven Racers." *MoTor* (New York), December 1903.

————. "Spark-Plugs for High-Speed Engines," *1917 Transactions.* New York: Society of Automotive Engineers, 1918.

Chevrolet Photo Album. From the Collections of the Richard P. Scharchburg Archives, published to celebrate the one hundredth anniversary of the Chevrolet Motor Company. Flint, MI: Kettering University, 2011.

"Col. Pope Passes Away." *Bicycling World and Motorcycle Review* (New York), August 4, 1909.

Chronicle of America: From Prehistory to Today. New York: Dorling Kindersley, 1995.

Editors of *Automobile Quarterly Magazine, GM: The First 75 Years of Transportation Products.* Princeton, NJ: *Automobile Quarterly Magazine*; Detroit: General Motors, 1983.

"Handling Quality Goods Brings Jobbers Success: Albert Champion Talked to Accessory Distributors of New England on Relations Between Manufacturer, Jobber, Dealer and Customer." *Automobile Journal*, April 10, 1918.

Harris, Stewart. *Have You Seen the Globe Today? A History of the Boston Newspaper.* Boston: Class paper for Boston University, 1981.

Hartmann, Gérard. *Clément-Bayard, Sans Peur et Sans Reproche*, 2006, http://www.hydroretro.net/etudegh/clement-bayard.pdf.

Herlihy, David. "The Bicycle Story: It Was Born in Europe, But American Ingenuity and Know-How

Helped Bring It to Maturity—and Affordability—in the Years before Automobiles Took Over." *Invention and Technology* (New York), Spring 1992.

"How the Gray Wolf Came to Grief." *Automobile Topics Illustrated* (New York), November 7, 1903.

Kimes, Beverly Rae. "The Dawn of Speed," *American Heritage* (New York) 38, no. 7 (November 1987).

————. "Launching the Chevrolet: The Early Years of the Marque," *Automobile Quarterly* (Kutztown, PA) 17, no. 3 (1980).

————. "Packard Gray Wolf." *Automobile Quarterly* (Kutztown, PA) 19, no. 3 (1981).

King, Jenny. "A Bow Tie for Everyman," *Automotive News, GM 74th Anniversary Issue* (Detroit), September 16, 1983.

Lane, Doris. *The Haunted House*. http://www.madammurder.net/shadylady/penthouse.html.

L'Homme Dans la rue. "Les Potins du Cycle." *La Pédale* (Paris), October 8, 1924.

"Motorettes" De Dion-Bouton "Motorette" Company booklet, *Something New*. Brooklyn, NY, undated, approximately 1900.

"Motorettes" De Dion-Bouton "Motorette" Company catalogue. Brooklyn, NY, February 1901.

Perrodil, Edouard de. *Albert Champion: His Triumphs, His Adventures, His Voyage to the United States*. Paris: L'Auto, 1904.

"Pneumatic's 21st Anniversary: Royalty Helps Honor It—Inventor Dunlop at Celebration, Which Recalls History of the Millions Made," *Bicycling World and Motorcycle Review* (Chicago), November 27, 1909.

Pritchard, W. A. "Albert Champion a Cycle Marvel: Wonderful Records Made by Manufacturer in His Younger Days Are Recalled." *New York Sun*, January 7, 1917.

Renault, Dennis. *Book Press Ink and Paper: The History of the Nineteenth Century Letter-Copying Book Process*. Sacramento, CA: Mockingbird Press, 1996.

Riggs, L. Spencer. "Carl G. Fisher, Indiana's Best Kept Secret," *Automobile Quarterly* (Kutztown, PA: Kutztown Publishing Company), May 1996.

Rimel, Bob. "Reed Martin's 1899 DeDion Bouton," *Classic Cycle Review* (Harrisburg, PA) 2, no. 4 (1994).

Ritchie, Andrew. *Charles Terront and Paris-Brest-Paris, Part Three of Three*. Sand Lake, MI: 1999.

Rothenberg, Al. "The Mystifying Millionaire: The Best Known and Least Known of GM's Leaders." *Automotive News* (Detroit), September 16, 1983.

Rutt, Walter. Unpublished memoir in a collection by Sammlung Wolfgang Gronen, Zentralbibliothek der Sportwissenschaften der Deutschen Sporthochschule (Cologne, Germany), Inventory Nr. 26.

Scharchburg, Richard P. "Albert Champion," *Encyclopedia of American Business History and Biography: The Automobile Industry, 1896–1920*. New York: Broccoli Clark Lyman1990.

————, ed. *The GM Story: Corporation Created by Dynamic Flint, Bold Men*. Flint, MI: General Motors Institute, 1981. Originally published as "GM Story" in the *Flint Journal*'s Golden Milestone Edition in 1958, celebrating the fiftieth anniversary of the corporation's founding.

————. *W. C. Durant: "The Boss."* Flint, MI: General Motors Institute, 1973.

Stranahan, Ann. *An American Chronicle: The Stranahan Chronicles*. Perrysburg, OH, June 2004.

Stevens, O. L. "Stabling Automobiles around Harvard," *Automobile Magazine* (New York), January 1901.

Wilson, S. S. "Bicycle Technology: This Humane and Efficient Machine Played a Central Role in the

Evolution of the Ball Bearing, the Pneumatic Tire, Tubular Construction, and the Automobile and the Airplane. *Scientific American* (New York), March 1973.

SELECTED NEWSPAPER ARTICLES

"America Enters Grand Prix This Year." *Evening Tribune* (San Diego), April 2, 1921.

"Both Killed: Miles and Stafford, Motor-Pace Riders, Slain on the Track at Waltham before Thousands." *Boston Journal*, May 31, 1900, p. 1.

"Boxer Fights A. C. Champion Widow's Will: Share in $6,000,000 Estate Demanded on Claim of 'Common-Law' Husband." *Detroit Times*, June 16, 1935.

Champion, Albert. "All Kinds of Machines at the Automobile Show." Special to the *Boston Traveler* (Boston), January 19, 1904.

———. "Uncle Sam Now Supreme in Two Speed Classes." *Duluth News-Tribune* (Minnesota), February 27, 1921.

———. "What Spark Plugs Means to the Motor: Facts Concerning Making of Important Little Contrivance," *Flint Journal*, February 23, 1917.

"Champion Co. Plans Branch Plants in France and England." *Flint Journal*, July 18, 1919, p. 1.

"Champion Divorce Decree Is Filed: Property Settlement Made Out of Court—Wife Goes to France." *Flint Journal*, November 1, 1921, p. 15.

"Champion Estate Suit Withdrawn: Brazelle's Alleged Claims Apparently Ignored." *Flint Journal*, June 25, 1935.

"Charge Boxer Enslaved, Beat Mrs. Champion." *Detroit Times*, June 15, 1935.

"Charge Terrorism in Champion Suit: Kin of Spark Plug King's Widow Accuse Former Boxer." *Grand Rapids Press*, June 15, 1935.

"Court Battle Opens over Champion Will." *Detroit News*, June 14, 1935.

"Cycling in France: A Word about M. Clément." *Westminster Budget*. (London), October 9, 1896, p. 28.

"Death Race: Two Riders Fatally Hurt at Waltham." *Boston Herald*, May 31, 1900, p. 1.

"Duesenberg Is a Great Machine: Old-Timers' Club Responsible for Start of Prominent Racer; Murphy Entered." *Harrisburg Telegraph* (Pennsylvania), May 22, 1923.

"Europe Respects U.S. Auto Craft: Albert Champion Finds Changed Attitude during Trip Abroad." *Flint Journal*, October 12, 1922, p. 13.

"'Fixed' the Motor: Tampering, Marks Thinks, Caused Waltham Tragedy." *Boston Post*, June 2, 1900.

"Flint Manufacturer Arrested in Hotel on Wife's Complaint: Mrs. Albert Champion Finds Husband in Company with 'Other Woman.'" *Flint Journal*, August 25, 1921, p. 1.

"40,000 Spark Plugs Champion Co.'s Daily Average." *Flint Journal*, November 30, 1918, p. 9.

"The French Dunlop Tyre." *To-Day* (London), July 18, 1896, p. 331.

"Gen. Motors Party Now Seeing Paris: Albert Champion Is Famous Guide, Says C. S. Mott in Letter." *Flint Journal*, September 20, 1919, p. 8.

"La Belle France on Wheels: How the Dunlop Tyre Came to France." *Westminster Budget* (London), July 17, 1896, p. 28.

Martin, Martha. "Sparkplug Millions Explode in Tragedy: Death Wipes out Triangle of Champion, No. 2 and Gigolo." *New York Sunday News*, April 26, 1936.

Mayfair, Tony. "Brazelle Bares Story of Love: 'Common Law' Hubby Fights for Estate." *New York Mirror*, April 26, 1935.

———. "Fatal Romance behind a Suit by a 'Common Law Husband': He Brings Suit for a Share in the $6,000,000 Estate His Lady Beloved Inherited from an Inventor-Husband, Who Died of a Paroxysm after Discovering Their Close Friendship." *New York Mirror*, July 7, 1935.

———. "Mad Dream Lovers Got Costly Nest." *New York Mirror*, April 28, 1935.

"Millionaire's Death Laid to Boxer's Punch in Suit over Champion Estate." *New York American*, June 15, 1935.

"Old-Timers Choose Albert Champion to Head New Auto Club." *Flint Journal*, January 22, 1921.

"Pacemakers Killed: Miles and Stafford on Motor Tandem Hurled to Death." *Boston Globe*, May 31, 1900, p. 1.

"Pride of Albert Champion and Her Sister Now in Motion Pictures—Both Former Kansas City Girls." *Kansas City Star* (Missouri), February 22, 1922, p. 3.

Pritchard, W. A. "Albert Champion a Cycle Marvel: Wonderful Records Made by a Manufacturer in His Younger Days are Recalled. *New York Sun*, January 7, 1917.

"Proposition Is a Big One." *Boston Herald*, March 6, 1918.

"Pugilist Painted as Sinister Guardian of Mrs. Champion." *Detroit Free Press*, June 15, 1935.

"The Romance of Business: A Word on the Birth and Growth of a New Industry." *Westminster Budget* (London), May 1, 1896, p. 26.

"Spark Plug Widow's Life of Fear Bared." *New York Daily News*, June 15, 1935.

Stevenson, L. L. "Champion Will Fight Delayed: Brazelle Suit Postponed to June 25 after Charges He's 'Despoiler.'" *Detroit News*, June 15, 1935.

———. "Charge 6 million Will Plot: Friend Begins Court Battle: N.Y. Club Man Says He Lived with Mrs. Champion for 8 Years in Penthouse." *Detroit News*, April 23, 1935.

"Suit over Champion Estate Is Settled." *Lansing State Journal* (Michigan), June 26, 1935.

"To Enter Grand Prix: American Cars to Compete for Honors in Famous Speed Classic in July." *Baltimore Sun*, March 13, 1921.

"Two Killed in Cycle Race in Waltham: Champion's Fall Forced All Three Other Racing Teams into a Tangle." *New York World*, May 31, 1900, p. 1.

"Two Women Hurt in Auto Accidents: Coupe Hits Truck." *Flint Journal*, August 2, 1921, p. 12.

"Under Fire of Aeroplane Guns of the Germans: Albert Schmidt Returns to Flint after Five Months in French Army," *Flint Journal*, January 20, 1915, p. 1.

Un Spectator des Troisièmes. "Le Coureur Champion," *Le Cycle* (Paris), April 12, 1896.

"Work is Albert Champion's Main Pastime—Says He Can't Quit Now." *Detroit News*, August 21, 1927.

PERMISSIONS/CREDITS

While every measure has been taken to contact copyright holders, the author and publisher would be grateful for information about any copyright material they have been unable to trace and would be happy to make amendments in further editions.

The cover photo of Albert Champion is used with the kind permission from the owner, Kerry Champion Williams. She also gave kind permission to publish photos of her great-aunt Edna Crawford Champion and Albert Champion relaxing with his dogs as well as the portrait photo of Albert that used to hang over the portal to the shop floor of his factory in Flint, Michigan. The photo by Boston portrait photographer Elmer Chickering of Champion riding his aero bicycle is reproduced with the kind permission of Lorne Shields.

Excerpts from William C. Durant's unpublished memoir *William C. Durant, In His Own Words, The Unedited Memoirs of William C. Durant*, are published with kind permission from Kettering University Archives, Flint, Michigan, William C. Durant Collection. Excerpts of reportage by *Boston Globe* reporter John J. Donovan were kindly granted by PARS International Corp., which represents the *Globe*.

The photo of Henry Ford standing with Barney Oldfield seated at the wheel of the 999 racecar is published with kind permission from the collection of the Henry Ford Museum. Permission to publish the photo of Tom Cooper was generously granted by Janet Brown and Roy Drinkwater. Photos of Alfred P. Sloan, Louis Chevrolet, and William Durant from the GM Media Archive are published under licensing with the kind permission of General Motors.

Photos of the brothers Frank Duane Stranahan, Spencer Stranahan, and Robert Allen Stranahan II have been used with kind permission from Ann and Stephen Stranahan.

Poster Photo Archives, Posters Please, Inc., New York, graciously granted permission to publish posters of the Clément Cycle Company of Paris, Toulouse-Lautrec for La Chaîne Simpson, Orient Cycles, and Gladiator Cycles. Cherry Champion gave kind permission to publish the photo of Prosper Champion.

444   PERMISSIONS/CREDITS

Gary McCoy gave kind permission to publish the photo of Champion riding a two-cylinder Clément Gladiator motorcycle. Bernadette Murphy graciously allowed publication of the image of Champion's mausoleum in Père Lachaise Cemetery. The Waltham Museum of Waltham, Massachusetts, gave kind permission to publish the image of Charles Herman Metz steering the ten-seat Oriten tandem. Buck Peacock granted kind permission to publish the 1900 photo of Champion riding on a motor-tricycle.

INDEX

Page numbers in *italic* indicate photos.
AC = Albert Champion in subentries.